Sidney Lumet

ALSO BY AUBREY MALONE
AND FROM MCFARLAND

*Writing Under the Influence: Alcohol and the
Works of 13 American Authors* (2018)

*Hollywood's Second Sex: The Treatment
of Women in the Film Industry, 1900–1999* (2015)

The Defiant One: A Biography of Tony Curtis (2013)

*Censoring Hollywood: Sex and Violence in
Film and on the Cutting Room Floor* (2011)

Sidney Lumet
The Actor's Director

Aubrey Malone

McFarland & Company, Inc., Publishers
Jefferson, North Carolina

LIBRARY OF CONGRESS CATALOGUING-IN-PUBLICATION DATA

Names: Malone, Aubrey, author.
Title: Sidney Lumet : the actor's director / Aubrey Malone.
Description: Jefferson, North Carolina : McFarland & Company, Inc., Publishers, 2020 | Includes bibliographical references and index.
Identifiers: LCCN 2019051388 | ISBN 9781476675534 (paperback : acid free paper) ♾
ISBN 9781476636733 (ebook)
Subjects: LCSH: Lumet, Sidney, 1924–2011. | Motion picture producers and directors—United States—Biography.
Classification: LCC PN1998.3.L86 M35 2020 | DDC 791.4302/33092 [B]—dc23
LC record available at https://lccn.loc.gov/2019051388

BRITISH LIBRARY CATALOGUING DATA ARE AVAILABLE

ISBN (print) 978-1-4766-7553-4
ISBN (ebook) 978-1-4766-3673-3

© 2020 Aubrey Malone. All rights reserved

No part of this book may be reproduced or transmitted in any form or by any means, electronic or mechanical, including photocopying or recording, or by any information storage and retrieval system, without permission in writing from the publisher.

Front cover image: Sidney Lumet on the set of *Family Business*, 1989 (TriStar Pictures/Photofest)

Printed in the United States of America

*McFarland & Company, Inc., Publishers
Box 611, Jefferson, North Carolina 28640
www.mcfarlandpub.com*

Table of Contents

Acknowledgments vi

Introduction 1

Beginnings 7

Moving to the Big Screen 17

On the Wing 28

Peaks and Valleys 37

That Vision Thing 51

Chameleon 61

Misfires 72

Pacino on the Double 81

The Mad Prophet 98

Workaholic 114

Mixed Grills 132

To Hollywood—Finally 150

Crime and Punishment 167

Final Surge 181

Chapter Notes 195

Bibliography 206

Index 209

Acknowledgments

I couldn't have written this book without the help of John Andrushkoff. He tracked down rare material by and about Sidney Lumet with the kind of speed one associates with Lumet himself. I'm deeply grateful for his tireless exertions on my behalf in bringing this project to fruition and for his vast collection of movie memorabilia.

I'm also very grateful to Edward Comstock, who never fails to provide me with research material from places where I would never have thought of looking. These often arrived unsolicited onto my computer screen, something Ned does as matter of course with constant good cheer.

Thank you to Kristine Krueger of the Margaret Herrick Library for her many suggestions as to where I might find background information on Lumet. Sincere thanks also to Debbie and Derek Savage for their tireless work beyond the call of duty. For visual material, I'm indebted to Dollie, Alexx Van Dyne and Jeff Mantor.

Introduction

A minuscule giant. A filmmaker who hated Hollywood. A lover of the stage who became a titan of the screen. The contradictions surrounding Sidney Lumet are manifold.

Maybe the sobriquet "actor's director" describes him best of all. Every director should be that, of course, but how many are? Maybe you have to be an actor yourself before you're one. And Lumet was. He'd been in the firing line so he knew how difficult it was.

"I like being described as the actor's director," he allowed, "because it comes from the fact that actors open up with me more than they do with most directors."[1] That was because they relaxed with him. He didn't throw tantrums or play the diva. He became closely involved in any problems they might be having with their characters or with the film in question.

If he was working with an insecure actor, he might say "Print!" on a bad take to boost them.[2] He always knew how to get the best out of an actor. Sometimes this was done by pushing them hard and sometimes by letting them work their way into a part. Sometimes it was done by thinking outside the box.

Lumet brought his work home with him. He thought about it while he was shaving, while he was doing the crossword, while he was driving to and from work. One could be forgiven for imagining he even thought about it while he was asleep. As well as being a great motivator, he was a wonderful psychologist. Often the two went hand in hand.

He was born into a show business family. His mother was a dancer and his father an actor. He started appearing in juvenile roles on Broadway in the mid–1930s while he was attending the famous Professional Children's School. Stage acting continued into adulthood. His subsequent fondness for plays as sources for his films were bound up with these early experiences.[3] Such fondness had the side effect of giving him negative feelings about Hollywood. From a young age, he held the belief that it was a place where "you'd make a lot of money and then get corrupted."[4]

In 1949, he formed an off–Broadway acting group but as time went on he found it to be too narrow in its focus. He left it to become a television director. TV was then seen as the illegitimate stepchild of radio. The following year, he was promoted to staff director at CBS. Here his hunger for productivity flourished. He directed more than 500 shows at CBS, employing more than 2000 actors during that time.

Lumet worked in television during its Golden Age. He was in good company, working alongside directors the caliber of John Frankenheimer, Arthur Penn, George Roy Hill, William Friedkin and Delbert Mann. Television gave all these wonderful people their start.

Like them, Lumet learned his trade in a crucible where one mistake could eat up a budget that equaled his salary and that of his cast and crew as well. Such pressure meant he was walking a fairly permanent tightrope, but challenges seemed to bring out the best in him. When his back was against the wall, his brain worked faster.

He migrated from live TV in the late '50s. By now it had lost much of its vitality for him, becoming replaced with "canned" programs. His path to cinema was swift. He hit the ground running with his first feature, *Twelve Angry Men* (1957). Here he exploited his ability to work fast and cheap on an enclosed set. In his subsequent films *Stage Struck* (1958), *That Kind of Woman* (1959) and *The Fugitive Kind* (1960), he moved away from a single set. *Long Day's Journey into Night* (1962) returned him to the confinement of *Twelve Angry Men*, a confinement he used to its best effect for intense character portrayals.

Not for him the wide open spaces of a John Ford or a Howard Hawks. He preferred urban dramas where the action was centered on emotions, on hollowed-out feelings, on psychological convolutions. As he often said, "I'm much more interested in a face than a mountain."[5]

He made the political thriller *Fail-Safe* in 1964 but it was dogged with problems from the get-go, mainly because its release coincided unhappily with Stanley Kubrick's more imaginative *Dr. Strangelove*. There was no way Lumet's wordy drama could compete with Kubrick's dystopian flamboyance.

He inherited a host of problems with *Fail-Safe*, not just because it wasn't as dynamic a film as *Dr. Strangelove* but also because its screenplay seemed to have been lifted from Peter George's novel *Red Alert*. George sued Eugene Burdick and Harvey Wheeler, who co-wrote the novel *Fail-Safe*, for plagiarism. The case was settled out of court but it left a bad taste in everyone's mouth.

Lumet had better luck with *The Pawnbroker* the following year. It was an artistic and commercial hit but gave him many headaches with the censors. *The Hill* (1965) began a partnership with Sean Connery that would extend to five films in all. When Lumet found actors he admired, he went back to them again and again. Often such partnerships spilled over into off-screen friendships. He was heartened by the fact that people liked coming back to him. Why wouldn't

The young Lumet on the cusp of a superlative career. He could hardly have known then that he'd still be going strong half a century on, and that his films would have been nominated for more than forty Academy Awards (Jerry Ohlinger).

they? His sets were always happy ones, at least when he was in control of them—which was most of the time.

The Hill was a fulfilling experience for both Lumet and Connery. Connery was deeply embroiled in James Bond films at this time but he found them limiting. He was trying to escape the Bond straitjacket when he started working with Lumet. The main problem with the film was the Scottish accents in it, which many viewers found difficult to make out. Lumet fought for authenticity in dialect just as he fought for it in everything else he did but it cost him money in this instance.

Afterwards he embarked on *The Group*, adapting Mary McCarthy's popular "women's novel" for the screen, but here again there was a problem. This time it was caused by the acerbic critic Pauline Kael, whom he mistakenly allowed on his set to watch him work. She wasn't impressed by his direction and conveyed her displeasure in dispatches to the media that amounted to character assassination. For Kael, Lumet never shed his TV roots in his "Lights, camera, action, cut, print" *modus operandi*.

A series of box office disappointments followed: *The Deadly Affair* (1966), *Bye Bye Braverman* (1968), *The Appointment* (1969), *The Last of the Mobile Hot Shots* (1970), *The Anderson Tapes* (1971), *Child's Play* (1972), *The Offence* (1972). Lumet earned critical kudos in these years but the public, while not exactly boycotting his works, attended them only in modest numbers.

That changed with *Serpico* in 1974. The film initiated his collaboration with Al Pacino, an actor who thrived under his open-ended direction. Lumet used Pacino again soon afterwards in *Dog Day Afternoon* (1975). In both films, Lumet showed not only his love of directing but, more pertinently, his affection for the streets of New York. He captured the pulse of the city in ways that influenced everyone from Paul Mazursky to Woody Allen. One can even see his influence in the works of Martin Scorsese. Lumet relished the Big Apple for its ethnic mix, its ebullient energy, even its crime. He captured its varying shades and moods with his loyal team of producers, art directors and cinematographers. His set was like an extravagant train set where everyone knew exactly what he expected them to do because he explained it in such detail to them. "New York can be anything and everything you want it to be," he declared.[6]

It's become something of a cliché to say that New York is like an extra character in his films but, like most clichés, it's difficult to refute. The city encapsulated the chaotic frenzy that acted as an ideal backdrop for his own undiluted energy. He loved it for its sense of change, its "closeness to destruction and infinite potential for growth."[7] It wasn't only New York that inspired him. Most cities did. They were capable of portraying any mood a scene required.[8]

Dog Day Afternoon was followed by *Network* (1976), the film with which Lumet is most associated today. Perhaps fittingly, it brought him back to the world of television. The difference now was that he was satirizing it instead of dining at its table. He was castigated for this but he explained that the film wasn't so much a critique of television as of the corporate tyranny that threatened America's lifeblood. When Peter Finch—who was so brilliant at transmitting that message—died shortly after the film wrapped, the surreal atmosphere it created seemed to have bled from the screen onto real life.

Lumet adapted Peter Shaffer's Broadway hit *Equus* for the screen in 1977. The critics said it failed to shed its theatrical origins, a familiar accusation leveled at Lumet and one that began to exasperate him as the years went on. The fact that he set such store by language didn't make his films any less cinematic, he insisted. One could compensate with lighting, movement and camera angles.[9]

Lumet was even more reviled for *The Wiz* (1978), an unwise foray into the world of a big-budget musical. He was ill-suited, even with Quincy Jones to ease his path, and icon Diana Ross and a young Michael Jackson singing the songs. The experience taught him that one shouldn't tamper with classics—in this case *The Wizard of Oz*—without good reason.

In *Prince of the City* (1981), he revisited the world of *Serpico*. Here again a man pits himself against police corruption from the inside with negative results. Despite Lumet's best intentions, it failed where *Serpico* succeeded. This was mainly down to the fact that it didn't have enough dynamism to sustain its three-hour running time. More worryingly, it didn't have Al Pacino to upgrade its human interest element. Lumet put everything he had into it and was devastated that it wasn't a hit. Maybe the problem was that he tried too hard. It was meant to be a thriller but he directed it like an art movie, shooting space in elongated or foreshortened manners with lenses of various sizes to accentuate the growing alienation of the main star (Treat Williams) from his colleagues. Not too many viewers were concerned about the fact that city blocks could be "twice or half as long" as they were in reality.[10] They just wanted to know if Williams' crusade against the system would bear fruit.

This was a theme Lumet explored many times. It reached its apogee in his 1982 feature, *The Verdict*. This produced one of Paul Newman's great autumnal performances as he pits himself against medical and legal structures to reclaim the sense of self-worth that deserted him after a mistake he made early in his career. Once again, as in *Prince of the City*, Lumet used his camera as a commentary on the action, employing cinematographer Andrzej Bartkowiak's burnished tones to underline Newman's renaissance.

From now on, Lumet announced, he was going to tell his stories in abstract terms.[11] It was as if he'd exhausted *realpolitik* and wanted to push the envelope in a different direction. "I don't want to settle into a particular style," he stressed, "because to me the style is determined by the material."[12] This left him in a kind of vacuum as regards the critics but it was a vacuum he welcomed. "I've never been a fashionable director," he said.[13]

For years he'd been seen as someone who worked on predictable canvases, even if his brushstrokes varied dramatically. "The typical Lumet flick," muttered Joe Hoberman, "is an overstuffed club sandwich filled with juicy parts, smeared with moral seriousness and garnished with New York local color."[14] Andrew Sarris, who was almost as vicious in his condemnation of Lumet, denounced him for a sense of "strained seriousness."[15]

This was something strongly in evidence in *Daniel* (1983), one of the most ambitious films of Lumet's career. Again, however, it appealed more to the intelligentsia than the general public. He explored the theme of capital punishment for political dissidents and the manner in which its fall-out infected the children of those executed.

His penchant for versatility continued to prove admirable but in films like *Garbo Talks* (1984) and *Power* (1986), his resolve to break out of the strangleholds that restrained most other directors sometimes stretched him beyond his ability. He made a reluctant trip to Hollywood for *The Morning After* (1986) but he didn't seem to have his heart in the film. It came across as a dutiful exercise, exemplifying the kind of blandness he associated with a town he often likened to a cultural boneyard.

In *Running on Empty* (1988) he revisited the "generational guilt" theme of *Daniel*, albeit in a more commercial manner. After that, it was back to another caper movie, *Family Business* (1989), and then another police corruption one, *Q&A* (1991). He continued to experiment with mixed results. He also scripted *Q&A*, which resulted in an Oscar nomination.

"All I was ever interested in was the next job," he confessed, which seemed to endorse Pauline Kael's vision of him as an artistic hack.[16] His love of work was well documented but the "all" is misplaced here because he was also interested in doing everything he could to make that job worthwhile. He needed to keep continually on the move but he never sold audiences short, even if he occasionally ventured into areas outside his comfort zone, or thumped the tub too vehemently on the "You can't fight City Hall" theme.

In *A Stranger Among Us* (1992) he demonstrated his Jewishness more prominently than he had for a long time. One had to go back to the days of *The Pawnbroker* and *Daniel* to witness this. Here it was trained on the Hasidic community in a film that acted as a cross-cultural romance mixed with a whodunit. Two years later he reprised the glossy urbanity of *The Morning After* with *Guilty as Sin*, another courtroom drama where he reversed the *zeitgeist* of *Twelve Angry Men*. No longer were innocent men presumed guilty. Now guilty ones could walk free if they could afford the right lawyer. *Night Falls on Manhattan* (1997) provided a more nuanced take on a similar theme and gave Lumet a chance to focus on something that also featured strongly in his work: the idea of filial loyalty.

Critical Care was made in the same year but it fell short of expectations as a medical satire, playing out like a second string Paddy Chayefsky from *The Hospital*. Likewise, *Gloria* (1999), an affectionate tale of a sweet-hearted moll on the run from the mob, seemed superfluous to John Cassavetes' venture into the same territory some years before, despite Sharon Stone's gallant efforts to break out of her *femme fatale* straitjacket for something decidedly more cuddly.

Age was now creeping up on Lumet. His mind was still razor-sharp but his energy levels weren't what they were. The man who'd made a film or more a year for most of his career only went behind the camera twice more, for *Find Me Guilty* in 2005 and *Before the Devil Knows You're Dead* in 2007. The former gave Vin Diesel an opportunity to show what he could achieve if he was asked to do more than change gears on souped-up vehicles. *Before the Devil Knows You're Dead* transmuted melodrama into something almost operatic under Lumet's octogenarian guidance. Even at 83, Ol' Man River was still rollin' along, still pushing the boat out for a whole new generation.

People wondered where he was now in his mindset. Had he dismissed the liberalism of films like *Twelve Angry Men* with *Find Me Guilty* and *Guilty as Sin*, two films where villains seemed to be able to play the system? It wasn't that simple. He never liked spoon-feeding audiences facile messages. That, he felt, would be to patronize them. He despised what he called the "rubber ducky" school of drama. This was the phrase he used to describe a scene where a character's motivation is accounted for by a childhood trauma: "Someone once took his rubber ducky away from him and that's why he's a deranged killer."[17] But he also said, "I go after vulnerability. I pick victims."[18]

His work was always as much about style as subject matter. Filmmaking for him was like a mosaic: "You take each little tile and color it. It's not until you've glued them all together that you know whether you've got a film or not."[19] Having said that, films weren't made in the editing room, as some people believed. The "tiles" had to be quality-studded for the gluing to be effective.

Though one of Hollywood's most prolific filmmakers, he confessed that he never fully knew why he said yes to a film.[20] He made choices instinctively, sometimes after just one reading.[21] He's commonly regarded as one of America's best directors never to win an Academy Award.[22] The present book is an attempt to understand why.

Beginnings

"I was born in Philadelphia," Lumet once said, "and had the good sense to leave when I was four."[1] In actual fact, he was only two. His father Baruch was a director-cum-actor who transferred his love of both disciplines to his son.

Baruch had grown up in Poland and trained as an actor there. He moved first to London and then to Philadelphia before finally settling in New York. There he appeared in many television plays and even wrote one himself, *Autumn Fever*. In both countries, he experienced anti–Semitism. His wife remembered Cossack raids.

Sidney was born in 1924. When he was young, his father brought him to the various theaters. There were 12 in all but they were past their glory days as he was growing up. Baruch told him about his days touring North America with his one-man show *Monotheatre Varieties*. Sidney saw him in his Broadway debut, *The Chinese Nightingale*, in 1934.

Sidney made his acting debut at the age of four through Baruch's association with the Maurice Schwartz Acting Group at the Yiddish Arts Theatre.

There was also a strong literary emphasis in the Lumet household. Baruch read *Hamlet* in Yiddish to six-year-old Sidney. Two years later, Sidney was dipping into the writings of Karl Marx. In the late 1920s and early 1930s, he acted in a series of radio dramas which his father produced. It was 15 minutes work five days a week. As well as a love of theater and literature, Baruch transmitted the work ethic to his son. He believed that work involved "a lack of self-indulgence."[2]

One of the radio dramas in which young Sidney appeared was called *The Adventures of Helen and Mary*. (It was later re-titled *Let's Pretend*.) Its cast fancifully featured everything from leprechauns to speaking animals. Another show on which he appeared was called *The Rabbi from Brownsville*. Baruch wrote, directed and acted in it with him. His mother was the leading lady. The weekly salary for the three of them was $35.[3]

Then the Depression hit. From now on, treading the boards became a necessary source of income rather than a labor of love. Times were tough but the Lumets didn't lie down under them. They didn't think of themselves as poor because most of the people around them were in the same predicament.

Sidney shared a bed with his sister until he was 11. The bathtub was in the kitchen. There were no luxuries, least of all in clothing. "You bought clothes a size too big for you," he recalled years later, "so you could grow into them."[4]

The family moved from apartment to apartment to save money. Landlords were so desperate to procure tenants they offered leases of a year with the first month being given free. Each year the Lumets would uproot themselves to take advantage of that offer. It was a saving of $30 every time. The moves usually cost about $15 so they were really only saving the other $15. That's how tight funds were.[5]

According to Lumet, they lived "in every borough but Staten Island" during these years, each change of address bringing its own pressures. Being both foreign and Jewish gave the local ruffians two reasons to dislike him: "If I walked a few blocks one way or another into a different neighborhood, I got beat up." This made him develop an alertness that would stand him in good stead for his directorial career: "You notice things pretty closely. The immigrant experience not only gives you a tremendous sense of time and place and limits; it also gives you a tremendous energy because you have to pay attention. All the time."[6]

Lumet developed a social conscience at a young age. As an adolescent, he was a member of the Young Communist League.[7] "To me," he said, "the subtext of the '30s was commitment, commitment to the best of all possible worlds. I remember Roosevelt and the Group Theatre and the Spanish Civil War."[8] All three espoused that sense of idealism.

He was only 11 when he made his Broadway debut in Sidney Kingsley's *Dead End*, a "social problem" play that saw wealth and poverty living tooth-to-jowl in Manhattan. The Dead End Kids were featured in it. Lumet would like to have been one of them but he was too short. He thought that meant he wasn't going to be in the play but Kingsley wrote another part for him. The playwright's kindness led to a lifetime friendship between them.[9] Kingsley was more amused by Lumet's shortness than anything else. So was Lumet himself. He once joked to a journalist, "I could have been tall but I turned it down."[10] He kept a diary, filling it with whimsical entries like, "I advise all the children who want to go on the stage to try to find a profession where the hours are more regular and the pay is better. The theater is no place for sissies or people who can't take it."[11]

He went on the road with the Group Theatre in 1939 and gained some invaluable experience there. His colleagues at "summer school" included many actors who would become major figures: Elia Kazan, Stella Adler, Harold Clurman and Lee J. Cobb. He educated himself through correspondence courses. In 1939 he appeared in William Saroyan's first play, *My Heart's in the Highlands*.

His first—and only—screen appearance occurred that year. It was in the Sylvia Sidney feature *One Third of a Nation*, directed by Dudley Murphy. Lumet played Sidney's troubled brother. The plot had a slum landlord being converted to the cause of decent public housing. It was an oddly prophetic debut for him considering it was set on the streets of New York and featured a social conscience theme: two benchmarks of Lumet territory in years to come.[12] In his next theatrical venture, he played Jesus Christ in Elmer Rice's *Journey to Jerusalem* in 1940. He followed that with *USA* in 1941.

He studied literature for a semester at Columbia University before America entered World War II. After the invasion of Pearl Harbor, he enlisted in the army. He wanted to join the Marines but he was rejected because of poor eyesight—an irony considering he would eventually make his living using his eyes. Instead he did a one-year training course in the Signal Corps studying radar. "I got everything I know about sound there," he enthused.[13]

His mind was always on the alert, always processing data that could be beneficial to him in whatever line of work he took up in the future. If he hadn't become a film director, he'd surely have used the experience he got there in some shape or form.

He stayed in the army for four years, a lot of his time spent at the Burmese front. "I would have preferred to be in Europe fighting Hitler," he complained.[14] In 1943 he was airdropped into China as part of a mission to teach signal communications to the Chinese, but Japanese troops overran the proposed landing site and that was the end of that. He spent the last two years in the jungles of Northern India with the same intention but this proved to be a largely worthless exercise as the mountains prevented the radar from working properly. The war years were wasted ones for Lumet apart from the basic technical knowledge he picked up from the Signal Corps.

They also left him with a lingering regret over an incident that took place one day in India, an incident that gave him deep feelings of shame about himself, some of which seemed to inform the themes of his films. It happened one day when he was on a train bound for Calcutta. He spotted a girl of about 12 standing on a platform. All of a sudden, a GI in the compartment behind her reached out and grabbed her. He pulled her into it.

Lumet went down to it to see what was going on. When he got there, he saw a bunch of GIs having sex with her, "just passing her from one to the other," as he put it. A man at the door said to him, "You want some? It'll cost you whatever." Lumet was so shocked he didn't know what to do. He knew he should have gone to her rescue, even at the risk of personal harm, or at least reported the incident to the authorities, but he didn't. The experience, he claimed, stayed with him all his life, filling him with a sense of self-loathing.[15]

When the war ended, he felt a sense of rootlessness common to many of those who'd enlisted. He didn't feel motivated to go back to work and his confidence was low. He was "five foot seven, no great beauty, not a leading man," and living in a time "before ethnic was beautiful."[16] In the end, he went back to what he'd been doing before the war: acting on Broadway.

In 1946, Lumet replaced a young actor called Marlon Brando in a production of Ben Hecht's *A Flag Is Born*. He would direct Brando in a film in the future and also become a friend of his. Brando, in fact, was one of his colleagues at the Actors Studio when it was set up in 1947. So was Maureen Stapleton. Both of them would star in *The Fugitive Kind* for Lumet some years down the road. He met them on opening night. Two other people who attended on opening night were Arthur Miller and Tennessee Williams. Both of these men would also feature in Lumet's future.

The Actors Studio provided an opportunity for out-of-work thespians to hone their skills. It flowered under the stewardship of Bobby Lewis but today it's mainly associated with Lee Strasberg. He injected a Freudian element into it. Strasberg was referred to as "the poor man's psychiatrist" because of the amount of psychology he brought to it.[17] It wasn't until 1948 that it became known as the Actors Studio. In Lumet's time, it was simply called "The Group"—a term that would have resonance for him when he came to film the Mary McCarthy book of that name.

They met in a dingy room on the top floor of the Old Labor Stage at Broadway on West 29th Street. How many luminaries cut their artistic teeth within these walls?

Montgomery Clift also was there on opening night, as were Kevin McCarthy, Karl Malden, E.G. Marshall, Patricia Neal, Eli Wallach and Beatrice Straight.[18] Years later, Lumet guided Straight to her finest moments on screen in *Network*.

The Actors Studio was focused on realism whereas Lumet wanted to experiment with different types of writers—Dostoevsky and the Anglo-Irish authors Farquhar and Sheridan. He felt the approach was too lazy there, and too repetitive. He didn't want to stage the old favorite *Waiting for Lefty*, he said, for the umpteenth time, "not to mention all the social plays from the 1930s that I could have played perfectly fine even if I had been woken up by surprise at four in the morning without any preparation."[19]

He was asked to leave the Actors Studio because he objecting to the way everything was analyzed to death there. "How long can you investigate one style?" he fumed. "Nothing could have been more boring."[20] He set up his own actors' workshop with some friends. Here the scope was more extensive, ranging from Shaw through Shakespeare and back to Greek drama.

It was run on a shoestring. Members made a token $5 contribution. It was an exciting time but there were some problems. The main one was that there were too many actors and no directors. And so a career was born. He decided to take the reins.[21]

He didn't make the decision lightly: "I knew that if I stayed in acting, the best I could hope for was getting the part of the little Jewish kid from Brooklyn who got shot down by the mean Japs or Nazis. Then Clark Gable would pick me up and with tears in his eyes would rush forward and single-handedly wipe out their machine-gun nest, That was an area of drama that didn't particularly interest me."[22] There was another reason he left acting: "I didn't want to keep revealing myself to 1500 strangers every night on a stage." He decided he'd prefer to do it through others.[23] He was tired of the emotional exposure.[24]

Even if Lumet didn't pursue acting as a career, his brief time before the cameras—and more importantly the stage lights—gave him an understanding of its traumas. "I was an actor," he said simply, "therefore I know where it hurts."[25]

By this time, a new medium had arrived: television. It was invading America with a vengeance, ushering in the "home cinema" culture that would explode into the video rental industry some decades hence. It started to have a major impact on entertainment in 1947. That was the year NBC began *Kraft Television Theatre*, offering productions of new and old plays.

Something else helped the new medium flourish: The HUAC investigations which put many Hollywood actors out of work. The following year, the Supreme Court decided that film studios should no longer be allowed own theaters, a ruling that threatened the dominance of the studio system. Actors and directors found their contracts terminated without warning as ruthless cost-cutting procedures were implemented.

If Hollywood was seen as a sell-out for theater people, television was regarded as an even bigger one. Lumet didn't subscribe to that kind of snobbery. He believed one could do good work in any medium. He grabbed the opportunities television offered with both hands, excited about the way it could propel his career forward.

He married actress Rita Gam in 1949. Born Rita Eleanore MacKay, she took her last name from her stepfather. Her mother was a Romanian Jewish immigrant and her father was also born to Romanian Jewish parents. She had begun acting in 1946.

The following year, he became an assistant director at CBS. He had Yul Brynner to thank for this as he'd been in the position before him. "Come on in," Brynner advised. "Nobody knows what the hell they're doing. It's a ball." So he did.[26] He watched Brynner and learned from him. "Yul was a brilliant director," he said. "People don't know that about him. His pose of cavalier disdain hid a deep commitment to the craft."[27]

Martin Ritt called Brynner the best director CBS ever had: "His innovations were so unique, the BBC sent two of their top men to study them." To achieve results, he used to "scream, torture and practically commit mayhem"—his own words. Instead of conventional rehearsals, he used baseball games to sharpen people's reflexes. A temperamental director, he was disturbed by noise from an adjoining room one day and thundered, "Who's responsible for that bloody racket?" When he was informed that it was a prospective sponsor for the show he was directing, he refused to apologize. Instead he said, "I will not continue until that idiot leaves!" On another occasion, when a CBS executive criticized the performance of a member of his cast, he roared, "Who is that creep?" When a terrified aide informed him that he was the company's vice-president, Brynner ordered him removed. "I detest anything concerned with vice!" he pronounced. How did he get away with such arrogance? For only one reason, according to Lumet: their awareness of his great talent.[28]

When Brynner eventually left, it was his own decision. He would soon begin making the film with which he would forever be identified, *The King and I*. CBS's loss was Lumet's gain—he ended up taking on the project Brynner was directing at the time, a murder series called *Danger*. He helmed almost 500 episodes before graduating to other programs.

Lumet became staff director in 1951. Two years later he was directing for the series *Play of the Week*, *Best of Broadway*, *Goodyear Playhouse 90* and *Studio One*. He learned to work fast and cheap, and about the vagaries of actors. He also learned about lighting and camera placement, things with which he would become identified in years to come.

He had original ideas from the start, being responsible for unique innovations like stringing cables from the ceiling rather than running them along the floor, something that wasn't generally done at that time but which made the working environment much more comfortable and safe. Television had drawbacks in terms of size but it also had advantages. The relatively small financial outlay and the cheapness of the sets allowed him the luxury of experimentation: "If we laid an egg, it was a $20,000 egg, not the $300,000 one it would be today."[29]

From another point of view, television was a tough school for him just as it was for Ritt and John Frankenheimer. "In live television, the director not only had to be good with actors," Lumet maintained. "He had to be a technician and editor as well, to be able to improvise, adapt with split second timing." He learned his trade by trial and error: "There were no rules as to what you could or couldn't do like there were in film-making." Lumet had to have "a sharp visual eye" and lots of stamina.[30]

Rod Steiger, an actor who would give perhaps the greatest performance of his career under Lumet in the years to come, was especially aware of the pressures of live television in the '40s. "When you did a half-hour show," he recalled, "you did it in five days." The area actors worked in was also very confined, like a bedroom or a kitchen. The night the show was aired was like an opening night on Broadway "and you had to get it right because the critics and the world were watching and if they didn't like you, you were finished. You had no chance to come the next day and correct things or re-rehearse them. It was the worst pressure you could possibly have: millions of people watching as the little red light went on in front of the camera."[31]

It was the kind of pressure Lumet thrived on: a minefield where, if anything went wrong, the whole country knew about it within minutes, as opposed to theater where mistakes were confined to one night, one building. He turned out work with the skill of an old hand. Deadlines proved to be a healthy challenge to him and so did tight budgets. He seemed able to get the best out of mediocre actors and equally mediocre scripts. He flattered material by his brisk efficiency and no-nonsense attitude. There was an honesty in what he did, an absence of bullshit. He might have been working at the lower end of the market but it didn't look like it. He alchemized the ordinary into something approaching art.

Pretty soon actors knew just what they had to do to impress him: solid work without any frills. He didn't want divas or distractions; neither did he welcome people with other things on their minds besides the job at hand.

He also insisted on passion in his stars. He once rejected no less a luminary than Grace Kelly for a TV film because she hadn't, as he put it, any "stove in her belly."[32] This was precisely the quality Alfred Hitchcock adored in her, the icy charm, but it didn't work for Lumet.

His television career coincided with programs like *Robert Montgomery Presents*, *Revlon Theatre* and *Philco Television Playhouse*. It was a time of great artistic ferment. This is how Arthur Penn remembered it: "You went on the air and there was no stopping, come hell or high water. A lot of guys had heart attacks. A lot of guys had bleeding ulcers." No such pressures existed in the world of cinema, where a scene could be re-shot as many times as it took to get it right. Another advantage of TV over cinema: Actors didn't have to project to the last row in the balcony. And there was the advantage of more close-ups to accentuate emotion.[33]

Piper Laurie played in two of Lumet's live TV shows, *The Deaf Heart* and *The Changing Ways of Love*. The first, based on a play by Mayo Simon, dealt with a woman who made herself go deaf to better understand the problems experienced by her deaf brother. Fritz Weaver played the psychiatrist examining her. The atmosphere on the set was relaxed. When Weaver's wife went into labor during rehearsal, Lumet had no hesitation in telling him to take the day off. In fact he took two, returning as a father. This was the other side of Lumet, the side that put humanity before a pressing deadline. He also believed in frequent breaks during rehearsals to allow the cast to recover from the intensity of the work.[34]

The Changing Ways of Love had Laurie playing three different characters. The first was from a Clifford Odets play, *Awake and Sing!*, the second from the F. Scott Fitzgerald story "Winter Dreams" and the third from Reginald Rose's *Three Empty Rooms*. She had to be on the alert to orchestrate the various entrances, exits and costume changes necessitated by the unusual task she undertook. Every second counted. The background team had it down to a fine art. Lumet oversaw the productions like a benign patriarch, enjoying the multi-tasking and the ordered chaos.

At this time, he was also directing a unique series of historical enactments for the series *You Are There*. Episodes made it seem as if the events of long ago were happening at the time it was being shot. One of them dealt with the Alamo, another with the death of Socrates. There were 60 or 70 shows a year. That meant, as Lumet recalled, over 400 actors and "God knows how many writers, video engineers and audio men."[35] The circumstances were ridiculous but they provided entertaining history lessons to those who craved such on-the-spot reportage. "I know it sounded crazy," Lumet admitted.[36] But it worked.

The show didn't make any claims to be realistic. Reporters "interviewed" Sigmund Freud while he accompanied Joan of Arc on her way to the stake. The juggled time frames also featured in the treatment of events like the trial of Galileo, the Salem witch-hunts and the Louisiana Purchase.

You Are There was hosted by Walter Cronkite, who later became something of an icon as a news anchorman and the voice of integrity. Lumet chose him, he said, "because the premise of the show was so silly, so outrageous, we needed somebody with the most American homespun warm ease about him." Each episode ended with the same refrain from Cronkite: "What kind of day was it? A day like all days, filled with those events that alter and illuminate our times. And you were there."[37] Cronkite was ideal for it because of the sense of sincerity he gave off. It made his career. He talked to the camera each week about milestone events. The show ran for two years. It made a lot of money for CBS. It was even sold to schools.

Paul Newman appeared on a number of installments. In its first season he was Brutus in "The Assassination of Julius Caesar." He played Plato in "The Death of Socrates." "Not right now, please," he says to a reporter confronting him with a microphone outside the prison where Socrates awaits execution.[38]

John Frankenheimer, one of Lumet's assistants on the show, remembered those days fondly: "Sidney was wonderful to me, and I've never forgotten that. He really taught me so much, and he was so patient with me."[39]

Lumet had intentions of filming the play *Wedding Breakfast* at this time. It had been a hit on Broadway with Tony Franciosa. Lumet wanted Franciosa and his then wife Shelley Winters to appear in it. He had many meetings with Winters to try and set this up. He wanted her to produce it as well and gave her $600,000 towards the cost of this. After eight weeks of shooting, Winters decided Franciosa was too unstable to handle the demands of a tight film schedule so she pulled out of the production. Lumet was furious with her and vowed never to employ her again. She paid back the $600,000 she'd been given, plus $7,000 from her own funds to cover the time she'd wasted on filming already completed. Lumet must have forgiven her because he later shot a TV show starring Winters and Farley Granger.[40]

Television continued to be both exciting and infuriating. He directed a film called *Tragedy in a Temporary Town* in which Lloyd Bridges flipped out on air one night, giving a performance of great power as his emotion got the better of him. All would have been well except for the fact that the feelings he was generating were so effusive, he departed from the script. He also used a lot of unacceptable language. Lumet was both fascinated and devastated as he watched the tears coursing down Bridges' face, knowing that the footage would be totally unacceptable to the vast majority of the people who viewed it.[41] Lumet knew the boundaries. There were certain things you could say and certain things you couldn't. There were also things you could say if you said them a certain way, and things you couldn't say under any circumstances.

As well as artistic license being limited, so were political attitudes. The stone cast into the HUAC river was still spreading its ripples far and wide. In addition to having to vet his actors for going over the top in their performances, Lumet also had to be careful scripts didn't contain inflammatory material that might be seized upon by Senator Joseph McCarthy's bulldog cohorts who were steamrolling anyone with even the vaguest hint of communist sympathies. Don Shewey wrote, "By the '50s, communism had metamorphosed from a vision of hope for working people into the enemy of American motherhood and apple pie."[42]

Lumet always fought for the rights of the downtrodden but he wasn't a "Red" in the sense McCarthy would have used the term. He claimed to have attended only one communist meeting in his life. (And he'd been asked to *leave* when he had the temerity to point out that Soviet society wasn't classless because artists lived more comfortably there than everyone else.[43]) He saw himself as a moderate but even moderates were now seen as being tarred with the Red brush.

He divorced Rita Gam in 1955. In the years since they married, she'd been signed by MGM but only had a minor career, partly due to her own doing. She turned down the female lead in the Dean Martin-Jerry Lewis comedy *Living It Up* in 1953 and was briefly suspended as a result. She was offered a role in 1956's *The Ten Commandments* but when she told Cecil B. DeMille she wasn't religious, he didn't hire her. Two years earlier she had appeared opposite Jack Palance in *Sign of the Pagan* and Gregory Peck in *Night People* but she didn't create much of an impression in either film. After the marriage to Lumet broke down, she became more known for talking about her friendship with Grace Kelly than anything she'd done on screen. She was bridesmaid at Kelly's Monaco wedding to Prince Rainier.

Shortly after they divorced, Lumet was introduced to the flamboyant heiress Gloria Vanderbilt by *Harper's Bazaar* photographer Richard Avedon. Sparks flew between them at a party they attended at his house. Vanderbilt had inherited $5 million from her father's railroad business when she turned 21. She'd previously been married to the conductor Leopold Stokowski. At 68, Stokowski was many years her senior. They had two children in their decade-long marriage, Stan and Christopher.

Avedon threw another party a week later and Lumet and Vanderbilt met up again. The chemistry between them was even more evident this time. When Lumet hugged her, Vanderbilt confessed to feeling "like a teddy bear." When they danced, she felt "the energy of his heart and soul" going through her like "warm honey." Before the party ended, he told her he had to meet his agent. He promised he would be back to her afterwards. "I bet a red rose you won't," she admonished, not shy about letting him know how keen she was on him. When he came back, he carried in his hand ... a red rose. She knew then that her feelings for him were reciprocated. They left the party together. From that moment on, according to Vanderbilt, they were "glued."[44]

Lumet became engaged to Vanderbilt just three weeks after meeting her. She couldn't wait to divorce Stokowski, whom she'd found to be overly possessive. She was then acting in the play *The Swan* at the time and casually dating Frank Sinatra. Sinatra offered to bring her to Hollywood if she was interested. She signed a contract to appear in three films with him but a "wildly insecure." Lumet begged her not to go. He was afraid that if she went, she wouldn't come back to him. By now the tide of dependency had swerved from her to him. As a result, she stayed put.[45]

There was no way Sinatra was going to put up with this kind of shilly-shallying. When she didn't make the trip to Hollywood with him, he refused to negotiate on her behalf from her New York base with Lumet. Patience was never one of the singer-actor's virtues and he also had a lot of other distractions at this time. He was exhausted, having just made the pulsating drug movie *The Man with the Golden Arm*.[46] Vanderbilt wanted to do the Western *Johnny Concho* but when she didn't audition for it, the part went to Phyllis Kirk.[47] Interestingly, *Johnny Concho* was adapted from a *Studio One* TV play of the type Lumet had been directing. Sinatra mentioned two other possibilities for Vanderbilt but she would have had to travel west to have any chance of beating all the other actresses in line for them.

The beautiful heiress Gloria Vanderbilt, whom Lumet fell in love with at first sight and married shortly afterward (Jerry Ohlinger).

Her decision not to go to Hollywood was one she would regret. She felt she should have made at least one of the three films that were offered to her but Lumet was determined to have her stay with him and she couldn't bear the thought of going against him. It was always her personality to please others. "I went with the flow," she said, "rarely having a plan or thinking seriously about the future." When she was in her teens, she said, her plan was to marry, have a big family, "and wear the apron in the kitchen, cooking like the mother in the Andy Hardy movies."[48] In later years, she resented that picture-book dream of matrimony. It was one Lumet never had, in any case. He may not have wanted his wife in the studio but neither did he want her chained to the kitchen sink. He liked to throw parties and socialize, playing as hard as he worked.

He married Vanderbilt in August 1956 in the plush ten-room apartment of Sidney Kingsley, his friend from the *Dead End* days. There wasn't much time for a honeymoon as he had a number of directing projects to consider. Licking her wounds from the aborted Hollywood trip, Vanderbilt settled for some stage acting. In fact, the night after her wedding, she appeared in a play called *The Spa* in Milburn, New Jersey.[49]

Vanderbilt never seemed to know what she wanted in life, either in matters of the heart or head. Lumet would have helped her with a film career in New York but he drew the line at Hollywood. Once she gave up on that dream, she changed her priorities altogether, devoting herself to more individual pursuits like literature and painting. "By nature I work best alone," she decided.[50]

Lumet's own work, meanwhile, went on apace—and *at* pace. People who disapproved of him said he cut corners but he didn't see it that way. He knew working fast had its advantages. He often got what he called a "hot take" as a result of it. That was when an actor did exactly what he wanted them to do on the first or second go. Sometimes it wasn't technically perfect but he accepted that. Correcting what was seen as a problem and asking for it to be done again made it artificial in his eyes. It might be the seventh or eighth take before the actor in question reached that level of emotion again.[51] "Good work is an accident," he liked to say. It was a director's job to prepare the ground for that fortunate circumstance to come about.[52]

His punchy style, Eric Luke remarked, managed to maintain audience concentration beyond the usual 60-minute mark that was then the norm in television. It also whetted people's appetite for more when a week's lay-off was called for during the many programs he made which were dependent for their drama on people talking about what might happen in the following installment.[53]

One of Lumet's 1957 shows exhibited just how exact he was in his style. In *Hans Brinker or the Silver Skates*, a musical version of Mary Mapes Dodges' children's story, a poor Dutch family struggles against adversity. Tab Hunter, who played Hans, had to play some of his scenes on a skating rink. At 27 he was an unlikely choice for someone supposed to be a teenage star but his facility on the rink—and his singing ability, which was also required—netted him the role. He was impressed with Lumet's punctiliousness, the fact that he pulled together an elaborate, fully choreographed 90-minute musical in just three weeks. This was down to his fastidious preparation. During rehearsals, he taped out the floor to the exact dimensions of the studio set.[54]

Lumet directed many productions like this in the mid–50s, sometimes knowing exactly what he wanted and sometimes "winging it" as he waited for a piece of unexpected magic to occur. He was happy with what he was doing but craved a bigger stage. When his friend and colleague Delbert Mann managed the crossover to cinema with his surprise hit *Marty* in 1955, Lumet looked on with interest. *Marty* had originally been a TV production. When it became a screen success with Ernest Borgnine, who wasn't regarded as a major star, Lumet sat up. Here was a film about an ordinary man, a butcher looking for a girlfriend. "What are you doin' tonight, Marty?" became a line people shouted at Borgnine in the street after seeing it. They felt an empathy with his lonely heart.

The film won the Best Picture Oscar that year (beating out works the caliber of *Picnic*, *Mister Roberts*, *The Rose Tattoo* and *Love Is a Many-Splendored Thing*) and Mann won for Best Director. If Mann could top directors like Elia Kazan and David Lean, who'd been nominated for *East of Eden* and *Summertime* respectively, Lumet felt that everyone had a chance to get into a new arena.

Maybe he could become another Delbert Mann, he thought. All he was waiting for was that "happy accident" to occur. Then he could enter a new arena too.[55]

Moving to the Big Screen

Lumet didn't have long to wait to follow in Mann's footsteps. He was now asked to direct a film based on a 1954 courtroom drama that had been a TV success. *Twelve Angry Men* was written by Reginald Rose. Lumet had directed some of Rose's scripts for *Danger* so he was familiar with his name. Likewise Rose with Lumet. He was the co-producer of *Twelve Angry Men* along with Henry Fonda, who was going to be its main star. He rang Fonda and mentioned Lumet to him as a possible director for it. Fonda was familiar with Lumet's work and liked it so he approved him.

Neither Fonda nor Rose had much time or money to invest in the project. That was partly why they chose Lumet to direct. They knew he worked fast and cheap. They were also aware that he had the human touch with casts. "I knew we had only two weeks to rehearse," Fonda recalled. Within that time frame, he felt confident Lumet could "get performances out of actors."[1]

Lumet was delighted to be given the opportunity to direct the film. "I didn't even have to audition," he beamed.[2] He appreciated what television had done for him but now it was time to move on. The main difference between television and cinema, he thought, was one of scale. Moving a 17-inch piece of glass onto a 35-foot screen meant a story had to be told in an entirely different way. The lens was the same but its frame was much more dynamic. "On the small piece of glass," he explained, "you lose the instrument of distinction between the wide shot and the close-up." The close-up was the only thing that really registered on television but it wasn't wise to overuse it. If you did, you had no relief from it: "It starts losing its value as a point of visual emphasis."[3]

One of the main problems with *Twelve Angry Men* was the fact that it never moved out of the jury room. To help him make this visually interesting, Lumet employed cameraman Boris Kaufman. Kaufman was already a legend in the film industry, having photographed *On the Waterfront*. In time he would become like Lumet's right arm, as important to him for cinematography as Philip Rosenberg would be for production design or Ely Landau and Burtt Harris as producers. Kaufman had the ability to make something out of nothing with his chiaroscuros, his atmospheric hues.

When Lumet's friends heard he was about to direct the film, they told him he was crazy. "How can you do a picture in a room?" they asked.[4] He couldn't understand their concerns. If the material was good enough, he reasoned—and it was—what did it matter where it was shot? He approached it with the confidence of a man who was, he admitted, too dumb to fear that a one-set movie could fail miserably.[5]

He procured his cast cheaply because, with the exception of Fonda, not many of them were that well known. Ed Begley had a modest reputation but actors Jack Klugman and E.G. Marshall weren't yet household names. Lee J. Cobb had made some strides in that direction with his Oscar-nominated performance in *On the Waterfront* but he wasn't a major star either. Some of the other cast members—Jack Warden, Martin Balsam, Edward Binns—would work with Lumet time and again in future years. One could argue that he made their careers. They also helped his by giving such powerful performances in his maiden cinematic voyage.

The plot concerned the trial of a young Puerto Rican from a poor neighborhood, accused of knifing his father to death. Did he do it? At the beginning of the film, 11 of the 12 jurors believe he did. They're not mentioned by name in the film, which increases its impact considerably. Only Fonda, "Juror Number 8," has doubts. He asks for a review of the evidence, to many groans. "We're talking about somebody's life here," he says. "What if we're wrong?" Though an architect by trade, he shows all the characteristics of a lawyer. Or maybe he just possesses a lot of common sense.

A jury was once defined as "12 people of average ignorance."[6] Fonda exposes such characteristics in his colleagues, harping on points that, while obvious in retrospect, were missed—or ignored—at the trial. For the prosecution, one imagines, if not the defense, it was an open-and-shut case. Nobody was too concerned about nuances. Poor people from racial minorities killed their fathers more often than wealthy ones from WASP homes.

Henry Fonda demonstrates how he thinks a killing might have occurred in Lumet's first feature, *Twelve Angry Men*. As "Juror Number 8," Fonda managed to sway the eleven other people in the jury room from a guilty verdict to an innocent one, in the process setting the tone for a career built on playing characters of great integrity (Jerry Ohlinger).

In another director's hands, this could have been stodgy fare. By drawing emotional performances from the cast, Lumet gave the script vitality. Cobb plays a bully who sees in the defendant his own rebellious son and has his judgment clouded as a result of that. Begley is a racist who thinks all minorities are "trash." Marshall is short-sighted—both visually and psychologically—but comes to "see the light." Another juror is exposed for wanting to get the verdict done quickly so he can get to a ballgame. Lumet shreds them all just as Fonda does, inverting the 11-to-1 for conviction to 11-to-1 for acquittal. The last man to change his mind is Cobb. When he breaks down, it's a life-changing moment for him.

For Fonda, the film was like a corollary to *The Ox-Bow Incident*, the western where three innocent men were hanged by a lynch mob. What made it interesting was the fact that the audiences isn't informed at the end if the teenager really committed the crime or not. For the film's purposes, it doesn't matter. It's the system Lumet puts on trial, not the boy. And the system is found guilty.

As the film begins, 12 people enter a room. They have wildly differing views of what constitutes justice. Over the next two hours, they argue with one another—and themselves—in sweltering July heat.

For Fonda, the deliberations are enlightening. He gets more and more ideas as he talks. He plays with the other jurors like a cat with a ball of wool, occasionally making wild suggestions to get them going. Once the suggestion of innocence—originally not even on the table—is posited, everything becomes possible. The supposed certainty of the boy's guilt peels away to reveal the flaws in the jurors' characters.

Fonda is like a Christ figure in the film. The fact that he isn't named adds to his mystery. If he's an "ordinary" man, he's one with a difference. It's only when the film is over that we realize we know less about him than any of the others. His focus throughout is on them, trying to find out why they're saying what they're saying, what reasons they could have for their views. If they're microcosms of society, as Lumet suggests, such reasons, when multiplied, become the death sentences of so many teenagers who went to the electric chair on spurious pretexts, or so many western heroes who were hanged without trial like those in *The Ox-Bow Incident*.

Because Lumet had so little to work with in terms of set-ups, he put a lot of emphasis on the "look" of the jury room, the little chinks of light from outside which the jurors glimpsed as brief respites from their own faces.

Fonda was originally unhappy with the external views visible from the room. Lumet used a painted backdrop from a photograph because of the tight budget they were on. "Christ!" Fonda exploded upon seeing it, "When I worked with Hitchcock, the backings were so real you'd walk into them because you thought they were three dimensional." Lumet's heart sank when he heard those words, which seemed so much like a putdown of him. Nonetheless, he promised to improve the look of the film with help from Kaufman.[7]

An outdoor shot had been scheduled for the following day. He waited from 8:30 a.m. to 4 p.m. to get the right lighting for Fonda now that he knew how much it mattered to him. "Hank doesn't sweat," he said, "but that was about as close as he's ever come." Both of them were tense as they viewed the rushes. "Hank steeled himself," Lumet recalled. "He walked into the projection room and sat down beside me. He watched for a while and then he put his hand on the back of my neck. He squeezed it so hard I thought my eyes would pop out." Lumet didn't know what reaction to expect from him until Fonda whispered quietly to him, "Sidney, it's magnificent." Then he dashed out. He never looked at the rushes again.[8] At that point. Lumet knew he had a movie.

Even this early in his career, we see the classic Lumet style here: the examination of urban life, the carefully delineated performances, the liberal social philosophy, the one against the many.[9] Because the budget was small, there was no room for experiment.

"Once a chair was lit," Lumet lamented, "everything that took place in that chair was shot."[10]

People born on the wrong side of the tracks, like Lumet, either try to subvert society or make it better by exhibiting the cracks in it. He chose the latter option. In *Twelve Angry Men*, which is really more like 11 angry men and one idealist, he made the first of many films exposing anomalies in the legal system. Fonda challenges the prejudices of the other jurors and rips their views to shreds, thereby unpicking the whole rationale of the jury system. The murder case that underpins their decisions isn't as important as what it unearths about the people adjudicating on it.

Fonda is brilliant as the man who puts his finger in the dike but so is the ensemble playing of the others. Lumet was used to dealing with large casts interacting with one another in a "cabin fever" atmosphere. The film was an ideal vehicle for him from that point of view. He let the emotions boil over repeatedly in the jury room, ending up not so much with a TV-play-on-film as a statement about a society.

The film wasn't shot in sequence. It was more economical to feature the actors in particular positions at the one time. After he worked out his angles, he got everything down to the *nth* degree, even going so far as to compute the amount of sweat drops that should appear on each actor as the atmosphere became more intense. "My script became a maze of diagrams," he stated. Some people felt this was unnecessary but he disagreed: "The diagrams came out right 396 times in 397 scenes." He only had to re-shoot one of them, when a juror looked the wrong way.[11]

Many courtroom dramas resort to flashbacks to relieve the tedium of a film set in a single room but Lumet welcomed the monotony. If an audience could experience the same restrictive conditions as the jurors, he reasoned, they would be in a better position to understand what they were going through.

To make the room look brighter, it was suggested that he put a glass top on the jury table. He knocked this idea on the head immediately, feeling the pressure cooker atmosphere was better served by wood. A further suggestion to have the room located in a basement where a set of pipes might lessen the monotony was also thrown out. "There's going to be no artificiality in this," he told his cast, "You're going to be the whole picture."[12]

He shot the first third of the film above eye level, the second third at it and the final third below it. This increased the sense of entrapment. "Not only were the walls closing in," said Lumet, "the ceiling was as well." For the final shot, as Cobb leaves the building, Lumet used a wide angle lens, wider than any he'd used up to now. "The intention," he explained, "was to give us all air, to let us finally breathe."[13] We'd surely earned it after two hours in such a heated furnace of bigotry.

A class war has been waged under the auspices of a criminal discussion. Many of the jurors would have almost had their minds made up that the teenager knifed his father as soon as they heard his address, or his nationality.

The film, as one writer noted, acted as a rebuttal of the political hysteria of the McCarthy era. If we read "Puerto Rican knifer" as a code for "left wing sympathizer," the film becomes a subtle critique of commie-baiting. Not only did Fonda atone for the ills of *The Ox-Bow Incident* with his interrogations, he also flew the flag for Everyman here. Once again he was Tom Joad, the "ordinary decent American seeking justice," *homo Americanus*.¹⁴ He achieves it not so much by browbeating the jurors as to get them to prise one another apart. Begley does this by protesting too much and driving everyone away from him. Cobb does it by discovering a softness within himself he didn't even know was there.

Fonda is also on a journey. It isn't only the other jurors he sways but himself too. When he starts the proceedings, it isn't because he believes the boy is innocent. Even at the end, he doesn't necessarily believe this. That wasn't what the jury system was about for Lumet. He pans the room for doubts, foibles, insecurities. Over the 90 minutes, his camera becomes, in effect, the thirteenth juror.[15]

Lumet thought Fonda was perfect for the role of Juror Number 8: "Hank always had the best of American liberalism about him," he said. "The idea of a man, fighting for justice, was enormously appealing to him." It wasn't a reach for Fonda but rather something that was already inside him: "His performances were heroic without him ever having to play the hero."[16]

Fonda became friendly with Lumet during the making of the film, which resulted in him inviting him to dinner at his house one night. Here Lumet met his wife Afdera. She was more lively than her husband in Lumet's view. So were her friends. There were gardenias on the table. At one stage of the dinner, they started dipping the gardenias in sauce and throwing them at the other diners. Lumet could see from Fonda's face that he was disgusted: "His sense of order had been violently disrupted." Fonda's virtues as an actor, for Lumet, were the very things that militated against domestic bliss for him: "His weakness, I think, is that he was perfect, if that is a weakness."[17]

He thought he was severely underrated as an actor. "His work was so good for so long," he said, "it became expected." On that account, it was taken for granted. Because he wasn't spectacular, he fell under the critical radar: "He never played the drunk running down Third Avenue. He never played the lunatic in the asylum. He never played the Hunchback of Notre Dame. The parts were calm, the performances were calm. They needed a little bit of looking at." This was one of the reasons Lumet thought it took the Academy so long to give Fonda an Oscar. Another possible reason was that Fonda was never among the great moneymakers in Hollywood. "In the past, how a picture did commercially has a great deal to do with the Academy Awards. Very often they went to the four or five biggest commercial hits of the year and Hank didn't have many of those." His art concealed art, Lumet thought. People came out of his films saying, "Oh, well, another great performance from Hank Fonda. So what?"[18]

"What's fascinating to me about Fonda as a talent," Lumet deduced, "is I don't think if you took a stick and beat him, he could do anything false. He's incapable. As a performer and as a man, he's pure. He's like a barometer of truth on the set. He has the inner resource to make the lines deeply true. Great actor. I don't use that term often."[19]

The film came in at $340,000. That was $1000 under budget. Though Lumet was very pleased with it, he didn't think it would do great business. Neither did Fonda or Rose. "We dreamed of putting it into a small East Side movie house," Fonda stated, "the kind that held a few hundred people at the most." They hoped word of mouth would spread from there, as it had with *Marty*. But that wasn't the way United Artists saw things.[20]

One day Fonda got a call from Arthur Krim, the head of United Artists, telling him he wanted to see him in a hurry. Krim had seen the movie and flipped over it. He wanted it shown in all UA's flagship theaters across the country. Fonda didn't think that was a good idea and neither did Lumet. Krim blew a fuse. "Are you out of your ever-loving mind?" he thundered at Fonda, "All you'd have to do is sit back and hire people to take the wheelbarrows of money to the bank."[21]

As things worked out, Krim didn't need any wheelbarrows. The instincts of Lumet and Fonda were proved right. It flopped in a mainstream theater and was pulled after a week. But then it was shown at the Berlin Film Festival and it won first prize. It also won prizes in Japan, Australia, Italy and Scandinavia. A pattern was set with Lumet that would repeat itself time and again: critical success, commercial failure. How could he relate to the marketplace?, he wondered. By making something less noble? By being more Lee J. Cobb than Henry Fonda?

Interestingly enough, he seemed to have an element of Cobb in him when he was called for jury duty after *Twelve Angry Men* was released. The case involved drug trafficking. Before it began, Lumet said he felt so strongly about the subject, he would have found it difficult to have a presumption of innocence for the defendant. On that account, he was ruled out for selection.[22]

"I wasn't interested in justice," he said mystifyingly of *Twelve Angry Men*. "I was interested in making a movie. It changed the law in England but that wasn't why I made it."[23] One finds it difficult to believe him here considering the passion he poured into it, a passion he would pour into many similar types of films over the next half century. Did he mean what he said or was he just being mischievous?

He was aware the film was a kind of fairy tale: "There's no way in the world that a nice attractive guy is going to turn 11 people around. It cannot happen." Neither was there any way that 11 people would leave a room when a bigot started talking, as also happened in the film. That didn't mean it was false. It led audiences to such a point that they believed this could happen: "We're dramatists, not documentary filmmakers."[24] There was "a lot of fakery in it."[25]

Notwithstanding all this, it put Lumet's name on the cinematic map. It became one of the most popular films of all time, an iconic exploration of the cornerstone of democracy. The scene where Fonda leaves the courthouse at the end and inhales proudly is also iconic. Talk show host Dick Cavett wrote about a trip to that building to protect John Lennon from deportation by Richard Nixon in the 1970s: "I knew the main court building, with those long steps from multiple viewings of Sidney Lumet's classic."[26]

Fonda was delighted with the way it turned out. He believed his performance was the closest he ever came to a theatrical one on screen. It had that intensity. If the film hadn't been shot out of sequence, he believed the cast could have performed it on stage.[27] He thought Lumet deserved more praise than anyone: "What I got was a bonus I didn't count on—his incredible use of the camera."[28]

Lumet was nominated for an Oscar but he lost out to David Lean for *The Bridge on the River Kwai*. That film also beat him to the Best Picture award. But he came away from the ceremonies with his head held high. He'd started his movie career with a claim for its highest honor. That had to bode well for the future.

He wondered what he would do next. Had he peaked too soon? He was afraid he might have. A gradual climb to the top was in some ways more to be savored than an instant hit. It knocked things out of proportion too much and threatened to give him a big head.

No matter how much praise came his way, however, studios weren't exactly jumping up and down to offer him another film. He wanted to direct *Marjorie Morningstar*, Herman Wouk's novel about a Jewish girl swept off her feet by a musical director, but when he flew out to discuss the project with Jack Warner, Warner told him flatly that he didn't intend to cast any Jews on it. This was so it would have "universal" appeal. Lumet was disgusted and walked out of his office.[29] It left a sour taste in his mouth about Hollywood which never really went away.

In the absence of any more obvious alternatives, he went back to what he was most comfortable with: a theatrical adaptation. Katharine Hepburn had won an Oscar for *Morning Glory* in 1933 and Lumet now decided to remake it. It was the story of a producer who takes advantage of a young actress, having a brief affair with her before rejecting her. In the end, she realizes her main love is the theater, not men. Lumet's title for the remake was appropriate: *Stage Struck*.

Henry Fonda agreed to star in it as a favor to him. He played the part that Adolphe Menjou had taken in the original. Susan Strasberg had the unenviable task of trying to emulate Hepburn in the leading role. The cast was rounded off by stalwarts Herbert Marshall, Christopher Plummer and Joan Greenwood.

Strasberg was riding high on the success of *The Diary of Anne Frank*, which she'd just starred in on Broadway. Lumet was excited to have Strasberg and Fonda working with him.

The early days of the shoot were happy for all concerned. "Both Sidney and I were rather hyper in those days," Strasberg recalled. Fonda, by contrast, was ice cool. "He was very kind to me," she conceded, "though everyone on the set thought he was aloof." She was self-conscious playing love scenes with him: "If you had to stand on an apple box wearing four-inch heels in order to kiss Henry Fonda, you wouldn't remember it. You're just happy you didn't fall off the box."[30] She put it in a different way to Fonda's daughter Jane, claiming that kissing him was like kissing her father.[31] (Her father was Lee Strasberg, the Method guru.)

Lumet thought she was miscast in the role, however. For him, she was essentially a dramatic actress. That meant her touch was too heavy for the kind of froth *Stage Struck* demanded.[32] He was passing the buck to an extent here because part of the problem was his own. He was uncomfortable in the genre of romantic comedy, something that would be evidenced in years to come in other ventures. The bottom line was that the film didn't measure up to *Morning Glory* and he knew it. He let his defenses slip when, asked if he'd seen *Morning Glory*, he confessed, "I didn't dare!"[33]

He fought hard to make *Stage Struck* realistic, right down to featuring the noises of trucks passing the theater in the film. This wasn't accepted by the sound department. They didn't want that much "vitality."[34] For this and other reasons, he was disappointed with the finished product. "I wanted to make a lovely little soufflé of a movie," he lamented, "but I'm afraid I came up with a bit of a pancake."[35]

The *New York Herald Tribune* thought he lingered too lovingly over Strasberg. The film was therefore hijacked by an actress "upon whom Lumet has concentrated the lens so often and so long that at times it takes on the quality of a one-woman recitation."³⁶ Citing the director of *Morning Glory*, the critic in *Films in Review* derided, "Sidney Lumet is no Lowell Sherman. His lack of polish would have been altogether fatal but for the fact that he had the luck to have two fine actors in key roles."³⁷ *Variety* praised Fonda for his "customary quiet authority" and thought Marshall "limned a warming portrait."³⁸ Such left-handed compliments once again left Lumet shouldering the responsibility for why it didn't work. The "honeymoon" of *Twelve Angry Men* hadn't lasted long, as he predicted.

Lumet's TV version of *All the King's Men* (1958) earned critical kudos, though not all of them for the right reasons. He shot one crowd scene where the lead character, a politician (Neville Brand) who becomes corrupted by the system, is speaking to a large number of people. Lumet was running low on money at this point and couldn't afford all the extras he wanted to have in the scene. As a result, they seemed very far away from Brand. Critics viewing the scene praised him for the way he appeared to distance Brand from the people who elected him. Lumet had to laugh. The "distance" was caused by a lack of funds, not anything artistic.³⁹

One is reminded of a conversation he once had with one of his favorite directors, Akira Kurosawa. Lumet had been fascinated by a particular camera angle Kurosawa used in his masterpiece *Ran* and asked why he framed it this way. Kurosawa replied that if he moved the camera an inch to the left, the Sony factory would have been seen—which he didn't want—and if he moved it an inch to the right, the airport would have been visible.⁴⁰ No doubt the critics saw some ulterior significance in that as well.

Lumet went into dangerous territory again with his next film, *That Kind of Woman*. Like *Stage Struck*, it was a romantic drama. But unlike *Stage Struck* it had Sophia Loren. Loren was one of the hottest actresses in Hollywood, at the forefront of the flood of sexy Italian stars who'd invaded the film industry, like Gina Lollobrigida, Silvana Mangano and Anna Magnani. Her husband Carlo Ponti was producing the film, which gave her extra clout. Her marriage wasn't recognized in Italy as his divorce from a previous marriage hadn't been formalized but this didn't affect her standing in Hollywood, nor his. The fact that, at 48, Ponti was twice her age had reverberations on the plot, which had her as the kept woman of a middle-aged George Sanders.

On a train to New York during World War II, Loren's character has a romantic encounter with a soldier (Tab Hunter) in a sleeping car. They part the following morning at Penn Station but Hunter is smitten by her and follows her all over New York to try and rekindle the passion of their night together. It was an inversion of the usual "one night stand" movie where the heroine usually pursued the hero, perhaps as a result of being pregnant. There was no way Loren would be running after Tab Hunter in *That Kind of Woman*. She was too busy living the high life with Sanders. The question the film asked was whether she would be capable of sacrificing Sanders' material comforts for the more earthy charms of Tab. Could love—and youth—beat money?

Hunter, as most people in Hollywood knew by now, was gay. How would Lumet get away with casting a gay man opposite an Italian sex goddess? (Answer: He wouldn't.) Even if audiences weren't aware of that fact, it would have been difficult for them to accept him winning Loren. He was, after all, a pretty boy, a "Hollywood product."⁴¹ But that didn't stop Lumet trying.

The film was originally supposed to have been shot in Texas but Lumet changed the location to New York. Once again he employed Boris Kaufman as his cameraman. The screenwriter was his friend Walter Bernstein, who'd been blacklisted by HUAC in the '40s for purported communist affiliations. Ponti was less concerned about this than a Hollywood producer might have been.

Freed from the constraints of *Twelve Angry Men* and *Stage Struck*, Lumet demonstrated his love of the outdoors to great effect in the film, shooting it everywhere from 125th Street in Harlem to Irish bars on Third Avenue, from the Brooklyn Bridge to Staten Island, from Sutton Place to Little Italy, from Fifth Avenue to Grand Central Station. Said Hunter, "The city became as much the star of the show as Sophia."[42]

Hunter's friend Anthony Perkins had recently starred with Loren in the Eugene O'Neill adaptation *Desire Under the Elms* and been blown off the screen by her. When Perkins asked Hunter how he felt about working with her, he said, "Under all that fire and sex, she's like a kitten."[43]

The film contains a subplot featuring Jack Warden and Barbara Nichols. Their predicament mirrors that of Hunter and Loren. Nichols faces the choice of having an economically comfortable life with a general or a more frugal one with the man (lowly soldier Warden) she loves. But Warden won't ask her to marry him and she isn't willing to wait forever. Her body clock is ticking. She wants a ring on her finger. Maybe the general will give one to her. Even if he doesn't, she'll have material bonuses with him, being a kept woman—like Loren.

Nichols' decision to sacrifice love to pragmatism drives Loren in the opposite direction. This is all somewhat contrived. Nichols' capitulation to consumerism makes Loren realize love is what's important after all. The film becomes mushy here. When she chooses Hunter in the last scene, it's like *Brief Encounter* with a bad jazz score. (Lumet was usually very good with music. What happened here?)

Their *Romeo and Juliet*-style coupling doesn't work for a number of reasons, the main one being that Hunter doesn't do enough to win Loren. She runs the full gamut of emotions in the film but he spends most of his time just gazing yearningly at her. She ranges from laughter to tears in the blink of an eye but Hunter has just one expression: strained intensity. There was also a problem with his voice. He sounded like Dennis Hopper more than himself. It was almost as if he was doing a Hopper impersonation.

"I can't give you what he can," he says, referring to Sanders. "All I can give you is me. But you'd have it all." These are big lines but Hunter isn't the man to deliver them.

Lumet had to push him to his limits to get the performance he wanted out of him. After one scene, he told him he was being too tame in his acting. "If you want to play it safe," he derided, "stay in bed all day long. That's the safest place to be but it's also the dullest."[44]

Despite the lack of chemistry between Hunter and Loren, they became good friends. It was a blistering summer and she invited him into her air-conditioned limo between takes to listen to pop music on her radio. Bobby Darin's "Splish Splash" was a big hit that year and they had great fun dueting on it. "Sophia had an incredible sense of humor," Hunter recalled, "and a magnetic personality that drew everyone to her. Her on-screen personality was very misleading. She was no more a man-devouring tigress than I was the naïve boy-next-door. She was a talented and guileless woman and everyone she worked with should be thankful to have known her."[45]

But Loren, too, had problems with Hunter's acting. One afternoon she told him she thought she was upstaging him. He didn't know if it was an apology or a rebuke. He knew she was the bigger star by far and became defensive in his response, telling her he felt he was going to be just as much a hit with viewers when the film came out as she would be. "Look, Sophia," he taunted. "Sooner or later audiences are going to get tired of your face filling the screen. It'll be like a refreshing breeze to catch a glimpse of someone else."[46] Sadly for him, that wasn't the way things panned out.

The film premiered at New York's Roxy Theatre, which seated almost 6000 people. Singers were employed to dramatize the night. Anyone who was expecting a hothouse drama was sorely disappointed. It only played for three weeks before being pulled from circulation. Hunter put its failure down to a combination of bad timing and misleading marketing. Paramount packaged it as a romantic comedy whereas Lumet had focused more on the "darker corners" of the story. Hunter felt his "new-realist" approach clashed with Ponti's attempt to draw in the younger audiences who had posters of Hunter on their walls, or who enjoyed Loren's most recent film, the Cary Grant comedy *Houseboat*.[47]

Hunter never looked like the type of man who could break down Loren's materialist spirit. *Saturday Review*'s Hollis Alpert was right when he wrote that she looked like she'd tired of "several Tab Hunters before cornering George Sanders."[48]

Lumet used too many close-ups of him, most of which highlighted his weakness as an actor. At times the film looked like a travesty of a silent movie.[49] As far as *Variety* was concerned, Hunter did little in the film but "gazingly look hurt."[50] The *New York Herald Tribune* felt that screenwriter Bernstein couldn't make up his mind if he was making a comedy or a serious drama.[51] *Time* hit it on the head about the lack of chemistry between Hunter and Loren with a pun on the film's title: "That kind of woman should never be mated with that kind of man."[52]

There was no way Hunter, the former *Photoplay* pin-up, could match Loren's 1000-watt sexuality. One reviewer blasted, "It's like watching a speedboat race a tricycle." Another one felt it was Hunter's homosexual orientation that stopped any chemistry taking place between them. Lumet agreed with this. "If you put Sophia in the arms of someone who's not responsive to women, or someone who can't pretend he is, there are going to be problems."[53]

Hunter thought Lumet's attitude was a betrayal of his trust in him when he gave him the role. Why did he hire him if he felt that way about him? Was he just being wise in hindsight? "Sidney had specifically asked for me," he pointed out. Paramount also wanted him, as did Ponti and Loren. When the film failed to live up to its expectations, he believed he was the fall guy. "If it had been a winner at the box office," he claimed, "nobody would have been questioning whether I belonged in Sophia Loren's arms or not."[54]

He was probably right there. As the old saying goes, "Failure is an orphan but success has a thousand fathers." It was unfair of Lumet to single him out. The real villain of the piece was Ponti, who turned the film into a different kind of one than Lumet envisaged, a blancmange comedy with a milquetoast hero rather than a May–December romance that asked serious questions about age. "The problems were studio-related," he said. "Ponti and I didn't get along."[55]

Loren was disappointed that the movie didn't fare better at the box office, especially since it had been directed by such a great artist as Lumet.[56] Considering she felt this way, why didn't she put a word in her husband's ear about the fact that it was mixed up in its intent and that as a result they were all about to lay an egg? The fact that Lumet ended up with a misguided sudser made him think this was life's punishment for the fun he had helming it: "To make up for the joy of seeing Sophia Loren every morning, God punishes the director with the mix."[57]

The film was edited savagely by Ponti. Even Loren's part was trimmed down. "It was one of the things that scared me about going to work for a major studio," Lumet told Peter Bogdanovich years later.[58] "The best scenes were cut out," he said elsewhere, "and the weak ones left in." *That Kind of Woman*, as a result, lost all the charm he'd tried to put into it.[59] "Not to be involved in the post-production of movies," he sighed, "is like the director suddenly leaving a play when it goes out of town."[60] This was one of the main reasons he shied away from Hollywood. Such dangers were greater there. (In later years, when he became more established in the industry, Lumet got "final cut.")

In 1959, he explained his reasons for staying in New York. First of all, he said, he didn't know of any director who got better after going to Hollywood. He cited Fred Zinnemann is someone who managed to produce great work without going west. Working in both Hollywood and New York wasn't a possibility because such a gypsy existence, with homes on both coasts, wouldn't have suited him.

Hollywood's traditional boast was that it had better technicians and shooting facilities than New York. Lumet claimed good technicians could be found anywhere. As for shooting facilities, a sound stage was a sound stage wherever it was. The fabulous back lots of yore were suitable for movies of the past, he allowed, but they wouldn't be accepted by sophisticated modern audiences: "You can't shoot on studio streets and pretend any more. It has to be real."[61] New York always gave him that sense of reality. It was a city that was "always changing and yet always remains the same."[62]

Another reason he stayed in New York was to avoid the patriarchal studio system which allowed studio heads to wander onto sets willy-nilly and make demands when they got there.[63] This to him was a gross invasion of professional privacy. It was also typical of Hollywood's bullish attitude. He described Hollywood generally as "a company town not fit for human habitation."[64]

A third reason for staying put was more personal: "I'm a city rat. When I leave New York, my nose starts to bleed."[65]

On the Wing

The failure of *That Kind of Woman* after the similarly under-performing *Stage Struck* made Lumet wonder if *Twelve Angry Men* had been a fluke. He needed another hit. To make one, he thought it was wise to go for another theatrical adaptation.

The Fugitive Kind was based on Tennessee Williams' play *Orpheus Descending*, which played on Broadway in 1955 with Cliff Robertson and Maureen Stapleton in the main roles. It was the story of New Orleans blues guitarist Val Xavier: He has a criminal past but at the beginning of the film he's decided to go straight. He wanders into a small Southern town where "Lady," the wife of the corrupt local sheriff, gives him shelter and arranges a job for him as a clerk at the local general store. Lady is attracted to Val and throws herself at him. He's also pursued by Carol, an outcast from a plantation family.

Martin Jurow, the producer of the film, was interested in Anna Magnani taking the part of Lady. She was living with Anthony Franciosa at the time, and wanted Franciosa to be her co-star, but Jurow didn't think he was a big enough name. He went in search of Marlon Brando instead. Brando was badly in need of money at the time, having been financially crippled by a recent divorce from Anna Kashfi. He was also having problems with his production company, Pennebaker, over the editing of his last film, *One-Eyed Jacks*. Brando had directed it but it ran to nearly five hours so he had to cut at least half of that. "I needed money," he said, "and it was the best role I could find in a hurry."[1]

Williams wrote the two main characters for Magnani and Brando to play on stage but both of them had turned down his offer—Magnani because of film commitments and Brando because he didn't think his character was developed enough. Magnani's one, in contrast, was. This meant that if he agreed to play opposite her, she would have "wiped me off the stage."[2] He thought the play contained some of Williams' best writing apart from the problems with Xavier. This ruined it for him: "He never takes a stand. I didn't know what he was for or against."[3]

Magnani was so anxious to have Brando in the cast that she asked Williams to make his part bigger and hers smaller. It was probably the only time in film history that a star asked for their part to be reduced rather than increased.[4] If that wasn't flattering enough, Jurow offered Brando $1 million, the highest fee ever made to an actor at that time.[5] Brando's eyes lit up. When he heard that Lumet was going to direct it, his eyes lit up brighter. He had a lot of respect for him.[6] He always admired directors who'd been actors because they knew how hard it was. He felt Lumet would be more sympathetic to any problems he had with Xavier, who came across to him as a kind of Stanley Kowalski without the spirit.[7]

It was Magnani who brought Lumet's name to Jurow's attention. She thought his background as a Group Theater director made him an obvious choice for Williams' script.[8] Lumet approached the project with a lot of enthusiasm. He was about to direct a film written by America's greatest playwright and starring its greatest actor. What was there not to love?

Boris Kaufman was again director of photography. Maureen Stapleton and Joanne Woodward were the two other female leads. Stapleton had played the Magnani role in the Broadway production but she wasn't bankable enough to reprise it on screen. Lumet was nervous asking her if she'd settle for the smaller role. In the end, it was she who rang him asking him if she could do it. She had no problem downsizing, which relieved him.[9]

Woodward played Carol, the outcast. Brando knew her, having dated her for a month back in 1953. She was also seeing Paul Newman at that time. She preferred Newman to Brando but Newman was married at the time, which complicated matters. He told her he'd marry her as soon as he could get out of his other marriage, which wasn't a happy one. Woodward's choice of Brando as a date seemed to come about as a result of Newman's circumstances. He hardly seemed like her type.[10]

The film was originally supposed to have been shot on location in the Deep South but Lumet didn't want to go there so it was filmed in a town near Poughkeepsie.[11] Magnani jettisoned Franciosa when he was dumped from the role, focusing her sights on Brando as a possible new lover. Brando wasn't attracted to her and he was also afraid of being upstaged by her, the same fear he had of the stage version that they both turned down. but he respected her talent. When you played opposite her, he declared, you had to either have a wonderful part or carry "a fair-size rock in your hand."[12]

He was late for the first reading, having missed a flight. Magnani thought this was a deliberate attempt to annoy her. When he started to read, it was in a voice so low as to be inaudible. She followed suit, as did Woodward. Lumet knew there was a kind of subtle "star wars" game going on but he said nothing. It was Williams who finally exploded with, "I'd need radar equipment to hear what you're all saying. If I can't hear my fucking dialogue, I'm going home." Brando and Magnani smiled at one another in a temporary *détente*.[13]

As was his custom, Lumet put his cast through two weeks

Marlon Brando curls up with Anna Magnani in his famous snakeskin jacket in *The Fugitive Kind*, Lumet's adaptation of Tennessee Williams' play *Orpheus Descending*. The film divided both critics and the public alike in its confused treatment of a raft of different themes (Jerry Ohlinger).

of rehearsals before filming began. This suited Brando, who liked to do multiple readings of a part to get a fix on his character. Magnani was less patient, feeling more and more drained after each one. She was also increasingly irked by the continuing "Marlon mumble."[14]

There were many ego clashes here. Brando wasn't the only Oscar winner on the set. Woodward and Magnani also held that distinction, Woodward for *The Three Faces of Eve* and Magnani for another Williams venture, *The Rose Tattoo*. All three seemed aware of their position in the pecking order, which led to a lot of friction. Brando also argued with Williams about *Orpheus Descending*, especially the demeaning way blacks were treated in it. Brando saw them as little more than props, or "window panes." He regarded this as a subtle example of racial discrimination in his part.[15]

But his biggest problem was Magnani. He was afraid of her making amorous advances on him ever since Williams told him she had feelings for him. There was a time he might have been interested in her but not now. He saw her as being sexually frustrated and past her prime.

She tried to get him on his own many times as they prepared to start shooting the film. One afternoon she succeeded at the Beverly Hills Hotel in an incident that became more farcical than anything else. She put her arms around him and started to rain kisses on him. He tried to pull away from her but she hung on for dear life, eventually biting his lip in her ardor. As her passion increased, Brando was reminded of "one of those mating rituals of insects that end when the female administers the *coup de grace*." His lip was hurting badly by this point, so badly that he grabbed her nose and squeezed it as hard as he could, as if he were squeezing a lemon. This startled her and enabled him to make his escape.[16]

A young screenwriter, Meade Roberts, collaborated with Williams on the screenplay. He wrote an interesting prologue to the main plot, which features Brando in a courtroom. For many people, this was the best scene in the film.[17] It gave Brando an opportunity to establish the character of Xavier in a way the rest of it fails to follow up on. He stands before a judge and explains to him why he got into a fight at a party. His guitar was stolen and this was like a personal violation for him. "Everybody's got something that's very important to them," he says, "and with me it's my guitar." Lumet doesn't show us the judge, which gives it a kind of Kafkaesque feel. Brando is excellent. Lumet lets him flow without—one imagines—any direction at all.

There was a lot of media speculation around the film. That happened any time Brando made a film. His reputation preceded him. The rumor mills were especially busy because of his behavior on the set of *One-Eyed Jacks*. The budget had spiraled out of control under his direction and he was blamed. There were also a number of stories circulating about his private life, which was generally the case with him.

Lumet was sympathetic to the fact that Brando was a man more sinned against than sinning. "We were in rehearsal a week," he recalled, "when I read that Marlon hadn't shown up yet."[18] He knew paper wouldn't refuse ink where Brando was concerned. It didn't matter if it was the truth or lies that was printed. His name sold papers.

Brando appreciated the fact that Lumet didn't show much interest in this kind of gossip. He also admired his work, so much so that a year or so before taking on *The Fugitive Kind* he'd asked him if he would have been interested in directing *One-Eyed*

Jacks.[19] On the *Fugitive Kind* set, they became good friends and empathetic colleagues. Lumet described Brando as "angelic" and described the aforementioned courtroom scene as containing "the best acting I have ever seen in a movie."[20]

Lumet showed a freewheeling attitude to his direction from the get-go. When it rained cats and dogs at the beginning of the shoot and everyone was feeling miserable doing nothing, he decided to shoot a later scene—which called for rain—to keep them occupied. To the incurable optimist, the bad weather turned out to be another one of his "happy accidents."[21]

Brando did every take differently, as was his wont. Lumet enjoyed this, but the same couldn't be said for the rest of the cast. Magnani got revenge on him by trying the same thing on him but there was always going to be only one winner in this kind of game.

Brando was slow to learn his lines and Lumet didn't discipline him for this. His self-indulgent behavior continued as the days went on. Jurow remarked, "He was a god and he knew it."[22] The mumbling also continued, and the pregnant pauses between his lines. Said Stapleton, "I could make dinner in all that space."[23]

The three women told Lumet that Brando was threatening to destroy the film, but the director didn't agree. "He's extraordinarily knowledgeable about his instrument," he said. By "instrument," he meant his intuitive gifts, which saw possibilities in scenes that few others would have. Lumet and Brando had endless conversations about how they should be done, to the growing indignation of the other cast members. Lumet liked the fact that he was constantly questioning: "It's thrilling to watch it and it's thrilling to argue with him and help him channel that extraordinary motor into the place that the script demands."[24]

"When you work with Marlon," he said, "you only have one job: release him, get him moving, get him afraid—yes, even Marlon is afraid. That doesn't mean you simply let him go. You must stay within the confines, heading towards an objective,"[25] So what was that objective? Sometimes Lumet wasn't sure.

He knew Brando was testing him, as he tested all directors, to see if they knew what they were doing. The test was always the same. He would do a scene two ways with only slight variations but within those variations lay his whole feeling. "He'll watch which one you decide to print," said Lumet, "and on that decision relies your whole subsequent relationship with him. Because if you don't know your job as well as he knows his, you've had it. In those performances where you've seen him just walk through a film, he made the test and the director flunked it."[26]

Meanwhile, the childish games between Brando and Magnani continued. Lumet was amused by these. In a scene where Magnani asks Brando to hand her a reference for a job he's seeking, he searched for the piece of paper in his pocket for an eternity. He also dragged out the process of taking it out of his pocket and smoothing it before handing it to her. Lumet cried out, "Cut! Let's try it again." During the next take, it was Magnani's turn to drag things out. When she got the reference from Brando, she took great care to smooth it out more and more as the camera lingered on her. Lumet knew what was going on in these "acting duels" but chose not to become involved.[27]

Brando wasn't the only problem for the increasingly distressed Magnani. One day she upbraided Kaufman for photographing her too harshly. To bolster her case, she brought some glossy pictures of Sophia Loren and Gina Lollobrigida to the set and showed them to Lumet, telling him that was how she wanted to look.[28] Lumet didn't have the heart to tell her that she wasn't a Loren or a Lollobrigida even in her best days, which were in the long-ago past. It wasn't Kaufman that was the problem; it was "anno domini." Lumet did the best he could to flatter her appearance without compromising the artistic integrity of the film. This involved a complicated use of chiaroscuros. Brando, in contrast, was usually shot against a light background to distinguish him from the darker hues of the dry goods store where he worked.[29]

Magnani found Lumet "too technical" in his direction. She thought he was limited by his television background. When he put chalk marks on the floor indicating where she was to move in a particular scene, she exploded. "What are these signs? I can't act this way. I'm not used to it. You must let me breathe." She suggested an alternative. She promised him she'd do the scene as he wished if it didn't work out. "But first time my way, please."[30] She knew he was giving more time to Brando than to her. This was true but Brando was where the money was. His salary had eaten up a quarter of the film's budget.

She both resented and admired Brando. "He's crazy," she blasted, "like me."[31] And elsewhere: "When I work with him, it's like I work with a wild animal."[32] Lumet never knew what to expect from her. "Sidney," she said to him one day, "you've got to realize I am not a trained actor. I'm either a miracle or a disaster."[33]

Her instinctive approach made her inconsistent for Lumet: "When that motor gets going, everything happens. When it isn't going, nothing happens." The language barrier was another problem. He had to employ a translator to know what she was saying, and for her to know what he was saying. Acting was agony for her, he believed: "She has to rip herself into pieces to get what she wants."[34] But when she was on fire, it was worth it. He didn't care how long it took until he got the right take. He knew the film centered around her character rather than Brando's, which dissipates in the last half of the action. From that point of view, the play's title was apt: Orpheus *descends*.[35]

Williams was renowned for his female creations, starting with Blanche DuBois. Brando and Lumet knew this. They tried to get him to flesh Xavier out but he couldn't, despite Lumet's urgings. "Whatever solutions I'd come up with," Lumet groaned, "would not work for Tennessee, and you can't force a situation. It had to fit organically into what he had in

Anna Magnani (left) and Joanne Woodward square up to one another in *The Fugitive Kind* as a bewildered Marlon Brando looks on (Jerry Ohlinger).

mind and what flows easily for him. That we never found, and to me it's the failing of the picture."³⁶ It had a Blanche but no Kowalski.

Lumet didn't think it had to be this way. He knew there were Kowalski-style lines in the script, as when Brando says to Magnani, "I see through you, Lady." Williams, unfortunately, refused to write more of these. He liked the script too much as it was and didn't encourage Roberts to change it. He also refused to discuss it with Lumet. He even avoided innocuous questions from him, as when he asked him if Xavier was meant to be a disguised version of St. Valentine. Instead of saying yea or nay, he just smiled "that enigmatic little smile."³⁷

To establish why Xavier wasn't more attracted to Carol than Lady, efforts were made to make Woodward look less pretty than she was. She was dressed in a baggy coat. Her eyes were smeared with white makeup, her eyes rimmed with kohl.³⁸

Woodward hated working with Brando. "He wasn't there," she complained. "He was somewhere else. There was nothing to reach out to."³⁹ As the film went on and their relationship degenerated, she said the only way she'd work with him again would be "in rear projection."⁴⁰

He usually only behaved this badly when he was bored on a set. That was probably the reason here too. Working people up diverted him. He did it more with Magnani than Woodward. Sometimes it verged on harassment. "Why can't she use Nair?" he asked Lumet one day when he spotted hair on her upper lip before they were due to kiss. "Why doesn't she take a shave?"⁴¹

Stapleton was the least angry of the three women in the cast. She loved working with Lumet. She couldn't figure out where he got all his energy. "It's like he's doing two movies at once," she said. All the waiting around that actors usually did wasn't for him: "It drives Sidney crazy." To avert it, he kept whizzing around the set. He didn't talk much, Stapleton noticed, but when he did, it was for a good reason: "His eye and ear are infallible."⁴²

Brando's sullen personality was used to good effect in the film. Instead of vying with Magnani, he chose to brood on the sidelines. That way there was less danger of her "wiping him off the stage." In this sense, he resembled the bird he speaks of in his main speech in the film, the one that lives on the wing. *The Fugitive Kind* is worth seeing for this speech alone. It was written beautifully by Williams and delivered with a sense of rhapsodic wonder by Brando. "You know," he says, "there's a kind of bird that don't have legs so it can't light on nothin'. It has to stay all its life on its wings in the sky. They just spread their wings and go to sleep on the wind. They never light on this earth but one time. Then they die."

He worked harder on the speech than anything else in the film, no doubt knowing it was his best chance to give some much-needed depth to his character. Apart from its poignancy, it also carried the film's title in it, which created extra attention for an audience. He had problems with it, though, and kept stumbling on the same line. It was a Friday and everyone was tired. He did take after take but he still couldn't get the line right. All the cast wanted to be away, including him. He was about to go to Kashfi for the weekend. He said to Lumet, "Sidney, do you think we could leave this until Monday?"⁴³

Lumet wasn't sure what to do. It didn't take a genius to figure out that he was having some kind of a block. Lumet feared it could worsen over the weekend. Brando's shirt was soaked with sweat from wrestling with the line.

"I could have told him what was blocking him," Lumet claimed, "because he kept going off on the same line every time. From a previous conversation between us, I knew what that was about." But he didn't want to play the psychologist. If he heard something from an actor about his personal life, he didn't feel he had the right to "use or misuse that in terms of the work."[44] It was almost like the seal of the confessional for a priest as far as he was concerned, a sacred ground one didn't traverse. So he didn't say anything to Brando about what he thought might be troubling him.

"If we don't get it now," Lumet said, "we'll never get it. I'd rather bullet through." Brando understood his reasoning. He took a deep breath, tried again and after some more false starts, finally got it—on the 34th take.[45] He hugged Lumet in relief when he finally said the magic word, "Print." Lumet thought this was because he hadn't invaded his space: "I let him fight through it himself. I didn't try to be a psychoanalytic smart-ass."[46] It was unusual for a man renowned for fast takes to be so patient. Neither was he a lover of improvisation. But he knew this was the most important scene in the film. That was why he allowed Brando such latitude.

Lumet allowed him latitude with time as well, letting him away from the set every now and again to try and sort out his divorce details with Kashfi or to try and fix the editing problems with *One-Eyed Jacks*. This didn't go down too well with the other cast members but Lumet felt it would have the effect of getting the best out of Brando when the time came to do his scenes. He knew there was no point in having him around if his mind was AWOL.

Sometimes, though, Brando's absence from the set taxed even Lumet's patience. One day he was nowhere to be found and the director was screaming, "Where is he? I want to shoot!" Eventually he appeared. When he did, he started apologizing profusely to all the people there, an uncharacteristic gesture for him. The apology, however, was directed more to the crew than the cast. "I know you guys are docked for being late and it affects your paycheck," he said. "That should happen to me too but it probably won't." He said nothing about Lumet or the other cast members, who were the ones mostly discommoded.[47] This, everyone felt, was in poor taste.

Magnani thought Lumet treated Brando with kid gloves, which made her more angry with him in the scenes they did together. Their rivalry continued right until the last day of shooting. In fact, it went on even afterwards, when the film was completed and the talk turned to billing. Brando said he would only allow Magnani to share top billing with him in Italy. In the U.S., he wanted it.[48] Magnani could do nothing but fume.

In the film, in contrast, Lady softens towards Xavier as it nears its end. To indicate this, Lumet used a longer lens for both of them in the final scenes: "He'd changed her life. She was now in his world."[49]

As the strange mélange of stars prepared to go their separate ways, none of them were fully sure what kind of film they'd made. It hadn't been a happy experience for any of them but that wasn't necessarily a yardstick. Smug sets sometimes produced bad art while tense ones often produced masterpieces. Would that be the way with *The Fugitive Kind*? Lumet hoped so. He knew all the performances were strong but also that they were delivered on an uncertain canvas. Roberts had changed Williams' script as much as he could but had he made it better or worse? Williams thought worse.

The film was previewed in December 1959 to boos and laughter from audiences. Williams was so incensed at what he saw as the bowdlerization of his work that he refused to speak to Lumet on the way out of the theater. Lumet was devastated too. He re-cut the film, trimming it by 25 minutes to try and give it more life. He thought the truncated version would work better but when it was released, the reviews were almost uniformly bad. The *Los Angeles Times* barked, "Too much is too much, even from Tennessee Williams." Brando's performance was described as being little more than "mumbling with marbles in his mouth."[50]

Lumet was aware most of the characters in the film were overdrawn—the volatile Magnani, the sex-mad Woodward, Magnani's bitter husband (Victor Jory), the brutal sheriff (R.G. Armstrong)—which meant he welcomed Brando's underplaying. The star's moodiness usually exploded into fury in his films but here it failed to. This meant it ended as it began, like a dormant volcano, despite the fire that claims Brando's life and gives him one of those martyred demises that were to become all too familiar in his career.

Despite the high-quality cast and the occasional writing riches, *The Fugitive Kind* had to be racked up as another Lumet flop. Was he too much in awe of his three Oscar winners? Hollis Alpert thought so: "His crime seems to be that he allowed the actors to do what they wished—pace and movement be damned."[51]

Films in Review was more vicious: "*The Fugitive Kind* is such a mess of technical incompetence and psychopathic misrepresentation as to be a disgrace to U.S. culture. It derives from one of the last scraps—let us hope—at the bottom of Tennessee Williams' barrel of degenerate plays. Why was such a witch's brew turned into a motion picture?" The critic went on to trash the (mis)direction of Lumet and the performances of an "incomprehensible" Magnani, a "facially gross" Brando and a misfit Woodward: "Her performance is so grotesque, one wonders if Lumet wasn't deliberately trying to ruin her career."[52] Lumet wasn't used to such mauling but he was playing for bigger stakes now than in his modest courtroom drama, his valentine to Broadway or his lightweight rom-com. The salaries alone took care of that. He was now a target.

David Shipman had mixed feelings about the film. It was effusive, he wrote, and had too many dangling ends, which meant that the themes of the play on which it was based were more often implied than stated. The overall effect for him was of "some modern myth, its curling edges unfamiliar."[53]

Maybe the main problem was that it wasn't cinematic. Responsibility for this had to go down to Williams and Roberts, if not Lumet.[54] Neither did the metaphorical parallels to Eurydice and Hades come off. The film didn't go much further than giving us a glimpse into an ugly town inhabited by mostly ugly people. It left a flat aftertaste, despite Kaufman's atmospheric photography and a moody Kenyon Hopkins jazz score. It was, unsurprisingly, the first Brando film to lose money—not something any director wanted to have on his CV, especially someone of Lumet's pedigree.

The surprise with *The Fugitive Kind* isn't so much that it fails to be great—it was, after all, based on one of Williams' most disjointed plays—but that it has any quality at all. The fact that Brando's character remained almost as undeveloped in the final cut as he did in Williams' first draft meant that his scenes with Magnani—the supposed "meat" of the movie—had all the life of a dead haddock. When Stanley Kowalski exploded in *A Streetcar Named Desire*, Blanche DuBois went into a shell. The Kowalski character here is Magnani. Somehow it doesn't work as well watching Brando as the DuBois clone. We await the moment where he'll reverse the roles but it doesn't come. His ambition in the film seemed to be to stop Magnani from stealing scenes from him rather than him creating some of his own to steal from her. To do this, he would have needed much better dialogue to work from. Lumet couldn't draw this from thin air so one was left with the opening scene and the speech about the bird as two beacons in an otherwise limp script.

Lumet believed Magnani was responsible for most of the problems. He thought Brando shone when he was away from her. "His scenes with Joanne Woodward," he contended, "contained some of the best acting he's ever done." Magnani, he thought, had too much vanity to be great. Her talent was dwindling, he believed, as her looks faded. Brando, on the contrary, was "Herculean—very giving," and yet he bore the brunt of the blame when the film failed to perform at the box office.[55]

This was over-generous. Even Brando knew he was under par here. He also looked distinctly uncomfortable playing a guitar in the film. As a prop, it didn't suit him; as a character tool, it didn't convince. He struggled to make something of the part. The fact that he did so in any shape or form was a testament to his screen presence. Even when his co-stars have superior lines—and he was aware that Magnani's were generally better—you're watching him.

One of the few complimentary reviews he received was from *The Daily Express*, which said that he exuded a "sulky pathos."[56] The fact that Williams created Xavier with him in mind was probably a disadvantage rather than an advantage. It didn't free up his pen but rather limited it. Lumet had to work hard to combat all these pitfalls.

Brando and Williams sniped at one another for everything that had gone wrong when the post mortems started. "I just wish he didn't remember Kowalski so well," Williams complained.[57] Brando thought precisely the opposite, that there wasn't enough of Kowalski in the part. This was closer to the truth. Williams was desperately searching for someone to blame besides himself. The fact that he was booed coming out of the preview of the film went hard with him. One of the crowd shouted out, "There's Tennessee Williams, the guy who wrote the piece of junk we just saw."[58] Some of the crowd even spat at him. Undaunted, Williams spat back at them.[59] He felt validated in this. The play that he was said to have loved even more than *Streetcar* was now a thorn in his side and he found that hard to countenance.

There were a few positive voices. Bosley Crowther lauded the film for a "morbid tempo that lets time drag and passions slowly shape."[60] The *New York Times* praised Brando and Magnani for their "poignancy and longing" in it.[61] *Film Comment* credited it with foreshadowing the turmoil of the South in the '60s.[62]

These were largely lone voices in a relentless sea of abuse. A bewildered Lumet could only throw up his hands in despair and sigh, "I tried to pour oblivion out of a bottle but it wouldn't come out."[63]

Peaks and Valleys

Depressed over the box office failure of *The Fugitive Kind*, Lumet went back to Broadway to direct Albert Camus' *Caligula*. Camus had always refused to grant permission for the play to be staged in America for fear of it being done badly, but he admired Lumet's work and changed tack when he heard he'd be helming it.[1]

After this, Lumet did another television film. In the summer of 1960 he directed *The Sacco and Vanzetti Story*, a two-part documentary about two Italian-born anarchists who were convicted of killing a guard and a paymaster during the robbery of a shoe company in Massachusetts in 1920. It was written by Reginald (*Twelve Angry Men*) Rose and starred Peter Falk and E.G. Marshall. If Lumet's pride had been dented by *The Fugitive Kind*, it received a timely boost with this film, winning an Emmy for it. The Sacco and Vanzetti case is generally regarded as one of the most shameful examples of legal negligence in American history, the two men in question being sacrificial martyrs to a communist witch hunt. It foreshadowed Lumet's later *Daniel* in the manner in which it calibrated socio-political themes.

In the fall, Lumet directed a theatrical version of Eugene O'Neill's *The Iceman Cometh*. This was a massive undertaking, a four-hour production starring Jason Robards, and Lumet did it proud. It was first presented on WNTA-TV on the *Play of the Week* series. Ely Landau produced it. It was a marvelous achievement to come to grips with the kind of emotions O'Neill had on display here within the confines of a television show. "I've seen some Shakespeare on TV," Lumet told Peter Bodganovich, "and it's disastrous. I wonder if the sheer physical size of the screen isn't something that rules out tragedy."[2]

It didn't do so here. The production was faithful to O'Neill's words, so much so that his widow, Carlotta Monterey, gave Lumet the rights to all subsequent O'Neill productions that she had control over.[3] Robards gave a crowning performance under Lumet's tutelage. Harry Hope's bar was recreated in all its dismal glory as the sad souls who inhabited it poured their hearts out. The cast also included a young Robert Redford.

Lumet was then offered *A Raisin in the Sun*, a film that would have been ideal for him, dealing as it did with the attempts of a black family in a Chicago tenement to retain some dignity within their straitened circumstances, but it would have meant going to Hollywood and he didn't want to do that. "I can improve by staying in the East," he declared. "I'll let Hollywood come to me."[4] With a few notable exceptions, that was how he would play out the remainder of his career.

He now turned his attention to another literary work. *A View from the Bridge* was an adaptation of Arthur Miller's poignant tale of Brooklyn longshoreman Eddie Carbone (Raf Vallone), who, with his marriage collapsing, harbors incestuous desires for his niece Catherine (Carol Lawrence). Maureen Stapleton played Beatrice, his wife. After Carbone manages to get two illegal immigrants into the country, and indeed into his house, he becomes tormented with jealousy when one of them falls for Catherine. As a result, he reports both immigrants to the authorities.

There were a lot of big emotions here. In some ways, Miller's script was like a Greek tragedy transplanted onto the wharves of New York. The simmering tensions were handled adeptly by him as he explored Carbone's sexual denial over the niece he and Beatrice have raised from childhood.

The main problem Lumet had with the film was the weather. He shot most of it on the docks, where the wind knifed through him. "When you got home," he gasped, "your shirt stuck to your neck caked with blood, rubbed raw by the material." When he was lining up a shot where he had to put his hand on a wheel, his fingers froze. "I had to get an actor to peel me off," he wailed.[5]

The film ended with Carbone's suicide. In another director's hands, this might have come across as melodramatic but Lumet kept it real, thanks largely to the strong performances of all the cast, especially Vallone. He made the New York docks look very authentic too, though there weren't enough exterior shots in the film for him to explore them in depth.

There are powerhouse performances from the whole cast but Vallone's stands heads and shoulders above the rest. He's almost primitive in his emotions. Carbone's torture is apparent whenever he watches Catherine with the man she loves, Rodolpho (Jean Sorel). When they announce their intention to marry, Carbone goes out of control. When he sees them in an embrace, he pulls them apart and kisses Rodolpho on the lips. Never before had a man kissed another man on the lips in a mainstream work. He does so not from homosexual desire but to imply that Rodolpho, a gentle person, could be gay. It's a desperate move but one he sees as his only chance to break up the pair. All of his subdued emotions come out now. As well as publicizing his hatred for Rodolpho he confesses his infatuation with Catherine.

Afterwards comes the reporting of Rodolpho and

Raf Vallone soliciting the advice of his lawyer (Morris Carnovsky) as he seeks to get rid of the young man who's fallen in love with his niece in *A View from the Bridge*, Lumet's adaptation of Arthur Miller's starkly evocative play.

the other immigrant, Marco (Raymond Pellegrin), to the police. Rodolpho has a chance of being allowed stay in the country because of his forthcoming marriage but Marco knows he's going to be sent back to his poverty-stricken life in Italy where he's going to find it difficult to support his wife and children.

Towards the end of the film, as Marco is being led to prison, he spits at Carbone. After he's bailed out, he goes to Carbone's house and challenges him to a fight. It takes place on the day Catherine is due to marry Rodolpho. Beatrice wants to go to the wedding but Carbone forbids her. He says if she goes, he won't allow her back to the house. When Marco arrives, Carbone goes out onto the street to confront him. Carbone grabs a dockworker's hook but Marco proves stronger than him in their duel. He brings Carbone to his knees. Carbone is full of self-revulsion at this point. In a final gesture of defeatism, he drives the hook into his own heart.

The film garnered generous reviews. The *New York Herald Tribune* commended it for its sense of tension: "Although the outright violence doesn't come until the climax, the threat of it sneaks into every line."[6] The *New York Times* said Lumet "drenched the drama in a proletarian atmosphere so absolute and authentic that actuality seems to pulsate on the screen."[7]

Other reviews were less effusive. *Variety* felt Lumet had a tendency to be theatrical, "hewing more to a series of dramatic incidents rather than letting them grow more harmoniously from the characters and their plight."[8] *The Saturday Review* thought the film veered uncomfortably from the "solemn neo-realism of Raf Vallone to the fluttering naturalism of Maureen Stapleton."[9] *Time* believed Lumet failed to find "in the moral slime of a slum episode the ink to write Greek tragedy as it was written in the golden age"—but the failure was "impressive."[10] According to *The New Republic*, the film "compensates in conciseness for what it lacks in depth."[11]

Buoyed by the success of *The Iceman Cometh*, Lumet decided to do another Eugene O'Neill play. He chose the obvious one, O'Neill's masterpiece *Long Day's Journey Into Night*. He didn't commission a screenwriter. His attitude was, if it was good enough for O'Neill, it was good enough for him. Ely Landau once again was the producer. Very early on, they decided Katharine Hepburn would be a good choice for the role of Mary Tyrone, the drug-addicted mother of the piece.

Landau rang her to ask her if she would agree to be in it. "Who's doing the script?" she asked. Without missing a beat, Landau replied, "O'Neill."[12] That was enough to get her hooked. (O'Neill was long dead by now but she got the point.) Once Hepburn committed, that was the green light for Lumet and Landau to raise the money for it.[13]

Marlon Brando had been Lumet's first choice to play Mary's husband but he refused. He'd been at a theater version of the play that Lumet had done in late 1956 and it had upset him greatly, the character of Mary being too similar to his own mother for comfort. She hadn't been addicted to drugs but she was an alcoholic and that rang similar bells for him. He was so traumatized by the play that he left after the intermission.[14]

The play struck a chord with Lumet, not only because of the brilliance of the writing but also because, like O'Neill, he was the son of a theatrical father. The "uncertainties and excitements" of the theater predominated both men's childhoods.[15]

Lumet and his cast did *Long Day's Journey Into Night* for "union minimum." He formed a cooperative with them where they each worked for a basic salary, agreeing to share whatever profits might accrue from the finished product.[16]

The set was simple: the Tyrone living room. Boris Kaufman was once again the director of photography. Ralph Richardson played Hepburn's husband, a washed-up actor. Jason Robards essayed the role of Jamie, his alcoholic son. Dean Stockwell was the other son, Edmund. His diagnosis of tuberculosis forms one of the driving points of the action. Lumet, as ever, informed his stellar quartet that he would be putting them through two weeks of rehearsals before filming began.

Rehearsals were common in television but not in films. The fact that he set such store by them put him apart from most other directors. Rod Steiger once said, "In 1957, to utter the word 'rehearsal' in Hollywood, they committed you to the insane asylum."[17] He was joking of course but the thinking of the time was that spontaneity was artistically preferable to contrivance, and rehearsals were seen as leading to that. They were regarded by many as a kind of filmmaking where no surprises could happen because the actors were over-prepared. Lumet didn't go along with that kind of thinking, seeing them as mere frameworks. They didn't have to dictate what happened afterwards, merely cut off unnecessary time-wasting on the set for issues that could be addressed before expensive crews were waiting to use their equipment.

Lumet didn't hit it off with Hepburn at their first meeting. She was living in John Barrymore's former house at the time. He stepped into what seemed to him like a 50-foot living room. She walked towards him without even saying hello. The first words out of her mouth were, "When do you want to start rehearsals?" He was shocked but he didn't show it. "September 19th," he replied. Hepburn said, "I can't start till the 26th." When he asked her why she couldn't be there earlier, she rasped, "Because then you would know more about the script that I would."[18]

Ely Landau was with him at the time. He was as shocked by Hepburn's rudeness as Lumet was. When she was out of earshot, Landau whispered, "Let's get somebody else." Lumet didn't think that was a good idea. He told Landau he was employing her as an actress, not a friend. Any problems he had to put up with as a result of her lack of social graces would be worth it "because she's the best person in the world for the part."[19]

He knew she spelled trouble but he didn't let it get to him. When rehearsals began, he spent his time with the other cast members. He wasn't consciously freezing her out, just letting her know she wasn't the only person in the film. And, more importantly, that she wasn't going to intimidate him. On the third day as they all sat at the table, a small voice cried out, "Help!" It was Hepburn. The mountain had come to Muhammad.[20]

Up until that moment, she thought she could do the part on her instinct but instinct, for Lumet, "only lasts for a short while and then starts collapsing under the weight of the emotional demand."[21] She needed technical support to join all the wheels of the machinery and that's where he came in.

Her performance was tight for the first fortnight. At the end of that time, she had a scene where Edmund is trying to tell her he has consumption while she's in denial about it. She didn't know how to react to the news. Lumet suggested she smack Edmund. She didn't want to do that. He had to talk her into it. "She's not a physical actress," he pointed out. "She doesn't clutch people. Physical violence isn't something that comes easily to her." She looked at Lumet for almost two minutes trying to psych herself up for the strange demand. Then she said, "Okay, I'll try it."[22]

After she smacked Edmund, she knew Lumet had been right. She felt a kind of catharsis. It was a defining moment for her, and for her relationship to Lumet. She now had more confidence in him. Because of that, she chilled out with him more, becoming more human with him. One day soon afterwards, he asked her if she'd like to look at the rushes. She said no, that she would have been too embarrassed looking at her sagging flesh. That humanized her even more for him.[23]

Hepburn was feeling emotionally distraught when she made the film. Perhaps that accounted for some of her rudeness. Her father was dying and the health of her longtime lover Spencer Tracy was deteriorating. Normally she didn't use personal emotions for screen ones but in this instance, instead of letting her vulnerability drag her down, she drew on all her resources to use it to improve her performance. As the shoot went on, it became like an all-consuming passion for her. "I couldn't let everyone down," she said. "I knew what financial backing had been raised on my name. We'd all taken almost nothing to be able to make the film."[24]

She drew on the memory of her mother for her performance. This exhibited itself mostly in the gestures she used to convey Mary Tyrone's demons. As Barbara Leaming

Ralph Richardson (left), Dean Stockwell and Katharine Hepburn in a scene from one of Lumet's early theatrical adaptations, *Long Day's Journey into Night.* His Broadway background made him an ideal candidate to helm Eugene O'Neill's classic play. He defended it to the hilt as being much more than "a play with the camera running," a taunt that was levelled at many of his films (Jerry Ohlinger).

wrote in her Hepburn biography, "She clutched herself defensively. She played with her arms. She touched her breasts. She tightened her jaw. She covered her lower face with her hand, curling her fingers inward. One moment her voice was taut and constrained; the next, she allowed all the pent-up rage to spew out. Now she turned down the sides of her mouth; now she flashed a broad, tense, heart-piercing smile." In another role, Leaming observed, such gestures might have seemed mannered but they "powerfully communicated" Mary's inner turmoil."[25]

Hepburn wasn't the only one suffering such turmoil because all of the Tyrones are dysfunctional in their way. All of them have secrets and addictions. None of them seem to be able to get out of the ruts they've dug for themselves. It's unusual to see four victims in the one family. What makes them distinctive is the fact that they're all in denial about their problems. They express such denial by deflecting them onto the other members of the family. The verbal parry and thrust becomes the stuff of tragedy—and occasional farce—as the single day in which the play takes place becomes a microcosm of their lives.

Lumet used different techniques to get the best from all four performers. Richardson was "old school" so he allowed him to declaim. That suited the hammy nature of his character. Hepburn had varying levels of intensity that he encouraged her to plumb in her own time. Robards was a combination of brashness and sensitivity. Lumet never knew what he was going to get out of him from day to day. Stockwell was the most complicated. Like Edmund, he was quiet. "Dean worked very internally," said Lumet, "he needed Strasbergian analysis of each moment in the character."[26]

Hepburn was more important to Lumet than the others because he saw her as the fulcrum of the play, the still point around which everything else revolved. She may not have had the most prominent role line-wise but her withdrawal into her drug-drenched world acted like a template which her husband and sons aped in different degrees. For Lumet, she was the play's moral center.[27]

To convey her withdrawal in visual terms, he used longer and longer lenses on her as the play went on, and wider lenses on the other cast members. He also shot her from above on occasion, which diminished her in size. This increased her sense of isolation from the others, who tended to be in fairly close proximity to one another most of the time.[28] The camera was like a scalpel cutting through their insecurities but Lumet also wanted to show compassion for a family that was in so many ways past rehabilitation.

He treated every nuance of the play meticulously—perhaps too meticulously. Richardson asked him a fairly simple question one day and it took him 45 minutes to answer it. After listening to his extrapolation, Richardson said, "I see what you mean, dear boy. A little more cello, a little less flute." After that, they communicated in musical lingo all the time. Lumet later discovered Richardson used to play a violin in his dressing room when he was appearing in theater to prepare himself for his performance: "He used himself as a musical instrument, literally."[29] Lumet felt as much a conductor as anything else with him as a result.[30]

The film, in fact, was like a musical symphony itself. Lumet shot Hepburn in long takes so that the "legato" feel of her scenes would help audiences drift into her narcotized world. Robards was shot in a staccato rhythm because Lumet wanted him to look disjointed and uncoordinated.[31]

Edmund presented different kinds of problems because he was based on the character of O'Neill himself. *Long Day's Journey* is O'Neill's most personal play so Lumet knew he had to be very careful with him. Edmund wasn't an unduly large part. Lumet tried to rescue him from invisibility in the film by emphasizing his relationship to his mother.

The most obvious problem the film had was the amount of dialogue in it. Lumet grew up on theater so he wasn't afraid of the length of O'Neill's speeches. Too many directors shied away from words whereas he embraced them. He didn't think they could hurt a film if the performances were good enough: "You do a very simple thing—you act the shit out of it. You come in loaded for beer. You've got the room to act the bejesus out of it."[32]

Everyone worked themselves to the bone throughout the shoot to help Lumet capture all the power and plaintiveness of O'Neill's drama. It ended with the Tyrone family still locked in their private hells, at war with one another and yet in a strange kind of bonding, imprisoned in their incestuous bubble as they use one another both to endorse their various addictions and to abuse one another about them. It's the ultimate womb-trap multiplied by four as the curtain comes down on the tragic ensemble.

The day, which has begun so promisingly, has now, thanks to an ominous medical diagnosis and a cozy immersion in mutual bickering, descended into disaster. As the fog begins to roll in from the sea and the long day journeys into night, the layers of respectability have been peeled away. Now all that remains is the illusory past and a woman who used to be happy once, for a time.

The film was shot in 42 days for $435,000. When it ended, they were all drained. Lumet felt as if he'd been crying for the whole 42 days.[33] Now he faced a bigger test: How would it go down with the public? His decision to stick with O'Neill's words may have cheered the purists but it was hardly going to boost its commercial prospects.[34]

His final cut ran almost three hours but he wasn't too worried. In an age of canned culture, he felt it was therapeutic to have to wait for epiphanies and catharses. "People are used to fingertip experience," he sniffed. Sometimes one had to "go around the same circle four times" to find what they're looking for, somewhat like a dog circling a mat before he lies down, or an owl biting into wood: "Finally something bursts."[35] He thought the climax of the film was all the more powerful because the audience had to wait three hours for it. The soliloquies building up to it became like a series of incantatory mantras for him.

He was chuffed to see it win all four acting awards at Cannes. Hepburn was commended for adroitly managing the transition from innocent romantic to world-weary drug addict but some critics questioned whether her emotions were real or manufactured. "There are times," wrote her biographer William J. Mann, "when Mary feels artificial, when the actress playing her feels too blueblood, too Protestant, to truly understand the conflicts of this weak convent girl who once dreamed of being a nun."[36]

Pauline Kael vindictively described both Lumet and O'Neill as "pedestrian." Kael had a grudge against Lumet—for whatever reason—but drawing O'Neill into the equation wasn't clever. It made her admonitions of the film lose their weight. She went on to say that Lumet "did well" with O'Neill's plays because they didn't depend on precision. They were simple, basic and forceful, "solid meat and potatoes so honestly served it's great."[37] Is "great" a word anyone should ascribe to "meat and potatoes"? Particularly anyone as po-faced as Kael? *Haute cuisine* might be "great" but hardly meat and potatoes. Her praise here, as one might have expected where Lumet was concerned, was grudging.

Her misgivings, however, weren't shared by many. Hepburn was convinced the film was the best thing she'd ever done. She secured her ninth Oscar nomination for her performance and campaigned with unusual vigor to win the gold, taking the uncharacteristic move of phoning gossip columnists for publicity. She'd won two Oscars already and told *Variety*'s Army Archerd, "I have to be the first to win three." Sheilah Graham observed that the normally reclusive star was suddenly becoming "almost as accessible" as Zsa Zsa Gabor.[38] All her efforts, alas, were in vain as Anne Bancroft won for *The Miracle Worker*. Another veteran, Bette Davis, had been favorite for *What Ever Happened to Baby Jane?* She took defeat worse than Hepburn.[39]

Lumet objected when *Time* called the film a stage play on celluloid.[40] This was too easy a criticism, he thought. It was also an obvious one because he'd stayed so close to O'Neill's text. The reality was that it was one of the most elaborately visual films he ever made, with imaginative use of lighting and editing to get inside the characters' skins.[41] Reviewers, he huffed, "didn't know technique from a hole in the wall."[42]

For all the imaginative camerawork, however, there was no way to avoid the fact that there's too much talking and not enough action in the film. This was always going to be the case the moment he said he was going to be "faithful" to O'Neill's text. As the *Saturday Review* critic wrote, "Films have a tendency to telescope. They can tell a great deal in relatively little time. The eye drinks in more detail, the ear listens more acutely. O'Neill's techniques, with its repeated lines and recapitulated situations, is the very antithesis of this."[43] *Time* magazine said something similar about O'Neill's quartet: "If there is revelation there is no development. In a kind of *folie a quatre* they go over and over the same ground and end where they began, like the serpent that eats his own tail."[44]

So was the film a masterpiece or a disaster? Or something of both? People never seemed to be able to make their minds up fully about Lumet's filmed plays. He did the best he could under the circumstances but he made a rod for his back sticking so doggedly to O'Neill's words over such a lengthy timeline. (The film was eventually clipped down from its original 174 minutes to a more palatable 136.)

By now Lumet had something else to concern himself with as well: his marriage was in trouble. Gloria Vanderbilt never denied that he was a good husband but they were highly incompatible. He was a family man and she a social butterfly. He wanted children and she didn't. She had two from her other marriage and that was enough for her. Lumet said to her one day, "You're not giving all of yourself to [the marriage]." "I am," she retorted, but deep down she thought he might be right. She was afraid to love too much for fear it would be taken away from her, as was her past experience. "My secret heart was locked away," she wrote in a memoir, "so that it could never be hurt again"[45]

A friend of hers said bluntly to her, "I don't know if the kind of happiness you're looking for exists anywhere." She agreed with that estimation of things. She felt she was looking for what Susan Sontag called "the inescapable longing for something you never had"—change for the sake of change, in other words.[46] Dorothy Parker put it slightly differently when she said, "They sicken of the calm who know the storm." Vanderbilt believed her life was formed by chaos and such chaos eventually became part of her, like a tattoo.[47]

Lumet began dating Gail Horne, daughter of the famous black singer Lena Horne. They very quickly became serious and started talking about marriage. Gail was excited about the prospect but her mother didn't share her enthusiasm. One of the reasons was Gail's age: She was 14 years younger than Lumet. Another was the fact that he'd been married twice already. Gail wasn't bothered by either of these considerations. She didn't think 14 years was a huge gap and neither did she think having two previous wives was "a necessarily immodest amount."[48]

On August 25, 1963, the day his divorce from Vanderbilt came through, Lumet felt overcome with exhaustion or depression—or both—and washed down some sleeping pills with vodka. Before drifting off to sleep, he rang Gail. She knew by his voice that he wasn't himself. "I took a couple of pills," he told her. Not knowing what to think, she rushed to his Greenwich Village apartment. When he failed to answer the doorbell, she phoned the police. They climbed a ladder to his window and opened it. When they got inside, they found him unconscious on the floor, dressed only in his underwear.

They gave him artificial respiration and brought him to a hospital where he was revived. In the newspapers the following day, there were stories of a suspected suicide attempt. Lumet denied them all, saying all he'd wanted was a good night's sleep. "I would have got it too," he added, "if I hadn't been bothered." He called Gail "a rather hysterical little baby," a remark that didn't impress Lena. It made her think her future son-in-law was "nasty and unstable."[49] Lumet played the incident down, telling reporters his unconsciousness was the result of nothing more ominous than "seven vodkas, a Miltown and idiocy."[50]

Lumet and Gail decided on November 23 for the Big Day. Early in the month, Lena went to the White House for a photo session with President John F. Kennedy. He'd been president since 1960 and was preparing for the 1964 campaign. The composer Richard Adler was rallying theatrical luminaries for a re-election gala to be held the following year and Kennedy was heavily involved in the preparations. In the course of the conversation with Lena, he asked how Gail was, and she told him she was about to marry Lumet. He asked her to congratulate her for him but then he said to Lena, "Do you approve of the marriage?" It was almost as if he had an intuition that she didn't. It was an intrusive question but, in her eyes, a "typically direct" one from the president.[51]

Kennedy was assassinated on November 22 by Lee Harvey Oswald at the beginning of an electioneering trip to Dallas. The country ground to a standstill, united in shock. Nobody could quite believe what had happened, least of all Lumet and Gail. The fact that the assassination took place the day before their proposed wedding date made their shock all the more palpable. They thought of cancelling the wedding but it was too late to do so. All the preparations had been made.

They were married in the New York apartment of Lena's friend Walter Bernstein and the reception was held at the Waldorf Hotel. It rained hard, which seemed to reflect everyone's mood. Lena wore a black suit. People didn't know if this was to suggest sadness for President Kennedy or a disapproval of Lumet.[52] Whatever the reason, the day resembled a funeral more than a wedding.

The entire country was in mourning on what was supposed to be a joyful occasion for Lumet and Gail. Half of the guests didn't turn up and Lena cancelled the musicians she'd booked to sing along with her during the reception. Gail couldn't enter into the spirit of the occasion at all. She was astounded when photographers asked her to smile. An Episcopal priest who was a guest led the glum gathering in a collective prayer for the dead president.[53] It was a day to be got through rather than enjoyed.

Under such circumstances, it's interesting that Lumet's next film featured an American president facing a crisis of huge proportions. *Fail-Safe* (1964) had a fascinating premise: a U.S. bomber is mistakenly ordered to drop two 20-megathon bombs on Moscow. When the mistake is discovered, the Americans are unable to countermand the order because the Russians are jamming their radio signals. The American president (Henry Fonda) tries to explain the situation to the Russian one. An advisor played by Walter Matthau believes this to be an ideal opportunity to eradicate the communist threat once and for all. He gets his wish when Fonda fails to make contact with his bombers before they destroy Moscow. America now faces retaliation from Russia unless he does something drastic to right the wrong. Fonda now makes the incredible decision to bomb New York.

Lumet loved the concept of a technological malfunction theoretically leading to Armageddon. "We're suddenly living with things that are out of control," he said. "All of a sudden we're helpless. We can't do anything. There ain't no answers. The machines are bigger than we are." Mankind was in a situation where an IBM machine was able to decide whether he was going to be blown sky-high or not.[54]

Lumet chose an opportune time for his film. Talk of nuclear war was in the air. It wasn't long since Russian warheads had been trained on the American coastline in the Bay of Pigs incident that led to a stand-off between Kennedy and the Russian premier Nikolai Khrushchev.

Fonda was brilliant in a challenging role. He spoke in a tense monotone, "as though every word was crushed by a burden of significance too great to bear."[55] This was a man everyone would want in their corner on the eve of a potential global disaster. No matter how reliable he was, however, he was in infinitely choppier waters than his 1957 turn as Juror Number 8 in *Twelve Angry Men*. He brought sanity to a difficult set of circumstances in that film but it wasn't just a man's life at stake in *Fail-Safe*, it was that of the

Henry Fonda looking solemn in *Fail-Safe*, as well he might. He's the president of the United States, facing down a potential nuclear holocaust (Jerry Ohlinger).

planet. To paraphrase Neil Armstrong after he stepped on the moon, that was one small step for a man; this was one giant leap for mankind.

In the end it proves beyond him, not because he does anything wrong but simply because the situation is too extreme. Nero can't fiddle while Moscow burns. There has to be retribution, and Lumet gives us the most horrific version of it we could ever envisage as his beloved New York is bombed by America's own president. As one writer remarked, his great love of the city must have made the contemplation of its destruction especially upsetting for him.[56]

Apart from the opening scene with its party atmosphere, the film was grim fare indeed. After a character says, "We have checks on everything," one senses everything is going to go pear-shaped. When it does, Lumet draws on all his abilities to create white-knuckle tension.

Pauline Kael alleged he took on *Fail-Safe* only because he liked to hustle quick jobs bigger directors didn't want.[57] Here as elsewhere, she regarded him as guilty until proven innocent on any film, a get-rich-quick opportunist who worked fast and cheap to get the job done instead of involving himself in anything more subtle or nuanced. Kael could never get beyond Lumet's television past. Because he worked in the lesser medium, he was always going to be a small man trying on a suit too big for him in cinema as far as she was concerned.

Having said that, human interest is lacking in the film. The opening scene apart, it's like another *Twelve Angry Men* in its claustrophobia—except here plot rules over character. The casting was uneven too. Fritz Weaver was credible as a general but Matthau seemed like a fish out of water. As the *New Republic* critic wrote of the sometime comedian, "He knows he must not look for laughs so instead spends his time wondering what he ought to look for."[58] Dan O'Herlihy was miscast as another general.

David Mamet praised Lumet's minimalistic treatment of the scene where Fonda speaks to the Soviet premier from his bomb shelter—a bare white room—as he directs his interpreter Larry Hagman on how to translate his words: "The fate of the world depends on his translation. Fonda tells him to take it easy, listen carefully, take his time. He does. In this remarkable scene it is nearly impossible to realize that they are but two actors in an imaginary situation in a set made of four white flats."[59]

Hagman conveys a certain degree of nervousness but not enough to suggest the end of the world might be nigh. We don't expect Fonda to show fear—he's Henry Fonda, after all—but Hagman is a mere mortal like the rest of us. An element of hysteria in his translations would have added some much-needed drama to the proceedings.

But there are some beautiful touches, like when, in the middle of the life-and-death discussions, Fonda says, "I wonder what it's like out. It looked like rain before." It's a great line, and nobody could have delivered it like he did.

Edward Binns plays Colonel Grady, the pilot who bombs Moscow. His wife appears near the end and makes an impassioned plea for him to turn back but he doesn't believe it's her that's speaking to him. This is a potentially fascinating scene but it's not made enough of. Neither is enough made of the fact that Fonda's wife, the First Lady, is in New York when it's about to be bombed. Why didn't Lumet highlight these elements more? It would have broadened out the film and made it more personal. The intensity that made *Twelve Angry Men* breaks *Fail-Safe*. We're drained by the end.

One hardly needs to mention the fact that the American government wasn't happy with *Fail-Safe*. As a result, it insisted Columbia add a coda to the closing credits: "It is the stated position of the Department of Defense and the U.S. Air Force that a rigid enforced system of safeguards and controls ensure that occurrences such as those depicted in this story cannot happen." It was the price Lumet had to pay to get the film released. Even at that, the government refused to help him in any way during production, even to the extent of stopping him from using stock footage. He had to edit creatively to get any sort of authenticity into the aerial shots, using trick photography to make one plane look like six of them, and so on.[60]

It was felt that paranoia might ensue if people thought a mistaken military order could cause World War III. Lumet's attitude was that films like *Fail-Safe* acted as preventatives. They alerted us to the dangers of such system failures as well as exploiting the situation for dramatic potential. The disclaimer might have satisfied the Defense Department but the audience hardly felt reassured by it.[61]

Fail-Safe died at the box office. It was too droll to intrigue over the running time and it had the added misfortune of being shot at the same time as another anti-war film, Stanley Kubrick's *Dr. Strangelove: Or How I Learned to Stop Worrying and Love the Bomb*. Lumet wasn't aware of *Dr. Strangelove* until he finished shooting *his* film.

Lumet frames Henry Fonda in his viewfinder to get the angle right for a scene in *Fail-Safe*. Also in the shot are cameraman Albert Jaffet on the right and cinematographer Gerald Hirshfield smoking a cigarette (Jerry Ohlinger).

Columbia, the studio that produced it, then bought the rights to *Fail-Safe* and delayed its release. This was an orchestrated move to prevent competition from it. It bought it, in effect, to bury it. "I knew we were dead as a movie as soon as Columbia bought us," Lumet lamented, "because I knew they'd done that to hold us off."[62] Columbia was adopting a ploy of, "Keep your friends close but your enemies closer." The big fish gobbled up the little fish and thereby ensured a monopoly on all things nuclear for 1964.

There was something else as well: a plagiarism charge. Before Columbia bought it, it threatened to sue its makers because of the similarity of the two plotlines. Written by Harvey Wheeler and Eugene Burdick, the novel *Fail-Safe* was an instant best seller. But Peter George, who wrote *Two Hours to Doom*, the book upon which *Dr. Strangelove* was based (it was re-titled *Red Alert* for the American edition), sued for plagiarism. He won an out-of-court settlement but *Fail-Safe* was still optioned by Hollywood. Fearing that it would precede *Dr. Strangelove* to theaters, Kubrick started to work faster than he normally might. He also decided to change the tone of the film, making it as outrageous as he could to separate it as much as possible from *Fail-Safe*. To this end he employed Terry Southern as his screenwriter. He'd read Southern's book *The Magic Christian* and felt he could make his movie into a kind of "hideous joke" to divert any threat posed by *Fail-Safe*.[63]

The buy-out removed any possibility of that. *Dr. Strangelove* went into release in January 1964 whereas *Fail-Safe* didn't open until September. It might have posed a small threat to it if it opened concurrently with it but six months later it was a non-event.

Kubrick created a satiric masterpiece in *Dr. Strangelove*; Lumet's overly earnest film seemed dull by comparison. It was deeply felt, but *Dr. Strangelove* tapped into similar reservoirs of apocalyptic dread with much more imagination. Kubrick won the New York Film Critics Award for it and he was also nominated for an Oscar. He should have won. He was denied by George Cukor for *My Fair Lady*. *My Fair Lady* also won Best Film that year. It was a victory of blandness over genius.

No matter how good *Fail-Safe* was, it couldn't compete with *Dr. Strangelove* in the drama stakes. Someone laughing in the face of doom is irresistible. Someone keeping a poker face, even if that someone is Henry Fonda, becomes stodgy by comparison.

Dr. Strangelove opted for farce as a way of whistling in the graveyard. "If nobody is going to do anything about Doomsday," it suggests, "we might as well greet it in good humor."[64] The closest *Fail-Safe* comes to such jollity is in the character played by Matthau, who advises Fonda to bomb the "Marxist fanatics" to smithereens. After all, as he remarks with eminent good sense, "We'll never have the chance again."

The basic difference between *Fail-Safe* and *Dr. Strangelove* is that Lumet's film tries to avoid nuclear meltdown with dull predictability whereas Kubrick's one embraces it with satanic glee. It's obvious which film is the more imaginative. We don't want our holocaust films to be sensible. We can get that on CNN.

In retrospect, maybe Columbia was right to delay the release of *Fail-Safe* until after *Dr. Strangelove*'s run. The world is ending. Slim Pickens is riding a bomb like a bronco. Vera Lynn trills, "We'll meet again," as a mushroom cloud forms. There was no way any film could compete with that kind of a finale, even one directed by Lumet at the peak of his powers.

Lumet thought a marketing opportunity was lost in not releasing *Fail-Safe* first. It could have been an appetizer for *Dr. Strangelove*. How could Columbia have seen it as a threat?, he wondered. It was more like a documentary than a drama. It was like the difference between *War of the Worlds* and *E.T.* One was a cautionary fable, the other an escapist treatise. For Lumet, "the wry comment would have worked more effectively after the serious one."[65] "Release the drama first," he exhorted, "and then the comedy."[66] It seemed to make sense. But Columbia wasn't listening. It had too much to lose if he was wrong.

The debates went on but at the end of the day it was *Dr. Strangelove* that got the gravy. Lumet missed the nuclear boat and had to live off the seconds. The battle of Kubrick vs. Lumet was a no-brainer.

Fonda admitted that if he'd seen *Dr. Strangelove* before making *Fail-Safe*, he wouldn't have been able to make it.[67] This despite the fact that he loved working with Lumet and looked forward to doing so again.[68] His problem was that he thought he'd given a one-dimensional performance as "The Conscience of the Nation."[69] Lumet disagreed. He repeated his familiar view that Fonda—like most viewers of him—took his great talent for granted.[70] He wasn't demonstrative; he was aware of that. It was his underplaying that gave things their resonance. When the premier says to him, "This was nobody's fault. No human being did wrong," Fonda looks him in the eye and says, "What do we say to the dead?" Nobody could deliver a line like that with the quiet power this actor possessed.

But maybe underplaying was what let *Fail-Safe* down. During his television days, Lumet made a science fiction drama called "Night of the Auk." It dealt with five men in a spaceship who returned to Earth from the moon. When they got back, atomic war had broken out. It was a melodramatic storyline but still powerful. *Fail-Safe* could have done with some of that kind of melodrama.

The film ends with a collage of images of a New York that's about to be bombed. Lumet effectively threads together a cross section of people going about their ordinary lives, lives that are shortly about to be ended in the most graphic manner possible. Except we don't see it. The film ends before it happens. We see the words "Directed by Sidney Lumet" and somehow feel shortchanged. It's not that we have an appetite for nuclear holocausts but after 90 minutes of talk, we needed something more visual than a half-minute of the quotidian. (Russian people might also be entitled to ask why we didn't see the destruction of Moscow, or even a jump cut hint of it. Was this city not as important to filmgoers in America?)

Any discussion of *Fail-Safe* in the context of *Dr. Strangelove* involves a similar one of opportunities lost and gained. Both films reminded us of the "hairline of human failure that separates our world from annihilation."[71] The fact that one did it with black comedy and another with somber melodrama shouldn't have rendered either expendable. Judith Crist insisted *Fail-Safe* was for "non–Strangelovians."[72]

Perhaps Lumet would have done better if he'd learned to stop worrying—and love the bomb.

That Vision Thing

In 1961, Edward Lewis Wallant wrote a novel about Sol Nazerman, a Jewish survivor of the Holocaust. Sol may have survived physically but he's psychologically devastated by the death of his wife and children in an Auschwitz concentration camp. Everything he loved was taken from him, he says in the book, but he didn't die.

Twenty-five years later he lives with his relatives in a Long Island suburb. He runs a pawnshop in the Spanish Harlem ghetto, offering minute sums to the downtrodden people who enter with their trinkets, selling them to him to keep body and soul together. The pawnshop is a front for a money-laundering operation run by a local black man, Rodriquez, who deals in drugs and prostitution. Nazerman is unaware of this.

The book was called *The Pawnbroker*. As it goes on, we learn that Nazerman's wife Ruth was raped by the Nazis before being murdered by them and that Nazerman was forced to watch the rape. He's always tried to suppress these memories but they re-surface in his dreams and nightmares.

His life means nothing to him. He expects it to continue like this but one day a young man called Jesus enters. He's Puerto Rican. Nazerman employs him as his assistant but he doesn't treat him well.

Jesus is dating Mabel, a prostitute who works for Rodriquez. Jesus is obsessed with money. Such an obsession makes her fear he'll end up in Rodriquez's clutches, trying to earn some in a hurry. In a central scene in the book, she offers her body to Nazerman in the hope that he'll give her a more generous "reward" for a trinket she's trying to sell to him, money she can then give to Jesus to stop him descending into crime with Rodriquez. Nazerman is shocked at her actions and at her revelations about Rodriquez. When he accuses Rodriquez of drug-dealing, Rodriquez tells him he's complicit too, simply by running the shop. Nazerman says he wants it all to stop but Rodriquez refuses.

Frustrated at how he's being mistreated by Nazerman, Jesus decides to rob the shop. He assembles some hoods and they confront Nazerman one night, demanding that he open his safe. He refuses, whereupon one of them threatens Nazerman with a gun. Jesus, standing in front of him to protect him, is fatally shot.

Nazerman is devastated. The death of Jesus becomes a cathartic moment for him. He realizes he's not the only person in the world to experience tragedy. He mourns Jesus in a different way than he mourned his wife, behaving more positively now. He realizes he still has something to live for despite what's happened. He vows to make the most of whatever time is left to him.

The book had a mixed reception. Some of its critics felt Nazerman's rehabilitation was too instant. Others thought the book was anti–Semitic. One person who was moved by it, however, was Roger Lewis, a former United Artists executive. He took out an option on it and shopped it around the various studios with the hope of it becoming a film. Most of them were leery about taking it on but Ely Landau kept pushing it. Eventually it got the green light to proceed under Lumet's direction.

He chose Rod Steiger to play Nazerman. Boris Kaufman became his director of photography once again. Lumet once asserted that Kaufman could get more tones into black and white than most other cameramen could with ten different colors or 100 different shades.[1]

The Pawnbroker was the first Lumet film to have a specifically Jewish focus.[2] Kaufman had a particular interest in the material. He'd been living in France when it fell to the Nazis. Staying there as a Jew meant almost certain death. He escaped to Canada and then made his way to the U.S., where career took off. Kaufman was in top form on *The Pawnbroker*, the richness of his lens drowning Nazerman in its soporific hues. Set designer Dick Sylbert created a sense of entrapment for Nazerman courtesy of a series of cage-like structures that surrounded him. There were bars, locks and wire mesh almost everywhere one looked.[3] Lumet employed the then-unknown Quincy Jones to do the music. It was "love at first sight," according to Lumet,[4] and they would work together many times in the future. *The Pawnbroker* owes a lot of its dynamism to Jones' brilliantly atmospheric jazz score.

The obvious problem Lumet faced was in tying together all the loose strands of the novel, particularly the Holocaust nightmares that periodically haunt Nazerman. He decided to replace these with what we might call "daymares," i.e., various scenes Nazerman witnesses in schoolyards or on subways which trigger memories of his wife's grim fate. They reach their climax in a scene which became one of the most controversial of Lumet's career. It also caused a seismic shift in the way films were viewed by the church, by censorship bodies and the general public.

It was suggested he use newsreel footage for the flashbacks but he thought that would be exploitative: "These people didn't die so I could make a movie out of it."[5] He preferred to make it particular to Nazerman's own memories.

The first flashbacks featured images that lasted less than a second each. After that, they gradually increased in length.

Rod Steiger was nominated for an Oscar for *The Pawnbroker*. He gave a brilliant portrayal of a man suppressing memories of a World War II concentration camp where he was forced to watch his wife being brutally raped (Jerry Ohlinger).

Then they become all-pervasive. Lumet found this to be the way things happened in his own life. When something he didn't want to deal with came bursting through, the suppressed content "kept recurring in longer and longer bursts until it emerged fully, dominating all other conscious thought."[6]

His jump cuts have now become part of movie lexicon. They've even become part of the advertising industry. When they're used here, they have a subliminal effect on viewers, making them unaware their subconscious minds have registered the name of a product because it stayed on their retinas for so little time—sometimes less than an eighth of a second. Lumet apologized for such chicanery.[7]

He used harsh lighting for the flashback sequences to stress the fact that for Nazerman the past was more real than the present. Steiger over-acted in some of these sequences, appearing to be fighting the light.[8] Lumet was aware of his tendency towards melodrama so he reined him in. "Rod has weaknesses of rhetoric," he remarked, so he had to try and curb this: "I explained that this solitary Jew could not rise to heights of emotion. He had been hammered by life and by people. The faith he had to find was in other people because God had betrayed him."[9]

In the early scenes of the film, Nazerman doesn't look anyone in the eye. The first time he does is when he's asked what the tattoo marks on his arm are for. He replies, "For walking on water." It was Steiger's favorite line in the film. What he means, he explained, is "You jackass."[10] (They were, of course, concentration camp insignias.)

Steiger was unsociable on the set. Some people perceived this as egoism. He wasn't bothered. He felt he needed the distance to stay in character: "I was trying to keep myself in some kind of calm and sadness."[11] Lumet approved. It was part of a slow build-up of tension, a tension that would explode in the film's climax. If it happened too soon, it wouldn't have had the same effect. It was important, he emphasized, "to make sure we weren't using fuel up that we might require later on down the line."[12]

In the film's most talked-about scene, Mabel (Thelma Oliver) strips to the waist to entice Nazerman to pay her more than he might otherwise do for a trinket. What she doesn't realize is that her act is totally non-sexual for him. Instead of titillating him, it convulses him with horrific memories of the Holocaust. He gives her $20 but she knows this isn't nearly enough so she tries to work her sexual charms on him more suggestively. "I'm good, pawnbroker," she teases, "real good. I'll do things you never even dreamed about."

Lumet cuts to a shot of women in Auschwitz being forcibly scrubbed for work in the camp brothel. Nazerman sees his wife naked on a bed as a Nazi officer stands over her threateningly. He doesn't want to look but he's forced to, his head being smashed through a window to give him a better view.

We go back to the present. "Look, look," Mabel invites. "It don't cost you nothin' to look." But it has. It's cost him everything. He covers his eyes but with his inner eye he sees Auschwitz again as his wife waits to be raped. He covers Mabel's naked body with his coat and thrusts some money into her hands.

Nazerman's next crisis, during the robbery scene, is even more traumatic. After Jesus is shot, he holds him in his arms as he waits for him to die. If Mabel's stripping recalls Ruth's rape, Jesus' death recalls her murder. He tries to scream but no sound comes out.

At the end of the film, in his last act of expiation, Nazerman drives his hand into a receipt spike. The pain allows him to feel something outside the confines of his head. He then walks out onto the street in a symbolic gesture of connecting with the world again, the world he's cut himself off from for so many decades. It isn't quite a rebirth but it's a first step.

It's significant that he impales his hand on the receipt spike. This is where he's been placing all his pawn tickets throughout the film. The action signifies the fact that he's renouncing consumerism, replacing the things of Caesar with the things of God. Nazerman—Nazi man—has become Nazareth man as he cradles "Jesus" in his arms.

Steiger came up with the idea of putting his hand on the spike. It was inspired by an incident that happened when he was a child. One day he got four of his fingers caught in the door of the family car: "Somebody slammed it and to this day I can't forget that feeling. I started to remember the color of the Packard, where it took place." He remembered holding his breath because the pain was so bad. As a result, his face went red. Thank God the film wasn't in color, he said, or he would have looked like a tomato. He was glad that Lumet didn't use dialogue in the scene. It meant he had nothing to "spindle" on but his instincts.[13]

Steiger took chances with the role, pushing his boundaries. He realized he would have looked foolish if the scream didn't come off.[14] Pauline Kael made fun of it, as she made fun of most things in Lumet's films, but it was fitting in the circumstances. To paraphrase the singer Morrissey, it was "at a pitch so high as to be beyond the range of human hearing."[15] This was what Steiger aimed for, and what he achieved.

He said the moment was inspired by Picasso's painting *Guernica*: "When I saw the painting, those figures he had with the painted tongues were some of the loudest screams I ever heard in my life. Obviously a painting can't scream. That moment came to me. It was a moment I'll never forget. Don't ask me why."[16] Steiger's biographer Tom Hutchinson thought he was also inspired by Francis Bacon's picture series *Screaming Popes*, which were taken from Eisenstein's *Battleship Potemkin*.[17]

In another sense, his breakdown is reminiscent of Lee J. Cobb's in *Twelve Angry Men*. A chink has appeared in the armor of indifference. Once again the "angry" man has given up his arrogance to let the light in. The manner in which he walks onto the streets, like Cobb—the final image in the earlier film—is a tenuous nod towards a new dawn.

Jesus dies but Nazerman survives. Survival is what he does. The last time, in Auschwitz, it led to nothing but misery. Maybe now it will be different. The savior has come to the Jew to save him from wandering. His Calvary is over.

The Pawnbroker was Lumet's first commercial hit but it was dogged by censorship difficulties. It was the first American studio film to contain nudity since the early 1930s, before the Production Code rendered such indulgences inadmissible. As such, it was obviously going to raise the hackles of church and state alike.

Like most directors who fought to keep their material intact, Lumet employed various stratagems over the years to deal with both of those institutions. He also used a third one: the studio system. Studio heads were often on his case asking him to shorten scenes for one reason or another, usually pragmatic ones. Sometimes he shot extra scenes in the knowledge that they would demand cuts. Then he could excise the extra scenes (which he didn't really want) and keep the ones he did. The corporate people would feel they'd "saved the movie," unaware that Lumet had intended to remove the offensive scenes anyway.[18] This was a variation of Alfred Hitchcock leaving mildly sexual scenes in his films as bargaining chips for more seductive ones. If he took out the former, he had a stronger case with the censors for keeping in the latter.

The Pawnbroker premiered at 1964's Berlin Film Festival. It gave rise to a lot of debate concerning racism and possible anti–Semitism but, significantly, there was no mention of the exposure of Oliver's breasts.[19] In the U.S., little else was talked about. The film was submitted to the Production Code Association in January 1965 and Geoffrey Shurlock, its main decision-maker, denied it a seal. But he appreciated its artistic merits and advised Landau to appeal his decision to the Motion Picture Association of America.[20]

Two scenes proved particularly problematic for Shurlock. The first had Jesus in bed with Oliver. The second was the infamous "bare breasts" scene.[21] Landau argued that both of these were integral to the story but Shurlock refused to budge. He'd recently had his fingers burned by the furor surrounding the granting of a seal to Billy Wilder's saucy comedy *Kiss Me, Stupid*, an experience which had hardened him. Upon Shurlock's advice, Landau appealed to the Production Code Review Board and here the film was granted a special exemption.[22]

The board's decision was influenced by the fact that Landau threatened to release the film without a seal if he had to. He also used *Kiss Me, Stupid* as a bargaining chip. How could it confer a seal on *that* and deny one to *The Pawnbroker*?[23] Lumet's pronounced disregard for sensationalism, as evidenced by his work up to this, was another factor in their decision.[24] There was also the fact that bare black breasts, for some reason, weren't deemed to be as reprehensible as bare white ones.[25]

The Legion of Decency proved a tougher nut to crack. It denied the film a classification and condemned it in strong terms, claiming that the nudity was an unnecessary ploy to achieve dramatic

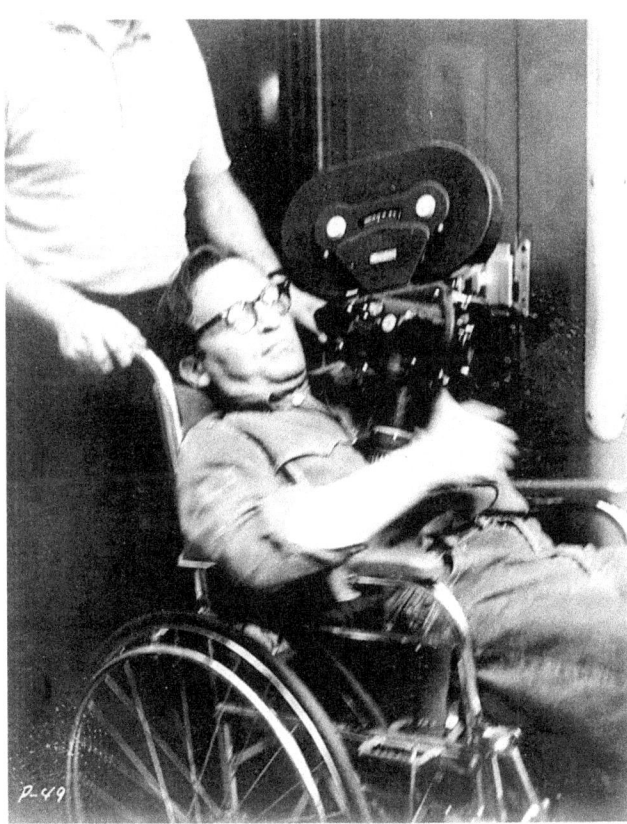

Lumet has himself wheeled into position for a "fish eye" shot in *The Pawnbroker*, a film in which he experimented with various camera techniques to amplify the film's grim scenarios (Jerry Ohlinger).

effect.[26] Monsignor Thomas Little, a spokesman for the Legion, thought that a decision to go easy on it could open the floodgates to any number of unscrupulous operators out to make a quick buck.[27]

A "Condemned" tag, however wasn't to be feared as much in 1965 as it would have been some years before. Between 1963 and 1965, the Legion had condemned 38 films, more than half of them from major studios, without creating much of a stir. By now it had lost its power to inspire fear or dread.[28] Neither did the refusal of a seal mean automatic box office death, as was once the case.[29]

Judith Stone asked in *Newsweek* how the Legion could be taken seriously when it had condemned "one of the few significant moral films made by Hollywood."[30] Joe Mankiewicz ridiculed Little's "dangerous precedent" angle by saying that if Fellini made *Oedipus Rex*, it would hardly open the floodgates to "quickie, tasteless tantalizers" like *My Son, My Lover* or *Daddy Does It Best*.[31] *Newsweek* wondered how it could condemn *The Pawnbroker* and put films like *Godzilla* and *The Earth Dies Screaming* on general release.[32]

Lumet was amused by the fact that his modest tale of death and resurrection got so many tongues wagging. It wasn't only the sex in it that bothered people. It was the perceived racism and the anti–Semitism as well. John Eastman quipped, "A film that offended so many guardians of morality had to be worth watching."[33] British film censor John Trevelyan had no problem passing it without any cuts.[34] Episcopal bishop James A. Pike went so far as to describe it as a "religious" film.[35] It was the first condemned production to play in a major theater in the strongly Catholic Albany, New York, since *Baby Doll* a decade before. (Bishop Pike had defended that too.)

In some ways, *The Pawnbroker* was the Legion's "last stand."[36] By now the International Federation of Catholic Alumnae was losing its grip on the film industry, so much so that it changed its name to the National Catholic Office of Motion Pictures. *Time* magazine praised it for dropping such an "arrogant and muscular" name.[37] Archbishop John Krol of Philadelphia emphasized the fact that the church was still deeply concerned about decency in films despite the softer title.[38]

The Pawnbroker also caused a sea change in the way films were rated. Jack Valenti, president of the Motion Picture Association of America, did away with the old Hays restrictions as a result of it, replacing them with the ratings system we still have today. Lumet and Landau could claim to have played a significant part in this phenomenon.[39]

Landau had some problems getting the film distributed because of its dark nature. After a few rejections, he decided to distribute it himself with two small companies, Allied Artists and American International.[40] That was the hard part. Once it hit the screens, everything came up roses. The critics were vociferous in their praise. Richard Oulahan of *Life* magazine described it as being "shockingly good."[41] *Film Daily* said it commanded "attention and respect."[42] Judith Crist praised it for its "unbearable cruelty and total heartbreak."[43] *Daily Mail* critic Cecil Wilson felt Steiger's performance seemed to encompass "all the agony ever inflicted on man."[44]

There were some dissenting voices. Robert Hatch of *The Nation* thought Nazerman wallowed in self-pity.[45] Andrew Sarris—no lover of Lumet at the best of times—dismissed it as "a pretentious parable that manages to shrivel into drivel."[46] Its release reduced the Production Code to "a mere scrap of paper" for Legion diehard William Mooring.[47] Pauline Kael dubbed it "a Jewish *Christmas Carol* trying to be *King Lear*."[48]

It's interesting to note that the Legion didn't issue its "Condemned" rating until after the film had been favorably reviewed by the critics. This probably explains the relative mildness of the condemnation. "Nudity is not in itself objectionable," it said. Not very long ago, it would hardly have held that view. Liberal Catholics generally saluted it. It was everyone else who seemed to be confused.[49]

Steiger was Oscar-nominated for his performance, as Lumet predicted, but Lee Marvin won against the odds for a quirky performance in the western *Cat Ballou*. Comedies didn't usually win Oscars for their stars and Steiger didn't see this coming. He hadn't been up for an Oscar since 1954 when he was nominated in the Supporting Actor category alongside Lee J. Cobb and Karl Malden for *On the Waterfront*. He was so confident he was going to win that when he heard the words, "And the winner is…" he got ready to stand up and approach the podium. He was crushed when the announcer said, "Lee Marvin." It taught him to never again take anything for granted.[50]

Devastated as he was, he tried to put a brave face on things, telling his friends that the nomination in itself was a victory, but his real feelings came out when he said, "When *The Sound of Music* gets an Academy Award, you know it's Hollywood's year."[51] He meant independent productions hadn't a chance against mainstream ones. *The Sound of Music* won Best Picture in a gross misjudgment. It had been up against *Dr. Zhivago*, another Steiger movie, so his pain was doubled. Lumet wasn't nominated. It was a shameful oversight but Lumet didn't mind. *The Pawnbroker* put him on the commercial map.

He wasn't quite as blessed with his next release, the made-in-Spain *The Hill*, which was shot before *The Pawnbroker* but didn't reach theaters until October 1965. (*The Pawnbroker* came out in April.) Based on a TV play by Ray Rigby and R.S. Allen, it was set in North Africa during World War II. It told the story of five British military inmates who are harshly treated by warders at a desert stockade. Sean Connery played Joe Roberts, a prisoner who decides to press charges against drill sergeant Williams (Ian Hendry), whose brutal treatment resulted in a man's death. Like all of Lumet's films thus far, it was in black and white.

Connery was producing it. Lumet flew to London to meet him. Connery had director approval but that turned out not to be a problem as they hit it off immediately. Some of the executives thought Lumet might not know enough about the British Army, a notion he found laughable. "The army is the army," he scoffed. "It doesn't matter if it's Pakistan or America."[52]

The film's theme, suggested by its title, recalls the Greek myth of Sisyphus where a character had to climb the same hill over and over again without any hope of reaching the top. It's 30 feet high in the film. Both Hendry and another tough sergeant (Harry Andrews) force the prisoners to climb it carrying packs on their backs. Andrews takes a special interest in Connery, who's been court-martialed for cowardice after refusing to go on a suicide mission. "The court-martial busted you," he gloats, "and I'm going to finish the job."

The main problem with the film was the climate. It was shot in the same desert in Spain where *Lawrence of Arabia* had been made. The temperature went up to 120 degrees during the day. It was important to drink to avoid dehydration. Lumet chose water but some of the cast members preferred alcohol. He joked, "You know how they say you shouldn't drink in hot weather? Well I had eight Scotsmen in the movie. They disproved that theory."[53]

He didn't go easy on his cast, making them run up the hill time and again to achieve the effect of exhaustion under the hot Spanish sun. Connery was excellent in the part, especially in the scenes where he breaks down. He harnessed his energy like a true professional, letting it out in a rush of emotion both at the climax and in a scene where he's being bullied by Andrews. The former 007 grew a mustache for the part to look different from previous characters. Audiences saw a side to him they weren't familiar with. This was much more cerebral than anything he'd done as James Bond.

Lumet got on well with him, as he did with most actors. Some directors found Connery stand-offish, which Lumet thought was their problem rather than his. "I know he's not a legend," he said, "because I go to the toilet with him."[54]

Lumet employed Oswald Morris for the photography rather than Boris Kaufman. Connery liked his work. He thought it gave the film a documentary feel: "There are no little lights under your face to take away the lines."[55]

He also liked Lumet's direction. "He doesn't waste time or waffle," he said. "He works his end." He became aware of Lumet's punctilious nature one day when he employed 350 extras as soldiers. He counted each and every one of them. When he discovered that a few were missing, he barked, "Okay, we don't go until all the soldiers are here." Said Connery, "He knows what a picture costs and he gets his money up to the hilt."[56]

The Hill occasionally spilled over into melodrama but it had few equals in its exhaustive treatment of the manner in which the human spirit can be pushed beyond bursting point. There was a lot of shouting in it and not much light relief. Everything was pared to the bone to give audiences the sense that they were "in" the experience. Morris' harsh lighting combined with Lumet's minimalism to create a sense of unmitigated torture.

There were no frills. Lumet even kept background noise to a minimum. He liked sound effects unless they were clichéd. "Can there be a country night scene without crickets?" he asked.[57] He demanded that one scene be done without any sound at all. Even the buzzing of a fly spoiled the silence for him until the sound editor explained to him that such buzzing intensified the sense of silence instead of disturbing it. Lumet never minded being corrected on something like this. "A good lesson," he concluded.[58]

Lumet loved Connery's performance in the film. After it wrapped, he said he felt there was "almost no telling where he'd go." He discounted the idea that Connery wasted himself in Bond movies. People thought they were just "flip easy stuff" but in his view this was one of the hardest kinds of acting and only a real actor could handle it. Never an artistic snob, Lumet felt the same way about Cary Grant: "People always assumed Grant was no actor at all, just a personality." He thought of Grant and Connery as severely underrated talents. They were two stars who'd never been given the proper credit because of being pigeonholed.[59]

Connery thanked Lumet for saving him from "Bondage fatigue" with *The Hill*.[60] Somewhat more extravagantly, he credited his direction with having what he described as "that vision thing."[61]

The film originally ran 122 minutes. MGM cutter Margaret Booth said this was two minutes too long. Lumet went through it with her but he felt he could only cut 35 seconds from it without, to his way of thinking, spoiling it. Booth grudgingly agreed. He was allowed keep the precious minute and 25 seconds that separated them. It's a measure of his perfectionism that he held onto that minute and a half like a parent with a child that was in danger of being taken away from him. He took a firm stand because he was aware of the ruthlessness of the people who sat in sharp suits behind executive tables—who weren't necessarily versed in the arts. "Once the studio puts its hands on a picture," he growled, "there's no way of knowing what will finally emerge."[62] But he respected Booth. Though powerful ("She owns your negative!"), he never thought she abused that power, tempering control with fair play.[63]

In the film's last scene, the prisoners kill Hendry. We seem to be gearing up for a happy ending, but Lumet was never going to go for that. He didn't want *The Great Escape*: "We know that in most areas [of life], the establishment keeps control. Nobody is going to tell me that in an army, much less an army prison, that isn't going to happen." He wanted to build hope that they were going to get out and then, "Bang! No they don't. The ending was deliberately caustic." It's a pyrrhic victory.[64]

When the film went into general release, Lumet was criticized for his "overly diagrammatic arguments about authority and rebellion."[65] He was accused of "besmirching" the good name of the British military.[66] When it threatened to win first prize at Cannes, Rex Harrison, one of the judges, wired the queen to alert her to this fact.[67]

Lumet had severe misgivings about how it was marketed. On the day it opened, he went to the distributor's office and saw an ad for it: a full-page drawing of Connery. He had his mouth wide open as if he was screaming. Above his head, a "thought balloon" showed a drawing of a belly dancer. Across the top of the ad, in big white letters, the words, "Eat it, mister!" were written.

He had no idea what any of this signified. Was Connery fantasizing about the belly dancer? If so, why did his face show rage? Was it sexual frustration? Were the distributors trying to play to the James Bond audience, who felt their man had to be thinking of sex even if he was in a prison in Africa? He couldn't believe this was all the marketing department had come up with after his months of hard work.

That night at dinner with his wife, he burst into tears. He told her he was tired of fighting. He'd fought for the script, the cast, the length of the film. He'd fought the heat of the desert and the exhaustion it caused. And now he was fighting about a stupid advertisement.[68] He thought the general quality of movie ads was abysmal. He felt the same about trailers, believing them to be filled with "the same breasts, kisses and explosions we saw the week before." As for press junkets and "made-for-cable, behind-the-scenes interviews," these amounted to a "stupefying dullness" that made his teeth ache.[69]

Most people realized how good *The Hill* was but it didn't do well commercially. Much of the reason for this was down to the unintelligibility of the dialogue. It failed in the U.S. when the British and Scottish accents (and vocabulary) proved indecipherable to many audience members.[70] This proved to be such a problem, it had to be subtitled in some parts of the country.[71]

Lumet said the difficulty of understanding the accents was the price one paid for authenticity. He didn't understand the logic of traveling thousands of miles to get a realistic look on a film and then put an "unrealistic" soundtrack onto it.[72] He had a point, but his artistic dedication cut little ice with the public. They found it all very tedious. Despite many critical kudos, it didn't make money for either Connery or Lumet.

"We both had a piece of it," Lumet revealed, "but neither of us got a cent."[73] He obviously meant apart from their salaries. Connery was paid £140,000 up front to star in it, which was almost as much as the rest of the cast put together.[74]

Chameleon

When Mary McCarthy wrote *The Group*, it signaled a seismic shift in the way women were perceived by men, and indeed by other women. It was a study of a motley crew of Vassar graduates who plow troubled furrows as they embark on their various life paths with dreams that more often than not turn to dust. Lumet always said happy endings were unrealistic, which was why he didn't want *The Hill* to have one. The pattern was continued with this film.

In another respect, it differed greatly from it. Up until now, he'd been working much more with men than women. That was why he wanted to make *The Group* a success, to prove he hadn't a blind spot there. Women, of course, were "eye candy" in movies, but how many of them represented them in their 3D reality? How many films featured them in large numbers as independent characters rather than accessories of men? How many of them had women as the centerpieces of the action rather than sidebars?

The most obvious film that sprang to mind when one thought of a "women's film" was *The Women* itself, the 1939 feature thrown to George Cukor as a sop by MGM when he was fired from the set of *Gone with the Wind*. It was a high-profile release with Joan Crawford and Rosalind Russell but Lumet didn't think much of it. "Rosalind was a caricature," he scoffed. "It was just a very broad comedy."[1]

He was determined to make *The Group* more cerebral. He admired the book for the manner in which it chronicled the young women's odyssey from innocence to experience. When they leave Vassar, the world seems to be opening up before them like so many blossoming flowers but by the end of the book, such flowers surround them like dead stalks. The challenge Lumet faced was to transfer that metamorphosis intelligently onto the screen.

He had a strong cast to help him: Candice Bergen, Joan Hackett, Elizabeth Hartman, Kathleen Widdoes, Shirley Knight, Joanna Pettet, Mary-Robin Redd, Jessica Walter. Many of them weren't known to viewers at this point. The film marked the debut of Bergen, Hackett, Widdoes and Pettet. The men in the cast seemed like drones by comparison: Larry Hagman, Hal Holbrook, Richard Mulligan. It was Holbrook's debut too.

Boris Kaufman was back as Lumet's cinematographer but he was unhappy working in color. This is something that would eventually result in the termination of his collaboration with Lumet. Most of the cast would have preferred black and white too but once the budget was set for color, it couldn't be changed.[2]

Lumet allowed Pauline Kael to be present on the set to watch him work, which turned out to be one of the greatest mistakes he ever made. Right off the bat she was aggressive to Sidney Buchman, the film's screenwriter. When Buchman said the theme of *The Group* was the fact that higher education didn't fit women for life, she shot back, "Does it fit *men* for life?"[3] The point was: The film wasn't *about* men. She seemed to be looking for a fight.

She saw Lumet as a sloppy director who didn't care about the finer points of direction. She thought all that mattered to him was to get a shot in the can as soon as possible and then to move on to the next one. She regarded him as a fast-track director who was more suitable to TV than cinema. On TV, budgetary constraints were paramount. It didn't permit the luxury of retakes, or discussions about underlying forces at work in scenes.

She jotted down notes furiously as she watched Lumet darting back and forth giving instructions to his cast about where they were to stand, how they were to deliver their lines, how to convey emotion. She wrote about his "ostentatious show-business street boy's manner." She said he didn't listen. She accused him of having no intellectual curiosity.[4] Was this simply because he hadn't read McCarthy's book? She thought he turned it into the stuff of soap opera.[5]

He was a commercial director greedy for the big time, she alleged, and would probably get it "because of a basic emotional vulgarity in his work that audiences may respond to." He also had "a bad ear for dialogue, and no eye."[6] More from Kael:

> He cannot use crowds or details to convey the illusion of life. His backgrounds are always just an empty space. He doesn't even know how to make the principals stand out of a crowd. If he moves the camera it's just a form of conspicuous expenditure—to prove he can do it. He has only TV foreground actions without intrusions. Although this looks fine when the movies later turn up on TV, it basically represents a loss of the whole illusionary delight of cinema.[7]

It's difficult to know how she arrived at these conclusions unless she'd reached them before she got to the studio because all of Lumet's films—and indeed his writings and interviews—testify to a great knowledge of precisely the things she castigates him for: his use of crowds, of space, of camera movement, of perspective.

She claimed he once told her he gave up acting because he thought it was "a faggot's career," something one finds very difficult to believe.[8] If he believed this, why

Pauline Kael castigated Lumet for misinterpreting Mary McCarthy's acclaimed novel *The Group* when he took on the arduous task of filming it. Having her on the set made the experience a tense affair for him but there were occasional light moments, as in the above photograph where he proudly displays a baby (Jerry Ohlinger).

did he spend so much time nurturing them, becoming friends with them, speaking highly of them whenever he got the chance? Either she misheard him or she made it up. He could even have said it to jerk her chain because he didn't like her and wanted to shock her.

Perhaps the greatest injustice she conferred upon him was her contention that, for him, the "little things" in a film didn't count.[9] If he had shortcomings as a director, lack of attention to detail certainly wasn't one of them. Pedestrian directors sometimes obsess over minutiae and miss the bigger picture. Lumet always had one eye on the scene at hand and the other on the finished product. The "little things" didn't get lost in this equation; he just didn't believe in making capital out of them.

Kael's problem was that she thought she could have made *The Group* much better than Lumet if she held the reins. Like many people who live on the sidelines, she didn't understand what it meant to be at the coalface. Ideas aren't facts. Lumet worked on his instincts. Sometimes something felt right and he did it. That didn't mean he was disrespecting McCarthy's book, or McCarthy herself, or women. It meant that his gut feeling told him where to go. He didn't always get it right but if Kael had directed the film, one imagines it would have become a dull feminist tract rather than a human story.

Kael never let up on Lumet, either with regard to *The Group* or anything else he did. To her, he was "everybody's second choice" for a film, the "driving little guy" who talked himself into jobs and finished them before producers even got to know him.[10]

She seemed to think he was a Roger Corman–type director, not somebody with a proven track record of classics like *The Hill*, *The Pawnbroker*, *Twelve Angry Men* and *Long Day's Journey Into Night* already on his CV when she met him. She equated his speed with lack of quality. Just because he often got things done in one take, did that automatically mean the take was bad? This seemed to be her (lack of) logic.

Lumet's mistake was to accord her too much respect. This had the effect of making him second-guess himself when he made a film. He would say to himself on the set, "What will Pauline think of this?" One day she claimed her function in film criticism was to advise him how best to direct. Lumet was flabbergasted when he heard this.

Lumet putting a baby into a cot between takes on the set of *The Group*. The nurse is Hildy Parks (Jerry Ohlinger).

"You've got to be kidding," he said to her. She didn't like him taking her on even this mildly. "She's never written a good word about me since," he noted.[11]

"From what I observed," she wrote, "his planning is based on the hope that he'll come out of the shooting with something he can pull together in the editing room."[12] Lumet set a lot of store by editing but he usually made sure he had what he wanted before he got there. Kael's comments smack of a predetermination to find something bad even in his virtues that she could jump on with her acid-dipped pen.

Any compliment that came from her was a left-handed one: "Lumet works best under pressure. If it isn't there, he creates it." "He operates on a wing and a prayer. For sheer guts, Lumet is awe-inspiring."[13] These comments seem willing to wound but afraid to strike; there was always that passive-aggressive air about her when she wrote about him or spoke to him.

On the *Group* set, she even accused him of being sexist to go with all his other weaknesses: "As I got to know him, I concluded that, for Lumet, a woman shouldn't have any problems a real man can't take care of. If she does, she's sick."[14]

It beggars belief that he allowed her to intimidate him like she did. When he told her he was thinking of directing an epic, she said that would be unwise because he wasn't good with crowd scenes. Instead of telling her what to do with herself, he said, "I know, but I can learn."[15] This kind of self-deprecating comment only filled her with more arrogance, and more belief that her criticisms of him were justified. As his future films were to prove, dealing with crowds was something that came very easily to him.

The Group has faults just as most films have. The question was, how big they were and, more to the point, how much Kael exaggerated them. Lumet thought the book had flaws as well after he got around to reading it. He felt this was where Kael should have started her search for soap opera, not with him. He did his best to overcome them but some of them proved insurmountable, which meant that parts of the film were two-dimensional.[16]

The screenplay was also problematic. Penelope Gilliatt wrote in the *London Observer*, "Buchman's script is disconcertingly scrappy, as though we were watching installments of a woman's serial. Tiny climaxes are reached every so often. The tone skids into chattiness and then a whole new episode begins."[17]

Whatever its strengths or weaknesses, Lumet tried to put them out of his mind when it was finished. Like most of his films, it was an experiment. He wasn't the kind of man to lie awake brooding about what he could have done better after he called "Cut" for the last time. When a film was over, it was over. He dusted himself down and moved on.

The following year, he was asked to direct *Funny Girl*, a prospect that didn't fill him with excitement, mainly because it was being filmed in Hollywood. "I went out there, and sat down at a budget meeting. There were 32 heads of department. That's clearly a crazy way to make a movie." In New York he didn't feel people were breathing down his neck to the same extent and neither were there as many moguls there: "The sheer physical distance discouraged them. They usually didn't like coming to New York. There were people in the streets and all those unpleasant things."[18] He spent some time on the set but left it after a disagreement with the film's producer, Ray Stark, about money.

By now his disaffection for Hollywood seemed to have reached fever pitch. He told a *Newsweek* journalist, "They have sets but not the genuine thing. Even the lampposts are wrong—they're made of Styrofoam. I hate being separated from life. There's nothing organic about Los Angeles. When it rains, the soil slides down; when it's dry, there's fire. The history of art is the history of great cities." New York was prime amongst these: "It's like sitting on a big lid ready to blow off. And this energy reaches the screen."[19]

Remaining in New York, he made *The Deadly Affair*, a quietly effective thriller based on a John Le Carré novel. It starred James Mason as an intelligence officer trying to find out if a diplomat committed suicide or was murdered. Simone Signoret played the diplomat's widow. Harriet Andersson was Mason's unfaithful wife. Maximilian Schell played a friend of Mason's from the war. Harry Andrews rounded off the cast as a semi-retired policeman helping to unravel the mystery.

Mason enjoyed making the film. He'd already worked with Lumet on three TV dramas, *The Hiding Place*, *John Brown's Raid* and *Silent Nights*. Lumet was extravagant in his praise for him: "I always thought he was one of the best actors who ever lived. Whatever you gave him, he would take it, assimilate it and then make it his own. The technique was rock solid." Every time Lumet read a script, one of his first thoughts was: Is there anything here for James? "He had no sense of stardom," he observed. "All he wanted was good billing and the best money he could get." After that, all he had on his mind was how best to play the part. He reminded Lumet more of an actor in a theater repertory ensemble than a film star.[20]

Lumet never got to know Mason well. He sensed an unhappiness in him but didn't delve into what might be causing it. There was "a privacy which one couldn't invade with James." Lumet thought he was like Henry Fonda: Both men were "profoundly reliable" but also somewhat aloof. The difference between them was that Fonda became a megastar whereas Mason was more like a "greasepaint gypsy, roaming the world in search of work." Basically he did two types of pictures, "the ones he despised and did for a lot of money and the ones he liked and did for very little."[21]

The Deadly Affair fell into the latter category. He was so convincing in it, he set one thinking he would have made a good fist of that other John Le Carré adaptation of the time, *The Spy Who Came in from the Cold*. Signoret was also at the top of her game as a supposed communist agent. Schell was equally two-faced in the convoluted plot, playing the very worst kind of "best friend" anyone could have. It was a pity that the high point of this downbeat film—Schell's murder of Signoret—wasn't even shown. We were left with a typically murky Le Carré finale where Mason kills Schell and walks off into the night.

It was hardly the type of film to make one dance with joy but Lumet directed it with grim determination. It bore all the hallmarks of a *film noir* in its grimy trawl through the underbelly of Cold War espionage but Lumet had now left monochrome behind and wouldn't go back. This was unfortunate as its jaded set of characters would have worked better in black and white.

There were also some problems with the plot. Schell doesn't only betray Mason professionally but personally, having an affair with Andersson. Andersson admits to this too readily when Mason tells her he suspects it. He also accepts it too philosophically. It's almost as if he's been expecting it. He even expresses concern for her as a cuckold: "I didn't want you to be hurt." Is this what a husband would say to a cheating wife? Hardly. Mason was a wonderful actor but no matter how wonderful one is, it's difficult to make implausible lines like that work.

The climax takes place in a theater. Mason and Andrews hatch a plan to trap Signoret and Schell into meeting at a play, thereby exposing their involvement with one another. This is where Schell kills Signoret. They're watching a play, *Edward II*, where violence is also unfolding. Lumet juxtaposes the two scenarios in a clever manner that calls up Hitchcock.[22] Is it too clever? Perhaps. The scene isn't helped by Andrews yawning. (His propensity for somnolence at dramatic times is a kind of mini-motif in the film.) It's a surprise ending but any regular filmgoer will probably see it coming. Lumet's gift was to handle it without melodrama.

He went from obtuseness to black comedy for his next feature, *Bye Bye Braverman* (1968). Based on Wallace Markfield's novel *To an Early Grave*, this is a poignant satire focusing on four Jewish writers who reminisce about a dead friend as they drive to his funeral on Long Island.

Leslie Braverman, the deceased writer, never sold out, in contrast to his survivors, played by George Segal, Jack Warden, Sorrell Booke and Joseph Wiseman. The film is really about them rather than him. The journey is more important than the destination. It's both psychological and geographical. The fact that they're late for the funeral—going to the wrong church in their confusion—underlines that.

The streets of New York were Lumet's home away from home and *Bye Bye Braverman* gave him an opportunity to spend more time in them than many of his films. Here he discusses a scene from the movie with George Segal (Jerry Ohlinger).

The film was a kind of precursor to *The Big Chill* in its exploration of elegiac friendships battle-scarred by life and the end of life. It's also a parable about midlife crisis but Lumet treads lightly on this, injecting as much humor as he can into the story. This is most apparent in the section where a car accident turns from a situation of anger to one of *bonhomie*. It's also apparent in a synagogue scene where Alan King shines as a rabbi. When they finally reach Braverman's grave, Segal pontificates on all the things that bother him in life, speaking both to the dead and the living in a tragicomic manner.

Bye Bye Braverman was Lumet's first foray into comedy and it showed. Some of the scenes have a clunky feel. He realized this but didn't feel equipped to do anything about it: "The script was so good, and I didn't fulfill its potential,"[23] *Time* magazine agreed, accusing him of turning Markfield's dark humor into Jewish situation comedy.[24] Judith Crist offered a more consoling viewpoint, praising him for capturing the essence of New York in the film's "day in the life" structure.[25]

Both viewpoints were tenable. Lumet saw the film as only partly successful, a tenuous tread into a genre in which he felt uncomfortable. He had to work hard at developing a light touch, something that troubled him not only when he was shooting but off-set as well. A perfectionist by nature, he brought his work home with him and brooded over lapses in it. How could he make certain scenes better? What might a character do that he wasn't doing? He liked to tease out various alternatives, ruling nothing in or out, but at the end of the day *Bye Bye Braverman* beat him in his effort to make it both deep and palatable to the masses.

He met Alan Pakula one day at Bloomingdale's department store after the film wrapped. It was at a time before Pakula had become a director. He was producing the

Lumet shows Godfrey Cambridge how he wants a scene played in *Bye Bye Braverman* as members of the cast and crew wait for it to start (Jerry Ohlinger).

Gregory Peck film *The Stalking Moon*, with Robert Mulligan directing. "What the hell are you doing here?" Lumet asked him. "Aren't you making a picture?" "I'm not needed on the set," Pakula replied. "Bob has everything under control." Lumet shook his head. He said with mock severity, "While Bob is working his ass off shooting, you're in here buying shirts." Pakula took the reprimand on board, even if it was only meant in jest. Lumet's gentle prod made him turn from producing to directing, which he'd always wanted to do. Within the year he'd helmed *The Sterile Cuckoo* with Liza Minnelli, a film that set him on his way for a brilliant career.[26] The incident showed how focused Lumet was, and how interested he was in other people's lives.

He next adapted Chekhov's *The Sea Gull* for the screen. It was a play he'd always admired. He put three members of the cast of *The Deadly Affair* into it: James Mason, Simone Signoret and Harry Andrews. "One of the joys of my life," he asserted, "is the fact that I never had an actor who didn't want to come back to me for a second time."[27] He also assembled Vanessa Redgrave, David Warner, Denholm Elliott and Kathleen Widdoes. Widdoes had already worked with him in *The Group*. He couldn't get clearance to film it in Russia so he had to shoot it in Stockholm instead.[28]

Lumet contended that it was a play in which everyone was in love with the wrong person: "Medvenko loves Masha, who loves Konstantin, who loves Nina, who loves Trigorin, who belongs to Arkadina, who's really loved by Dr. Dorn, who's loved by Paulina."[29] This made it interesting for him. It was true to the way things happen in real life, even if the extent of the unfortunate associations was too much. He had his work cut out for him trying to make this credible. Another problem was trying to make the "Who's Who of British Cinema" in his cast sound like 19th-century Russians.

He'd been trying to get *The Sea Gull* onto the screen for some time before it came about. The cast actually met one another a year before filming began. When he told them it was finally going to happen, he also informed them of his customary rehearsal arrangements. Those who'd worked with him before weren't surprised; the new recruits were.

Before shooting began, he explained his work methods to them in some detail. He didn't like hanging about, he said, because it tired actors. They spent enough time waiting between takes without him adding to the problem by fussiness. Because of his theater and TV background, he liked to have his homework done before the cameras rolled. Failing to prepare was preparing to fail: "I'm trained to make the dramatic selection in advance so I rehearse and then commit to one attack." This approach also helped people to stay "hot."[30]

He liked to get to know actors, and to help them get to know one another, before filming began. That way they relaxed and got the best out of themselves. Henry Fonda told him that when he was making *Once Upon a Time in the West* for Sergio Leone, he came on the set the first day and received a big surprise. Leone said to him, "Mr. Fonda, this is Miss Cardinale," indicating his co-star Claudia Cardinale. Five minutes later, they were in bed together. That would have been unthinkable on a Lumet set.[31]

The rehearsals helped all of the performances, just as they had in *Long Day's Journey Into Night*. Lumet loved this film just as much as the other, and for similar reasons. He had total control over the production. It was free of the chaos that attended most films. His familiarity with the text and what it was trying to convey gave him time to address its nuances. At 141 minutes, it was a daunting experience for audiences, but Lumet's devotion to Chekhov, and theater in general, shone through every frame.

For Signoret, playing Arkadina was one of the most fulfilling experiences of her career. Each day on set was like a drug to her. "There are people who take LSD in order to go on trips," she said. "We took Chekhov, and after we had, the world could collapse. We were on vacation from our real world and in the process of telling how the world whose story we were telling would collapse." She echoed Lumet's comments about the film's themes: "No one loved the person who loved him; what happened if you abandoned your lands and were bored far from Moscow; how to commit suicide and miss, and finally not miss." More positively, it was an exercise in "how you could believe in yourself as an actress, and how to let time go by while you did nothing—that is, how to live in Czarist Russia in 1896." She transported herself back into that time frame with 100 percent dedication.[32]

James Mason played Trigorin. He hadn't been in a theatrical role since the 1930s. *The Times* thought he gave a reasonably good study of "a weak-willed, unworldly man who is only really happy when writing or fishing," but thought there "had to be more to Trigorin than this surprisingly dull impression of a second-rate literary lion."[33] That was always the problem with playing Chekhov: falling into the provincial rut one was depicting.

Many critics felt the film had the same problems as *Long Day's Journey Into Night*, being movingly filmed but suffering from a certain tedium in its pace. Once again the "play on film" accusation reared its head. Those who liked to go to the cinema for escapist purposes found little to intrigue them in Lumet's forensic immersion in the tortured lives of reclusive folk. He was rewinding the tape of *Long Day's Journey* and for some the anguish was too much.

Time magazine rubbished it: "Chekhov called *The Sea Gull* a comedy, but any traces of wit have been pretty well destroyed by Lumet's lumbering technique."[34] Lumet saw it differently: "There are only two films I've made in which I wouldn't change a thing—*Long Day's Journey Into Night* and *The Sea Gull*."[35]

Signoret experienced withdrawal symptoms when the film ended. She woke up many mornings afterwards with just one thought on her mind: "How sad—I'm not filming *The Sea Gull* today."[36] Lumet and Mason were also depressed that it was over. They were almost in tears as they flew back to London together. They held hands on the flight, "aware that we'd come to the end of something very important in our working lives that we were probably never going to get the chance to recapture."[37]

Lumet was due to direct *The Confessions of Nat Turner* now but the plug was pulled a few months before filming due to financial problems with Twentieth Century–Fox. The studio's other feature, *Hello, Dolly!*, hadn't performed up to par at the box office despite being nominated for Best Picture, and Lumet took the brunt of the blame.

He would have been well advised to follow *The Sea Gull* with a lighter effort but instead he went for a meditative venture called *The Appointment*. Omar Sharif starred as a lawyer who suspects his wife (Anouk Aimeé) of being a prostitute. There wasn't much more to it than that.

Lumet admitted he hated the plot, if you could call it a plot. He only made it, he said, because he wanted to improve his use of color. He hadn't been happy with Boris

Kaufman's transition from black and white in *The Group* and *Bye Bye Braverman*. If he was going to continue using it, and he knew he'd have to, he needed to find someone of Kaufman's ability in the color mode.

He found that man in Carlo Di Palma. Lumet had been impressed by Di Palma's work in the Antonioni film *Red Desert* and gave him a call. He told him he needed someone to get him through his "color block." *Red Desert*, he said, had used color to deepen the characters and further the story. When Di Palma agreed to do the movie, Lumet happily signed him up.[38] He knew he'd got the right man. Di Palma was such a perfectionist, he once painted grass greener for Antonioni to get the shading right.[39]

Di Palma gave Lumet an important piece of advice one day which made the color problem seem less worrisome to him: "Just pick the right place," he said, "and the location will do the work for you." It was simple and yet ingenious. As Lumet listened to Di Palma speaking, he realized he had to be sure from now on that the locations had what he needed in them. The color of the places in question would help him to tell his stories.[40]

The Appointment was an interesting departure for him. The plot was wafer-thin but that didn't bother him because he saw the film as a mood piece. In it we can see the influences of Antonioni, Fellini, Godard, Buñuel, even Visconti. There are lots of sumptuous sets and meaningful glances. Its basic issue—is Aimeé really a call girl?—is interesting for a while but when it takes the film over to the exclusion of everything else, it becomes tiresome. How could Lumet not have anticipated this?

The dull plot failed to justify the evocative music score, the elaborate costumes, the lush set designs. As was the case with *The Sea Gull*, people hadn't the patience to sit for 114 minutes watching a man who looked almost too emotionally disturbed to smoke a cigarette, let alone find out the truth about his wife's morality. MGM dumped it on the market and let it die.

Martin Luther King was assassinated while Lumet was making it. King had been a hero of his life, and also one of Lena Horne's. His assassination reminded both of them of the Kennedy assassination. Robert Kennedy was horrified by it too and Lena was touched by this. She felt that, in time, Robert would also be cut down for his idealistic principles and she was right. Not too long afterwards, he too fell prey to an assassin's bullet.

Lumet and Gail were in London when it happened. That meant they'd been out of the U.S. for the two assassinations. For some reason, that made them feel worse about them. Their daugh-

Omar Sharif was tortured by the idea that his wife (Anouk Aimeé) might be a call girl in *The Appointment*. Unfortunately, audiences ended up being tortured by his *angst* as well.

ter Amy was now four. She'd spent a lot of her young life on the move (Italy, London, Stockholm). Gail asked her where she'd prefer to live from now on. Her answer was music to Lumet's ears: "New York."[41] That was all he needed to hear. He decided to travel less outside his home country afterwards.

He also decided he wanted to honor the memory of King in some way. He did so through a documentary which he co-directed with Joseph L. Mankiewicz: *King: A Filmed Record ... Montgomery to Memphis* chronicled his life from 1955 to his assassination. There's some brilliant footage focusing on his visionary speeches but the film is marred by a series of celebrities like Paul Newman and Burt Lancaster delivering overly earnest platitudes. Harry Belafonte, Charlton Heston, James Earl Jones and Ben Gazzara also feature in these segments. The "I have a dream" speech is the highlight of the film but there are others almost as eloquent. There are many scenes of King and his team going about their ordinary business and even being jocose before the shot rings out and puts an end to it all. The contrast is startling. It emphasizes the bigotry in the outpourings of those who printed slogans like "Colored Entrance" on storefronts.

The documentary is valuable as a slice of history as well as a paean to an icon. We see the arrests of those who opposed segregation on public transportation and elsewhere. We see the "persistent agitation" of those who were regarded as a menace to peace simply because they aired their views. We see messages like this outside a café: "Khrushchev Could Eat Here. Why Not American Negroes?"

"We hold these truths to be self-evident," King pronounces, "that all men are created equal." In an ideal world, the world Abraham Lincoln also dreamed of, this might have been possible, but Lincoln was also mowed down in cold blood.

King's winning of the Nobel Peace Prize becomes tragically ironic in the overall context of the film. The march to Washington, and the much-talked-about march to Selma, become twin chimeras that show us a "black and white together" cosmos is a long way away. The abiding memory of the film is that of bombings and self-righteous lynch mobs going about their business nonchalantly as their black brothers smother in "air-tight cages of poverty."

A black man's first name in life is "nigger," King tells us, and his second is "boy," no matter what age he is. A century after Lincoln, America was still back at square one as deluded optimists sing out "We Shall Overcome" to unhearing multitudes.

"I have seen the glory of the coming of the Lord," King declares before a bullet stops him in his tracks. As the dream ends, the funeral begins. Here Lumet is respectfully muted in his direction. In another scene we see a Ku Klux Klan member spreading his hatred. A swastika is displayed as a symbol of white power. King promises to use the force of his soul rather than bricks and bottles to achieve justice but in the end "the breastplate of righteousness" proves no match for the assassin's gun.

The film ends with Anthony Quinn quoting Ernest Hemingway's moving speech from *A Farewell to Arms*. Hemingway didn't write it with blacks in mind but rather all humanity. Even so, its power is strangely applicable to the black America cause: "The world breaks everyone and afterward many are strong at the broken places. But those that will not break, it kills. It kills the very good and the very gentle and the very brave impartially. If you are one of these you can be sure it will kill you too but there will be no special hurry."[42]

Misfires

A screenplay by Gore Vidal based on a play by Tennessee Williams, with photography by James Wong Howe and music by Quincy Jones. What could go wrong? Answer: everything!

The Last of the Mobile Hotshots was based on Williams' little-known play *The Seven Descents of Myrtle*. Lumet knew it wasn't one of Williams' better works but he felt a below-par Williams was still superior to most playwrights at their best.[1]

Jeb Thornton (James Coburn) and Myrtle Kane (Lynn Redgrave) meet in the audience of a TV game show in New Orleans. If they agree to be married on air the following Wednesday, they'll qualify for either a trip to Hollywood or a $3500 cash prize with $5000 of electrical household appliances thrown in. They opt for the latter. The morning after their lucrative nuptials, Jeb utters the immortal words to his new bride, "What is your name?"

Myrtle is a sweet, red-haired klutz who can't seem to stop jabbering. This is in marked contrast to the more pensive Jeb. She used to be in a five-piece girl band based in Mobile; hence the title of the film.

The newlyweds make their way to Waverly, Jeb's rundown family plantation in Louisiana. He lives there with his bi-racial half-brother Chicken (Robert Hooks) but they don't get on. They had the same father but different mothers. Or was it the other way round? The full details aren't revealed until the end. Both of them insist they're entitled to inherit the rights to the plantation and this causes most of the animosity between them. Chicken usually seems to get the better of their arguments. He describes himself as "half-light, half-dark, all bastard."

Jeb tells Myrtle he wants to restore Waverly to its former glory. But he's running out of time. In fact, Jeb is dying of lung cancer. The first inkling we get of this is when Myrtle throws off her wedding dress and goes topless for him. He tries to make love to her but gets a coughing fit that interrupts this. "I want an heir," he says, as if this is more important to him than anything sexual in their lovemaking. Myrtle doesn't seem to mind either way, being the type of woman who takes everything in her stride.

When she meets Chicken, he both entertains and frightens her, mixing the singing of songs with threats to drown cats and slaughter pigs. Meanwhile, the weakening Jeb sits in a chair contemplating the past. Lumet displays this to us in a series of blood-red flashbacks that have a psychedelic look about them. In one of them, a *ménage à trois* takes place, with Chicken getting most of the action.

There's a lot of unexplored sexual tension. The battle for the mansion is accompanied by a different kind of battle for Myrtle. She seems attracted to Chicken. Will she fall for him?

Inheritance talk continues. Chicken has forced Jeb to sign an agreement to deed the plantation to him after Jeb dies. Jeb wants to destroy this. He tells Myrtle to get Chicken drunk and then take it out of his wallet. If he can get rid of it, he's confident the estate will go to her after his death even if he doesn't live long enough to produce an heir. Anything would be better than having it fall into Chicken's hands. He doesn't want to die "without issue" but he may have no option. Maybe he's even impotent. A lot of things are left hanging in the air.

The Last of the Mobile Hotshots, based on a largely unknown Tennessee Williams play, was one of Lumet's most ill-judged projects, though he admired it himself. Here he's pictured with the film's two main leads, James Coburn and Lynn Redgrave (Jerry Ohlinger).

The three-way relationship is handled with a sense of the offbeat by Lumet against the backdrop of a river threatening to overflow its banks and flood them all out. Most of the dialogue concerns the agreement. Myrtle asks Chicken for it. He then asks to see her marriage license. Is she really Jeb's betrothed or just a game show wife? The pair of them flirt. Jeb stays upstairs playing records. Tragedy mixes with comedy in the familiar Williams manner. Lumet captures its flavor with bizarre enthusiasm.

Jeb puts on his great-grandfather's Confederate uniform. He lies on the floor as Myrtle becomes concerned about his rapidly declining health. He takes down his great-grandfather's gun from the wall and stumbles downstairs with it. Pointing it at Chicken, he demands that he hand over the agreement. Chicken does so and Myrtle promptly burns it.

Robert Hooks, James Coburn's biracial half-brother in *The Last of the Mobile Hotshots*, teases out a point with Lumet.

But then Chicken explains that the agreement is irrelevant to the inheritance rights as Jeb is misinformed about his roots. All his life he's believed his father was responsible for the half-brother situation. Chicken now tells him that it was their mother who was the sexually active party. The shock of this revelation causes blood to spurt out of Jeb's mouth. He falls to the floor and dies.

Neither Myrtle nor Chicken seem unduly perturbed by his death. In fact, nobody in the film reacts to anything in the way you might expect. It's one of Williams' weirdest plays and one of Lumet's weirdest movies. You watch it out of a perverse sense of curiosity.

Before it ends, a virtual tsunami gushes toward the mansion. Chicken grabs Myrtle and tells her they have to go up onto the roof to avoid drowning. Going up on a roof is a Williams metaphor for having sex. It turns out Chicken was conceived on a roof. Now he wants Myrtle to conceive a child by him there. Is she fertile? You bet your boots she is. Before they venture upwards, she tells him she's had five children already—all of them adopted. The pair of them wend their way to the roof as the water engulfs everything in sight.

Needless to say, audiences didn't know what to make of it all. It only had a limited release. To this day it's a film few people have seen, and not surprisingly. There are elements of *Cat on a Hot Tin Roof* in it and also *A Streetcar Named Desire* but it shouldn't really be mentioned in the same breath as either of these.

All the same, Lumet gets good work from his cast. Coburn doesn't look sick enough in the early stages but he gives a strong performance nonetheless. So does Redgrave. She does the part like Karen Black playing Blanche DuBois, making a ditzy character totally credible to us no matter how incomprehensible her dialogue becomes. But despite the effort everyone put into the film, it was avoided by the public and derided by the critics. They saw it as a piece of grave-robbing, another example of someone gathering together the last remnants of discarded Williams' works as get-rich-quick gambits.

Neither did Lumet have much luck with his next feature, Columbia's *The Anderson Tapes*. After serving a ten-year prison stretch for safecracking, "Duke" (Sean Connery) plans to rob a luxury apartment. He goes about this unaware that his every move is being monitored by the law. Dyan Cannon plays his former mistress.

Lumet said he made this caper movie for novelty purposes. "For someone like me," he chuckled, "with a tendency to be introverted, every four or five films it's important simply to make an action-packed story just for fun."[2] The problem was, it wasn't really funny. It was also too far-fetched. Not only is Connery being monitored by the law, so are lots of other people in the apartment complex where he lives with Cannon. What's the likelihood of this? One of them is an electronics expert called The Kid (played by Christopher Walken, looking near-angelic in his first role).

Casting Connery against type worked in *The Hill* because it had a strong script. Here there are too many resonances of Bond to make the transition credible. When Connery says to Cannon after coming out of jail, "I haven't been laid in ten years," it's hard to believe it. The glint in his eye is straight out of 007. The film's "Big Brother Is Watching" elements undermine its thriller aspect. A criminal can hardly complain that his civil liberties are being encroached on, which means that Lumet's Orwellian message goes for nothing.

The film fares better when it captures Connery's bewilderment at the brave new world that has come into being while he was "inside." Lumet would have been better off to make it as a straight-up heist movie without harboring pretensions to be a parable on a police state. The *Fail-Safe* message of "the machines are winning" didn't work.[3] Francis Ford Coppola would handle this much more adeptly in *The Conversation* (1974).

The film also lacks a sense of direction. We don't get to know anything about the characters beyond their situation. There's no pace, no plan, no vision. In its latter stages, the limp attempts at humor degenerate like a slow puncture.

Lumet, as usual, brought it in on time but Columbia didn't like his ending. He originally had Connery escaping. Columbia worried that this might affect its future sale to television. Moral laxity was more of an issue on TV than it was in the cinema. On the small screen, criminals still had to serve time for their sins. Lumet wasn't pleased but he had to defer to the studio's wishes. Whose bread he ate, their song he sang. In the revamped version, Connery was caught.[4]

The film had some compensations. Alan King was mildly amusing as a Mafia don, as was Martin Balsam as a gay antique dealer, even if he camped it up too much. Today it's noted mainly for being Walken's debut. Gary Arnold issued it a brief sop when he wrote, "*The Anderson Tapes* compensates in energy for what it lacks in style."[5]

Dyan Cannon was seen as little more than Connery's squeeze in it. *Newsweek*

Lumet shares a joke with Sean Connery on the set of *The Anderson Tapes*, one of Lumet's misguided "caper" films (Jerry Ohlinger).

huffed, "She has nothing to do but undress."[6] In *Newsday*, Joseph Gelmis wondered why the so-called professional safecrackers behaved like amateurs, and why, since Labor Day was chosen for the heist because nobody would be at home ... everyone was at home.[7] It wasn't like Lumet to overlook practical issues like this.

His next feature *Child's Play*, based on a successful play by Robert Marasco, posed different kinds of problems. Set in a Catholic boarding school in New York, it dealt with the violent behavior of the pupils and the rivalry between two teachers (James Mason and Robert Preston). Beau Bridges was a former pupil of the school who becomes a PE teacher there. Preston portrays himself as a Mr. Chips figure to Bridges while he's anything *but* that. He poisons Bridges' mind against Mason, whom he eventually drives to suicide. When Bridges finally realizes that Preston is the villain of the piece rather than Mason, he tries to alert the pupils to that fact but they've become too brainwashed by Preston and they turn on him as they turned on Mason, presumably killing him. (We don't actually see this happen.) At the end of the film they turn on Preston too, circling him threateningly in a church. Lumet leaves us in little doubt that the evil he's unleashed on them is about to snowball back on himself.

Marlon Brando was originally supposed to play the Preston role. Brando told his friend Wally Cox he would also be in the film, playing the role of an alcoholic priest who teaches at the school. What Brando didn't tell him was that Lumet would be auditioning him. Cox was shocked when he got to the set and learned this was the case.

Lumet said to him, "You used to play Mr. Peepers, a schoolteacher. Marlon says you're also an alcoholic so you should be just right for the role."[8] Again Cox was shocked. A dark part of his life had been used to garner him the role. His drinking problem was private, he assumed, something between himself and Brando, but now it was public property. It was out of character for Lumet to talk like this, so Brando must have told him Cox wasn't embarrassed about his problem.

What goes around comes around: Brando now had a problem of his own. Lumet hadn't worked with him since *The Fugitive Kind* and he'd had a string of flops and fallen dramatically since then. He was about to have a renaissance with *The Godfather*, which he'd just finished, but it hadn't come out yet.

As soon as Brando arrived on the set, he started demanding changes to the script, which was fairly typical of him. Lumet was sympathetic to his concerns but the film's producer, David Merrick, wasn't the type of man to indulge the star. "He wanted to make basic changes in the story," Merrick told the *Los Angeles Times*, "and I couldn't accept that."[9]

Lumet was caught in an awkward position. He liked Brando and wanted him on the film but Merrick was calling the shots. He'd just produced *Child's Play* on Broadway and he knew exactly how he wanted things done. He wasn't adaptable like Lumet. It was a case of "take it or leave it" as far as he was concerned. The script was set in stone. Brando couldn't accept that so he was told to leave the set. Who knows how the film would have fared out with him in it. Merrick could have made a big mistake. Or maybe it would have been a failure anyway.

It would probably have worked better if the Mason and Preston roles were reversed. Preston didn't have the screen presence to convince us he would have been able to hypnotize his pupils as the script demanded whereas Mason would have. He was in a different league to Preston as an actor. He was also excellent in the part he was given. He gives one of his best performances as a man whose life—and sanity—is slipping away from him under a welter of sexual peccadilloes and a mother fixation.

Lumet was less comfortable with the terror aspect of the film, using exaggerated sound effects and gimmicky camerawork to convey the ominous nature of the goings-on. He performed better when he was exploring the tensions between Mason and Preston, if not the pupils. These become vague figures hovering at the edge of the action, making us wonder if they're to be pitied or feared, whether they're victims of brainwashing or aggressors in their own right.

James Mason (center) had both his life and career destroyed by Robert Presto (right) in *Child's Play*, Lumet's attempt at a demonic drama set in a New York school. Beau Bridges is the third teacher in the photograph (Jerry Ohlinger).

There are many vague elements in the film. "*Child's Play* is about as much or as little as you care to have it about," wrote Charles Champlin in the *Los Angeles Times*, which sums it up.[10] We shouldn't look for easy answers here any more than we should have in Marasco's play. Not many people would have tried to cross *Rosemary's Baby* with *Goodbye Mr. Chips* and gotten away with it. Lumet just about does, despite the ponderous melodrama and "zombie killer" aspect of it.[11] It carried echoes of everything from *Lord of the Flies* to *Unman, Wittering and Zigo* and in the end probably bit off more that it could chew.

Mason drew positive notices for his performance, most notably from Pauline Kael, who took a break from her customary Lumet-bashing to praise the film. She said Mason "transforms an initially irritating bundle of neuroses quite miraculously into a fig-

Lumet was always a "touchy-feely" type of director. He liked to get close to his stars professionally if not personally to help them maximize their potential. Here he sits beside Robert Preston on the set of *Child's Play* (Eddie Brandt's Saturday Matinee).

ure of human dimensions." She liked the way Mason wore his suit, the way he grimaced, the way he shuffled when he walked. Everything about him, she maintained, "bespeaks the terrors of lonely old age and the painful self-denial of a cramped life."[12] Rod Steiger said more generally, "There was something oddly tragic about Mr. Mason. You felt things in life were eating away at him, that he was always in a tremendous kind of emotional pain which he was bravely trying to hide."[13] From that point of view, he could be seen to be playing himself in the film, or at least a version of himself.

Lumet didn't come out of it as well as Mason. It was seen as an amateur horror film that creaked with quasi-grisly undertones. Having pupils with their eyes being gouged out, or tied to crosses in church, clearly had him out of his depth. *The Exorcist*, which worked a similar beat with a degree more heft, wiped it out at the box office.

His next project was equally dark. Based on a play by John Hopkins, *The Offence* (1972) suffered from many of the same problems as *Child's Play* in the sense that it wasn't typical Lumet territory. He took it on because it was proposed to him by Sean Connery. He had such respect for Connery for his work on *The Hill* that he didn't like to refuse.

It was a bleak story about a police officer (Connery) who beats a suspected pedophile to death in a London station while interrogating him on suspicion of molesting a child. Connery's Sgt. Johnson is an angry and embittered man obsessed with pinning the crime on the suspect Baxter (Ian Bannen). Vivien Merchant played Connery's wife and Trevor Howard his superior officer.

Why does it mean so much to Connery to find Bannen guilty? Probably for the same reason it meant so much to Lee J. Cobb to find the defendant of *Twelve Angry Men* guilty—to sublimate tensions inside himself. Both men project their conflicts onto an external source to try and expiate them but in the process only increase their discomfiture. Cobb finds release in the end under Henry Fonda's stubborn probing but Connery has no such catalyst to usher in his reformation here.

Connery's father died shortly before filming began and it had a devastating effect on him.[14] The anger we see on screen is partly the anger of bereavement. In a strange way, it helped his performance. It goaded him on to new levels of vindictiveness in every other scene. At times Lumet felt more like a spectator than a director. Connery was in his own world, reminding Lumet of Brando being "somewhere else" on the set of *The Fugitive Kind*.[15]

The way Lumet foregrounded Katharine Hepburn in *Long Day's Journey Into Night* is repeated here with Connery. Such a foregrounding isolated Hepburn; here it serves to make Connery more fearful. His anger rises in torrents, overflowing like lava. John Huston said the last 40 minutes of *The Offence*, where Connery totally disintegrates psychologically, was some of the best footage he'd ever seen on film.[16]

The problem with the disintegration is that it's too piecemeal. Because of the film's flashback structure, we don't get a chance to become as involved in Connery's anger as he does. It's splintered, which lends an air of contrivance to it. Lumet would have been better advised to keep it all together. In that way, he could have worked up better to a crescendo.

Where it's most interesting is in the comparisons it draws between Connery and Bannen. When Connery calls him a "filthy pervert," Bannen replies, "It takes one to know one." At times Bannen appears to analyze Connery even more than Connery analyzes him. By the end we still don't know if Bannen is guilty or not. Maybe it doesn't matter. The film is more about Connery than him.

It came in ahead of schedule and £80,000 under its $1 million budget but it bombed. Connery felt it might have had better success if it was released into arthouse cinemas.[17] It might, but how many people would have gone to see the man who played James Bond in such a venue? It wouldn't have been practical.

It wasn't released until a year after its completion, a detail

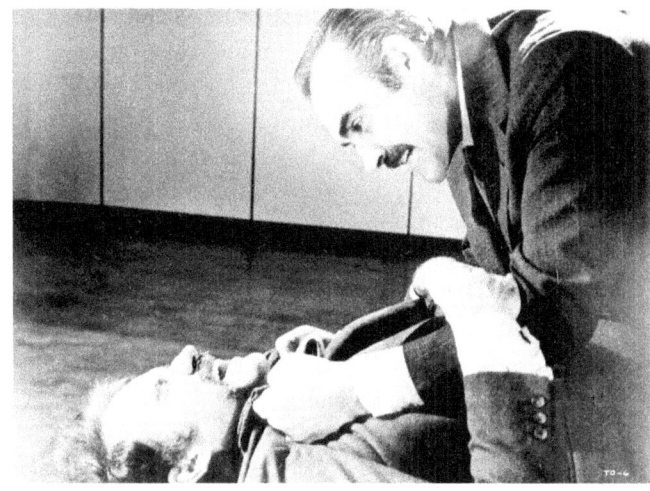

Sean Connery (right) struggles with Ian Bannen in *The Offence*, trying to exorcise his own demons in the process (Jerry Ohlinger).

that was indicative of the studio's lack of confidence in it. According to Lumet, "I don't think United Artists even spent $3,000 advertising it. They had no faith in it."[18]

The critical reaction was mixed. Some reviewers castigated Lumet for his heavy-handed treatment of the material and the set-ups he used, like the mammoth circular light under which Connery quizzes Bannen. Christopher Bray lambasted him for his "radical theater workshop" atmosphere, his "Dadaist abstractions," his "Pinteresque take on the police procedural."[19] These were legitimate accusations. Mix in Hopkins' overwritten script and the result was an arguably melodramatic package. Even Connery suggested Lumet had "gone a bit European on us" with his techniques.[20] He overplayed the Freud card and, in Connery's eyes, that made it difficult for the film to succeed outside the U.S. "The British have always been so anti-analysis," he said.[21]

There were other reasons why *The Offence* failed. It fell between the Scylla of mainstream drama and the Charybdis of an art film. Some of the Connery-Bannen exchanges also seemed too theatrical. The acting was of a high quality but the scenes of physical violence had a posed look about them.

When we consider Connery's rages, we could even argue that there was too much talk mixed in with them, which dented their credibility. In this sense he was himself a proponent of the over-analysis he talked about. As for Bannen, he was too forthcoming with information about himself to a man who was beating him to a pulp. If this was done from fear, it might have made more sense but he appeared to enjoy telling Connery about himself. At times the pair of them almost seemed to be becoming friends. That's where the Pinter element entered. One was never quite sure if the dialogue was going to morph into violence or not.

Lumet was interviewed for *Films in Review* after it was released. He smoked nonstop during the interview. In between cigarettes he gobbled pistachios. The interviewer said she could see how his manic energy had managed to produce so many films in such a relatively short span of time. He said *The Offence* was basically the story of two people who were like opposite sides of the same coin. Connery beats the criminal to death because he sees himself in him and can't face it.[22]

The fact that the film didn't make a profit, Lumet insisted, didn't bother him, even if this was the priority of most people in the film business.[23] How did he feel about films in general? The industry had changed exponentially, he said. The old Hollywood had collapsed and everyone was running scared. Big budgets seemed to be a thing of the past. So were lifetime contracts. Films were being made "on spec" now, on an *ad hoc* basis. "Step deals" had made their appearance.[24] That meant directors could be fired at any time.

He tried not to let such concerns get in the way of his work. "All I want to do is to get better," he maintained. Sheer volume of output, he thought, could help him solve whatever problems he had in direction. He said, "I'm thrilled by the idea that I'm not even sure how many films I've done." He based his decision on whether to do a film or not on different things: "If I don't have a script I adore, I do one I like. If I don't have one I like, I do one that has an actor I like or that presents some technical challenge."[25] Inactivity was his only enemy. That was death to the spirit.

"He finished a film on Friday," Jay Presson Allen remarked, "and he wants to go to work next Monday on another one. It's what he lives for."[26]

A journalist said of him once as he watched him entering a room, "A small whirlwind called Sidney Lumet just swept through here."[27] He was amused by the comment. "I guess it's my metabolism," he explained. "I never walk down a hall. I bound."[28]

He would have an extra pep in his step over the next few years because one of the screen's most exciting talents was about to enter his life.

Pacino on the Double

Al Pacino already had an impressive body of work behind him when he took on the role of Frank Serpico for Lumet in 1974—including, of course *The Godfather*—but he wasn't yet a superstar. That was all set to change over the next few years. He would have Lumet to thank for a lot of it.

Based on a book by Peter Maas, *Serpico* dealt with a real-life drama involving two police officers, Frank Serpico and David Durk, who told a *New York Times* reporter that they had ample evidence of police graft and corruption. Publication of their story led to the appointment of a commission to investigate their allegations.

The screenplay was written by Waldo Salt. John Avildsen was originally supposed to direct but he fell out with producer Martin Bregman in a dispute over locations. The job then fell to Lumet. He admired what Serpico did and looked forward to the challenge of telling his story. He knew the shoot was going to be "physically brutal and emotionally tough." He was determined to get "all that intensity up on the screen."[1]

"The script was chaotic when I arrived," he recalled. It was 240 pages long, which would have meant a 4½-hour movie. He asked Salt to collaborate with another writer and chop it in half. He chose Norman Wexler for that job.

Lumet didn't meet Serpico until three days before filming began. He was very taken with him, finding him witty and fun to be around. There was only one problem: Serpico expected to be allowed to stay on the set for the whole film and that wasn't feasible. Lumet understood his eagerness. It was, after all, the story of his life. But it would have made Pacino too self-conscious. He took it quite badly when Lumet told him he'd have to leave.[2]

Dino de Laurentiis was adamant that the film needed a score but Lumet wasn't in favor of this. He liked De Laurentiis' choice of scoring on some films but on this one he was afraid of overkill. He didn't want two and a half hours of music, which he believed was what he would get with this man. De Laurentiis would have given the film "wall to wall carpeting" in sound terms.[3] Instead he opted for Greek composer Mikis Theodorakis. Lumet liked his work—he had *Zorba the Greek* to his credit—and also his politics. He'd spent most of his life opposing right-wing elements in Greece. When Lumet met him, he wasn't long out of prison for his principles.

The opening line of the film is spoken by Pacino as he lies on a stretcher in a squad car after being shot in the face. "Did a cop do it?" he asks. Lumet is preparing us for a world where everything is back to front, where police make the problems instead of solving them, where an honest cop becomes an oddball, where anything he does to try and root out the corruption drives him deeper and deeper into danger.

Serpico is a lone wolf trying to put his finger in the dike of a system that has long pre-dated him. He's told the force is "as clean as a hound's tooth" but in reality it's rotten to the core. He refuses his first bribe from a colleague and reports it but he's discouraged from taking the complaint any further. If he does so, he's informed, he'll either be hauled in front of a grand jury—or found "face down in the East River."

Taking the high moral ground alienates him from his colleagues. He's seen as a prima donna, a white knight on a horse singing "Ave Maria." His girlfriend tells him a story about a king who refused to drink from a poisoned well. Anyone who drank from it went mad. The king was called mad because he wouldn't drink from it. Then one day he did—and went mad. And the people said, "The king is well again."

The message is clear. If Serpico is to survive, he needs to be "on the take." "It hurts nobody," he's informed gleefully. But he refuses—unlike the king in the fairy tale. Will he testify against others taking the bribes? He's not sure. His conscience drives him towards this but he knows it might be dangerous.

The film could have been a boring propaganda treatise were Serpico not an eccentric. He wears kooky hats and keeps a white mouse as a pet. He has a laidback attitude to life when we first see him but that soon disappears. Moving from uniformed cop status to plainclothes one is the first step. Then he goes undercover. When he enters the narcotics division, it's a game-changer for him. Suddenly he's playing for much bigger stakes.

His childhood dream of saving the world goes west. He needs back-up but he doesn't get it. People in high places pay lip service to his integrity but they do nothing. The promises they make him ring false. Behind the scenes they discredit him. At one stage he's called "a fag" and threatened with official sanctions against him. He knows he needs to move—either geographically as a policeman or to another job completely. Not taking bribes becomes a bigger crime than taking them.

When he's lying in hospital after being shot, a young policeman is about to visit him when another one says, "Don't talk to him. He's no fucking good." He receives a "Get Well" card with the message, "Best wishes for a slow death. Die, you scumbag." Afterwards he's presented with a Gold Shield, an honor for bravery. It's something he's always wanted but now he tells them to shove it. This puts one in mind of Gary Cooper at the end of *High Noon* throwing his marshal's badge on the ground in disgust before he leaves the town that has betrayed him. An endnote informs us he moved to Switzerland after testifying to the grand tribunal. Maybe he was lucky he only got shot, that he didn't end up "face down in the East River."

Serpico is a film that wears its heart on its sleeve. Pacino's dawning awareness of the corruption surrounding him isn't novel celluloid fare but the conviction with which he plays the part makes for compulsive viewing. Theodorakis' gentle score is an ideal backdrop in the early scenes as we get to know Serpico the man rather than the campaigner for justice.

There were certain logistical problems with the film. Serpico grows a beard in it so the later scenes were filmed first, thus reversing the chronological order of things. The backgrounds of scenes had to be reversed as the film was set in winter but shot in

Al Pacino's whistle-blowing policeman in *Serpico* carried undertones of messianic zeal. The film set Lumet up for a series of "man against the system" crusades as he thumped the tub for the Old Left (Jerry Ohlinger).

summer. Lumet could hardly have made things more awkward for himself. He also found it difficult to guarantee the use of police precincts for scenes as a result of the fact that such precincts were often the objects of his main character's anger. This reminded him of the problem he had getting military footage for *Fail-Safe*.

He worked very closely with Pacino, making him privy to the way he set up shots and executed them. This was something Pacino wasn't accustomed to. "With *Serpico*, I was more on the inside," he enthused.[4] Under Lumet's collaborative process he became consumed by the part, so much so that when a friend of his showed him a poster from the film one day and said, "Hey, Al, that's you," he replied, "No, that's not Al Pacino. It's Serpico."[5]

On one occasion, he went so far as to make a citizen's arrest on the set. He was sitting in a taxi and the weather was unusually warm. He was bothered by the amount of fumes that were coming out of the driver's exhaust pipe. "Why are you putting that crap in the street?" he yelled at him. "Who the hell are you?" the driver yelled back. "I'm a cop," Pacino said, "and you're under arrest. Pull over!"[6]

Serpico's idealism was commendable but there were times it appeared to be out of sync with the circumstances of the film. At times his reaction to policemen bending the rules bordered on naiveté. We're asked to believe, for instance, that a man who's grown up on New York's streets is going to be shocked by a policeman being given free meals in a restaurant.[7] Serpico overplays his hand in scenes like this, especially when he has much more serious breaches of the law to deal with.

Lumet was captivated by Pacino in the role:

> Al felt the same sense of obligation to the material that I did, which was part of the reason for his sensational performance. The other part is built into him as an actor. There are only a handful of actors who are literally incapable of doing anything false and Al is one of them. He never says, "I can't do what you ask because it would not be true to me." He simply gets into a character and doesn't come out.... [He's] a complicated man and he uses himself brilliantly. He's an instinctive animal but he makes slow decisions. Maybe it's because he's a street person that he likes to keep his options open. He's totally consuming, totally committed, and you have to match his dedication.[8]

Lumet kept the relationship between them professional. He thought that was the best way to get an optimal performance from him:

> I know very little about his life. I never ask personal questions. One of my cardinal rules is never to invade the actor personally. If he's got sexual hang-ups or whatever, I don't want to know about it. If he's got problems about knowing who he is, the same [applies]. I want to work it out of craft and if we can't do that, fuck it.

Lumet had a few conversations with Pacino about his upbringing but that was it: "The little Al has volunteered, like being in his house alone for years, being brought up by his grandmother, that's all I know."[9]

One commentator on the film saw Serpico as a Christ figure, "a god-man doomed to suffer for his love of humanity, a cop who found his apostolate on the streets."[10] Lumet had a different view. For him, Serpico was more a rebel without a cause: "If he hadn't been able to protest against corruption he would have found a reason to protest about the color of his uniform."[11] Serpico, in other words, had an attitude problem. He would have been resentful of anyone over him in any walk of life. He didn't have to be a cop. He was going to be a pain in the ass for any authority figure.

Pacino once asked Serpico why he did what he did. He replied, "I don't know. I guess I have to say that if I didn't, who would I be when I listened to a piece of music." Pacino was blown away by that answer. "What a way of putting it!" he enthused.[12]

Lumet did up to 35 set-ups a day for the film, an incredible tally. He had a gift for mobilizing large crowds and having them photographed from unique angles. One of his cinematographers was amazed at his ability to keep control of them all. "A cameraman is like the first fiddle in an orchestra," he said, "The director is the conductor."[13]

Serpico had over a hundred speaking parts and almost as many locations but Lumet still managed to bring it in on time and on budget. It was a fulfilling experience for everyone concerned. Lumet was particularly happy with Pacino. "I could work with him forever," he beamed.[14] Jack Kroll described Pacino as being "almost a mythic incarnation of metropolitan chivalry."[15]

The film was a box office success, providing a much-needed boost for Lumet after his recent run of clunkers. Some directors tended to be sniffy about commercial success but not this man. It didn't take a genius to work out the fact that if nobody went to see your work, you wouldn't have a job to go to. "I'm not one to be cool about a hit," he confessed. He made no effort to disguise his glee.[16]

Pacino was nominated for an Oscar for his performance. The previous year he'd been nominated in the supporting category for *The Godfather*, a decision that annoyed him. His co-star Marlon Brando was on screen for less time than him in the film and

Anthony Perkins sits with Lumet on the set of *Lovin' Molly* while Blythe Danner stands between them with her head down. The film was based on a novel by Larry McMurtry but failed to reprise its folksy charm (Eddie Brandt's Saturday Matinee).

yet he won the Best Actor award. Pacino lost to Joel Grey on that occasion and he failed with *Serpico* as well, the award going to Jack Lemmon for *Save the Tiger* (which was directed by John Avildsen, who'd been rejected for *Serpico*). Lumet wasn't nominated for Best Director and neither did *Serpico* garner a Best Picture nomination. *The Sting*, a work of much less substance, won Best Film. This would be the shape of things to come for Lumet but he took it on the chin. Pacino was more upset, stuffing tranquillizers into his mouth during the ceremony to try and cover up his anxiety.[17]

Whenever directors—or actors—have success in a particular genre, they tend to be flooded with similar scripts in the months and years to come. Lumet was no exception but he generally tried to avoid re-visiting old pastures if he could avoid it. For his next undertaking he decided on something as different from *Serpico* as it would be possible to imagine: a sprawling romance spanning the early decades of the century.

Based on a novel by Larry McMurtry, *Lovin' Molly* was the story of two men (Anthony Perkins and Beau Bridges) who vie for the love of the same woman (Blythe Danner) over a period of 40 years. For Perkins, the film was a godsend. Much of his career since 1960 had been a kind of footnote to *Psycho*. Lumet was impressed with the "Gary Cooper quality" he'd shown in the William Wyler film *Friendly Persuasion* and thought he might reprise it here. Perkins was delighted with the "transitional" opportunities the role afforded.[18]

Shot mostly on location in Bastrop, Texas, with interiors completed in New York, the film was independently produced by Stephen Friedman. Friedman had brought McMurtry's most successful adaptation, *The Last Picture Show*, to the screen three years before. He'd also written the *Lovin' Molly* screenplay. Could Lumet repeat *Last Picture Show*'s success here?

At first sight, it didn't look like it. The film's attempt at folksiness went awry and the casting also left something to be desired. Perkins wasn't leading man material and Bridges was equally poor riding shotgun. It was left to Danner to drive the story forward. Lumet gave her too much responsibility in this regard, Momentous events jostled with trivia in a mixed grill of love and tragedy.

Lumet had problems with Friedman's script. He felt it lacked muscle. Very soon the cast got the feeling they were on a treadmill to nowhere. "There was no money for art," Lumet complained.[19]

The most obvious pitfall was having the main stars age as much as they did in the book. Lumet ruled out the idea of using three different sets of actors. This laid most of the responsibility at the door of his makeup artist, Phil Leto. Leto was his third choice for this job, the first two being unavailable. It was an unhappy omen for the film in general.

Everyone marries the wrong person in *Lovin' Molly*. This might have been more interesting if the voiceover didn't distance us from the action. Such a voiceover has the effect of making the events being described seem flat. We don't become involved in them; we're dispassionate viewers more than anything else.

Lumet was off-key here and he seemed to know it. He didn't direct with his usual verve. The film didn't do for Beau Bridges what *The Last Picture Show* did for his brother Jeff. That was because *Lovin' Molly* didn't have *Last Picture Show*'s elegiac quality. Apart from Danner's free-spiritedness, there wasn't much to become intrigued with. Having said that, her performance had inconsistencies. She under-reacts, for example, to the death of the son she has by Perkins. Everything seems to happen at a remove, which means the passage of time, which is a crucial aspect of it, loses its impact. From 1925 to 1945 there's hardly any change in the appearance of the characters apart from their hair. Ten years further on, there is. At this point, the changes become *too* dramatic. *Variety* compared the later Perkins to "an emaciated Gregory Peck." It accused Denner of being "not unlike Perkins playing Mrs. Bates in *Psycho*."[20]

A related problem—the one that had affected Tab Hunter in *That Kind of Woman*—was Lumet trying to persuade audiences to accept a man of ambivalent sexuality as a romantic lead. There were rumors about Perkins being gay for years. They abated when he married, shortly before *Lovin' Molly* was made. This gave him confidence in the love scenes with Danner, but not everybody "bought" these. The *New York Times*' Vincent Canby was most damning in his comments: Perkins acted mostly with his jawbone, he alleged, and aged "in the stiff-faced manner of a person who'd had too many facelifts." Canby intimated that the relationship between Perkins and Bridges seemed stronger in many ways than that of either of them to Danner. Was she a kind of "sexual surrogate" to something homosexual going on between them?[21]

The film was a misjudgment by Lumet both in style and tone. One admired his desire to keep trying new things but no more than a learner driver venturing onto the main motorway there were tripwires to be avoided. *Lovin' Molly* wasn't a disaster but it tried to piggyback on the coattails of *The Last Picture Show* and fell woefully short.

Undaunted by its failure, Lumet stayed with nostalgia for his next offering. If he had his fingers burned by *Lovin' Molly*, one would never guess this from the enthusiasm with which he approached Agatha Christie's *Murder on the Orient Express*.

Lumet was aware that he didn't have much of a reputation for light-hearted fare and was anxious to change that perception of him. It might sound unusual to refer to a murder mystery as light-hearted but that was how he saw it. It was "a lively soufflé." He wanted to "glam it up" rather than present it as a "small," realistic film.[22]

He gathered together a Who's Who of the British and American stage and screen for his cast. Sean Connery was his first thought. Once he was "in," he felt he could rely on him to persuade the other people he wanted to climb aboard. He thought Alec Guinness would be suitable for Poirot but the actor wasn't available. Neither was Paul Scofield, his second choice. He believed Albert Finney, talented as he was, was too young for the part but Finney—and the makeup people—allayed his fears on that score. He was such a good actor that with some simple gestures, like a tilt of the head, he

Playing a man twenty years older than him in Hercule Poirot guise, Albert Finney (center) is joined by Martin Balsam (left) and George Coulouris in Lumet's valentine to Agatha Christie, *Murder on the Orient Express* (Jerry Ohlinger).

looked older even without makeup. With his pomaded hair and his impeccable grooming, he *became* his character. The scene where he retired to bed with both his hair and his mustache encased in hairnets was classic Poirot.

Jacqueline Bisset was flattered to be in the film but thought her part, like most people's apart from Finney, was insignificant. "There's no such thing as a small part," Lumet chastised, quoting the old adage "only small actors."[23]

He also recruited John Gielgud, Richard Widmark, Anthony Perkins, Michael York, Martin Balsam, Wendy Hiller, Vanessa Redgrave, Lauren Bacall, Rachel Roberts, George Coulouris and Ingrid Bergman. Widmark claimed to have taken the part just to meet all the other luminaries.[24]

The mixture of film and theater stars resulted in tension. At the first reading, everyone spoke quietly. Lumet found them inaudible. He didn't know what was going on for a few minutes and then the penny dropped: "The movie stars were in awe of the theater stars and the theater stars were in awe of the movie stars. A classic case of stage fright."[25] It didn't matter what these people had achieved in the past or how long a media shadow they cast; the collision of their two worlds had caused them, as the phrase went, to "corpse." This despite the fact that people like Gielgud had inhabited both worlds. At the time of the reading, he was appearing in the West End. So were Hiller, Redgrave and Roberts. A bemused Lumet asked, "Do I detect two snobbisms here?" That eased the tension.[26]

Accents were important in the film. Bergman did a perfect Swedish one. Rachel Roberts, playing a German, copied hers from Marlon Brando in *The Young Lions*. She was word-perfect during the takes but being the fun-lover she was, she liked to "send her Teutonic character up rotten" between them.[27] Roberts was a functioning alcoholic by this time, well able to do her work but never wasting too much time after it was done to wet her whistle. This was made blindingly clear to Lumet one day. She'd just left the set when it struck him that he needed a close-up of her. He wanted it done there and then because it was a reaction shot so he had her called back. When she appeared, he was shocked to see she was drunk. (Only a little time had elapsed since she'd left the set.) Gentleman that he was, he pretended not to notice. He told her he didn't need to do it until the following day.[28] The anecdote demonstrates how needy she was for a drink and how quickly it took effect on her when she'd had it. She would commit suicide some years later. By then it had destroyed both her life and her career.

Maybe Perkins was the most surprising cast member considering he'd just appeared in a Lumet flop. The director didn't blame him for that. He liked the work he'd done in *Lovin' Molly* and was happy to employ him again. He encouraged him to experiment with the part, imbuing it with his trademark tics. These were all too familiar to anyone who'd seen him in *Psycho*. Here, unlike in *Lovin' Molly*, he had some kind of license for them, being a murder suspect.

Lumet was a great lover of realism but here, because of the genre in which he was working, he dispensed with it. In fact, he asked production designer Tony Walton to make things artificial. "He wanted costumes to look like costumes instead of clothes," said Walton. The film was all about style. Some of the stars felt what they wore was more important than what they looked like. They had a point, but because Lumet was directing, it was also about camerawork. For one scene, Bacall worried that her hat was so steeply angled and the camera wouldn't be able to pick up her face. Lumet had to assure her it would.[29]

One of the most interesting characters in the film was played by Bergman. Lumet originally wanted her to play the aging Princess Dragomiroff but she preferred the role of Greta, a Swedish missionary.[30] He was surprised at this. He believed she could have done more with the Russian part but she wasn't interested. "She was sweetly stubborn," he said, "but stubborn she was." The more he pleaded, the more indignant she became. Eventually she said, "Well, if you don't want me to be in your movie…."[31] Lumet relented at that point. He wanted her so much, he joked, "She could have played Poirot if she wanted."[32]

Because her part was small, he decided to film it in one take. She loved that idea and threw herself into it wholeheartedly. It ran for almost five minutes. Even though she'd been a great screen beauty, there was never any effort on her part to glamorize herself. She just played Greta like the funny old character she was. A lot of actresses in her place might have demanded special lighting but not this one. Lumet admired her lack of vanity.[33] Her costar Michael York agreed. Actresses, as everyone knew, generally went into the make-up room to make themselves look prettier. Bergman went there for the opposite reason: "To have her luminosity removed," said York.[34]

Lumet saw *Murder on the Orient Express* as a chance to indulge his mischievous side. Orson Welles once described a film set as being like a boy playing with an expensive train. That was almost literally true for Lumet here. Like Welles, he was an intellectual but he was happy to dumb himself down for Christie's pulp fiction. He was shifting gears once again to confound those who imagined they were able to predict what he would do next. Every film he made seemed a stretch of one sort or another for him, either within a genre or between two or three of them. Sometimes it was difficult to know what he was trying to achieve in such transitions but not here. Everything in *Murder on the Orient Express* screamed *déjà vu*: the costumes, the dialogue, the overwrought plot. He was going back to his childhood again like Welles, having fun with his overpaid, overdressed cast.

It wasn't a thriller so much as a crossword puzzle. He builds an opulent house of cards and knocks it down with relish. Anybody could be the villain, as seems mandatory for Agatha Christie. We don't chew our fingernails awaiting the final revelation. It isn't a whodunit so much as a "theyalldunit." He approached it with a "Let's do a '30s movie" attitude. If reality got in the way, to hell with reality.[35]

For his music score he employed Richard Rodney Bennett. Bennett devised a waltz to accompany the train as it moved. Or rather danced. The man who recorded the actual sound of the train whooshing along was dismissed, to his chagrin, because no way could a mechanical sound like the grinding of wheels produce the "soufflé" effect Lumet was after. "We weren't making *Psycho*," Bennett remarked wryly.[36] With music, Lumet enthused, Paul Newman could become Tom Mix. Jane Fonda could become ZaSu Pitts.[37] That was the beauty of *kitsch*. He said he was determined to make the film "gay"—meaning light, rather than homosexual—"if I had to kill myself and everyone else to accomplish it."[38]

The gods smiled on him for the shoot. Not only was it completed in 42 days but everything went exactly according to plan. Nobody tried to upstage anyone else. It worked a treat as an ensemble piece. The weather even behaved itself. He prayed for snow for a scene he was shooting in France and it arrived on cue.[39]

The film wasn't just a love note to the past; it was also a love note to a certain form of transport. "I'm a train freak," Lumet admitted. "I've had some of the most glorious times of my life traveling on them."[40] Having said that, he knew there was a big difference between boarding one for pleasure and making a film with one at its center.

There were logistical problems. To deal with them, parts of it were shot in a railway repair yard in Paris. It was the only place he could get the effects he was looking for. He wanted a feeling of enclosure for the carriage scenes, which brought him back to the claustrophobia of *Twelve Angry Men*. This time there were a dozen murderers instead of a dozen jurors. He placed them all in a carriage he found in a Belgium museum. (The actual Orient Express, had long ceased to run.)

Everyone in the cast seemed to share his good humor as they threw themselves into the action. Murder in Christie's novels often seems more like a parlor game than a horrific event and this was no exception. We marvel at Poirot's verbal linguistics so much that we almost forget what he's alluding to. The multiple stabbing plays second fiddle to the convolutions of his mind.

After the identities of the murderers are revealed in the last scene, Lumet still wasn't finished. He decided to end the film with a curtain call in which the cast toasted one another with glasses of champagne. These are dignified killers. The gory bloodfest is followed by a frothy denouement.

The public loved the film. There were lines threading their way around corners at some of the showings. It was a critical success too but there were, as ever, some negative noises. *Newsweek* thought Lumet had "no feel for high style."[41] This was a ridiculous comment. Another critic accused him of choosing to film one of Christie's silliest novels.[42] Again the comment didn't make much sense. If Hollywood didn't film silly novels, very few films would have be made. Silly novels often made for great films just as great novels often made for silly films. A more pertinent observation was made by the man who said *Murder on the Orient Express* was a forerunner of the mid–1970s vogue for disaster films.[43] Whether that was a good or a bad thing was a separate issue.

Its respectability was enhanced when it was nominated for a spate of Oscars: Best Actor (Finney), Supporting Actress (Bergman), Costume Design, Score, Cinematography and Screenplay. Only Bergman won. Obviously, she knew something Lumet didn't when she fought so hard for the part.

Bergman didn't think she deserved her statuette. In her acceptance speech, she said she thought the award should have gone to Valentina Cortese for Francois Truffaut's *Day for Night*. Cortese blew her a kiss but the other nominees sat frozen-faced. All too late, Bergman learned that an act of kindness towards one person could be considered ungracious towards another.[44] The point was that in praising Cortese, she was implicitly criticizing the other nominees as well as herself. She watched the look of horror on the faces of Madeline Kahn, Diane Ladd and Talia Shire as the realization of the implied insult sank in. "I often spoke first and thought afterwards," she confessed.[45]

Bergman had already won Best Actress Oscars for *Gaslight* (1944) and *Anastasia* (1956). Her hat trick was a sore point with the other nominees who had no awards at all on their shelves. They would have been angry with her even if she was right about

Cortese, and many people thought she was. Lumet didn't give his view as to whether he thought it was a fair or unfair division of the spoils. He was on too much of a high from his own personal journey.

Lumet had dinner with Anthony Perkins one night and Perkins tried to persuade him to remake *M*, the classic Fritz Lang thriller with Peter Lorre as the child killer. Perkins wanted to play the lead role. Lumet considered it but concluded there was no way he could equal Lang's genius so he dropped the idea.[46] Perkins was devastated. His career hadn't had many high points since *Psycho*, a film that defined him in a negative way. He frequently returned to deranged roles, believing this was what audiences expected of him. *Lovin' Molly* hadn't really worked as an antidote. That was probably why he approached Lumet with his dark project. He would return to *Psycho*-style roles often in future years when other wells ran dry. His death from AIDS in 1992 provided a grim coda to a storm-tossed life where he struggled with gay leanings despite being married with children.

Lumet's next undertaking, *Dog Day Afternoon* (1975), was inspired by a *Life* magazine article about a heist that took place in Brooklyn in 1972. The man behind it was John Wojtowicz, whose birth name was Ernie. In the film he's called Sonny Wortzik. He has two wives in the film, one from whom he's divorced and the other a pre-operative transgender woman. He robs the bank to get the money to pay for a sex change operation for the latter. If the plot hadn't been based on fact, people would have called it too farfetched.

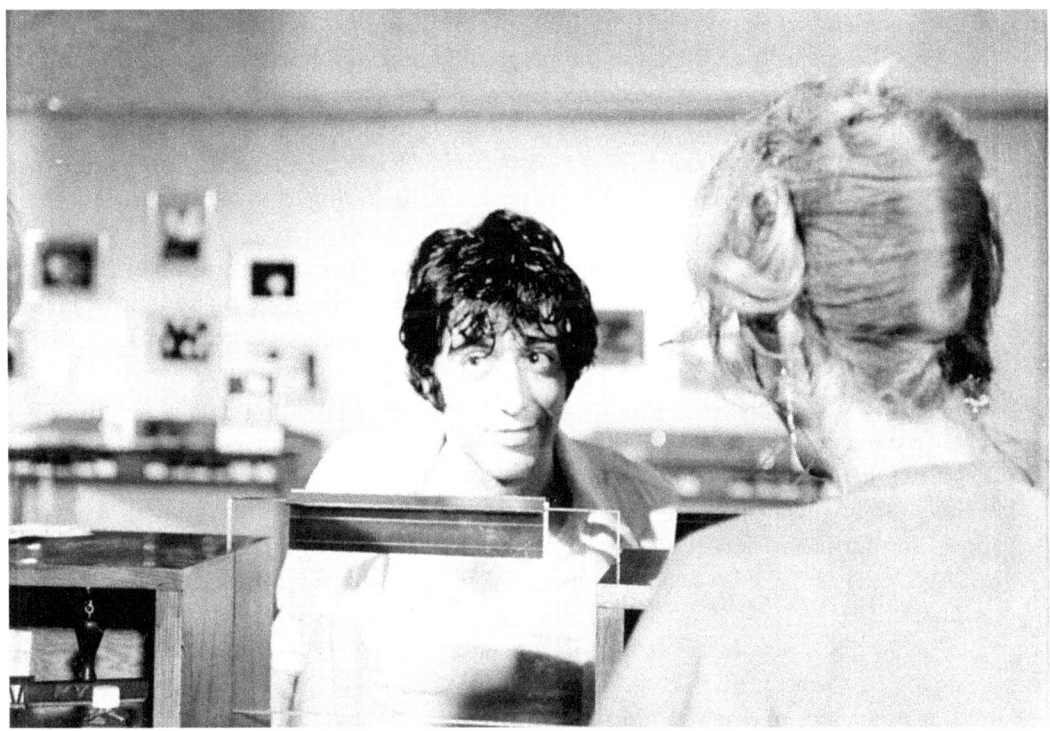

Al Pacino in puckish mood with bank teller Penelope Allen in Lumet's pulsating thriller-cum-love story, *Dog Day Afternoon* (Jerry Ohlinger).

Sonny bungles the robbery. The kind of money he imagines is in the bank isn't there. He helps himself to some traveler's checks. He burns them in a trash can but the smoke is spotted by people working across the street and they raise the alarm. Things become even more zany when he holds the bank manager and his staff hostage inside the building as the police lay siege to it in the sweltering heat. Sonny doesn't look like he is going to do anyone any harm. He's as inefficient as Paul Newman's Butch Cassidy or Warren Beatty's Clyde Barrow, so he becomes something of a folk hero for the crowd that has started to gather around the police. The robbery turns into a circus, what one writer called "a Marshall McLuhan media nightmare run riot."[47]

The heist has hardly begun before Sonny trips the alarm system. From now on it becomes a comedy of errors in which he shows himself to be a lovable pussycat. His mind is never really on the robbery. It's on the operation he's trying to fund. Later, it becomes focused on the problems of the bank staff, on the air conditioning, on the pizzas he orders to feed them. His partner Sal (John Cazale) exudes a certain amount of danger but he's also a naïf at heart. Like Sonny, he seems to have an emotional imbalance. But he's quiet, which makes the police wary of him. He looks like a bomb waiting to explode. Sonny is exploding all the time.

Sonny's mother was played by Judith Malina, a veteran of the Living Theatre. It was Pacino's idea. Lumet hadn't seen her for over a decade. He didn't even have a phone number for her. He tracked her down through the Living Theatre to her Vermont home. She was in poor circumstances, unable even to afford her fare to New York. But she was brilliant in the part. Pacino's long memory, and Lumet's interest in pursuing quality to whatever lengths he needed, bore fruit.

The film opens with a lengthy montage of scenes of a hot summer afternoon in New York. There are boats at the docks. A dog rooting through garbage. A kid jumping into a swimming pool. Construction workers digging in the street. People playing tennis. Such workaday images, for one writer, conferred a "baptismal blessing" over the city, setting a "charitable tone of forgiveness" over it and preparing us to feel at one with the events we were about to witness.[48]

Pacino showed courage in playing a gay man at the time. He was one of the first mainstream actors to take such a plunge. It wasn't a decision he made lightly. He'd received Oscar nominations for three of his last four performances and he was a household name. A role like Wortzik could have jeopardized that. He thought long and hard about taking on the part, changing his mind a few times before he finally committed to it. "We weren't just talking about a major star playing a homosexual," said Lumet, "but also portraying that whole insane framework."[49] It was a set of circumstances that, in the wrong hands, could have turned into the stuff of farce. "Since none of us ever knows how an audience is going to react," said Lumet, "I usually ignore them. However, on *Dog Day Afternoon* I was as terrified as Al because the subject matter was so sensationalized."[50]

Pacino didn't see Sonny as a bank robber. For him, he was just a confused lover trying to do a favor for his partner. This caused a problem with Lumet when he refused to wear sunglasses to disguise himself going into the bank. His reason was because he felt Wortzik "subconsciously wanted to get caught." Lumet originally disagreed with him and insisted the scene be shot with him wearing the glasses. When he thought about it, however, he realized Pacino was right and he reshot it without them.[51] Lumet was never too proud to concede a point like this to an actor for the good of the film.

He said of Pacino, "Everything stems from some incredible core inside of him that I wouldn't think of trying to get near. It would be like getting somewhere near the center of the earth. What comes out of his core is so uniquely his own. It's the only thing he can trust. It's quite clear Al is a loner."[52]

Sonny starts to become a folk hero when he chants "Attica! Attica!" at the crowd, a reference to the suppression of a revolt there in 1971 which resulted in the death of 42 prisoners when police opened fire on them. From now on, they align themselves to him. He becomes, like Frank Serpico, a self-styled crusader for the little guy fighting the machinery of state.

Sonny may be immature but he's a model compared to the number of dysfunctional people in his life: the lost-in-his world Sal who doesn't know Wyoming isn't a country; the mother who never wanted him to grow up; the wife who's lost in a haze of obesity; the second wife who alternates between suicide bids and transgender dreams. In such a context, the deluded bank robber comes across almost like the "normal" one.

Lumet allowed Pacino take his character in as many directions he wanted and at whatever speed: "Rather than tell Al to slow down, I'd put the cameraman on roller skates and have them pulled."[53] He walks away with the film in his pocket, his wild eyes dancing in his head in a mixture of mischievousness and confusion. If *Serpico* was characterized by Pacino's holier-than-thou hipness, *Dog Day Afternoon* has his crazier-than-thou passion.[54]

Lumet thought Sonny was enormously talented "but had no place to put it."[55] In the film, he finds that place, learning how to work the crowd, to whip up empathy from strangers, to bond in a strange way with the bank staff. Not since Woody Allen's *Take the Money and Run* has a man waved a gun around with less of a threat attached to it.

He treats the bank staff more sympathetically than the manager does. The security guard has an asthma attack and is subsequently released. The bank manager needs insulin for diabetic shock. Sonny teaches one of the staff army drill with a rifle. When he's tying another one up with rope, he asks, "Are you comfortable?"

Moretti (Charles Durning), the head of police, tries to keep a lid on the situation but doesn't make a very good job of it. After a while, he becomes the villain to Sonny's hero. Sonny may be innocent but he doesn't fall for Moretti's initial concessions to him. "Kiss me," he taunts. "When I'm being fucked, I like to get kissed on the mouth."

When Sonny throws money at the crowd, he has them in the palm of his hand. They get behind him to such an extent that he almost becomes high on their support. He's added a new dimension to their lives, exciting them by his daring heist. We feel we get to know these people just as we get to know him. They become more important than anything that's going on in the story.

As the film progresses, these people become more like cast members than faces in a crowd. Lumet worked them just as Sonny did, whipping them up into a frenzy to help the movie. "By the second week of filming we didn't have to tell anybody how to react," he said. "They just did what came naturally and it was wonderful."[56]

All these qualities made the film seem more like a documentary than a thriller. Lumet used handheld cameras for some of the scenes to amplify that effect.[57] He was

Marcia Jean Kurtz blows a bubble for Lumet on the set of *Dog Day Afternoon*. She appeared in five of his films, a tally equalled by a number of his favorite stars—Sean Connery, Jack Warden, Ed Crowley, Les Richardson and Harry Madsen (Larry Edmunds Bookshop).

at his happiest on this kind of set, barking out directions in the open air, moving people around and creating a frenzy of excitement. One writer described him as being similar to "a patrolman on a lifetime's beat."[58]

Pacino makes two phone calls to his wives in the film. Lumet wanted to shoot them in one take to help him build up a head of steam but the scenes ran for 14 minutes in all. His camera was only good for ten so he had to get a second one. Pacino did the 14 minutes, becoming more excited as the take went on. When it was finished, Lumet said to him, "Let's go again, Al." Pacino felt he was burned out. He looked at Lumet in disbelief. Lumet thought he was going to kill him but then his expression changed. He realized why he was making the request: He wanted him to start the calls in the same excited tone as he finished them. In effect, the 14 minutes was a kind of warm-up for him, an unofficial rehearsal. So he did them again, this time even better. Afterwards, a delighted Lumet gushed, "I knew he had another take left in him because he's got such an emotional reserve there."[59] Lumet was so moved, he began to weep. When Pacino saw him, he started crying too. Lumet let the camera run as Pacino covered his eyes. "It was an amazing moment," Lumet said, "as good a moment of directing as I've ever had in my life."[60]

Chris Sarandon played Sonny's transgender wife, Leon. Lumet wrote some of the dialogue for his phone call to Leon, allowing Pacino and Sarandon to improvise it after he'd finished, which increased its effectiveness.[61] After Sonny gets off the phone, the

FBI tell him they'll agree to his demand that they drive himself and Sal to the airport so they can fly to the tropics. This is a lie. As soon as they get to the airport, the FBI puts their own plan into operation, killing Sal and disabling Sonny. The drama is over, law and order has returned. Or rather it would have if this were an ordinary cops'n'robbers yarn. But it isn't.

The bank robber, with his poignant private life and his concern for the bank staff, has by now become the human center of the film. The police are the inhuman circumference. Because of this, we don't want Sonny to get caught. We want him to fly to the tropics with Sal.

The gun-toting FBI agent, played by James Broderick, is much more threatening to us than him. When he shoots Sal—the man dressed in dark killing the one dressed in white—what we're looking at is an inversion of the natural order. The defenseless faun has been mown down by the clinical tiger. So law and order has been preserved. So what? Sonny might not get the money but he gets the adulation of a city, a city in which even a pizza boy can become a "fucking star."

Pacino knew he'd given one of the performances of his career. It was especially gratifying because of his initial apprehensions. An actor was only as good as the chances he took. Every challenge carried the risk of falling on one's face. It was frightening to go into oneself, to take hold of the reins without knowing how it was going to pan out.[62]

For Lumet, the most moving scene was where Sonny dictated his will to Leon, aka Ernie. He was particularly taken with Sonny's line, "And to Ernie, who I love as no man ever loved another man, I leave..." He went so far as to say that the whole goal of the film was to make that line work. Pacino certainly did that, even for "the kind of audience that filled Loew's Pitkin on Saturday night."[63]

Pacino praised Lumet for the strength of his performance. "He was the one who made me understand the camera," he said, "and to get comfortable with it." He described him as being "stagey," but in a good sense: "He frees the actors instinctively by setting up his cameras and lighting and allowing them freedom within that framework."[64] Such freedom helped him discover depths within himself that he

Lumet in frenetic mode on the set of *Dog Day Afternoon* as Al Pacino wears that "rabbit in the headlights" expression that characterized his performance in the film (Jerry Ohlinger).

didn't even know were there. His friend Charles Laughton—not to be confused with the other Charles Laughton—said it was like pulling a pin out of a hand grenade and waiting for it to explode.[65]

Dog Day Afternoon wasn't universally adored. One critic felt Sonny was made more sympathetic than his actions merited by having his opposition "oversimplified, vilified, dehumanized."[66] The film was seen as exploitative by Liz Eden, the character upon whom Leon was based. Vito Russo joined Eden in calling it "the ultimate freak show, a film that used the sensational side of a story to titillate a square audience."[67] That was hardly fair in view of Lumet's direction and the empathy Pacino showed for Sonny.

Andrew Sarris, an outspoken critic of Lumet's work, castigated it for its "sentimental leftism." The crooks in the film, he said, were "cuddly," the honest citizens "boobs and bores and bullies."[68] One wonders why Sarris targeted Lumet with this and not a legion of other directors. Was "sentimental leftism" not at the root of almost every crime film made since the days of James Cagney? *Vogue* magazine was more fair. Pacino, the reviewer said, moved through the film "with the epic nobility of a Greek tragedian and the sashay of a pitiful comedian."[69] *Variety* praised Frank Pierson's screenplay for combining "warm human comedy with dramatic pathos."[70]

Pierson won an Oscar for his script but a lot of the dialogue was improvised. Lumet insisted on this to make everything feel more natural. He also asked the cast to wear their own clothes in the film for this reason, and to go without makeup.[71] He wanted it to have a *cinema verité* look throughout. Apart from the airport scene at the end, it was shot totally in Brooklyn. Lumet found a quiet street just a few blocks from the place where the real incidents took place and rented a building there, turning it into a bank.[72]

The film was nominated for a number of Oscars, including Best Actor for Pacino and Best Director for Lumet, but only Pierson won. Lumet didn't mind. Pacino acted as if he didn't, watching the ceremonies in his sweatshirt and jeans in a Greenwich Village restaurant. It was his third loss in a row. According to the cliché, being nominated was a kind of victory in itself but he didn't see it that way: "You feel good being nominated, then you get turned into some kind of loser when you don't win it. You've been feeling terrific and suddenly you've got all these people consoling you. It's real strange."[73]

Dog Day Afternoon has aged well. It continues to intrigue audiences with its diverse parameters. It alternates between moments of hyperbolic absurdity, as one critic wrote, and real tragedy, capturing the "swirling passions" of people and history, with a "brilliant immediacy."[74]

Both here and in *Serpico*, Lumet caught the "teeming, squalid energy" of New York. Owen Gleiberman wrote, "It was a working class outer borough energy. Lumet's streets were just as mean as Scorsese's but his seemed plain rather than poetic. He channeled New York's skeezy vitality with such natural force it was easy to overlook what was truly involved in the achievement."[75]

The film made Lumet's name. If *Serpico* was a good Pacino movie, this was a great one. If Lumet retired after making it, the history books would still list him among the seminal directors of his time. The fact that he sandwiched a hoary old yarn like *Murder on the Orient Express* in between *Serpico* and *Dog Day Afternoon* confused people. Who was the "real" Sidney Lumet, the man who gave us a new icon in Pacino or who wanted to do something different every time he turned his camera on? Versatility was a dangerous game to play, and one fraught with difficulty. By definition it worked against building up a fan base because it was so individualistic. But if the individual films were good enough, maybe the fan base could be individualistic too.

He was about to prove that to be the case with his most ambitious film to date.

The Mad Prophet

Paddy Chayefsky had always been leery of television. He referred to it as the "cathode ray tube" that imbued the American nation with a ten-minute concentration span.[1] It was always going to be only a matter of time before he turned his acerbic sense of humor on it. When he did, the richness of his writing found an ideal target.

Network explores the manner in which television sacrifices the lives of its operatives on the altar of ratings. Personifying the crusade against this holy grail is Howard Beale, an Elmer Gantry–style evangelist, albeit a secular one, putting his career—and life—on the line as he attacks the big guns in the only way he knows how, using the medium as an instrument to bring about its own destruction.

When Lumet was mooted as a possible director for the film, the prospect didn't meet with unanimous approval. Mike Medavoy, the vice-president of production at United Artists, asked, "Are you serious? When was the last funny movie you saw from Sidney Lumet?" He reminded Chayefsky of the final scene from *The Pawnbroker* where Rod Steiger impaled his hand on a paper spindle. Chayefsky took exception to this line of thinking. He was drinking a cup of soup at the time and threw it through the air in anger. Medavoy said, "If you feel that strongly, he's probably a really good director for this." And so the deal was sealed.[2]

Lumet didn't hem and haw about the offer, reading Chayefsky's script the moment he received it. He rang him the following day to say, "It's magnificent! Let's do it."[3]

Everything moved quickly after that. Chayefsky and Howard Gottfried became producers. Then began the search for a cast that would do justice to the material. Lumet was flattered by the number of people who were clamoring to work with him. He started to get a big head until he was brought down to earth by the remark, "What about Edward Arnold? He's dead, but I hear he wants to work with you."[4] Lumet always enjoyed jokes like that.

The initial searches were for Beale and the TV anchorman at the film's center, Max Schumacher. Another central character was Diana Christensen, a ruthless executive.

Chayefsky and Gottfried wanted George C. Scott in the film. He was hot from an Oscar nomination for *The Hospital*, which Chayefsky had scripted. They thought he could play either Beale or Schumacher. When they contacted him, the first thing he said was, "Who's playing Diana?" He wanted Trish Van Devere, his fourth wife, to play her. When Gottfried told him she wasn't a big enough star, Scott said gruffly, "Then I'm not interested."[5]

Scott's biographer David Sheward didn't go with this version of events. He said Scott didn't want the part simply because it wasn't big enough.[6] Lumet thought it was because of a personal problem Scott had with Lumet himself, which could have gone back to an incident in the distant past.[7]

Henry Fonda and Paul Newman also passed when they were offered the role. Lumet scratched his head. Who would he get for Beale? Walter Cronkite, a real-life anchor, was a friend of his from the *You Are There* days. He considered him for a while. John Chancellor, another anchor, was a friend of Chayefsky's and he too was approached. Neither of them took up the offer, which made Lumet conclude they didn't think the film was "dignified" enough. Then Peter Finch's name came up. Would he be suitable for it? Nobody was exactly jumping up and down with excitement at the prospect.

Finch was in semi-retirement, living on a banana farm in Bamboo, Jamaica. He was out in the fields, hacking away with a machete, when the script arrived. He read it immediately and was entranced. He tried to contact the people who sent it but couldn't: There had just been a hurricane so the phone lines were down. When he finally got through to them, he conveyed his enthusiasm. He agreed to fly to New York at his own expense and even subject himself to the relative ignominy of an audition to secure the role.[8]

When Finch's name came up first, it was thought he would be more suitable for the part of Schumacher. William Holden eventually took this role, but Lumet felt Finch would work better as Schumacher and Holden as Beale. It's fascinating to speculate how that might have worked out. After a while, they were flipped around.

Everyone knew Finch was a great actor but there were some concerns over whether he could do a credible American accent. To prove he could, he got in touch with Lumet through his agent, Barry Krost. Krost asked Lumet to send him tapes of Cronkite and Chancellor. When Finch listened to them, he found he liked Chancellor's voice better. He decided to copy that.

The accent, like the general delivery of the dialogue, was as important to Lumet as it was to Chayefsky. Said Lumet, "Paddy and I always had a very clear picture of what we wanted in the character of Beale. First we needed someone with a great understanding of language: the rhythm of language, the use

"I'm mad as hell and I'm not going to take it anymore!" screamed Peter Finch in one of the most quoted lines in film history in *Network*, Lumet's pungent satire of a world obsessed by television's sensationalism. Here Finch broodingly contemplates the fate that awaits him from his nefarious studio bosses in the wake of his quasi-apocalyptic outpourings (Jerry Ohlinger).

of language, and its sense." It was unusual for a film to have speeches that ran over four or five pages but Beale had a number of these and they contained his convoluted parabolas for Lumet: "We needed someone who could convey the fact that, although Beale is a madman, he makes the most sense of all the characters in the film." It was vital to see his "underlying humanity" coming through the lines.[9]

Lumet now had another challenge facing him: Who was going to play the inflammatory role of Diana Christensen? Despite the scarcity of good roles on offer for women, he still expected this one to be turned down by at least "ten actresses" because of Christensen's ruthlessness.[10] It was worth remembering that Louise Fletcher got the part of Nurse Rached in *One Flew Over the Cuckoo's Nest* only because many A-listers didn't want to be associated with such a repugnant character. Lumet expected the same conservatism to apply with Christensen.

It was first offered to Jane Fonda but she showed the same indifference as her father had with Beale. When Lumet suggested Vanessa Redgrave, Chayefsky said he didn't want her. Lumet said, "She's the best actress in the English-speaking world." Chayefsky snarled, "She's a PLO supporter." Lumet was shocked at his attitude. "That's blacklisting!" he exclaimed. Chayefsky said, "Not when a Jew does it to a Gentile."[11]

Redgrave was so anxious to be in the film, she visited Lumet in his office to try and bring this about. He let her know in no uncertain terms that it wasn't possible but she still persisted. In the end, he had to put on her coat for her and escort her out.[12]

Faye Dunaway showed immediate enthusiasm, seeing it as an opportunity to stretch herself. Lumet liked her work but before he gave her the part he wanted to be sure she shared his perception of it. He told her, "I know the first thing you're going to ask me is, 'Where's her vulnerability?'" Before she had a chance to say anything, he said, "Don't ask. She has none." Dunaway was stunned into silence. "Furthermore," Lumet went on, "if you try to sneak it in, I'll get rid of it in the cutting room so it'll be a wasted effort." She paused for a moment and then burst out laughing. Lumet took this as agreement so he gave her the part.[13]

Her ardor cooled when she heard Holden was going to be appearing opposite her. They'd worked together in *The Towering Inferno* and hadn't got on. She didn't want a repeat of the experience. She suggested Robert Mitchum to Lumet as an alternative. She thought he had the "irascibility" necessary for the role. This was a surprising word for her to use as it's hardly the first thing that springs to mind when one thinks of Mitchum. Marlon Brando was also mentioned but Lumet ruled him out. Not because he didn't think he wouldn't do the part well—Lumet revered Brando—but he knew that, like Mitchum, his larger-than-life persona would upset the balance of the film. Brando was also unpredictable. "No tantrums, no bad behavior" was Lumet's philosophy on this film. He wanted the cast to fit together like "disparate pieces of a puzzle."[14] In the end, she had to accept Holden—and he her—so they made a tentative détente. "Half aloof," Holden joked, "is better than none."[15]

Now that the main roles were cast, Lumet started to work on the subsidiary ones. He originally thought of Candice Bergen for the role of Schumacher's wife Louise. He'd been impressed with her in *The Group*. But Beatrice Straight tested for it and bowled everyone over. Lumet was relieved that she was so impressive as she was a cousin of his former wife Gloria Vanderbilt and it might have been seen as nepotism on his part if she was anything less than great. Robert Duvall was chosen to play Frank Hackett, the man who finally decides Beale's fate. (For "Hackett," read "hatchet.")

Ned Beatty was suggested for the role of another ruthless executive, Arthur Jensen. Beatty conned his way into the part by telling Lumet he had another part waiting for him if he didn't get it. "It's for more money," he fibbed. If he wasn't selected for Jenson, he said, he had to call his agent immediately to cancel and tell him there was a question mark about him taking the other role. He left Lumet's office to make the (non) call. "When I come back," he threatened, "I've got to know." His ploy worked. Lumet conferred with his colleagues and they made a quick decision: The part was his if he wanted it. When he came back in, Lumet told him he had it. "I was lying like a snake," Beatty admitted afterwards, adding significantly that they might have suspected what he was up to and saw it as something Jensen might do. Such slyness was in his "lexicon."[16]

Before shooting began, Lumet assembled his cast and, as ever, told them he was going to be rehearsing with them for a few weeks before the cameras rolled. He knew he was dealing with seasoned performers but there was a lot of money riding on the film, and a lot of expectations for it, so any misjudgments of style or tone could be catastrophic.

Dunaway was nervous approaching her part. It was significantly different from anything she'd done before, even *Bonnie and Clyde*. Lumet sympathized with her state of mind. He told her she was trading on all the goodwill she'd built up in films like *Chinatown* and *Three Days of the Condor*. *Network* was going to be an antithesis of these but also an extension of them. "I'm not sure if I could have taken Diana to the edge," she conceded, "if Sidney had not understood that."[17]

As the film begins, Beale is about to be dismissed from his job because of poor ratings. On a farewell show he tells the audience he's going to blow his brains out on air. The transmission is cut here, but everyone around the country has heard what he said and been mesmerized by his words. The network chiefs see that he's sent the ratings soaring so they ask him to stay on. They tell him to be as outrageous as possible in his next broadcast. He's happy to oblige.

Uttering one of the most quoted lines in film history, he says, "I'm mad as hell and I'm not going to take it any more." His notoriety increases after each broadcast and the ratings continue to soar. He becomes a guru to millions of viewers but inside himself he's imploding, just one step away from meltdown.

This was Chayefsky at his best, writing a scorching script with all his pet obsessions and passions. Everyone wanted to know what—if any—influences were behind it. If *Fail-Safe* had its origins in *Dr. Strangelove*, the embryology of *Network* could perhaps be traced back to 29-year-old Florida broadcaster Christine Chubbuck, who shot herself on air in 1974 after a long battle with depression.

Chayefsky was working on his screenplay when Chubbuck died. She had similar concerns to Beale about the manner in which the dignity of people's lives was being sabotaged by network chiefs. Her final words to camera were, "In keeping with Channel 40's policy of bringing you the latest in blood and guts, in living color you are now going to see another first—an attempted suicide."[18] A moment later she produced a .38 caliber Smith & Wesson from a shopping bag at her feet and shot herself behind the ear. The word "attempted" was interesting. Could one shoot oneself at point blank range and expect to survive? Did she want to? Hardly.

Chayefsky's original script had Beale saying that he was going to shoot himself in the middle of the seven o'clock news, "just like that girl in Florida." He later changed this.[19] He never mentioned her to anyone afterwards. Neither did he make any reference to her in his screenplay, but her circumstances are eerily similar to those of Beale. He could also have been influenced by the British cult film *Peeping Tom* (1960), which featured a deranged man who filmed himself committing suicide at the end.

Both Chubbuck and Beale desperately sought news stories for years and finally found them in their own tragic lives. Chubbuck's was more downbeat: She had broken romances and feelings of hopelessness even outside her work. Beale is more elated than depressed. He may have run out of bullshit, as he says, but he never runs out of vitality.

His disenchantment with television culture—or rather lack of it—is shared by many members of the public. They're just as disgusted by its "infotainment" ethos as he is. The irony is that he uses television as the instrument to do it down. And then it does him down. It becomes his weapon as well as his execution chamber.

What he plays into isn't just disenchantment; it's also people's need for fun, as in the mock–suicide attempts of those who pretend they're going to throw themselves out their windows upon his recommendation. They join him in exposing the sensationalism of the network. They're as much his friends as the people who cheered Sonny Wortzik in *Dog Day Afternoon*. *Network* is like a footnote to the Pacino movie in that respect. In both we have eccentrics trying to make their voices heard by a restrictive system. They convince us that a "good" person may rob a bank just as a "good" person might want to blow his brains out as a protest against falling ratings.

For Chayefsky, television was a vampire that sucked the life out of anyone in any way connected with it. As its prime emissary, Diana Christensen becomes the chief bloodsucker of the film. But just like we get the politicians we deserve, so it is with television programs. Audiences lap them up like baying mobs. When they discover a sacrificial lamb like Beale, they offer him the opportunity to self-destruct as they savor the details from the comfort of their living room sofas.

Chayefsky knew a lot about the medium because he spent so many years working in it. So did Lumet. In some ways they were like carbon copies of one another. They were close in age, and from similar backgrounds. Frank Beaver wrote in his study of Lumet, "They had weathered World War II and the McCarthy period and had emerged from such experiences with similar hopes and fears about America. They had watched the political pendulum swing from the right to the left and back again. Vietnam, Watergate and the like seemed to call for a response, a statement. *Network* promised to be a vehicle that could make such a statement."[20]

Chayefsky disagreed with Lumet on the way certain scenes should be done. When Beale first tells audiences that he intends to kill himself, Lumet wanted all the people in the control room to express shock. Chayefsky thought it would work better if they weren't even listening to him. Lumet agreed and that was the way the scene was shot.[21] In the scene where Beale says he's "mad as hell" and incites people to shout out their windows that they are too, Lumet wanted to do "a hundred things" over two nights

Peter Finch exhorted people all over America to open their windows wide and scream out their disgust at the way society was going in *Network*. Here the "mad prophet of the airwaves" is again in Elmer Gantry mood, though his message seems wasted on one viewer, at least (Jerry Ohlinger).

whereas Chayefsky suggested a more muted approach. "Paddy was always a good man with a buck," said Lumet. "He wanted the scene shot in one night and not two." But again he gave in.[22] This wasn't just cost-cutting on Chayefsky's part; he didn't want it to look too melodramatic. The circumstances in themselves had enough drama. There was no point going for overkill.

Finch wasn't able to make it through his "mad as hell" speech because of a bad heart. Lumet wasn't aware he had that problem and Finch didn't tell him. He just stopped halfway through and said he couldn't do any more. Lumet didn't want to put him through the trauma of another take as he was already on the second one. Instead he used Take One for the second half of the speech. He preferred the way he did the first half of it on Take Two so when we watch the film what we're seeing is the first half of the speech from Take Two and the second half from Take One.[23]

Finch liked to rehearse in the bathroom of his hotel, which led to some amusing incidents when the maids came in to make the beds. As they turned down the sheets, they must have wondered what was the cause of the raucous utterings emanating from behind the bathroom door. "They think I'm absolutely insane," he chortled—which was good for his character.[24]

David Denby once said that a Lumet film is one in which a man enters a room shouting, stands there and shouts some more, and then leaves the room at the top of his voice.[25] Nowhere is this more evident than in *Network*. Even so, the film has an undercurrent of humor. Lumet's mixture of melodrama and black comedy had already been in evidence in *Murder on the Orient Express*. In fact, he went so far as to say, "I couldn't have done *Network* without *Orient Express*."[26]

As was the case with the earlier film, he decided to experiment visually as well as every other way. With this in mind, he used three different visual styles to depict the different moods of Beale. The first third of the film was naturalistic, the second third realistic and the final third what he called "commerical."[27] Because the film was about corruption, he wanted to "corrupt" the camera as well. His use of artificial lighting became more prominent towards the end.[28]

In front of the camera, meanwhile, there were performances to be worked on. Lumet wasn't happy with Dunaway in some of the early scenes. She fumbled so many of her speeches, he even considered replacing her.[29] Walter Cronkite's daughter Kathy, who appeared in a minor role, also struggled with some of Chayefsky's lines.[30]

Lumet had no such problems with his male leads. Finch and Holden got on famously. The two veterans hadn't met before but when they did, they formed an immediate bond. Both were legendary characters, both had had illustrious careers and both were getting on in years. They could now drop their leading star credentials and invest themselves totally in their characters, with all the psychological bruising that entailed. The fact that each of them had problems—with drink, relationships, career, etc.—made them even more attached to one another. Lumet spent more time with Finch than Holden for obvious reasons: His story was the message of the film.

Chayefsky adopted a hands-on approach to the film, unlike many screenwriters who might not even have appeared on the set. There was one scene where Beale came into the studio drenched from the rain and asked a guard to take his coat. Lumet wanted the guard to act surprised at his saturated condition but Chayefsky said drolly, "This is TV. He wouldn't even notice him." Once again, Lumet was won over by the insight. When the scene played in cinemas, it drew a bigger laugh than it would have if the guard fussed over Beale.[31]

But Lumet drew the line when Chayefsky tried to intervene in the scene where Holden tells his wife he's leaving her for Dunaway. As Chayefsky started to make a point about how he thought the scene should be played, Lumet put his hand up and said, "Paddy, please. I know more about divorce than you do."[32] It was a rare personal comment from a man who always separated his work from his home life.

Finch's wife Eletha, an avid film fan, loved being on the set. She wasn't averse to putting in a word for him to Lumet. One day after viewing the rushes, she went up to him and said she thought Finch could have done with a few more close-ups in one scenes. Lumet was amused. "Yeah, pussycat, yeah," he said, hugging her affectionately. She wasn't impressed with what she saw as his condescending attitude and persisted in her demand but Lumet was unrelenting. There could only be one boss on a film set, he knew, no matter how much he loved Finch—or Eletha.[33]

Everybody knew they were making a wildly inventive film. They devised different ways of getting into character. Maybe Duvall's was the most unpredictable. He mooned. A technician gaped in shock as he watched him thrusting his bare buttocks out a window and screaming at the people on the street below. He went up to Lumet and said, "Your actor's going a little over the top."³⁴ They were on the 22nd floor of a building. Duvall was remembering his antics on *The Godfather* with Marlon Brando and James Caan. On that film, the three of them mooned almost on a daily basis to let off steam. Here Duvall was tapping into a similar outrageous sense. He claimed he tried to play Hackett like "a vicious President Ford."³⁵

Lumet was on fire most of the time. Camera operator Fred Schuler was amazed at his speed. "Cut, print and move on" was Lumet's slogan. He would already be walking away from a take before Schuler had time to turn off his camera. Director of photography Owen Roizman had to stay on his toes too. He imagined he'd have worn out a pair of sneakers before the film was finished.³⁶ Tom Priestley, another camera operator, described Roizman as being "soaking wet" with the sweat he expended. Script supervisor Kay Chapin wrote in her diary that Lumet was like a tiger as he told grips how to move the crane or scheduled the actors for the following day's shoot.³⁷

Dunaway was also impressed with his energy. He seemed to whiz about on invisible roller skates, she thought, nudging and prodding people with "Sweetie this" and "Sweetie that." But he never cut corners: "He just seemed to be able to get it right more quickly than most."³⁸ She also admired his perfectionism. The first scene she had with Holden took place in Holden's office, with the RCA building visible in the background. It was late at night and Lumet was worried the lights in the building would be turned off before they finished shooting, which would have ruined the effect. To prevent this, he dispatched an assistant director somewhere—perhaps to an executive to ask a favor—and he got his wish. When the scene finished some hours later, the RCA building was still "ablaze with light."³⁹

Dunaway told Lumet she wanted to play Christensen as a sexy woman to offset the clichéd image many people had of the female executive being cold or androgynous. He thought that was a good idea. She carried it off by wearing long hair and sexy skirts. One thing Lumet asked her to do differently than most women was to eat savagely. He thought it would be in character for Christensen to cannibalize food like she did people. Dunaway ate ravenously in one scene. "We chose a huge hamburger and French fries," she recalled, "It told you something about how voracious this woman was."⁴⁰

"All I want out of life," Christensen declares, "is a 30 share and a 20 rating." This is what Beale represents for her. It's the reason she's willing to tolerate him until he outlives his usefulness to her. Beale doesn't mind, immersed as he is in his odyssey towards some psychedelic nirvana.

When she isn't having Beale pouring his heart out, she does features on terrorism and bank robberies. These strike a chord with audiences fed up hearing about Watergate and Vietnam. Ahead of her time, she taps into a dumbed-down mindset predating the era of Jerry Springer's "reality" TV. Beale's rants ally with her lust for audience excitement. It's only when he threatens the body politic that she decides he has to be liquidated.

Schumacher has more divided feelings about him. He refuses to cut him off the air because he agrees with a lot of his pronouncements. "He's saying life is bullshit," he proclaims, "and it is." Christensen likes his anger but she wants it to be fabricated, not real. The fact that he embodies it rather than merely mouths it make him a liability for her.

Dunaway once asked Chayefsky why he didn't make Christensen into a man considering she has so much testosterone. He replied, "I needed a love story."[41] Dunaway didn't then say, as she perhaps should have, "So why didn't you make Schumacher a woman?" A better answer from Chayefsky would have been, "Because we've seen too many men behaving like this in films over the years. It's more of a novelty to see a woman doing it."

Even in sex, she behaves like a man. It isn't "Wham, bam, thank you, ma'am" but "Wham, bam, thank you, *man*." By transposing her gender, Chayefsky made a conventional scenario unique. Norman Mailer often said that if feminism taught us anything, it was that women were entitled to behave just as badly as men had been doing for centuries. Christensen takes him up on that offer as she emasculates Schumacher.

Schumacher, in a sense, is the film's fulcrum. His involvement with its two polar opposites, Beale and Christensen, gives him a foot in both camps. His position of power at the television station allows him to fire Beale while his humanity grants him a stay of execution.

On the surface, he's the "straight man" of the film, but as it goes on, he develops almost as much angst as Beale. Lumet said Holden didn't know the role was going to take so much out of him: "Compared to Peter and Faye, he thought his part was simpler, that of an older leading man, but once we started rehearsals and he saw the process that was going on, he was kind of stunned."[42]

The most problematic scene was the one where Holden and Dunaway are in bed. Dunaway dominates it just as she dominates Holden's life. Unfortunately, she tried to dominate Lumet as well. She made so many stipulations about how she wanted the scene done, it almost came to a court case. She didn't want too much of her body on display and put enormous pressure on Lumet about the camera angles. Lumet sympathized more with Holden, who was very much second banana in the scene. For a star of his stature to lie under Dunaway and not be allowed any reaction to her motions and mutterings was difficult. She goes on top, needless to say, which means Holden is suffocated under her. It was brave of a former macho hero to subjugate himself to this erosion of his masculinity but he did it.

Lumet understood Dunaway's discomfiture too, especially considering the scene called for her to reach a sexual climax: "She'd never done this before," he said. "To show an orgasm is tough." At first she refused to do it. He kept telling her, "It has to be, Faye, it has to be," and she kept saying, "I can't, Sidney, I can't." Frustration grew among the producers at her hesitancy, resulting in Gottfried calling her agent Sue Mengers and telling her, "Faye is out of the picture. She's getting fired. We're not kidding." Under threat of being liable for production costs if the production had to be shut down while a replacement was sought, she finally began to relent. "We played brinkmanship," MGM producer Dan Melnick admitted.[43]

Lumet promised her the scene would be done delicately. "We would open with a high shot of the two of them in bed, then the camera would dolly in behind her. I assured her that the bed sheet would be high enough that we would see no crack of the ass. As we moved in closer, her arm would be at such an angle it would cover her breast." He stuck to that agreement to allow her to concentrate on her lines rather than on how much of her anatomy was going to be displayed.[44]

Holden's main problem with the scene was that he had to go nude for it. He'd never done that before. "There are certain things that require privacy," he pleaded. Actors weren't people who "urinated in the streets."[45] He could have been accused of double standards here. Women had been stripping for decades and nobody thought anything of it. Could they not have made the same argument as he did?

Lumet shot the scene with a series of cuts. They suited the staccato nature of Christensen's life. Sex, for her, was a perfunctory sideline between meetings. "We filmed it a piece at a time," Dunaway recalled, "from every angle, and yet in the editing [Lumet] was able to make it look continuous and fluid from the minute we get in the car to when we finish." He relaxed the two of them by treating the scene like any other one in the film, a piece of business to be got through. When he had what he wanted, he shouted "Cut!" suddenly. It was over. Dunaway was relieved. She expected a lot of retakes but she should have known who she was dealing with: "One-Shot Lumet." She'd worked with a lot of directors who kept fumbling for better takes. Lumet was different. He was able to say, "This one is it. We've got it."[46]

There are elements of farce about the character of Christensen just as there are about that of Beale. Watching a woman have a sexual climax as she thinks of a television program is an unlikely as watching a man fantasize about committing suicide on air. But in Lumet's hands, as in Chayefsky's, the outlandish becomes credible. It's all about the way the events are portrayed. We suspend disbelief because we want to. We're having too much fun whistling past the graveyard.

Lumet gave some of the scenes between Christensen and Schumacher a quasi-romantic look to emphasize how incongruous they were together. For such contrivances, he employed "the proverbial 180-degree dolly around the table, the wood-burning fireplace in the background." Such details were designed to make their dates look like ad commercials.[47] He used '50s clichés to make them appear farcical. If Christensen had grown up on television, it seemed fitting that her sex life would also resemble something from "the boob tube."

Schumacher accuses her of having learned life from Bugs Bunny. This wasn't the best reference point for him to have used as the cartoon rabbit was primarily a cinematic phenomenon. It's doubtful it would have been an influence on her even from a chronological perspective. She grew up in the '50s but Bugs Bunny was really developed as a character in the '40s.[48]

Maybe we shouldn't nitpick. Chayefsky's line sounded good, and sometimes that's as important as literal relevance. Holden also delivered it brilliantly, as he did all of his lines in the film. His most powerful one is where he talks about intimations of mortality, about being nearer to the end of life than the beginning, and panicking about that fact. The terror is manifest in his eyes. (The fact that Holden died just a few years after making the film gives this scene added poignancy today. His death was just as absurd as something that might have featured in *Network*: He slipped on a mat when drinking heavily and cracked his head off the side of a bedside cabinet, bleeding to death afterwards.)

It's been obvious from the outset that Schumacher doesn't love Christensen any more than she loves him. What he's in search of is his own youth. That's something Louise can't offer him, even if she can offer him everything else. Even so, he must know inside that the relationship with Christensen can't last. She knows this too. If she thinks happiness can be gained by switching TV channels, Schumacher is just another channel to switch to—or from. When he's leaving her for the last time, he nails her cold with some classic Chayefsky lines: "You're indifferent to all suffering, insensitive to joy. You're madness incarnate. Whatever you touch dies with you."

The scene ends with a series of close-ups. He's burned out; she's merely blank. Dunaway saw this blankness as "the quintessential expression" of her character. "With those few seconds," she noted, "you knew she was completely unable to love."[49] It would have been perfect if it wasn't for the fact that a problem arose in the focusing process. Holden's face wasn't as foregrounded as it should have been. The editor, Alan Heim, noticed this and told Lumet the shot was too "soft." Lumet put his arm around him and said, "Don't worry about it, boychik." Heim was surprised that he wasn't being his usual perfectionistic self. "Sidney," he said, "was not a great believer in doing an extra take for safety." In this instance, it worked against him.[50]

As the film enters its *1984*–style phase, Lumet ups the satirical ante. When Beale discovers that the Communications Company of America is about to be bought out by a Saudi Arabian conglomerate, he launches a tirade against the deal, encouraging viewers to send telegrams of protest to the White House. Hackett is outraged at this and orders him to stop. Beale agrees but as a result, the ratings drop. This means he's back to the position he was in at the beginning of the film: expendable. But he can't just be fired now. The public would object. He has to be killed. This is no problem for Christensen. The only thing that concerns her is how to do it. The means she decides on displays a sense of the imaginative that one wouldn't have associated with her. She chooses a group called the Ecumenical Liberation Army.

If love is a piece of business for her, so is death. Lumet structures the scene beautifully, leading up to the murder plan with a few minutes of mundane chatter. When this is finished, she suddenly blurts out, "Let's kill the son of a bitch!" The words resonate more chillingly than they would have done if Beale's extermination was being discussed all along. Roger Ebert wrote: "We have entered the madhouse without noticing."[51] Up till now, we've been listening to Hackett saying things like "I want to hear everyone's thoughts on this" as if he's discussing how many cups of coffee his staff might want during meetings. This is different. They're finally cutting to the chase.

Dunaway thought Christensen's decision to kill Beale took her character too far into a criminal area. To deflect attention from her murderousness—in contravention to her promise to Lumet not to try and make Christensen in any way sympathetic—she admitted inserting a human element into her character now and then. "I had to sneak it in," she said, "to do it very, very obliquely."[52]

The last lines in the film are the weakest. After Beale is assassinated, a voiceover tells us, "This was the story of Howard Beale, the first man killed because he had lousy ratings." Up until now, Lumet has been keeping his agitprop cards close to the chest. He's been more *Dr. Strangelove* than *Fail-Safe*. But with this endnote—a cheesy line too tempting to resist—he blows his cover. And patronizes his audience.

The producers originally wanted an ending that wouldn't involve the assassination of Beale, only the return of Schumacher to his wife. Lumet felt this would be a betrayal of Chayefsky's vision. After thinking about it, he decided to finish the film like a commercial, with a lot of fast cuts. When it was all put together, he said, "I knew I was in hog heaven, that it would be a powerhouse."[53] How right he was—apart from the endnote.

Network has often been praised for its pace. Though it's two hours in length, it doesn't seem anything near that. That's because so much is happening, so many stories taking place in tandem. Lumet was aware he was making an important film, maybe the most important of his career. No scene was less important than any other one, even those involving the minor characters. This was especially so in the one where Beatrice Straight refuses to give up her husband. Lumet only spent three days rehearsing Straight and a further three shooting her. It was a lucrative week's work for her.

Like Straight, Ned Beatty had only one major scene. He too nailed it, without Lumet having to give him much direction. He was an actor with a history of playing "heavies," and it was right up his alley. The gritty language was familiar to him as he'd worked on a Chayefsky script once before, the drama *The Tenth Man* (1968). Beatty remembered him as "that little guy who smiled every three or four years or so."[54]

Because of Chayefsky's inspired writing, *Network* was more a film of words than action. This didn't bother Lumet. When he was working on a primarily visual movie, he set great store by camera angles but there wasn't such a need of that here. He preferred to give the words their due provenance. There were times, Dunaway said, when a picture was *not* worth a thousand words. Sometimes a word was worth a thousand pictures.[55]

There was one scene, however, where a picture *was* worth a thousand words. It was where Christensen was worried about a ratings drop and Schumacher walks into her apartment. Their affair is just after reaching a crisis and he's desperate to get it back on track. Christensen, as ever, is more concerned about the network. "What do you want me to do?" she asks him. He replies dolefully, "I just want you to love me, Diana." Dunaway had another line of dialogue to follow that but Lumet yelled, "Cut!" When she told him she was getting ready to deliver her line, he said, "No, no. All you need is the look. You looked at him as if he was from Mars. It's perfect."[56]

Lumet was nearly always in good form on the set, addressing people as "angel" or "pussycat," but even he succumbed to pressure on occasion. One day he lost his patience with an actor who asked what a scene was about. He threatened to fire him. The actor in question had only one line in the scene and had only been provided with a page of the script. Lumet was such a professional, he demanded that even actors with just one line made a point of reading the entire scene in question.[57]

Faye Dunaway, a woman who's learned life's lessons from Bugs Bunny, at least as far as her part-time lover William Holden is concerned, gets serious with him as their affair starts to go pear-shaped (Jerry Ohlinger).

But now all such details could be forgotten about. The film was in the can. Would people like it? He didn't know. It was going to be either a huge success or a huge failure. No other option was conceivable.

Because Beale was so outrageous, Lumet was afraid that at some point the audience might switch off and say, "Oh God, it's too bloody much. He's crazy. Why listen?" Finch's dexterity would hopefully counteract that. Lumet said, "The essential quality in all Peter's work was tenderness, an extraordinary vulnerability and a deep humanity. It was that humanity that enabled Beale never to lose his connection with the audience." Finch was a "director's dream," Lumet continued, because he had "an incredible instinct and a back-up of formidable technique." The combination meant he didn't have to stay on a uniform level in the different guises his character took on. He could instead "reach higher and higher in performance."[58]

The test showings were met with rapturous applause. Audiences stomped their feet and erupted into uninhibited cheers and whistles.[59] People wanted to know everything about the film: how it originated, what it was really about, what motivated the characters. Holden was asked at a press conference how a fundamentally decent person like Max Schumacher could have been attracted to someone as venal as Diana Christensen. His answer was worthy of Chayefsky himself: "When a man gets an erection, his brain slides into his backside."[60]

It was released into theaters in November 1976. Many people working in TV hated it but with almost everyone else it was a runaway success. Vincent Canby wrote in The New York Times that in its "wickedly distorted" view of the medium, it gave us "a satirist's cardiogram of the hidden heart."[61]

"Paddy found the perfect image for talking about America," Lumet stated. Television, in his view, said more about the country than anything else, even the automobile. Ever since it became people's cheapest available baby-minder, they "drowned" in its "garbage."[62] "Television has taken over our lives," he said, claiming that since the mid–70s people had been addicted to it. That was the first generation that didn't know what life was like without it. Such things frightened him.[63]

In another interview, he said *Network* wasn't so much about television as corruption in the human spirit. It would have been boring to make it into a polemic. Chayefsky got around the problem by making the most creative person in the studio a lunatic.[64]

Christensen's character came in for criticism from women's groups. Many of them didn't seem to understand the difference between art and life. Deborah Rosenfelt, co-chairperson of the Modern Language Association of America's Commission on the Status of Women, said, "The Bitch has moved out of the house and into the corporate structure."[65] Danny Peary thought she was evidence of misogyny on Lumet's part—a lazy and obvious jibe.[66]

When science fiction author Ray Bradbury saw the film, he said it shouldn't have ended with Beale's death. There should have been another scene showing his funeral, he suggested. It should have been a state funeral, which would have driven his ratings higher again. Beale should have been buried in a grandiose tomb. Bradbury maintained, with "an immense sculptured rock in front." After three days, the rock should have been rolled away and the tomb found empty. This would have set the stage for his Second Coming. Then it could be revealed that his assassination was a fraud, that fake bullets had been used, that he'd been in a rest home in Florida since his "death." Lumet loved these ideas and promised to run them by Chayefsky. "Among other things," he wrote in a letter to Bradbury, "it gives us a chance for *Network 2*." He thought they might even be able to plug it as a TV series. Beale could be shot every week and be resurrected in the guise of whatever was in fashion at the time—a black militant, an esoteric film director, "or Bella Abzug." Nothing every came of Bradbury's proposals.[67]

In the final analysis, *Network* becomes the very thing it purports to condemn: a riveting advertisement for television. One reviewer wrote, "It's a damning portrayal not just of the television providers but of us, the compulsive television viewers. It's enough to make you want to unplug your set and toss it out into the street but we can't. The sensationalism and the tawdriness of TV is exactly what keeps us coming back to it. It's all about the numbers, which is what we are."[68]

Chayefsky and Lumet were accused of biting the hand that fed them by satirizing television. They didn't see it like that. Having spent as many years as they had working in the medium, they felt they were the best people to comment on it. "To Paddy and me it wasn't satire at all," said Lumet, "it was reportage." Most things in the film had happened to them in one way or another—apart from being shot on air. Lumet sighed, "Let's give that a couple more years."[69]

Walter Cronkite didn't like it, branding it a fantasy and a burlesque. "It doesn't bear any relationship to reality," he sniped, "and they cut my daughter's part down to nothing."[70] The last part of his statement is perhaps a Freudian slip. She'd been cast as a Patty Hearst–style terrorist, one of Christensen's tasty sidebars to Beale in the ratings-grabbing stakes. We can see a strong whiff of sour grapes in his salvo. It also begged the question of what exactly was "reality." Cronkite had been a newsman all his life. Sometimes that had the effect of limiting one's perspective on what constituted facts. In the Donald Trump era, we talk of "fake news." Art is on a different level. Maybe it's a kind of "supernews."

The question of how it might be presented to the Academy was the next thing on Lumet's mind. It was first suggested that Finch be put forward for Best Supporting Actor, with Holden as the candidate for Best Actor, considering he had a slightly bigger part. Finch balked at that idea, as well he might have. It's his film, not Holden's, regardless of how many lines each has. Even when Finch isn't on screen, we're thinking about him. Holden's part is tangential to the film's main thrust, despite the great power he invested in it. "Howard Beale was not a supporting role!" Finch insisted.[71]

He worked his socks off promoting himself for the Oscar, doing a whopping 300 interviews on both coasts. No doubt such a workload, combined with his bad heart, led to his coronary. This happened, with a grim irony, as he was about to appear on a TV program. Due to appear on *Good Morning, America* with Lumet, he arranged to meet the director at the Beverly Hills Hotel so they could walk to the studio together. At nine a.m., shortly before they were due to go on air, Finch collapsed.

Finch was sitting in the hotel lobby as Lumet came down the stairs from his room. "I was walking down the staircase toward him," he said, "and I saw him go right over." Lumet started to give him mouth-to-mouth resuscitation. Paramedics couldn't revive him. He was unconscious when he was taken into the intensive care unit of the L.A. Medical Center. A short time later, he was pronounced dead.[72]

Howard Beale died on television and Peter Finch almost did. Life imitated art right down to this fatal foreclosure on a brilliant career. It made the circumstances of the film even more devastating, even more pungent. A coronary had brought about in one fell swoop what Diane Christensen had to marshal all her forces—and an exotic terrorist group—to expedite.

The film represented Lumet's finest night at the Oscar ceremonies, at least for his cast if not himself. It had built up a head of steam in the trade papers and now, because of Finch's freakish death, it was on the front pages of the tabloids as well. Lumet was nominated for Best Director and *Network* for Best Picture. He wasn't unduly optimistic about winning. "To me," he said, "the Academy Awards are like trying to catch lightning in a bottle." Chayefsky was equally leery. "I'm worried about that *Rocky*," he declared.[73]

He had a right to be. Sylvester Stallone's film was upbeat, the story of a man getting to the top against all odds, the kind of thing Tinseltown romantics loved. Lumet's blackly comic parody of consumerism was second favorite to the Neanderthal slugger.

Network's cast members were nominated for Oscars in all the main categories. Finch and Holden vied for Best Actor and Dunaway for Best Actress. Ned Beatty was nominated for Best Supporting Actor despite only working a day on the film. Beatrice Straight got a Best Actress nomination for what amounted to just one scene. It was expected that Finch and Holden would split the vote but this didn't happen. Finch won, and so did Dunaway and Straight. Chayefsky got the nod for Best Original Screenplay. Once again Lumet was bridesmaid at Hollywood's gala event.

Finch hadn't been expected to win. The only other posthumous nominees in the past—Spencer Tracy and James Dean—had both fallen short. Chayefsky took the award for Finch and then called Eletha onto the stage. He acted as if it was an impromptu gesture but it had been rehearsed. In fact, he'd even written a speech for her. It was a lovely gesture to the wife of a man who'd made his words sound so coruscating. William Friedkin, the director of the ceremonies that year, had advised Chayefsky not to bring her on stage for fear of casting a discordant note on the ceremonies but he knew it was the right thing to do.[74]

Rocky won Best Picture and Best Director (John Avildsen). Lumet didn't begrudge it to him even though the award was nonsensical. Avildsen had also beaten the likes of Ingmar Bergman (for *Face to Face*) and Alan J. Pakula (*All the President's Men*) with his pugilist picture. They were in an august company of losers. *Taxi Driver* had also been in the running for Best Picture. *Network*, *Taxi Driver* and *All the President's Men* exposed the worm in society's apple, but a feel-good fairy tale like *Rocky* was more to Oscar's taste. It was Sylvester Stallone's baby, a film he wrote as well as starred in. He refused to part with the script for any money unless they cast him in the lead role. His gamble paid off. His story was like the real-life one of Rocky Balboa. Howard Beale wasn't the only man whose life spilled out of theaters into reality.

For one writer, *Network's* defeat by *Rocky* for the Best Picture crown proved that the Hollywood tide had "turned back toward the bankrupt, emotionally fake triumphalism and reductive soap opera sentiments that Stallone had come to embody."[75] Perhaps, but grand sentiments like these couldn't change what would always be the case for populist events. As consolation, Lumet won a Golden Globe for Best Director. The Globes were often better barometers of quality than the Oscars.

Lumet was delighted at the way the film had performed overall. Dunaway had been fancied by some pundits but Straight was a bolt from the blue. Finch was a dark horse from the point of view of being on screen for so little time. Some people thought he got the sentimental vote. This charge should have been leveled at Stallone, not him. There was very little sentiment in *Network*.

Straight's win was sweeter to her than it might otherwise have been by dint of the fact that her scene was almost deleted. In the original script, it came before the Holden-Dunaway bedroom scene but it didn't work there because it took the pace away from the film. Lumet was tempted to excise it before Alan Heim said, "I'll move it." He put it in after the sex scene and it looked much better there. Straight was giving out to a man who'd just cheated on her with a woman young enough to be her daughter.[76] She was gracious in her acceptance speech, saying that Lumet was the kind of director who made one want to act forever. She acknowledged the fact that if you blinked, you would probably have missed her part.[77]

Dunaway's win had an interesting aside. She spent all night partying with her partner, photographer Terry O'Neill. He snapped her the next morning sitting beside a luxurious swimming pool with a "What was that all about?" expression on her face. It's an antithetical pose to what might have been expected from the rapacious Christensen, a wry commentary on the futility of material gains.

This photograph has become iconic. It's a commentary not only on *Network* but on consumerism across the board. It shows Dunaway poolside at the Beverly Hills Hotel, sitting alone in a satin robe, surrounded by newspapers testifying to her victory and Finch's death. On the table beside her is the Oscar, a cup of tea and a glass of Coca-Cola, both untouched. She has a faraway look in her eyes, what she called "an almost *dolce vita* decadence."[78] Howard Beale would have enjoyed it.

The story of *Network* doesn't end there. Despite the fact that CBS once told Chayefsky it would never be shown on television, in June 1977 that station paid $5 million for three showings. Asked to comment on the about-face, Chayefsky deadpanned, "They'll do anything for a good rating, even eat their young."[79] In the televised version, the Holden-Dunaway love scene was excised. The repeated use of the word "bullshit" was also a problem.[80] Fortunately, a suggestion that it be replaced with "bullsoup" wasn't accepted.[81]

When the dust settled, people came to see how prescient the film was. The idea that a news channel could behave in a show biz manner was dismissed as fiction by newspersons when the film was made but in no time at all Chayefsky's predictions came to pass. Lumet said, "He had a kind of Talmudic logic, that uncanny ability to see where everything was leading."[82]

Even so, he needed Lumet to bring it home. Roger Ebert wrote that, in another director's hands, *Network* might have "whirled to pieces" as a hodgepodge of dissonance but in Lumet's, it became a touchstone.[83] Television had grown from being the poor relation of cinema to its major rival. By the beginning of the 1970s, as Barry Norman pointed out, the film world had thrown open its sound stages and studio lots to it: "TV had not needed a Trojan horse to infiltrate the movie world; it walked in brandishing an embossed invitation."[84]

Workaholic

Not one to rest on his laurels, Lumet wanted to get into something else fast. He always said he became depressed if he was inactive for any period of time. Occasionally that meant taking on work that fell below par. "I don't believe in waiting for masterpieces," he liked to say. "Masterful subject matter comes up only rarely."[1] So he kept working. Whether it was a good film or a poor one, he always got something from the experience that he could use later.

When films ended, he was often so burned out that he'd take to bed and spend all day there, watching ballgames between snoozes.[2] Being a workaholic meant his leisure life was always put in second place. When he was shooting, weekends were for unwinding rather than doing anything elaborate. On Fridays he might have friends over. Saturdays were "goof-off" days. Sundays were the newspapers, the crossword, the acrostic and, in the fall, more ballgames. It might have sounded boring but it was the best way to store up energy for his next celluloid onslaught.

When that came about, the amorphousness of his "downtime" was replaced by an almost military-style discipline. He had his body so well trained, he often woke even before his alarm went off. A coffee got his energy level up—and Lumet was all about energy. He would think about whatever scene he was directing on his way to the set. By the time he got there, he would already be working out where people moved, how they should say something, how they might change the way they did so from the last time to improve it. He liked suggestions for departing from prepared scripts but he wasn't a fan of improvisation *per se*. There had to be a good reason for it. His television background was probably behind that attitude. Retakes cost money.

People were amazed at the way he seemed to be "on" all the time. When he was working, nothing else existed. If there was an earthquake next door, that was next door. His priority was what was in front of him, the pragmatic exigencies of getting from a to b. Such pragmatism extended to the way he dressed. Sneakers helped him to move around faster. Levis were better than pressed trousers because he worked so much on the streets. That meant he picked up a lot of dirt and dust. Nobody wanted to wear out a Savile Row suit on a film set.

If people thought he was boringly practical, that didn't bother him. He never saw himself as a genius. He would have admitted he was usually a man more of perspiration than inspiration. Films were more about preparation than the "happy accidents" that could happen if you were lucky. Such preparation meant keeping his scripts buttoned down, and he himself as trim and healthy as he could.

He ate as fast as he did everything else, gobbling up his lunch (usually an egg salad sandwich) in five minutes and then snoozing for the other 55 in the hour's recess from shooting that he usually allowed himself: "I'll be asleep within minutes of lying down, a technique I learned in the army during World War II. I wake up about a minute before lunch hour is over and go back on set."[3]

Even though he was anxious to get back shooting after *Network*, he knew the long knives would be out for him, the way they always were for anyone who had a hit, wondering if he'd follow it with a dud. The higher you climbed on the Hollywood tree, the more of your backside you showed.

He considered taking on Paddy Chayefsky's screenplay of *Altered States*. This was another unusual film. William Hurt was slated to play a researcher who uses himself as a guinea pig for research into mind-bending rituals. Lumet discussed it with Chayefsky but they disagreed about the financial aspect of it. Chayefsky was as tight with a buck as he'd accused Lumet of being on the set of *Network* and he gave Lumet a hard time from this point of view.

"I had a deal on *Network*," said Lumet, "and I wanted the same for *Altered States*." It was a reasonable demand but Chayefsky refused to commit to it. He wanted Lumet to agree to a lesser percentage of the profits than he'd received on *Network*. Lumet thought that was silly "because you never see percentages anyway." Of course they *had* on *Network*. That was probably what was in Chayefsky's mind. He kept stalling Lumet with a consolatory "We'll work it out, we'll work it out," to which the infuriated director replied, "When Paddy, when?"[4] The "when" never came. Ken Russell took over the direction instead and made a mess of the film. In his hands, it became a hallucinogenic piece of nonsense that Chayefsky disowned. He probably regretted not giving the job to Lumet.

Instead Lumet settled on *Equus*, a film based on Peter Shaffer's powerful play about Alan, a sexually frustrated boy who blinds six horses and then submits himself to the scrutiny of a psychiatrist, Dr. Dysart. Peter Firth took the part of Alan and Richard Burton played Dysart. There was a lot of symbolism in the text and also many Freudian undertones that Lumet was anxious to explore.

Anthony Perkins had played the Dysart role on stage before Burton took the film role. He was hoping to get the movie role but once again Burton thwarted him when he expressed an interest in it. Burton's contract gave him first refusal on it if it became a film. Lumet wanted an English actor for Dysart—*and*, in his view, Perkins was too young to play him.[5] Some studio bosses thought Burton's drinking problem might impair the production, or even make him uninsurable, but in the end they went for him.[6]

Lumet did his best with the film but it was always going to be an uphill struggle trying to make the material cinematic, especially in view of his love of words. Many people found the plot too far-fetched, especially when it turns out Alan blinds the horses because they see him having sex with a young woman. Is he trying to sublimate gay tendencies and resents their intrusion on his efforts to do so?

Film producer and author Julia Phillips thought Shaffer's play was "a crock of faggot shit."[7] Lumet tried to put it on a different plane, seeing it more as the story of Dysart than Alan. For the director, it was a study of extreme sensibilities. Dysart is too inhibited whereas Alan represents untamed sensuality. There's no middle ground. The irony is that Dysart envies Alan his passion. That makes his job of trying to tether it self-defeating. The two characters can be read—even alphabetically—as being coded manifestations of Apollo and Dionysius. Or, put another way, sanity vs. madness. One critic asked, "Is madness a healthier virtue than sanity in a society where mediocrity and safety are the inflexible molds?"[8]

Lumet's problem, he said, was trying to get the Dionysian side of things on a more realistic level, "so that it could be presented squarely in both its horror and its magnificence."[9] It was a tall order. Not many people were going to find equine mutilation "magnificent." He tried to make it, as he put it, "orgasmic," by shooting it in one take. He described this as "four and a half minutes at full gallop."[10]

Originally he wanted to make the film in black and white: "There's something about the nature of color that's so unreal, it prevents you going through a major tragic experience."[11] But that wouldn't have been practical. Neither would it have brought in audiences. Lumet's monochrome days were behind him.

Burton had eight long monologues in the film, all of which he spoke to camera. They allowed him use that mellifluous voice—his main acting tool—to its best

Richard Burton (left) sought to "cure" Peter Firth in *Equus* but secretly envied him his lust for life (Jerry Ohlinger).

effect. Never a man to hang about, Lumet filmed them all in a day.[12] Burton was in good form on the shoot. He felt better than he had in years, having given up drinking.[13] His performance was solid.

Equus failed to perform well at the box office. Despite Lumet's best efforts, it remained a theatrical piece. This was always an occupational hazard when one employed Burton: He could never stop emoting. Here, though, he had a license for it. He also looked the part. He had a kind of creaky compulsiveness in it, his face bearing the scars of 1001 hangovers. In contrast with most of the other '70s film projects with which Burton had been involved, it was a huge step up. He was coming off a run of flops and needed a fillip. His most recent effort, *Exorcist II: The Heretic*, had him playing the role of a pagan priest employed by the Vatican to exorcise the mind of a young child (Linda Blair—again) using a therapy called "synchronized hypnosis," which involved the use of electrode headbands. It was as bad as it sounded and got the reception it deserved. People laughed it off the screen. Angrier viewers threw their refreshments at it.[14]

Burton was nominated for an Oscar for his *Equus* performance. Like Lumet, he'd been bridesmaid but never a bride at the Oscar wedding many times now. The years were also gaining on him. Would *Equus* break his bad luck? He felt there was a fighting chance it would. People told him it was his best work since *Who's Afraid of Virginia Woolf?*

Lumet backed a campaign for him. United Artists ran ads for him, and arranged to have the film shown on TV. But it all proved futile as he was edged out by Richard Dreyfuss for *The Goodbye Girl*. As the name "Richard" was read out, Burton started to leave his seat. When it was followed by "Dreyfuss," he slumped back into it again. Realistically speaking, it was his last chance for an Oscar. "I believe I am the most nominated actor in film history not to have won," he remarked.[15] (Actually he wasn't—Peter O'Toole had eight unsuccessful nominations.)

The film wasn't a success with the press. "If ever there was a play that has no business being a movie," Frank Rich wrote, "*Equus* is it. Strip the stagecraft away and all that remains is two and a half hours of talky debate and shopworn ideas. The play stumbles and falls before it can break from the gate."[16]

Melvyn Bragg thought it was "shackled to the word."[17] David Parkinson said it was "as flatly staged as a party political broadcast." He felt Lumet had too much respect for the text.[18] Such accusations had cobwebs on them, going back to *Long Day's Journey into Night*. The director found this kind of thinking one-dimensional. Nobody seemed to care about depth of character any more. Were the days of "serious" filmmakers numbered? Along with his old television colleagues Martin Ritt and John Frankenheimer, Lumet had tried to entrance audiences with thought-provoking scripts, often to no avail. He knew he was living in the era of action movies, explosions, special effects. Audiences wanted stars, not psychologies. They wanted *Star Wars*. R2D2 was better known in most American houses than Shakespeare—or Sidney Lumet.

Hollywood had changed. To quote Rod Steiger, the film business was now being run by "kids with computers."[19] Human interest films were at a premium. Budgets dictated scripts. Big stars earned phenomenal sums. Quality played second fiddle to profit. People who knew nothing about the history of cinema were in pole positions, telling iconic figures what to do. If anything stepped outside the norm, it ran the risk of failure. Even Grade-A stars were feeling the pinch. "*Bobby Deerfield* had Al Pacino in it," Lumet noted, "and it still went to the shit house."[20]

He licked his wounds with another change of pace. This time he moved even further out of his comfort zone. *The Wiz* was an all-black musical version of *The Wizard of Oz*. It had been a Broadway hit with Stephanie Mills as Dorothy. Motown Productions made a deal to turn it into a film for Universal and it was going to be produced by Rob Cohen, the head of Motown.

Mills hoped she'd be cast in it until Diana Ross expressed an interest. Ross had become excited about it after watching the Judy Garland original of Frank Baum's classic one night on video. Afterwards she phoned Berry Gordy, her producer, and proclaimed without preamble, "I want to play Dorothy." Berry replied, "Have you been drinking? You're too old to play any damn Dorothy. Now go to sleep." He hung up on her. Outraged, she then rang Cohen and he expressed an interest in the idea. Cohen now made some phone calls himself. He learned Universal was interested.[21]

He rang Berry and told him the studio was happy to offer Ross $1 million to play the role. Berry was shocked—but impressed. The smell of money made him do a 180-degree turn on his original attitude. At this point, Cohen told Berry he thought Ross was too old to play the part. Things were getting comical. Both men had started to reverse their positions.

"This character is one of America's beloved icons," Cohen declared, "To cast Diana in the role may, in fact, be condemning the movie to being hated." Berry took his point but pointed out that Ross wasn't the kind of woman to back off from a decision once she'd made it.[22]

Whatever each man's reservations were, the project was now up and running. The next step was to find a suitable director. John Badman was the first to come on board but he departed prematurely. He too had a problem with Ross' age, and went on to make *Saturday Night Fever* instead.

Lumet stepped into the breach, employing Joel Schumacher as his screenwriter. His attitude, as ever, was, "Why not?" He'd tried his hand at most things up until now. The prospect of an all-black musical wasn't going to scare him off.

He didn't regard Ross' age as a problem. For him, the story was a search for identity, and he maintained, "Dorothy's trip to Oz is really her trip to self-knowledge."[23] That sounded like a non sequitur. He was going to be making a film about a 24-year old teacher (played by a 32-year old singer) who'd never yet been south of 125th Street in her life. It didn't seem to add up.

Was desperation forcing him to make this radical departure from what he was accustomed to? He felt he'd gone as far as he could with earnest realism and was looking for something completely different. This would be his first extravaganza. He hadn't read *The Wizard of Oz* as a child. "At eight I read Karl Marx," he chuffed, "but not Frank Baum."[24]

Lumet didn't just want to remake the film. He wanted to reinvent it. It was a good idea in theory. Nobody could improve on the 1939 version any more than they could on the original *Gone with the Wind*. He decided to turn it into a contemporary fantasy using—not

Lumet on the set of *The Wiz*, his most expensive flop. A man who thrived on experiment, sometimes he took on projects manifestly unsuited to his talent. This was one such, despite the number of musical divas on display (Jerry Ohlinger).

surprisingly for this man—actual New York locations. As a result, the World Trade Center became the Emerald City. His Yellow Brick Road was really miles of linoleum laid on top of the streets of the city.

He appointed Quincy Jones as his musical director. Initially Jones didn't want to do it, finding it difficult to believe that audiences would "buy" a revisionist version of the film. He conveyed his reservations to Lumet but he still took it on. He felt in some way beholden to Lumet because he'd given him his first film scoring job (*The Pawnbroker*).

The story begins with Dorothy being whisked off to Oz by a blizzard. Here she's joined by the Lion, the Tin Man and the Scarecrow. Lumet wanted to cast comedian Jimmie Walker as the Scarecrow but Walker couldn't sing so that ruled him out. Cohen fought hard for Michael Jackson for this role and he got him. Jackson was just 17 at the time. Ted Ross played the Lion, Nipsey Russell was the Tin Man and Richard Pryor was the Wiz.

Lena Horne, Lumet's mother-in-law, played the Good Witch. Her selection was seen as nepotistic by some. In her one scene, she sings a song, "Believe in Yourself," to Ross, who wasn't even there at the time. Ross' lines were shot separately and intercut.[25]

Horne never felt she got a fair shake in films. "I'm 'in' Hollywood but not 'of' it," "because I'm Negro," she complained. "I'd like to do a good serious role in a movie instead of being confined to café singer parts."[26] Her *Wiz* role was neither but at least it had potential.

The cast worked six days a week. Jackson's makeup took five hours to apply. He enjoyed the procedure, telling people he needed it to hide his acne. (Already he was showing an interest in re-designing his face.) In addition to the makeup, he had a false nose and a wig made of steel wool pads. Ross believed all this damaged his skin and gave rise to many of the problems he had in later years.

Rehearsals for the dance sequences took place in July 1977 at the St. George Hotel in Brooklyn. Jackson was more adept at the moves than Ross. This annoyed her. "You're embarrassing me," she barked at him at one stage, "You're learning the dances too quickly." Her comments made him uncomfortable. Gentleman that he was, he fumbled his next ones to make her feel better.[27]

Lumet was enthralled by him, labeling him "the most gifted entertainer to come down the pike since James Dean." One doesn't usually think of Dean as an entertainer. Lumet went on to say that he was a "brilliant actor and dancer." This was another confusing comment as Jackson hardly regarded himself as an actor. It's as if he got the terms "entertainer" and "actor" mixed up for both performers.[28]

What Jackson liked most about the Scarecrow was his confusion; "He's not like other people. No one understands him."[29] He took the role because he identified with his character in the same way as Ross identified with Dorothy. In many ways they were playing themselves, with their favorite hobbies—singing and dancing—thrown in for good measure.

Ross' marriage to Robert Silberstein had just broken down at the time the film was being made so her emotions were all over the place. She'd moved from Detroit, her marital home, to New York. She felt impersonal there but saw the city as a challenge. She was confident Lumet's movie could be the gateway to a better future.

"As I dived headlong into my new project," she wrote in her autobiography, "I began to realize an incredible connection between my life and Dorothy's. The sheltered girl who suddenly finds herself in a strange land without any of her old friends." Both physically and metaphorically, she thought, the role was a gift to her. It was a lesson about how to overcome fear by pushing herself to her boundaries and returning to a kind of original innocence.[30]

Maybe she identified too much with Dorothy. Such an identification gave her excessive expectations as to how the film would perform. Her analytic attitude continued with her co-stars, all of whom she related to herself. The Scarecrow became a representative of her hunger for knowledge. The Tin Man personified her craving for love. The Lion was her protective coat of armor. The Good Witch was another protector, "the subconscious part of her that saw through the illusion of separateness, that already knew the answers and that was already there to show her the way."[31]

Ross was one of the few people who didn't like Lumet's practice of rehearsing. She thought he overdid it, resulting in the film losing some of its magic.[32] She was probably right about this. When one is dealing with a watertight script, rehearsals can help the actors hit their marks, but different rules applied here. Considering it was a musical, Lumet might have been better advised to let Ross have her head. His system inhibited her. She liked him as a person—he eased her into the Big Apple by inviting her to many of his legendary parties—but she thought his approach to directing snuffed out her appetite for experiment.

She felt he shot the film as if it were a play and she also thought he made it too scary. She believed the fear factor was overdone and also that some of the faces of the characters were too alarming. As a result, she didn't allow her children to watch the film when they were growing up. But she admired Lumet's near-hallucinogenic depiction of New York with its fogged-over clouds of smoke. And, like so many others, she was awed by his sense of detail. This even applied to his approach to costuming: "Every component would be carefully thought out. Which buttons to use, whether or not there would be ruffles, the color and style of Dorothy's hair, how it would complement the outfit."[33] Such talents would have found a better home elsewhere. Lumet transformed New York into a magical mystery land but the film attempted too much to succeed. Revisionism often comes with a price and this proved too be the case here. In trying to expand the text, he lost it, his stylistic grasp exceeding his reach.

Urbanization took away the magic from the Yellow Brick Road. New York worked as a stage set for dancing and singing in films like *West Side Story* because the drama that underpinned it was so powerful but here we just had four cartoon characters in a glorified pantomime, none of them particularly interesting. Ross' attempted transition to a character half her age became embarrassing. By 32, one imagined, she would have known who she was without having to resort to clown clones for sustenance. The special effects were dazzling in a Busby Berkeley kind of way but people were looking for a story to be grafted on to them. All they got was a misdirected fairy tale.

Just this once, New York proved to be Lumet's downfall instead of his saving grace. It's workaday streets didn't suit the glossy overlay they got. In effect, he was making a Hollywood film without going to Hollywood. To that extent, he compromised himself.

Which isn't to say Ross and Jackson didn't perform to their best abilities. They did, but they were handcuffed, or "footcuffed," by their circumstances: Ross by her age and Jackson by a costume that seemed to interfere with his mobility.

All of this played into Pauline Kael's hands, giving her yet another Lumet movie to slaughter. She described the songs as being similar to "free form traffic jams." For her they were shot "the way a fagged-out TV crew arriving at the scene of a riot in the streets might grab whatever it could from behind the police barriers." Was Lumet, she asked, "trying to get the whole block in every shot?"[34] She had a point. His love of New York seemed to make him want to show too much of its riches to the detriment of the cast.

Patrick E. Horrigan agreed with her: "[Lumet] stands back, surrounding his actors with empty, unused space. The camera rarely interacts with them, and what good is singing and dancing if you can't feel it while you're doing it?" The people in the songs, he wrote, looked "shrunken, scrawny, a forest of undifferentiated arms and legs."[35]

He thought Jackson was practically invisible behind his nose, his wig, his baggy shirt, his pants and his floppy shoes. Lumet needed to be more inventive overall, in his view. If he was, that would have given him a greater insight into who Dorothy was: "We get no idea of what she thinks or how she feels about the seductive bodies all around her. Do they turn her on? Which ones does she desire to have? To be? How many layers of clothing would she have to peel away before she arrived at some irreducible core of her sensual self?"[36]

Lumet learned a lesson with *The Wiz*: Sometimes you can't re-invent a classic, even with two iconic performers in your cast. Ross' determination to do it was so great, it blinded her to her basic unsuitability for the role. Unfortunately, nobody in her inner circle had the gumption to apprise her of that fact. Her fame was so great at this point she could almost have demanded any role she put her mind to—if not for a million, at least for a sizable salary.

The Wiz became Lumet's *Heaven's Gate*, his *Waterworld*. It taught him that big budgets and big hits don't always go hand in hand. Sometimes they're more like a bad marriage. The film was the worst financial loss of his career by a mile. It wiped out much of the profit Universal had made from *Jaws 2*, which had swollen the studio's coffers to the tune of some $55 million earlier in the year. Even its positive aspects, like Mabel King singing "Don't Bring Me the Bad News" with the Flying Monkeys, and Horne's fine rendition of "Believe in Yourself," failed to take off.[37] The catchy Jackson-Ross duet "Ease on Down the Road" was the film's best song by far but it didn't even get into the Top 40 in the charts.

Everyone was dejected by the experience, especially Cohen, who lamented, "It was a big dream that got away, a brilliant idea gone wrong. The knowledge that two years of my life, $23 million of Universal's money, thousands of man hours of labor and all the hopes and dreams of everyone involved went into a movie that didn't stand a chance makes me sick."[38]

The bigger they are, the harder they fall. Lumet wasn't accustomed to working with outsized budgets and maybe that was a factor too. He was like the poor boy who won the lottery and blew it on a mad spending spree. No doubt he was better trying to fit minimalist scripts into tight formulas than expanding flimsy scripts like *The Wiz* into potboilers.

The coat was too big for him but he knew it was the way the industry was going. Budgets weren't being spread thinly any more. "When we were shooting *Dog Day*," he recalled, "Warner's was going to take a 30-second ad during the Super Bowl for $250,000. And we were saying 'Boy, they must really believe in the movie to spend that kind of money.' But now I think $250,000 is about what you pay for a double or triple truck ad in the *Sunday Times*." One day Sherry Lansing said to him, "Sidney, I can sit you down and show you why we're better off in most instances spending $100 million on one picture with an international star than doing ten $1 million movies."[39]

A pensive-looking Lumet engaging in a discussion about *The Wiz* when the film started to develop problems (Jerry Ohlinger).

No matter how much or how little it cost, it wouldn't have worked. It was saccharine, and contained too much "message" talk about Dorothy finding herself. People don't usually go to musicals for messages. They go for the music. The film had some good songs but not enough of them. Ross' age stopped them from working as they should have.

If Ross was too old, Jackson was too young. He danced and sang brilliantly but his acting was weak. He underplayed his character, which meant the charm came across but not the power. There was a kind of uniformity in all his scenes, as there was with Ross. For all the talk about realizing one's potential, both of them seemed to be the same at the end as they were at the beginning. Their journey is really just a geographical one, a jaunt across town to the over-elaborate sets. It's difficult to create credible characters when they keep breaking into song or mouthing platitudes about what home really means to them. Quincy Jones did everything he was asked to do on the spectacle front but Ross seemed to be making a different film than he was, one that conveyed her off-screen problems too forcibly.

In the scene where she met the Wiz, she had to look into a bright light for a long time. This burned the retinas of both her eyes. She had to go to a hospital and have patches put over them so that the damage wasn't permanent. For a time she was worried that she might go blind. She was informed that the healing could take anything from a few days to a few years but within a week, amazingly, she was back at work.[40]

The Wiz was "dead on arrival" in theaters.[41] It was denounced by critics and the public alike. People seemed to go out of their way to find bad things to say about it. Lumet was accused of making Ross both look and sound bad. This was unfair. Her

Lumet preparing a scene on the Emerald City set of *The Wiz* (Larry Edmunds Bookshop).

appearance was unsuitable because of her age. As for her voice, she sang a third-octave higher than she ever had in her life. That should have been seen as a good thing.[42]

Lending his voice to the number of people who had theories about why the film tanked, Cohen came up with one of the more intriguing ones: "Joel, Sidney and Diana had an interpretation of Dorothy that was sort of on the neurotic side. In their telling of the story she was to be a scared adult, a peculiarly introverted woman. Joel and Diana were involved in EST at the time and before I knew it, the movie was becoming an EST-ian fable full of buzzwords about knowing who you are and sharing and all that."[43]

This puts a different perspective on it. It suggests that Schumacher and Lumet were so much in awe of Ross that they allowed her to bring a fuzzy New Ageism to the project, which ultimately did it in. It's easy to understand such awe. Ross was a living legend and Lumet coming to music as a rookie. But he shouldn't have given her such power over him. Whatever the musical aspects of the movie, he didn't have to defer to her for its underlying premise. Lumet also admitted that he should have brushed up more on special effects before he appeared on set. It was an aspect of filmmaking with which he was relatively unfamiliar.[44]

Something else knocked him out of his rhythm: He divorced Gail during the shoot. They hadn't been getting on for some time. She thought part of the reason was her recent conversion to Catholicism. She revealed, "Sidney and I were not on the same wavelength, religiously or otherwise. I became a different person. We had nothing in common."[45] Her mother took a harder line on him after they broke up, branding him "a bastard" in an interview she did in *The Village Voice*. She even told the *Voice* journalist that she had no problem with him printing that word. Lumet was in shock when he saw the interview. In future years, he froze at any mention of Lena.[46]

He started seeing Gloria Vanderbilt again. They still had feelings for one another. Her husband, Wyatt Cooper, had just died of a heart attack so she was free. She asked Lumet if he still had the wedding ring from his marriage to her. He said no, at which point she said she had it. Before they separated he'd left it in the drawer of a night table beside their bed but forgot doing so. The fact that she brought it with her into the marriage with Wyatt spoke volumes about the fact that she'd never really left Lumet in her heart.

They became intimate with one another again. He even asked her to marry him at one point. She felt he was moving too fast, as he did everything too fast. "Sidney couldn't be alone," she declared. "Most men can't."[47] They moved back and forth between their separate homes as they discussed where they might go from here. One thing that impressed her about him was the devotion he showed to her sons Stan and Chris from her marriage to Leopold Stokowski.[48] She was confident that if they made a go of things, he would have shown the same devotion to the two sons she had by Cooper—Anderson and Carter. (Anderson went on to become a CNN anchor; Carter committed suicide by jumping from the family's 14th floor apartment in New York in 1988.)

But it wasn't meant to be. She was with him one night at his house when he made a comment that shocked her. They'd invited Neil Simon and his wife Marsha Mason to dinner and were waiting for them to arrive. Vanderbilt said she was surprised Simon married Mason so soon after losing his first wife. She'd died not long before. "Let the dead be dead," Lumet said dismissively. The remark stopped her in her tracks. She thought it sounded callous. It made her wonder how deep his feelings for her went. Was he just expressing an interest in her because her husband had died? Such a fear made her re-think their whole relationship. They still continued to see one another, but for her the spark was gone. Truman Capote sniped that they were only going out together again because they had nobody else in their lives.[49]

Vanderbilt would later express the view that, in many ways, divorce was like death. Such a thought was prompted by the night she had Simon and his wife over.

She told Lumet she thought they should slow things down a bit, that it might be an idea to spend some time apart before they made another major commitment. He took this as a sign that she wasn't interested in getting back with him so he started dating other women. She was right about him not being able to be alone. Within a year, he was married to Mary Gimble.[50] He stayed with her for the rest of his life.

Lumet followed *The Wiz* with a lighthearted feature, *Just Tell Me What You Want* (1980). It starred Ali MacGraw, an actress who wasn't exactly regarded as a doyenne of the film industry, but Lumet was never put off by reputations. He always took people as he found them. The film also starred Alan King, an actor he'd worked with a number of times and liked a lot. Lumet was so friendly on set, King recalled, he practically kissed people every morning: "You had to have mouthwash ready to hand when you worked with him."[51]

King played Max Herschel, a business magnate who drives his executive mistress Bones Burton (MacGraw) into the arms of a playwright, Steven Routledge (Peter Weller), as a result of his boorish treatment of her, and then spends the rest of the film trying to win her back. It was scripted by Jay Presson Allen from her own novel. Myrna Loy, in her last role, played Herschel's secretary. It was sad to see her bowing out this tamely. Dina Merrill gave a carpet-chewing performance as Herschel's neurotic wife.

All the ingredients were there for the kind of sophisticated comedy we associate with someone like Woody Allen but they failed to jell. At almost two hours long, the film needed at least 20 minutes edited out to give it the pace it needed. As it stood, many of the jokes fell flat, despite the best efforts of King to invest them with his customary *chutzpah*. It had a jaded look about it despite the glossy sets, and the plotline was also too conventional, which was surprising from someone as original in her thinking as Allen. The ending was at variance with what went before, giving things the kind of soft center one associates with "safer" directors than Lumet.

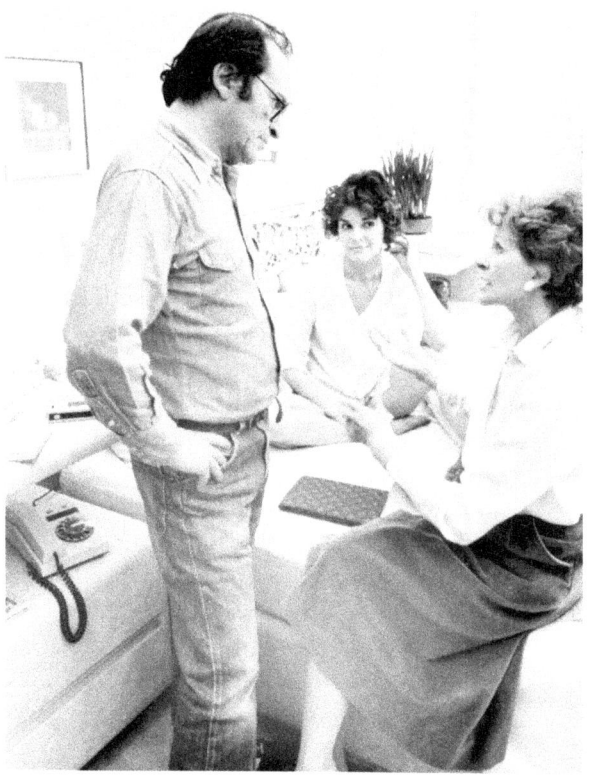

Lumet discusses a point with his screenwriter Jay Presson Allen on the set of *Just Tell Me What You Want* as the film's main star Ali MacGraw looks on (Jerry Ohlinger).

MacGraw was surprisingly good. She'd recently come through a turbulent relationship with Steve McQueen. She fell in love with Weller during the shoot and he gave her back some of the self-confidence McQueen had eroded in her with his explosive temper and repeated putdowns. Lumet gave her a different type of confidence before the camera. She said, "Sidney is the consummate actor's director, and he coaxed a real performance out of me." She also liked his rehearsal system: "This is an unusual luxury in films where, more often than not, the actors arrive on the set with just a few days of rehearsal time before the panic of filming. Sidney's way of working gives the actor a chance to stretch out and explore, and therefore give a richer performance. By the time the actual shooting begins, many of the mistakes and most of the fears are gone."[52] She spoke of him as "every actor's dream."[53]

The script had some racy language, which MacGraw's mother helped her learn. A refined lady by nature, MacGraw was surprised by the relish with which her mother corrected her on the line, "Fuck you, asshole, that's a lot of shit." The elder MacGraw told her she got it wrong. It should have been, "You shit-ass, go fuck yourself."[54]

MacGraw was proud of her performance, particularly the scene where she has to beat King up and in the process destroy thousands of dollars worth of products from Bergdorf Goodman's store.

Lumet rehearsed it like a dance scene. The floor of the studio was marked off with different colors of masking tape to indicate the various steps so that the cinematographer and he could plan the camera moves before the cast arrived. MacGraw was delighted: "As a result, the fight went as smoothly as one, two, three, kick poor Alan King, four, five, six, bash him with my handbag, seven, eight, nine, smother him with my huge fisher coat ... and so on until the whole ground floor of Bergdorf Goodman was demolished." By the end of it all, she was drenched in sweat. King's nose was pouring blood. "My goodness, dear," MacGraw's mother said, "I had no idea you worked so hard."[55]

Shortly after shooting was completed, Lumet received some devastating news: Paddy Chayefsky, 58, had died of cancer. The pair of them went back a long way and had a huge amount in common, both in television and outside it. "Of all the people I've worked with," he said at the funeral, "the only one who's irreplaceable is Paddy."[56] If he'd lived, he surmised, "He would have been after everyone with such hilarity. He had the ability to see the ridiculous, to see the madness."[57] And yet Chayefsky was besieged with doubts right through his short life. Despite his vast canon of work, he thought he'd be forgotten, that he'd be lucky if people even remembered his two most famous lines, "What are you doing tonight?" from *Marty* and "I'm mad as hell and I'm not going to take it any more," from *Network*.[58]

His death made Lumet reflect on the small number of quality films being made at the time. "There's a reveling in mindlessness," he told an interviewer. What used to be called "the silly season" now seemed to go on all year. The "summer fluff" movies were being made in winter as well, which meant one only had the early months of the year "for your flop serious comedies."[59]

Such disenchantment hurled him into the cauldron of one of the most ambitious films of his career, a 160-minute epic about police corruption in New York called *Prince of the City*. It was based on a book by Robert Daley and starred Treat Williams as Daniel Ciello, a character based on real-life policeman Robert Leuci. Ciello works in the Special Unit of Investigation (SUI) and goes undercover, like Frank Serpico, to expose the corruption. He also rails against the kind of legal wrongdoing that sees assistant DAs plea-bargaining Murder One charges down to misdemeanors.

Brian De Palma was originally supposed to direct the film with John Travolta starring. Then Robert De Niro was suggested for the lead. If De Niro said yes to something, according to Lumet, "They'd have filmed the phone book." Lumet wanted Al Pacino for the part but Pacino thought it resembled *Serpico* too much and passed. Williams was less bankable than the other two, so Lumet knew he would have to work harder on his performance on that account to make it work. Lumet knew he needed someone who'd give it 100 percent commitment. "We're going to rub his nose in shit," he proclaimed, "because he's been living in shit."[60]

Lumet was pleased to be working with a relatively unknown actor like Williams. If he cast a Pacino or a De Niro, he reasoned, the character of Ciello would automatically have been elevated to hero status, which would have diluted the film's impact. As it

Prince of the City was a film into which Lumet poured his heart and soul but it proved more of a hit with the critics than the public, a familiar problem for the director. This was both due to its inordinate length (167 minutes) and the fact that Treat Williams (pictured with him) didn't have enough star appeal. He played a morally compromised policeman who turned state's witness to expose corruption within the force *à la Serpico* but nobody seemed to care (Eddie Brandt's Saturday Matinee).

stood, one wasn't fully aware if Ciello was hero or villain until the end. Lumet himself said he wasn't even sure until he saw the completed film.[61]

He admired Williams. He'd seen him in Milos Forman's *Hair* (1979). He was impressed by his "innate sweetness and naiveté," qualities he felt would be put to good use as Ciello.[62] He didn't always have to have big stars in his films, he insisted. The trouble with them was that they ate up too much of a film's budget. He preferred to keep that money for other things. But unknown actors didn't sell films. That was something he'd have to expect, no matter how good Williams was.

Frank Cunningham, in his study of Lumet, said that the director interviewed more than 5,000 people for the smaller parts in the film, something one finds difficult to believe even for someone of this man's thoroughness.[63] One thing we do know for sure, however, is that he cast unknown actors in these roles. Out of 125 of these, 52 were filled by people who'd never acted before. Lumet thought this helped the film for two reasons. The first was that audiences wouldn't have preconceptions about them. The second was that they gave the film a "disguised naturalness."[64] He planned to erode that as time went on.

He also worked hard at finding the right extras for the film, as he had in *Dog Day Afternoon*. He had an attitude to extras that was unlike any other director. He believed they inspired casts merely by being there. They saved the professional actors from "theatricality."[65] Such an attitude was a measure of his great democratic sense, his absence of any preciousness about himself.

He cast Lindsay Crouse as Williams' wife. Counteracting views that she wasn't "cinematic" enough, he said "Cinematic is what reveals human behavior. And Lindsay does that better than almost any actress working today."[66] She proved that in the many times she worked for him. He seemed to get emotions from her that no other director could.

Tony Walton was the film's production designer. As was the case with most of his crew, Lumet solicited his advice frequently. Said Walton, "Working with François Truffaut I wasn't allowed to look through the lens but for every film I worked on with Sidney Lumet, he encouraged closeness."[67]

This was director of photography Andrzej Bartkowiak's first film with Lumet. Lumet gave him very specific instructions about what he wanted from him. *Prince of the City* was a film about deceit, he told him, so he wanted the camera to be deceitful too. He'd used the same technique in *Network*. He told him not to use normal lenses but rather long-angled ones to create a disorienting effect.[68]

Once again, Jay Presson Allen was the screenwriter. The theme of police corruption isn't one we generally associate with women but she was able to turn her hand to most subjects without breaking a sweat. She brought an extra dimension to a man's world because she was seeing it from outside.[69]

Lumet had a vested interest in filming *Prince of the City* as he himself could have been tempted to inform on some of his friends on an occasion in the past. It happened when he was working at CBS during the McCarthy hearings. After he directed a drama called *The First Salem Witch Trial*, he was named as a Communist Party member by Harvey Matusow, a "friendly" government witness. Soon afterwards, Lumet was asked to meet with Matusow and a McCarthy ally called Victor Riesel. As Lumet prepared himself, he wondered if he would cave in under questioning and name some of his friends from the "organized left" in order to keep working. By the day of the meeting, however, such fears were replaced by anger when he realized he'd been mistaken for someone else.[70] As he entered the room, he started roaring at Matusow. "Don't get in an uproar." He then said to his colleagues, "He's not the one."[71] But that was precisely why he was roaring.

The experience shook him as much for the way he questioned his resolve as for the injustice he'd experienced. He knew how difficult it would have been to be faced with the choice of naming names or losing his career. That's why he felt sorry for Elia Kazan, who sang like a canary. "I wasn't sure if I'd grovel or tell them to go fuck themselves," he admitted.[72] It was the theme of so many of his films, including *Prince of the City*.

"It's my most grown-up piece of work," Lumet beamed.[73] He described it as a film that was about "picking up that $70,000 that's on the table." Or, more to the point, *not* picking it up. The temptation was always there. Ciello resisted it and, by doing so, made himself a target for those who didn't. They were threatened by him because he could expose them.

Pacino was right; it was the *Serpico* theme all over again. The difference this time was that Ciello almost became part of the corruption. Lumet also introduces a Mafia element when Ciello gets caught in the crossfire between criminals and the police. Who's going to protect him since he's turning against his own?

What starts as an ideal becomes a game of trying to stay alive. Ciello turns over a stone and finds the slime beneath. But some of the slime has his fingerprints on it. Did he really think he could be selective on who he would betray? As the saying goes, when you lie down with dogs, you get up with fleas. He was naïve to think he could ask the SUI to do things his way. Once he signed his name on the dotted line, they called the shots. "Leuci fell into a classic trap," said Lumet. "He tangled with powerful forces believing he could manipulate them. The results were catastrophic."[74] In the end, they started to control *him*.[75]

Lumet used a change in the set design of *Prince of the City* to convey Ciello's growing isolation from his colleagues just as he had with Katharine Hepburn in *Long Day's Journey into Night*. Early in the film, he filled the streets with people and cars. If a scene took place in an office, the walls were crowded with pictures and flags. The courtrooms were also full at this point. But as the film progressed, it changed. Office walls became more Spartan and streets emptier. For the climactic courtroom scene, there were no spectators, just bare wooden benches. This reinforced Ciello's loss of human contact as he betrayed one colleague after another.[76]

The number of set-ups meant Lumet and his crew were always on the move. He likened them to an army with "54 trucks." The logistical maneuvers, he said, were worthy of "World War II combat strategy." He had to know about one-way streets, traffic flow, the various routes he could use to save time on a given scene. In all, he featured 135 locations in the film.[77]

He collaborated with Allen on the script as she was too busy with other projects to finish it on her own. She said to him, "Sidney, why don't we divide up the work? You do the nuts and bolts. Break the book down and set it up structurally." He did it so well that she then asked him to work on some of the dialogue. He wasn't comfortable doing so but he grew into the job as it went on. He ended up writing almost half of the dialogue in the film.[78]

If *Prince of the City* is a modern-day tragedy, maybe we should evaluate it in Shakespearean terms. Shakespeare wrote about the *hamartia* of his characters, the fatal flaw that brings them down. For Hamlet it was procrastination, for Othello jealousy, for Lear over-possessiveness, for Macbeth a lust for power. Danny Ciello's *hamartia* was the belief that he could handle any situation he created. He stopped being able to do that when he got in over his head. The Lumetian "white knight against the system" hero—his trademark—gets added shading here due to Ciello's moral compromises.

Prince of the City was one of his proudest achievements, even if the critics—and the public—didn't agree with his estimation of it. Maybe he believed in it too much to see its flaws.

Williams loved working with him. "He was a ball of fire," the actor recalled: "He came to work with all barrels burning." Williams called him the most "prepared" director he'd ever worked with. His foresight meant that "[e]veryone got home for dinner."[79] Elsewhere he said, "He made you feel safe."[80]

In one scene, a character spits in Williams' face. When Lumet was rehearsing it, he spat at Williams to get him to work up the rage he wanted in him and it worked. It wasn't an extreme he usually went to, but in this instance he felt it was justified.[81]

He'd done something like this early on his career and deeply regretted it afterwards. He was trying to get an actress to cry. He pushed her harder and harder until he eventually struck her on the face. Not only did the tears come, but the actress was overjoyed. She thanked him. He may have got the scene he wanted but he disliked both himself and the actress for the manner in which it came about.

"I'd made the most intense violation of her," he said, "and from then on I never wanted to see her again. If her self-respect was that little, she was nobody I wanted to be around." The experience was beneficial for him because it changed the way he behaved towards actors afterwards. He made a vow never to lie to them and never to be going for one thing when they thought he was going for something else: "If we can't get it out of mutual craft, I'd rather let it go."[82]

Prince of the City didn't fare as well as *Serpico* at the box office but it went deeper into its theme, helping us to understand why policemen make the compromises they do. They aren't distant figures here; they're family men with real needs. Lumet doesn't condone their actions but he devolves their responsibility. To make Frank Serpico a martyr, the police had to be the villains of the piece. Here they're neither martyrs nor villains; they're just people.

So what does that make Leuci? Probably more of a survivor than anything else. Serpico went into exile in Switzerland but he stayed in the force. That was a more pragmatic difference. To this extent, *Prince of the City* is more realistic than *Serpico*. One might describe it as "*Serpico* for adults."

Leuci informed on 70 men. Fifty-two were indicted. Two committed suicide. One went mad. Did Ciello clean up the city or merely make a cosmetic change? "The only difference between you and the guy with a stocking over his head," his brother tells him, "is you got a badge." Lumet seems to align himself with this viewpoint at times, framing him as someone who's as much a part of the disease as the cure.

Lumet stayed close to the facts of the matter even thought he fictionalized them. This enabled him to ask the kinds of questions Daley did in his book. For instance: Did the SUI do its business correctly? Was it right to give narcotics to its informants in exchange for testimony? Should it have given Leuci immunity from prosecution for crimes in which he himself was implicated? The film asked more questions than it answered. Lumet's moral landscape is so blurred, we end up with a set of circumstances that are skewed in their emphasis.

In the final scene, as Ciello talks to a class of new policemen, a cadet says, "I don't think I have anything to learn from you." We've waited nearly three hours for some sort of a conclusion and this is all we get. Have we been shortchanged? It depends what we're looking for, a scenario wrapped up in ribbons or a complex tangle of thwarted dreams.

Williams gave it everything, but everything from this man wasn't the same as everything from Pacino or De Niro. Was Lumet being defensive when he said he wanted him more than them? Perhaps. When you don't get what you want, you have to want what you get.

At the end of the day, Lumet was left with a film that lacked focus. People left theaters with their heads spinning. Lumet put too much into it and forgot about his audience. It's an earnest film for connoisseurs rather than a crowd-puller. Its failure to make a mark left him disheartened. He'd gone back to the streets to pursue a favorite theme, but it backfired.

Andrew Sarris said it was less a movie than "a surgical incision into the corpus of our society."[83] Another critic believed it had "no heroes." In general it was seen to be fuzzy in its depiction of the police force: "Five percent are honest and 5 percent dishonest. Ninety percent go whichever way the wind blows."[84] Such ambivalence also summed up Ciello's character. Audiences needed a firmer grasp on who he was. Because he wasn't sure himself, and because Lumet wasn't, the film became too modulated for its own good.

Did Lumet know who he himself was? The chameleon in him continued to evade definition. His last four films had been a literary adaptation, a musical, a comedy and a drama. There was no pattern except for the fact that it was the same man behind the camera.

His versatility seemed to suggest he was an *auteur* but this wasn't a term he liked. Its implication, i.e., that the director was the "author" of a film, didn't mean anything to him. It was inaccurate, he believed, because you couldn't say that of someone working on a film like you could of someone working on a book. A book author had a certain amount of control but there were too many variables on a film set. "When we shoot," he explained, "I'm dependent on the weather, on the drunk who won't get out of the shot until we pay him off. What am I really in control of?"[85]

That was where the *auteur* theory sprang a leak. "A movie is not a novel," he went on. "It is not a painting. It's not you working by yourself. You're at the mercy of the sun. You're at the mercy of the labs. You're at the mercy of a negative cutter. I've had shots torn so badly that they couldn't be repaired. You wait for an actor to have breakfast. You take a lunch break yourself. A writer doesn't take a lunch break if he doesn't want to and neither does a painter. A film is not one person's thing."[86]

Mixed Grills

Lumet often followed heavy films with light ones. Such transitions helped him recharge his batteries—and earn some money. He hadn't had a hit since *Network*. It often happened that films that won Oscars, or were nominated for them, were followed by flops. So it proved with him. After the disappointment of *Prince of the City*, he thought he would look for a potboiler to prop up his spirits. He found one in *Deathtrap* (1982).

Written by Ira Levin, it had been a stage success. Lumet liked it for the same reason he liked *Twelve Angry Men*: its tight construction. Everything took place in an enclosed area.

Levin's play had been running on Broadway since 1978. Lumet once again chose Jay Presson Allen to adapt it for film. She kept most of the play's script but inserted some deft touches to make it more cinematic.

Michael Caine plays Sidney Bruhl, a playwright who's just had another flop. His protégé Clifford Anderson (Christopher Reeve) has written a brilliant play and is about to show it to Bruhl for his approval. Bruhl senses it's going to be a hit. He suggests to his wife Myra (Dyan Cannon) that it might be a good idea to bump Anderson off and claim the glory for himself. She's not sure if he's joking or not. Neither are we.

Lumet was interested in the fact that a writer could also be a murderer, that there was a thin enough line separating creativity from destruction. "There's a life force," he opined, "that makes one person turn out a hell of a painting and somebody else stab his cousin."[1]

Reeve wasn't regarded as one of the great actors of his era but Lumet saw something in him he liked. "What seemed such a simple, artless performance in *Superman*," he observed, "was the finest kind of acting. Reeve's timing—and humor—had to be just about perfect to make the character come off."[2] Small wonder, then, that he wanted him for *Deathtrap*.

Pauline Kael once said that Lumet liked to get very capable actors into his films so that he didn't have to do much with them; they sank or swam on their own.[3] We can see how wrong she was when he talks about stars like Reeve or, in his early career, Tab Hunter. These were actors who were castigated for being pinups rather than serious performers. The point about Lumet was that, unlike Kael, he never prejudged anyone. Whatever reputation stars had before coming on his set didn't matter to him. He took them as he found them, and usually discovered something in them that other directors either missed or didn't bother with.

He felt the same about Reeve as he did about Sean Connery in *The Hill*: that he was a much better actor than people gave him credit for. James Bond was Connery's Superman from that point of view. If British fans found it difficult to get past the guns and the gadgetry with Connery, the American ones couldn't get past the cape with Reeve. Both actors were unfairly stereotyped.[4]

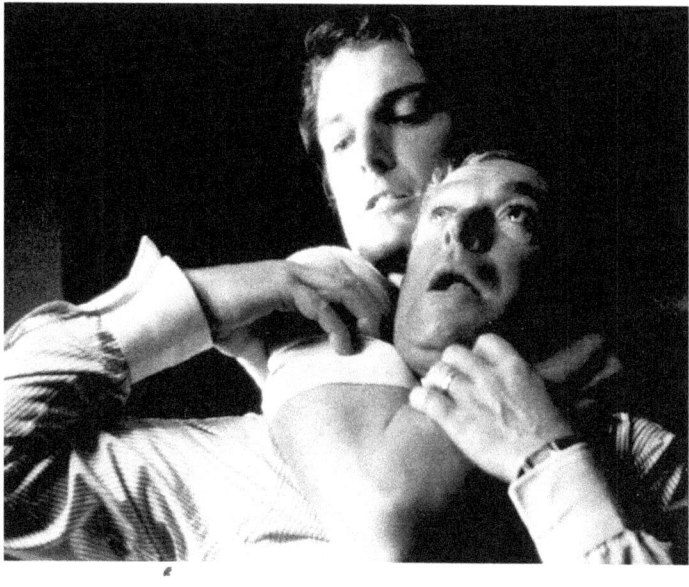

Lumet explored the antinomies of a gay relationship that went wrong when both parties became too greedy for their own good in *Deathtrap*, his adaptation of Ira Levin's black comedy. Here Christopher Reeve tries to strangle his partner in crime, Michael Caine (Jerry Ohlinger).

Reeve liked the way Lumet worked: "He knows how to speak a variety of languages, be they technical, Method or improvisatory." Caine knew exactly what he wanted to do in a scene before it started shooting but Reeve liked to work his way into it. Lumet welcomed this. Lumet kept making suggestions about how Reeve might play a scene before throwing himself into it. "Sidney often came up at the last minute and gave me a new idea," he recalled. This might not necessarily have been a major change. It was often just "something fresh to put on my plate."[5]

Reeve described Lumet as a "benign dictator." Working with him, he said, was like "one of those exercises where people stand backwards on a table and fall off, trusting the group will catch them. You do that with Sidney and he catches you." He described him as "part counselor, part psychiatrist and part technical director."[6]

Cannon also liked him and felt secure with him because he gave her the freedom to fail: "He always made me feel like I could make a fool of myself and it would be all right. He made me feel like I could gamble and never come up losing. That's a pretty amazing thing for somebody to be able to instill in you."[7]

The film has more twists than a corkscrew. Some of these are more contrived than others but if you suspend disbelief, as you must for something like this, they have a crazy kind of logic. Alone they don't work but as a thread they jell. The film creates its own rationale. One writer compared it to a snake eating its own tail, largely because of the play-within-the-play-within-the-play format.[8] A big surprise occurs when we learn that Caine and Reeve are in a gay relationship—and that they plan to murder Cannon. Afterwards they turn on each another.

The script alternates between ominous forebodings and Oscar Wilde–style one-liners ("Nothing recedes like success") as a demented Caine struts and frets his hour upon the stage in search of past glories. We're never too far away from farce even when people die or come back from the dead. It's played out with such good cheer under Lumet's frolicsome direction that you can't help forgiving its excesses. The robbers get robbed, the murderers get murdered and we end up with a finale not even seasoned whodunit specialists would have anticipated—unless they're like Irene Worth, who plays a psychic. She, of course, has the last laugh. This is only fitting. But even here we wonder if there's another twist coming. We've been so pummeled by them up until now.

Lumet with Jay Presson Allen on the set of *Deathtrap*. She was the executive producer and also wrote the screenplay (Larry Edmunds Bookshop).

The implausibilities of the plot aren't a problem because there are so many of them. When something is played as ham-fisted as this, the sky's the limit. The demented wife, the crumbling literary career, the gay boyfriend and the psychic are all put into the melting pot and stirred mischievously by Lumet. He teases us at every turn, rolling back his Russian dolls until we find the "real" one, the one that will explain all the others. It's hardly his most sophisticated film but, *Murder on the Orient Express* apart, it's probably the one on which he had the most fun.

Caine and Reeve had to kiss one another on the lips in one scene. This might be commonplace today but in 1980 it was unusual. To gear up for it, they both drank brandy. When Lumet shouted, "Action!" Caine said to Reeve, "Whatever you do, don't open your mouth."[9]

The kiss was probably remembered longer than the murder they cooked up. A hostile Denver audience booed it at a test showing. This was reported in *Time* magazine, which spoiled the surprise for a lot of people. Reeve referred to it as "the ten million dollar kiss." He estimated the film lost that amount due to *Time*.[10]

Deathtrap was unashamedly far-fetched. Reeve felt it succeeded because he and Caine had played it without apology."[11] Lumet also directed it that way. But the film wasn't a success. LGBT audiences felt it trivialized the gay theme whereas straight ones were put off by it. Maybe Reeve was right in his view that the *Time* article hurt its earning power. He also said, "I don't think America was ready to see Superman kiss another guy."[12]

Lumet next considered directing a film called *Scarface*, an updated version of the 1932 Paul Muni film. He was in consultation with Marty Bregman, its producer, about the prospect. Bregman wanted him to give it a "zap, bang, pow" emphasis instead of his more familiar "introspective, culturally dense" approach.[13] Lumet wanted to locate the story in present-day Miami. He suggested making the title character an exile from Castro's Cuba. That, he thought, would be an interesting launch pad for a man who was going to be "king of the cocaine mountain."[14] Bregman sent him a script written by Oliver Stone and asked him to read it and give him his view of it. Lumet didn't have time to do this so he put it on the long finger. By now he had another project on his mind which was more of a priority for him.

The Verdict was the story of washed-up lawyer Frank Galvin, framed for jury-tampering and almost debarred as a result. He's now descended into the depths of depression and drink. As he slides slowly into oblivion, he's presented with a case that looks like easy money.

A woman has been left lying in a coma after being given the wrong anesthetic by doctors at a powerful Catholic hospital in Boston. The hospital offers her sister $210,000 in compensation. All Galvin has to do is take the money and run. It seems to be an open-and-shut case but it turns out to be something quite different as Galvin digs deeper.

When David Mamet first submitted his screenplay to Twentieth Century–Fox, the producers didn't like it. They asked Jay Presson Allen for a second opinion. She said she thought it was brilliant but they didn't accept her view. They asked her to write a different version. When she did, it was offered to Robert Redford, who hummed and hawed about doing it. The producers, in the meantime, asked Lumet to direct it. Lumet

Paul Newman excelled as an ambulance-chasing attorney in *The Verdict*, Lumet's high-voltage drama about medical negligence and a damaged man's attempt to regain his dignity against legal and ecclesiastical authorities that seek to thwart him. So does Charlotte Rampling, at least when she isn't trying to lure him into her arms (Jerry Ohlinger).

had just seen Mamet's play *American Buffalo* and was impressed with it. He asked Mamet if he'd done any writing for film. Mamet showed him the screenplay of *The Verdict*. Lumet read it and loved it. He told Fox that was the version he wanted to do. As a result, Allen's was dropped. Fox, ironically, ended up with the screenplay they'd originally rejected.[15]

The lead role was turned down by stars William Holden and Dustin Hoffman. Frank Sinatra campaigned for it but he wasn't seen as a serious enough actor. Paul Newman now expressed an interest in it. He was looking for something to stretch him. Recent years had been fallow in that regard. He wanted to break out of the "pretty boy" image he still had with the press, even in his middle age.

His son Scott had recently died from a drug overdose. That hardened him. So did his forays onto the racetrack. "Racing has destroyed every iota of conservatism that was in me," he claimed. "Only at this point in my life could I have been such a splattered character as Frank Galvin. Any time before, I'm afraid I would have held back and played him much too cautiously."[16]

It was a relief for him to be able to "let it all hang out."[17] He took the part 48 hours after getting the script. It blew him away with the raw pain of its main character: "As the curtain rises, he's face down in a urinal. Sensational."[18] Shortly afterwards, we see him scanning obituary columns as he looks for possible clients among the bereaved. In the evenings he cruises the bars. He once studied for the legal one; now he prefers the other kind. Some poor decisions in the past have turned him into a lounge lizard.

Newman wears his hair longer than usual in the part. He has lines on his face. This is a man who's lived, who's seen the seamy side of life. He tries to conceal his depression under a barrage of barroom banter. Only when he's on his own does the real Galvin emerge.

Newman saw the film as a kind of coming-of-age for him. "I'm just now beginning to learn something about acting," he said, stressing the fact that he wasn't being falsely modest. He often compared himself to Marlon Brando, saying acting came easily to Brando and therefore he had a bigger responsibility to be great. As for himself, "I don't think I ever had an immediate, spontaneous gift to do anything right."[19] When he looked at his old films, he realized he'd always been working too hard to create the emotions. In *The Verdict*, he didn't want to let the "machinery" show.[20]

Jack Warden played his friend Mickey Morrissey. James Mason took the role of Concannon, the ruthless law firm boss (Morrissey refers to him as "the Prince of Fucking Darkness"). Mason was originally supposed to play Morrissey, with Burt Lancaster as Concannon. When Lancaster dropped out, Lumet offered Concannon to him. Mason's wife advised him to ring Lumet at the outset to see if there were any parts in the film he might be able to play. Mason knew Lumet liked him but he wasn't sure how much. Lumet had once said Mason was his favorite actor but after *Network* he changed his choice to Peter Finch. Mason felt hurt about this.[21]

He was so anxious to get the part, he went to the lengths of reading scenes from the film to Lumet over the phone to prove he could do it. Lumet was eventually convinced, which resulted in the switch from Warden.[22] This, no doubt, helped the film immensely. His Machiavellian performance provides an apt nemesis for a man trying to crawl out of the gutter.

Lumet discusses a point with Paul Newman on the set of *The Verdict*. Both of them were nominated for Oscars for the film but neither won. By this stage they'd become accustomed to being bridesmaids at the Oscar wedding (Jerry Ohlinger).

The Verdict reminded Newman of *The Hustler*, another film where he had to pull himself out of "the habit of failure." The difference this time is that he's lost his boyishness. He's closer to desperation: "There's a new hurt look in his eyes, a sound of willed sincerity in his voice as he bulls his way through lies, tricks, evasions."[23]

The manner in which he does this to get justice for the comatose woman is his catharsis. The film is also a manifesto against the church, a church that says it was "God's will" that the woman in question was turned into a vegetable when it's all too well aware that she was given the wrong anesthetic before her surgery. When it engages "the prince of fucking darkness" to defend it, we have a royal battle on our hands: ecclesiastical chicanery vs. the rugged dignity of a disgraced barrister.

Lumet's view of the Catholic hierarchy offers us "a stern corrective to the pluperfect cheerfulness and laughable impracticality of the Irish priests in *Going My Way*."[24] This is a more lethal clergy, tooth-in-jowl with the equally unscrupulous legislature. Both believe Galvin can be bought off with a generous settlement. The moment he refuses this—to the anger of the girl's family—is the moment when he starts to believe in himself again, when he stops being an "ambulance chaser" and engages the enemy in a duel to the death.

Standing in his way is Concannon, and a woman he sees first as his savior but who later turns out to be a plant of Concannon's, the duplicitous Laura (Charlotte Rampling).

Filming began with high hopes from Lumet and his cast for a high-quality piece of work but after his customary two-week rehearsal period he wasn't satisfied that Newman had "got" his character. He felt he was holding something back, some vulnerability. Newman said things would probably come together better when he had his lines memorized. Lumet said he didn't think it was anything to do with the lines.

The two of them lived near one another so they drove home together that day. Newman was silent on the journey. He'd obviously taken Lumet's words to heart. This was on a Friday. When he came back to work the following Monday, he gave a reading to Lumet that was superb. He'd opened up all his buried feelings over the weekend and was now ready to "become" Galvin. Lumet was delighted. He knew Newman was basically a shy man, like many actors. He had to be pushed to give his real self. When he did, he exceeded even his own expectations. "Paul's always been one of the best actors we've got," Lumet said, "but because of that great stone face and those gorgeous eyes, a lot of people assumed he couldn't act."[25]

Now minus his inhibitions, Newman threw himself into the role 110 percent. For a scene in which Lumet asked him to be out of breath, he ran around a sound stage repeatedly to make himself exhausted. When he gave his heart-rending court speech towards the end, a shocked Lumet found a piece of dirt on the film which required it to be re-shot. Newman didn't balk at this any more than Al Pacino had in similar circumstances during the shooting of *Dog Day Afternoon*. In fact, he did it even better the second time.[26]

When Frank Capra had his "John Doe" style heroes threaten the establishment, he used "ordinary" men like Gary Cooper and James Stewart to make the David-and-Goliath nature of the encounter more effective. Lumet did the same with Newman here, pulling him down from his superstar status to play a shop-soiled anti-hero. This is a do-or-die case for Galvin, as important for him to win as it is for the family of the woman in the coma. It's his Last Chance Saloon. If it goes wrong, he knows his career is over.

The crunch moment is when he refuses the $210,000. In real life he wouldn't have had the right to do this. It wasn't his to refuse. Strictly speaking, it belonged to the sister of the woman in the coma. Lumet uses poetic license here to make the plotline more dramatic. The sister of the woman is furious with him and so is her husband. They aren't well off. He's gambling with their financial stability as well as his own dignity.

Because *The Verdict* was a film about a man haunted by his past, Lumet asked Ed Pisoni, his art director, to imbue it with autumnal colors and shades. These, he felt, would give it an aged look. Pisoni obliged. He dispensed with bright colors like blue, pink, green and yellow, concentrating instead on russets, burnt orange and burgundy red. If a location had an unwanted color or hue, it was repainted.[27]

The color motif affects an early scene in a graphic manner. This occurs after Galvin goes into the hospital to see the comatose woman. At this point he's wavering, wondering if he'll accept the money. He's taken a photo of her and watches it develop. As it does so, he "develops" too. Seeing her in her vegetable state is what spurs him on to fight the case. Lumet loved the way Newman conveyed his growing transformation from victim to protagonist. "I could feel the present breaking through," he said, "for a man who, up until then, had been trapped in the detritus of his past life." It was the intercutting between the developing Polaroid and the close-ups of Newman that made that transition palpable."[28]

Newman admired Lumet's symbolism at times like this. Elsewhere he enjoyed something that Lumet was more noted for: the speed at which he worked. Lumet, he joked, was the only director who could double-park in front of a whorehouse and not get a ticket. Lumet countered with, "Paul is wrong. I would never do that outside a whorehouse."[29]

Charlotte Rampling proved to be the film's big surprise as Laura, who appears to be accelerating Galvin's odyssey from hell but who is in effect plotting with Concannon to keep him down there. Lumet beautifully milks the moment we learn this, panning his camera around Concannon's room to reveal her presence at the end of the sweep. An equally dramatic moment occurs when Newman punches her in the face after he realizes she's Concannon's patsy. The idea of a man striking a woman, especially a "gentleman" like Newman, might have come across as unseemly in another director's hands but here we cheer along with him as he decks her.

Mamet's original script lacked conclusiveness, the final verdict left hanging in the air. Lumet doubted that audiences would accept this after two hours of heavy drama so Mamet agreed to insert a victory for Galvin over Concannon. (This wasn't to Grisham-ize it; merely to give us some relief from the pulverizing nature of the foregoing.) How Mamet brings this about is intriguing. A doctor who knows the truth about the wrong anesthetic is lined up as Galvin's star witness but he goes missing prior to the trial. Now Galvin has to dig deeper. A conscience-stricken nurse who also knows the truth fills in at the eleventh hour. The "surprise" witness is a familiar ingredient of courtroom dramas but Lumet wasn't shy about including one here. She admits that times were changed on crucial hospital records to exculpate the medical staff from charges of negligence.

Lumet was aware he was using poetic license again in the scene. He knew her testimony would have been inadmissible in the real world. Audiences were familiar with such revelatory plot devices in an infinite number of Perry Mason–style dramas but he felt he was entitled to such a liberty in the scene. There had been so much pain leading up to it.[30]

Fittingly enough, the mystery witness lives in Lumet's beloved New York rather than Boston, the film's seat of corruption. Galvin has to travel there to find her. She's played by Lumet stalwart Lindsay Crouse. Like Galvin, she too has had a reformation. Her part is small but resonant. She and Galvin are like mirror images of one another, two lost souls struggling with their consciences.

In the last scene, Laura rings Galvin but he doesn't pick up. All through the film, he's been chasing her. She represents his perch on the ladder of respectability, his tenuous hold on a life he desperately wants to resume. But now, with his court victory, he's back there. The balance of power has shifted. She lies on a bed with a bottle of whisky beside her. She's the loser now, a kind of female Galvin. He's usurped the kind of control she used to have as he begins Phase Two of his life.

Rampling's character is perhaps the most beguiling in the film. Does she develop feelings for Newman after agreeing to spy on him? It would appear so. She encourages him to stick with the case at a point when he feels like giving up. Lumet doesn't explore this angle, save to suggest she takes to drink at the end after Newman gets over her. Is this due to depression over losing him or failing at her task? We're not sure. We suspect the former, which makes her more a pathetic figure than an evil one.

The general critical consensus was that Lumet was back to his best form on familiar turf. Newman also received generous notices, even for his voice. According to *Time*, it had "the breathy rasp of a drinker, his walk the uncertainty of a strong man going down." Mason was credited with giving his most "delicately modulated" performance in a decade.[31] Andrzej Bartkowiak's camerawork was also praised, his "rich browns and mahoganies" giving the film an elegiac look while avoiding the "impenetrable" quality of *Prince of the City*.[32]

Some critics carped about the fact that Lumet reused the old yarn of the small man trying to beat the system against the odds. But if he was a latter-day Capra, it was acknowledged that he avoided "Capracorn": "Like Capra, he manipulates his audience, but with a few more kicks in the groin before the happy ending."[33] Neither does he go the James Stewart route of stammering under pressure. Instead he has the more extreme symptoms of palpitations and anxiety attacks.[34] One writer saw a metaphor for Lumet's own life in *The Verdict*, the "New York filmmaker in an industry dominated by Hollywood, the successful director snubbed by critics, the teller of truths no one wants to hear."[35]

Both he and Newman were Oscar-nominated but both lost. Ben Kingsley took the Best Actor award for the earnest but plodding *Gandhi*. Lumet didn't mind losing but he thought Newman was "robbed."[36] Many other people shared that view. Clint Eastwood felt Newman was "too popular" to win an Oscar. Solemn films like *Gandhi* were more to the taste of the Academy voters.[37]

Newman had been nominated many times before to no effect but he took his defeat on the chin, saying, "I flew to the coast only to prove I'm a good loser."[38] Kingsley's award completed a sweep for *Gandhi* but the division of the spoils left many people nonplussed. They felt the movie was confused with the man, the film with the philosophy. Vincent Canby huffed, "*Gandhi* is a laboriously illustrated textbook."[39] Kingsley had also seen off the challenges of Jack Lemmon (for *Missing*) and Peter O'Toole (for *My Favorite Year*). Like Newman, O'Toole had been nominated many times and now looked set to end his career without a statuette. Would Newman end his one the same way? A few days after the ceremonies, a man called Ed Jones went so far as to place a *Daily Variety* ad addressed to the members of the Academy: "I would like you to see *The Verdict* once more and tell me what Paul Newman has to do to win an Academy Award."[40] Indeed.

Lumet: "Paul leads one of the most generous and honorable lives of anyone I've ever known. Between his popcorn and salad dressing and his other merchandising, all for charities he's created—not to mention his movie work—his days are packed. But he does it all and never seems pressed."[41]

The broken-down character Newman played in *The Verdict* was at odds with a public service commercial he did at this time. It reminded drivers to "belt up" for safety. If the commercial was done to gain a higher profile for himself during the run-up to the Oscar ceremonies, this was a mistake because it gave mixed signals to people about him. *Newsweek* saw it as part of an Oscar campaign but Newman's PR people denied he was involved in one.[42]

It hurt Lumet to lose again. He'd worked hard on the film, harder than on anything he'd done for years, and had nothing to show for it. Critical kudos were fine but you couldn't put them on the mantelpiece. He couldn't resist a poke at the industry, asking, "Why does Hollywood always ignore me at Oscar time? It can't be just that I live and work in New York. Look at Woody Allen, who's a complete independent spirit." Maybe, he speculated, his films didn't have the kind of eccentricity Allen's had: "Woody has his own kind of talent that's like no one else's. I haven't. I make commercial pictures. I'm in the marketplace." His Oscar-less status, from this point of view, resulted from his similarity to Hollywood *people*: "I could almost be one of them, which is what gets under their skin."[43] Another possibility was that it was difficult to put him in a category. The Academy always liked doing that with those it honored.

This could also have been a factor in Lumet's serial losses on Oscar night. "I always subjugate myself to the material," he maintained. From this point of view, *The Verdict* differed markedly from, say, *The Deadly Affair*: "I would like to think that if you saw them, you wouldn't think they were directed by the same person."[44] The bottom line was that his technique differed from film to film, depending on the theme he was dealing with. He thought this upset people. It upset them because they had a narrow-minded definition of what constituted style. Most people, he contended, didn't even know what style *was*. In his view, it was the most misused word in existence—apart from "love."[45]

It was unusual to see him coming out so strongly about his feelings as he usually kept them to himself. Maybe it was a build-up of years of frustration. He did an interview in which he became even more revelatory. During the course of it, he was asked what he was passionate about. He replied, "Work, a sunset, my wife, my children, politics, conflict, effort."[46] The order was interesting. Work came before nature and nature before his personal life. This despite his reputation as an old-fashioned family man with two daughters, Amy and Jennifer. He was a good father but he played this down just as he did his directorial gifts. In fact, he saw a connection between parenting and directing. Both of them involved control but also, finally, a lack of control. Just as one couldn't be an auteur on a film set, neither could one be a control freak within the confines of a household. Both activities were magical, he believed, because nobody could pin down what made them work. "There are two great secrets for raising children," he joked, "and nobody knows what they are."[47]

Considering the film he'd just made rocked both civil and religious boats, he was asked if he was worried about being pursued by the systems he debunked. "Not really," he said. "The thing about greedy people is that they love money. As long as my movies make money, they leave me alone. It doesn't really bother them if people criticize their institutions. They're not that secure."[48]

After the excitement surrounding *The Verdict* had abated, he finally got around to reading the Oliver Stone treatment of *Scarface* sent by Marty Bregman many months before. He still wasn't sure if he wanted to be involved in this project. Brian De Palma was also in the frame for directing it now. Lumet liked some elements of it but not others. He wanted to make it more political, exploring the CIA's involvement in drugs as part of their anti-communist drive. Bregman wasn't interested in that, which led to conflict between them. Lumet felt Bregman wanted to make a "comic strip" kind of film, a view that offended Bregman. It led to him deciding that Lumet wouldn't be the right man for the job, so he gave it to De Palma. "De Palma and I had no intention of making a comic strip," Bregman insisted. "We wanted to give the thing a larger-than-life quality."[49]

They got that as *Scarface* turned out to be a wonderful work in the end, an Al Pacino film that was up there with anything he'd done for Lumet. It hurt Lumet when it went on to become a cult hit. Sometimes his urge to make "message" films warred against a more exciting vision. It happened in the tussle between *Dr. Strangelove* and *Fail-Safe* and it did so again here. In Lumet's hands, would *Scarface* have become the cult success it did? It's unlikely. His talents lay in other areas, which is perhaps why it was best he walked away from it.

Instead he made *Daniel*, a film that was infinitely more important to him. It explored many issues close to his heart, like the right to free expression and the wrongful conviction of innocent people. It turned out to be one of the films of which he was most proud in his career but, like *Prince of the City*, it was probably too intense to be commercial.

Based on the 1971 E.L. Doctorow novel *The Book of Daniel*, it was inspired by the execution of Julius and Ethel Rosenberg for atomic espionage in 1953. This was the only instance of Americans being executed in their own country during peacetime.

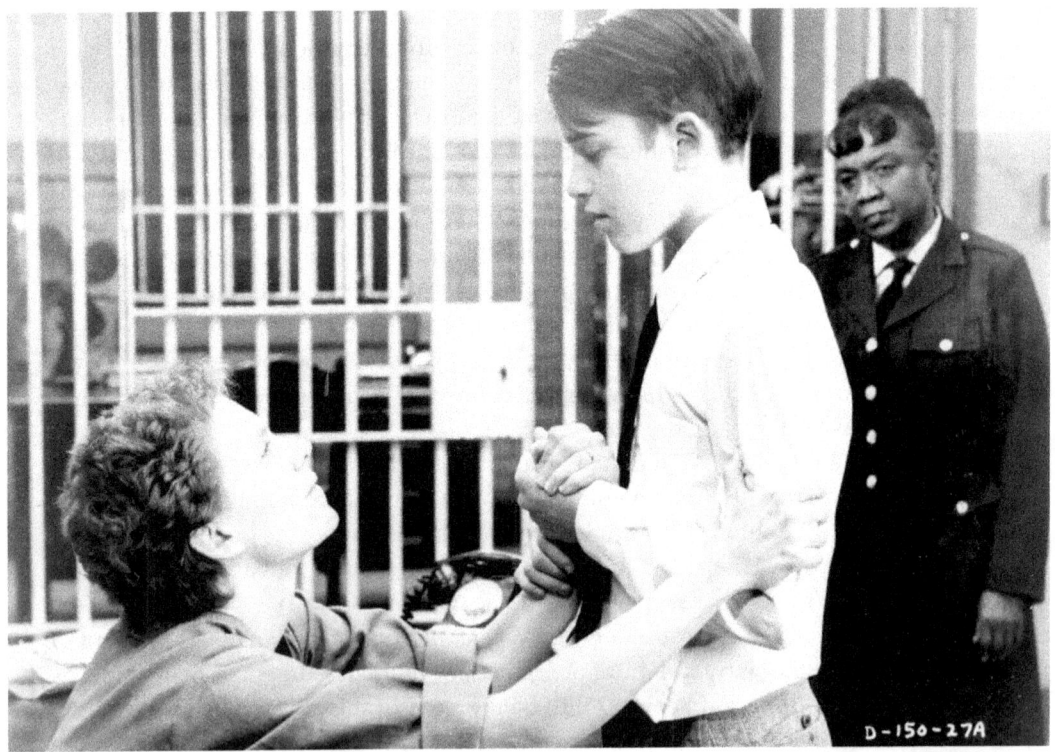

Lindsay Crouse being visited in jail by her son (Ilan Mitchell-Smith) in Lumet's scorchingly intense *Daniel*. Rosetta La Noire is the prison matron watching over them (Jerry Ohlinger).

Mandy Patinkin and Lindsay Crouse played Paul and Rochelle Isaacson, the executed pair. (Crouse had also been in *Prince of the City* and *The Verdict*.) The main story concerns the search of their son Daniel (Timothy Hutton) for the full facts surrounding their conviction and death. Were they guilty of the crimes for which they were charged or were they framed?

Daniel's immersion in the events is out of character for him as his past has been non-political. He becomes politicized as a result of the social activism, and eventual suicide, of his sister Susan (Amanda Plummer). Susan has been heavily involved in rallies against the Vietnam War before she collapses mentally and kills herself. Daniel is traumatized by her death, which he sees as an offshoot to the deaths of his parents.

The story is told with the use of flashbacks. Lumet's treasured cinematographer Andrzej Bartkowiak—working with him for the twelfth time here—used impressive color filters to make these stand out. The music score carried a number of Paul Robeson's spiritual songs. The most effective one is "This Little Light of Mine," heard during a moving scene where the young Paul and Susan (played by Jena Greco and Ilan Mitchell-Smith) have trouble finding their way back to their home along New York's busy streets.

Lumet spent over ten years preparing the film. Every time it seemed to be going to happen, something got in the way. It was important for him to set the record straight on two people who fascinated him, or at least as straight as he could with the information available to him. Hutton was also totally committed to *Daniel*, turning down much more lucrative offers for other films to make it. His salary was a modest $30,000.

Like Doctorow, Lumet made no attempt to be historically accurate in his depiction of the events that unfold before us. It's a speculative film that changes the circumstances of the Rosenbergs' lives—and deaths—so he can bring other elements into the equation to suit his purposes. In real life, it was Ethel's younger brother, David Greenglass, who was her main accuser. Here it's a dentist. Greenglass confessed to giving Julius notes and sketches in 1945 on the design of the "implosion principle" atomic bomb that was later exploded in Nagasaki. Ethel typed them up for him. He was sentenced to 15 years in prison for his complicity in the alleged conspiracy and served nine and a half. Both Julius and Ethel took the Fifth when they were asked in court about their links to communism.[50]

Lumet draws a brilliant performance from Hutton in the lead role. He doesn't have too much to do but his face conveys great passion. Here again Lumet shows how he can transform an actor who hadn't a back catalogue of this kind of work into an A-league performer. Patinkin and Crouse are also excellent. The scene showing their execution is harrowing, especially since Ethel has to be electrocuted twice after a systems malfunction.

Pauline Kael drew on all her reserves of venom for Lumet, accusing him of fostering hysteria.[51] For good—or bad—measure, she added that he made Susan look "rodent-like" in the course of it.[52] These were unfair and gratuitous remarks.

Lumet thought *Daniel* was more about the debt of history than anything else. It was the story of a boy "who buries himself with his parents and then spends the rest of his life trying to climb out of the grave."[53] Though the connection was somewhat strained, the issue made him wonder about his failings with his own family, not because of any criminal activity but simply as the result of work. Had this deprived his daughters of his company over the years? "Why can't artists' children ever seem to pull their lives together?" he asked. "How much do my kids have to pay because I've done 31 movies in 25 years?"[54]

He directed at his usual frenetic pace. One day he shot a six-camera set-up with 10,000 extras. He also dressed 3000 extras for the next scene and shot it with three cameras, all before lunch.[55] This was standard operating procedure for him.

Daniel is thematically linked to *The Pawnbroker*. As one writer noted, if the anti–Semitic madness of the Holocaust destroyed Nazerman (Rod Steiger's character in that film), the anti–Semitic madness of McCarthyism and the Cold War killed Daniel's parents.[56]

Lumet kept an open mind on the actual circumstances surrounding the lives of Daniel's parents. Were they engaged in minor crimes, as their lawyer suggests to Hutton at one point? Were their crimes exaggerated to make them face the chair? This is possibly what happened but Lumet doesn't go into it any more than he reveals if the young Puerto Rican in *Twelve Angry Men* was guilty. The details aren't as important as the witch hunt. Red-baiting was a cottage industry at the time they died. That's all Daniel needs to know. He can connect the rest of the dots later on if he wishes. Whatever his parents did, as one writer remarked, "our government did worse."[57]

Daniel was an intellectually draining film. Despite Lumet's protest that he wasn't agitprop, how could it be described as anything else?[58] The socio-political ballast is too dutiful, too earnest. The script doesn't get a chance to let its emotions through, replete as it is with history lessons, monologues to camera, dour flashbacks and Lumet's familiar Old Leftism. "The acting is good," wrote one critic, "as long as you don't demand that these people make you care for them."[59] Aye, there's the rub. Lumet is so immersed in the documentary overtones of the piece, he runs the risk of losing its sentimental center.

Doctorow was present on set as it was being shot. On the first day he was so overcome with emotion he cried. He couldn't believe his novel had finally made it to the screen as he'd been trying to make this happen for many years. Lumet was glad for him and not made uncomfortable by his presence, as he had been by Frank Serpico on *Serpico*. Doctorow was more like Paddy Chayefsky, a creative artist who could help the production along by making suggestions.

That wasn't always the way with writers. Lumet had had negative experiences with some of them. One screenwriter who appeared on the set of a film he made fell hopelessly in love with the leading lady and had to be ordered to leave. Another one was so obsequious to the actors that he did multiple rewrites of the script at their behest, which worked to its detriment. He had to be removed as well.[60] Lumet knew that without writers, there could be no movies. When he found one he got on with, like Doctorow, he held on to him like a vise.

Daniel, like so many of Lumet's films, was admired by the connoisseurs but didn't do much business at the multiplexes. This wasn't surprising. What he served up was a convoluted chunk of history without much in the way of entertainment. It wouldn't have been right to have an entertainment element in it but anyone in the business of making films needed to return a profit to stay afloat. The worry with Lumet was that he would make one too many labors of love for comfort.

He worried about the plethora of films being produced that hadn't any psychological stimulation. Too many of them appealed to the lowest common denominator of public taste without having any other ingredients. "The number of pictures out today that don't trust their audience's attention span is amazing," he railed. "Every seven seconds there's a cut." No wonder so many people suffered from ADHD. They had their reactions shredded by non-stop action and poor characterization.[61] But he couldn't go on making films like *Daniel* if he wanted to keep pace with movie "brats" like Martin Scorsese and Francis Ford Coppola. This new breed of directors, and their "indie" counterparts, were crafting films that made Lumet look too heavy-handed, too conventional. He knew he needed to cut loose with a project that would have a more instant appeal. Joe Hoberman wrote: "After the Talmudic weightiness of his 'What Is the Law?' trilogy—*Prince of the City*, *The Verdict* and *Daniel*—he was ready for a schmaltz break."[62]

That came in the form of *Garbo Talks*. It was an antidote to *Daniel* in the same way *Deathtrap* had been an antidote to *Prince of the City*. Estelle (Anne Bancroft) is dying of cancer and has one wish before she dies: She wants to see her idol, Greta Garbo. Her son Gilbert (Ron Silver) spares no effort in bringing that about. Gilbert is unhappily married. In the course of the film he falls in love with another woman, Jane (Catherine Hicks).

Carrie Fisher plays his materialistic wife, Lisa. We're told that she speaks two languages, English and Gucci. This line sounds like it came from Woody Allen. It's actually from rookie screenwriter Larry Grusin. If the film had more of these, it might have had a better chance at box office success.

In a film like this, almost everyone has to be endearing to make it work. Most of the cast—Dorothy Loudon, Harvey Fierstein, Hermione Gingold, Howard Da Silva and Hicks—play characters who are. The only fly in the ointment is the bitchy Lisa. Within the film's soap-operatic dynamic, she becomes the Wicked Witch who must disappear to make way for Jane's appropriation of Gilbert. She'll console him when Estelle passes on.

Estelle is a woman of strong principles. She missed Gilbert's wedding, for example, because she refused to cross a picket line. She's one of those ebullient Jewish mamas who have become something of a staple in films; it's a pity to see Lumet falling into the stereotype trap with her. Try as she might, Bancroft always seems to sound like someone else. She rants and raves about the trivia of her days while carefully concealing her heart of gold. How could Garbo refuse to see a woman of such vivacity and wit? A woman who can utter lines like, "When your head's in the toilet, don't blow bubbles"?

Not only is she witty and warm, she even looks great. Ali MacGraw holds the record for being the most healthy-looking cancer victim on screen as a result of her performance in *Love Story* but Bancroft runs her a close second here. Whatever she's on could power Manhattan. Silver, by comparison, looks positively anemic.

In a central scene, Garbo visits her in hospital. She doesn't speak, in a kind of joke on the film's title. The scene fails because of Bancroft. She should be more awed by her idol being physically there before her but instead she embarks on a nostalgic speech about her own life. This would have been fine if she showed some excitement at Garbo's arrival but instead she goes straight into her reminiscences. This self-obsession conflicts with the Garbo obsession we've been hearing so much about. She doesn't even sit up in her bed when Garbo enters the room.

This candid was taken on the set of *Garbo Talks*, a gentle film about a terminally ill Jewish mother (Anne Bancroft). Her dying wish is that she meet her idol, Greta Garbo. Her son (Ron Silver) arranges it (Eddie Brandt's Saturday Matinee).

Garbo, obviously, is played by somebody else. The fact that she's shown only from the back was probably necessary—who could they have found to look like her?—but in this crucial scene it means we're not really seeing anything different to her previous appearances from a distance. After the big build-up, there's a sense of "So what?"

If *Garbo Talks* sounds like Woody Allen, it lacks his spirit and verve. Maybe that's due to the fact that at 100 minutes it's about 15 minutes too long. Feel-good films like this, with the central character dying, have an automatic contradiction built into them. Do we laugh or cry? Lumet does his best to keep the tearjerker element in check but it's always there, even in the scenes where Bancroft doesn't appear.

The Jewish element is strong in the film and for most of the time it's amiable. Lumet does his best to keep the tearjerker element in check with scenes like the one where Bancroft takes on some wolf-whistling construction workers. Here as elsewhere, Silver is in her shadow. His unhappy marriage and new romance play out like perfunctory sidebars to her plight. It has some charming scenes but overall one feels that Lumet is working in a genre in which he feels uncomfortable. He tries his best but we feel we're watching a cheeky joke at a party. We laugh more from duty than amusement.

For his next film, he was back on more familiar terrain. *Power* (1986) was a political drama centering on the fall of a public relations spin doctor. It had three A-list stars, Richard Gere, Julie Christie and Gene Hackman. The quality cast was rounded off by Kate Capshaw, Denzel Washington, Beatrice Straight and E.G. Marshall.

Gere came to the project on the back of his recent flops *The Cotton Club* (1984) and *King David* (1985). He'd wanted to work for Lumet for some time, as a lot of actors did. When he met him, he said, "Why did you want me for the part?" Lumet was surprised at his modesty. He'd never been asked that by an actor, even those much less famous than Gere. He chose him, he said, because the film was all about appearance: "Richard had that, and also a wonderful technique which suited the part. When an actor is as beautiful as he is, it's difficult to be taken seriously but I felt he'd come through that and was ready for a heavier role."[63]

Christie was another member of the Beautiful Club. She was "the sex object of the '60s, reckless, charming, shy, glamorous and relentlessly pursued by the paparazzi." By the time *Power* came along, she'd become tired of that kind of attention. She was ready for a film that sought to unpack—if not unpick—such a culture. As one commentator remarked, Christie didn't want to be Christie any more.[64]

Lumet on the set of *Power*, the poor man's *Network*. As was the case in that film, he tried to portray the vacuousness of the media but the ploy didn't work within the film's political parameters and it sank without trace (Eddie Brandt's Saturday Matinee).

Wearing a mustache that was presumably designed to make him look slick but which had precisely the opposite effect, Gere played Pete St. John, a PR consultant employed by politicians wishing to inflate their profiles. Christie, his ex-wife, was an investigative reporter with *The Washington Post*. "My job is to get you in," he tells his clients. "Once you're there, you do whatever your conscience tells you to do." The people he generally deals with don't seem to be too troubled by their consciences.

Gere took the part so seriously that he employed a real PR man, Roger Ailes, to help him with it. Ailes had spearheaded the Republican campaigns of the 1980s. Gere sat in on meetings with him now, taking copious notes about the way his clients walked and talked, and even the way they dressed. He noted the way they smoked, the kind of ashtrays they used. This was a Robert De Niro type of preparation, a Method approach unusual for the star. It was a gesture of respect for Lumet that he was putting so much into it. Ailes thought Gere would have made a great politician if not a PR guru—at least for 20 minutes anyway. "Then, like me, he'd want to deck somebody."[65]

Maybe that was the problem with the film. One couldn't swallow Gere whole. For all his dedication, you felt this was a man playing at being a medical consultant rather than being one. His immersion in the role didn't go any further than the time it took him to play it.

Power is like *Network* without the human interest factor. It sinks under the weight of techno-fuzz. From early on we get the message: Gere is in over his head in it and Christie is equally vapid. Hackman tries to inject some vitality into the proceedings with his world-weary humor but a supporting player can't carry a film. An air of empty gloss surrounds it just as it surrounds Gere. It's all dressed up with nowhere to go.

How could it have failed so badly with its gilt-edged cast and Lumet at the helm? Maybe for this very reason. It was a case of too many cooks spoiling the broth. It tried to be a satire of a McLuhanesque culture but descended instead into a blob of verbiage and gimmicky camerawork.

Maybe it would have worked better in the hands of someone like Robert Altman. Altman was adept at creating worlds where depersonalization has set in and people wander about looking vaguely bewildered. This wasn't Lumet's forte; he was too much of a dynamo to be interested in stasis, or that kind of existential void where people have everything to live for except a good reason to get up in the morning.

In the same way as Lumet tried to be something he wasn't in *Garbo Talks*, he was equally adrift here. It's boring looking at Gere thinking about Arabian anti-solar policies or governorships of New Mexico. Watching him whizzing about the place in private jets impresses as little as the sight of him playing the drums, in a vague attempt by Lumet to give another dimension to his character. This is as annoying as the jazz score the film employs, which distances us further from the action. The relationship with Christie also fails to take off. Will they get back together? Do we care?

It's easy to see what Lumet is getting at in the film—maybe too easy. "The whole political process has become dehumanized," he claimed, adding, "Even movies look as if they were put together by a polling organization."[66] Maybe that's the problem with *Power*: It has that look too. Richard Combs wrote in *Monthly Film Bulletin*, "As Michael Ritchie's *The Candidate* is there to prove, it's difficult to make a film about the soulless merchandizing of media wizards without the film itself becoming part of the problem."[67] *The Candidate* succeeded because it gave us a succinct verbalization of Robert Redford's "rabbit in the headlights" moment after he becomes elected. "What," he asks bemusedly, "do we do now?" Gere isn't as interesting because he's the puppet master rather than the puppet.

His reformation in the finale doesn't ring true either. His character as presented up to this is that of an amoral film flam man. He's someone who's willing to doctor footage of a New Mexican candidate's clumsiness on a horse to make him look skillful, or even manipulate a terrorist act so that it becomes a photo opportunity for a candidate whom he asks to cradle a victim. Such a person would hardly undergo the Pauline conversion he does. It's as if Lumet is trying to create a Frank Galvin for yuppies.

The elements are there for a moral tale but there are too many of them crowding in upon one another to little avail: the Latin American socialist, the oil sheik, the investment scam in which a Senator's wife becomes embroiled. (She's played by Beatrice Straight, if only to remind us how much the film falls short of *Network*.)

It was said that Richard Nixon lost the 1960 presidential election because of his five o'clock shadow. Gere exhorts his clients to trim down, smarten up and get on their Nautilus machines to avoid such pitfalls. Unfortunately, he leaves out one part of the equation: They have to be credible too. It's not enough to look like one just walked out of the pages of *Esquire* magazine—as he does—to hold the reins of power. If St. John's love of gloss does him down, Lumet's attempt to transmit such a message is equally superficial. Sheila Benson put the failure of the film in a nutshell: "If power is the ultimate aphrodisiac, why is Sidney Lumet's *Power* the sexless diatribe that it is, all high-tech visuals and no emotional grounding?"[68]

Screenwriter David Himmelstein was a former political journalist so he knew the territory, but just as Gere is no Gene Krupa, neither is Himmelstein a Paddy Chayefsky. There are nuggets of well-written dialogue (Kate Capshaw says of a dull gubernatorial candidate on a podium, "If this guy was up there masturbating, his hand would fall asleep") but they're few and far between. Lumet relies too much on Andrzej Bartkowiak's glitzy cinematography to make up for the vacuousness of the characters. The annoying clutter of subplots fail to mask this, as does Gere's bouncing between South America, Washington, Seattle and Santa Fe as if he's on a caffeine high.[69] The point is that Lumet needed to make significant things happen in these places. Otherwise it just becomes movement for its own sake, a kind of relentless posturing.

Despite its problems, the film politicized Gere. Christie had long been involved in human rights campaigns for the underprivileged when she made it, working in Nicaragua, Honduras and El Salvador. During the shoot, she encouraged him to visit Central America to see the suffering caused by American support for the Contras. He did this after the film wrapped and it morphed into his later involvement in human rights issues in Tibet.

For Lumet, it was a case of another experiment that went wrong, but he didn't brood over it. This wasn't in his nature. His attitude was, you win some, you lose some. The important thing was to keep trying, to keep looking for that moment of serendipity, that "happy accident" that could transform base metal to gold. Everyone knew he still had what it took. It was a matter of finding the right vehicle upon which to unleash it.

In 1985, he received the Bill of Rights Award from the American Civil Liberties Union, an acknowledgment of the underlying themes of so many of his films. It came as something of a surprise to him as he never intended to be a flag-waver for any particular cause, merely to show conflict in people who struggled with their better—and worse—natures. To his mind, the fact that so many of these conflicts involved political and/or social issues was after the fact.

That wasn't the way the ACLU saw it. As far as this organization was concerned, Lumet was a crusader just like Frank Serpico and Robert Leuci, a seeker after truth like Daniel Isaacson and Howard Beale. The fact that he used celluloid as his road map towards that truth rather than a pulpit or a political platform didn't diminish it one whit in their eyes.

Maybe it even enhanced it.

To Hollywood—Finally

Lumet never denied that great films could be made in Hollywood; he just felt it was more unlikely that they would be. The hierarchical structure of the place militated against it. From a study of other directors, it seemed to him that they produced lesser work there than elsewhere. "A city that relies on just one industry can lead to catastrophe," he believed.[1] It was also a fact that at the beginning of his career, there were demagogues in Hollywood who had so much power, the very fact of being anywhere near them on a film set depressed him. He knew they could have overruled his instructions to people like the set decorator or the director of photography, and he didn't want that.

New York, in contrast, kept him in touch with people, with the hubbub of life going on. It made him feel real, energized. When the studio system fell apart in the early '60s, it gave him even less of a reason to leave the city he loved. Afterwards his children started to arrive: Amy in 1964 and Jennifer in 1967. As they grew up, they told him they liked living in New York just as much as he did. This was a source of much relief to him. It would have been a problem if they wanted to move. Neither did he want to uproot them from their schools. As time went on, he began to hear more and more horror stories about Hollywood. These convinced him his early misgivings about it must have been accurate.

James Mason believed Lumet had signed a pact with himself never to work in California.[2] This was something of an exaggeration but he thought L.A. had no ferment of creativity. There was nothing there to stimulate people. It was "inorganic."[3] Besides, he didn't like "company towns."[4] It also disappointed him from a filmmaking point of view: "In Hollywood, actors learn to act from watching television. In New York, people learn by walking down the street."[5]

In 1986, however, he broke the habits of a lifetime to make a film there, *The Morning After*. It began with Jane Fonda, an alcoholic actress, waking up next to a man with a knife in his chest, looking very dead. Who was he? Did she kill him? She was so drunk the night before, she couldn't remember.

Lumet liked showing characters at the end of their rope. It made them more human. This was especially important for someone like Fonda, a role model to many people. Lumet wanted to divest her of her image. She thought this would be a kind of liberation. She didn't have to be Jane Fonda in the role. She could be her character, Alex Sternbergen.

Lumet gives directions during the shooting of *The Morning After*, his first foray into Hollywood after a lifetime of excoriating its shortcomings from his preferred New York (Eddie Brandt's Saturday Matinee).

Lumet sympathized with women for the way they were judged on the basis of their appearance, the way they were regarded as sex objects by film directors so often:

> They may be able to bare their breasts and/or bottoms, or both. They know they'll have to lose ten pounds before shooting starts. They may have had collagen pumped into their lips, undergone liposuction to take fat out of their thighs, changed hair color and the shape of their eyebrows, had tucks behind the ears to tighten the skin around their necks. They've been evaluated purely—or rather impurely—on physical terms before a mention had been made of what emotions they might be expected to call up in their performances. And to top it all off, they know that when they hit 40 or 45 there will be fewer and fewer offers.[6]

With *The Morning After*, he hoped to reverse that spiral.

Fonda was nervous taking on the role. "Playing drunk had always frightened me," she admitted. "If there was even a short scene in a movie where I had to be tipsy, I dreaded it."[7] Facing the challenge of doing what she most feared was what impelled her to do the film. It was like a gambler who got a thrill from losing more than they could afford to while having a chance to also win: "That's what you live for, that moment. The crapshoot. If it's easy, what's the point?"[8] There was another reason she did the film: "We got Sidney Lumet to direct."[9]

Fonda's character had once been an actress. She said she modeled her on Gail Russell, who'd been found dead at the age of 36 surrounded by empty whiskey bottles. As part of her research, Fonda hung out in seedy late night bars and attended AA meetings.[10]

Lumet first met her through her father on the set of *Twelve Angry Men*. He tried to get her into a number of his films over the years but didn't succeed until now. He'd also worked with Jeff Bridges' father, Lloyd, during his television days, and with Jeff's brother Beau in *Lovin' Molly* and *Child's Play*, so the present cast was almost like an extended family reunion for him.

For many people, Jane Fonda was much too glamorous to play a down-at-the-heel alcoholic in *The Morning After*. Some thought she looked as if she'd come from the beauty parlor rather than the drunk tank (Jerry Ohlinger).

He could have made the film more dramatic, but his emphasis lay elsewhere. Right from the off, we know he's in an impish mood because the program that's playing on the television as Alex discovers the dead body features the man himself. He's talking about a group of women who are engaged in some Fonda-style work-outs. At this point we're entitled to ask: Is Lumet making a thriller or a comedy? One thing is for sure. Whatever it is, it isn't going to have the depth of *Twelve Angry Men*.

The film descends into farce as Alex removes the knife from the corpse with the line, "I'll just tidy up. You keep on doing whatever you're doing." We now know for sure that Lumet isn't so much celebrating *noir* as upending it. We're in black comedy territory. If you wake up drenched in blood, lying beside a man with a knife in his chest, it's likely you'll scream. What does Alex do? With commendable presence of mind, she phones her hairdresser husband Jacky (Raul Julia).

The marriage is over but they're still in contact with one another. "What happened last night?" she asks. She mentions the dead body almost by-the-way. (Oh yes, perhaps it was the drink. It's well-known that alcoholics frequently plunge knives in their lovers' chests and forget all about it until "the morning after.")

It isn't long before she's using her female charms at an airport to try and wheedle her way onto a flight without a ticket. Somebody is following her. Is it the police? The killer? She runs outside. Who should be fixing his car in the parking lot as she tries to escape her pursuers but Jeff Bridges. He plays a character called Turner, a former policeman. He had to leave the force because of injury and is now doing odd jobs to earn a crust. Maybe one of those "odd" jobs will entail joining Alex in her newfound sleuthing career.

Los Angeles confirmed all of Lumet's prejudices about it during the shoot. "The attitude of the Beverly Hills police was abominable," he complained. "They actually tried to interfere and place obstacles in our way, despite the fact that all our licenses and permits were in order."[11] What he decided to do, with the help of Andrzej Bartkowiak, was turn the city into a kind of Disneyworld. For this reason, the sets looked like something out of a Batman cartoon. Bartkowiak's hues were heightened to such an extent that we felt we were looking at a colorized version of an old movie. Lumet had fun satirizing the city he'd reviled so much in print over the years. We're far from the stink of the New York streets but under L.A.'s Edward Hopper–style glitz lurks an even greater evil.

The artifice extends from the buildings to the characters. Fonda doesn't look like a lush any more than Bridges resembles a disabled ex-cop. In fact, she looks like she just walked out of a health spa. Was Lumet so awed by her diva status that he didn't insist she keep the makeup off? Did she not want to do this herself? Was she afraid to lose a figure that had been gained over so many agonizing hours of aerobics? Casting a keep-fit guru as an alcoholic had about as much chance of success as a man who loved New York moving to L.A. to test himself in its kitschy milieu.

Lumet leaves gaping holes in the plot. Roger Ebert noted that the police should have found the bloody sheets she hides under her sink.[12] More off-putting is her efficiency at cleaning up the murder scene. This would have been difficult enough for a teetotaler. Alex goes at it like Joan Crawford on steroids. Is that a glass of gin in her hand or is it spring water? Has she just come back from the gin mill or the gym?

Fonda tries her best to recreate the Bree Daniels of *Klute* in the film but she seems more like Miss Marple with better hair. Lumet fared better when he turned Hollywood icon Paul Newman into an alcoholic in *The Verdict*. His attempts to portray Fonda as a woman on the edge ends with her insistence on looking glamorous even with hangovers. Neither are matters helped by Bridges riding over the ridge to help her clear her name.

Did Lumet really expect us to buy this amateurish whodunit? It doesn't take a genius to figure out that Jacky is somehow involved in the murkiness. We manage to put this to the back of our mind during Lumet's frequent detours from the main plot as Alex and Turner bond with some would-be amusing dialogue. (Alex: "Can you stay until morning?" Turner: "I live here.")

Bridges' character seems incongruous. He's probably the first redneck bookworm we've ever seen on screen. He's the crumpled hero who turns up in most poorly made thrillers to rescue innocent women on the run from cops and/or robbers, though not usually in the parking lots of airports trying to get their car going without the aid of a key. (The door that doesn't open properly is also *de rigueur* for crumpled heroes in films.)

Sex and death is a potent combination in theory but here the treatment is more Mickey Spillane than Raymond Chandler. Blood is replaced with blandness as Alex starts to unload her past on Turner. She's had some rough years. So has he. The two misfits are a fit for one another as they go in search of the villain of the piece.

For Fonda, this is no retread of *Klute* or *They Shoot Horses, Don't They?* even though the circumstances may suggest such a walk on the wild side. She looks like the most dangerous thing she might get up to on a night out is chipping a nail. This is an L.A. yuppie playing an L.A. drunk. Not even Lumet can bridge that divide. It would have made more sense to have her as a high society lady suffering from amnesia rather than alcoholism. Amnesiacs, after all, can look as good as Fonda does here, and it would have made the plot seem somehow sensible.

Bartkowiak's sets compound the artifice with their multi-shaded buildings and cerulean blue skylines. Where's the Lumet of *Network* or *The Verdict*? All the old subtlety is gone. Instead, as one critic remarked, "He moves the camera like Brian De Palma skulking outside the girls' locker room."[13]

There's a serious story to be told here, but he constantly dilutes it with stilted attempts at humor. His puckishness is evident even in the dialogue. Alex manages to convince Turner that she was a famous actress at one point. "I could have been a contender," she coos. Up until now, he doesn't think he's seen her in anything but like most moviegoers he's been to *On the Waterfront* so he gets the joke.

If we're to give Lumet the benefit of the doubt for this farrago, we could say it was his revenge on Hollywood's moral bankruptcy, a revenge necessitated by watching one too many third-rate thrillers in the past. Throughout it all, Alex seems to be more focused on her divorce from Jacky than the threat of spending her life behind bars—the punitive kind, that is, rather than the liquid ones.

At one point she tells Turner she was once groomed to be "the new Vera Miles." Filmgoers will recall that one of Miles' most well-known roles was in *Psycho*. Is Bridges "the new" Anthony Perkins from that movie? Filmgoers will also remember he was the killer in Richard Marquand's *Jagged Edge*, made just two years previously. Lumet throws a few red herrings at us in this direction but without much conviction. We feel the eventual denouement has to be somewhat more convoluted—and it is. Jacky, in the end, turns out to be behind it all.

There are some effective touches, like the cat that casually washes itself in the studio loft just after Alex discovers the dead body. If we had more of these, it could have held its own as a post–Hitchcock web of intrigue instead of a ho-hum love story with one too many dangling threads.

It's surprising Fonda earned an Oscar nomination for her performance. One imagines this was because of her being cast against type rather than anything sensational in her acting. Actors playing alcoholics usually do well on Oscar night even when they're below par. They have more to work with when they have a glass in their hand, even if we suspect—as in this case—that it's something strictly non-alcoholic.

Lumet informed her of her nomination. "She wasn't expecting it," he emphasized. Neither were many other people. Dave Kehr wrote in the *Chicago Tribune*: "She has the best muscle tone of any alcoholic in history."[14]

The Academy of Motion Picture Arts and Sciences gave Lumet a special tribute the following year. It seemed to be an apology for not awarding him an actual Oscar throughout his lengthy career. He was entitled to feel aggrieved but he was too much of a gentleman for that. Instead he embraced the occasion. "What amazed me was how clearly everyone stood out," he enthused of his audience. "It made everything seem so intimate. All nervousness disappeared. A wonderful sense of pleasure and kindness seemed to be spreading up from them." He said he understood the words Sally Field uttered upon her Oscar win (which struck some as cringe-inducing): "You like me, you really do."[15]

He now wanted to film Norman Mailer's novel *The Deer Park* but the deal fell through. It was one of the many near-things of his career. Instead he made *Running on Empty*, a movie about a pair of university radicals who commit a crime and fail to face the consequences. They're played by Judd Hirsch and Christine Lahti. River Phoenix and Jonas Abry play their sons Danny and Harry.

Eighteen years ago, Arthur (Hirsch) and Annie Pope (Lahti) set a factory on fire as a protest against the use of napalm in the Vietnam War. (That chemical was produced in the factory in question.) They didn't intend to harm anyone but a janitor was in the building and he was blinded in the subsequent explosion. Since then, they've been on the run from the FBI, moving from town to town with their children under assumed names.

The script was written by Naomi Foner, better known today as the mother of Jake and Maggie Gyllenhaal. Lumet loved it. It reminded him of *Daniel* in its theme of guilt transferring itself from one generation to the next. He was so enthusiastic about doing it, he took less than his usual salary for it.[16]

The film allied itself to his Old Left principles. The fact that Arthur and Annie are still fighting for their '60s values all those years later, albeit from an incognito standpoint, gave the lie, he believed, to the idea that the hippies of yesteryear were the yuppies of today.[17]

Arthur and Annie are, however, running out of road. Aware of the fact that their

River Phoenix shares a gentle moment with his mother (Christine Lahti) at a birthday party in Lumet's parable of generational guilt, *Running on Empty* **(Jerry Ohlinger).**

picaresque lives can't go on forever, they keep delaying the inevitable. Then one day Danny expresses the wish to become a concert pianist. His love of music has been instilled in him by Annie but now, by a cruel irony, it could be the thing that drives them apart when he's offered a place in a prestigious college. Registering entails filling out official documents. This will mean coming out of the closet, as it were, with the upshot that Arthur and Annie—and of course Harry—will have to go somewhere else without him. Arthur doesn't even like classical music. He calls it "decadent bourgeois crap."

Danny is also falling for the well-to-do daughter of his music teacher, Lorna (Martha Plimpton). He could have a good life with her, he knows, and with his music, were he to reveal his true identity and enter Juilliard, the prestigious college. Annie wants him to do this but Arthur proves a tougher nut to crack. When a fellow fugitive from college is shot, the story moves towards its climax.

Lumet captures the daily goings-on of his underground family with as much naturalism as possible. They do the things we all do, but with the constant fear that every phone call, every knock at the door may mean a midnight flit to a new town where all four will take on new identities. Danny and Harry will attend new schools and Arthur and Annie will try to get new jobs. And so the circle will turn, year in and year out.

What's surprising in such a scenario is the amount of nonchalance Lumet manages to conjure up in the interchanges between the foursome. When movement is the norm, stability becomes the exception. Danny and Harry have become as accustomed to the necessity of change as their parents. They take it in their stride, never blaming Arthur and Annie for the fact that they're the collateral damage of their mistake. Phoenix brings a sense of peace to the role, which means Lumet can document his burgeoning affection for Plimpton in the same laconic manner as everything else in the film. Its most touching scene occurs near the end when Annie meets her father for the first time in 18 years. At first he's hostile to her, telling her that the last time he saw her she called him "an imperialist pig, personally responsible for the war in Vietnam." Lumet leads us to believe he will continue to be intransigent towards her but her tears bring on his own and we realize by the end of the scene that his love for her prevails over the pain she's caused him by her crime.

For all their problems, the Popes are a united family. There's an understandable undercurrent of tension in their exchanges but there's also a goofy side to their behavior that makes all four of them seem like children at times. In this sense, the hippie credentials Arthur and Annie continually espouse have descended into their offspring. It's as natural for Danny to take a day off school because a class photograph is being taken as it would be for another child to go absent because of sickness. He doesn't see himself as a fugitive; merely someone who doesn't live by the rules that govern most other people's lives. The pay-off is that he probably gets more love at home than most other children. Arthur and Annie guard him preciously because they know how easy it would be to lose him. The same goes for Harry.

Having said that, they don't pamper them. This family is neither the Waltons nor the Barretts of Wimpole Street. The Popes are "just folks." They go to baseball games like the people on the next block. The only difference is that the people on the next block continue to live there.

Lumet looks distressed as he tries to work out the best way to direct a scene from *Running on Empty*. River Phoenix, the sensitive teenager around whom the film revolves, listens intently to the old master (Jerry Ohlinger).

As far as their friend Gus (Kit Carson) is concerned, Arthur and Annie have gone soft. He still believes in an armed struggle against the forces of law and order. Lumet doesn't develop his character and perhaps it's just as well because it's really Gus who is the anachronism, not them. His bumper sticker solution to society's problems are as dated in the film's terms as a protest against the long-ended Vietnam War.

In the end, *Running on Empty* is a story about moving on, about the fact that nothing ever really goes away unless we address it. It's also, surprisingly, a story about domestic harmony. Lumet captures the world of the Popes in simple but touching ways, like when they sing that iconic '60s song from James Taylor, "Fire and Rain." And it's a story about sacrifice. Most of the emphasis is on the sacrifice Danny's parents have to make to let him go, but it's a sacrifice for him too if he signs up for the piano college. He's giving them up just as much as they're giving him up.

Lumet took the theme to heart and ran with it—though not "on empty." The "wandering Jew" takes another twist here, embraced as he is into middle grade suburbia. There are no Nazi concentration camps, as in *The Pawnbroker*, or gruesome executions like in *Daniel*. What we get is a debt that takes 18 years to pay. And after that time is up, the payment is really just beginning. "We'll never see him again if he goes," Arthur tells Annie, as if he needed to. But Annie knows the time is ripe for his future to begin. Eighteen years is enough for anyone to spend in an "outdoor" prison.

Lumet never strains after effect and never over-sells his points. He lets the story tell itself. It works itself out in its own time and in its own way. There's a curious mix of tension and laconicism in the Pope household, perhaps born of the sense that these people know all too well each moment in a given community—or any community at all—may be their last. Their deracinated lifestyle has formed them and, in a way, relaxed them. Because, when you think about it, how else should hippies live but on the move? "It's wonderful having a new name every six months," Danny tells his mother in one scene, a line that encompasses the adventurous manner in which Lumet handles an off-kilter tableau. Phoenix plays it just as adventurously. His performance reminds one how much the film world lost by his early death. Penelope Dening called him the "emotional dynamo" that gave the film its high voltage charge.[18]

Lumet was now asked to direct the thriller *Sea of Love*. It would have been another opportunity to work with Al Pacino after the disappointment of losing *Scarface*. He liked elements of the script but generally found it too exploitative. The story, he thought, didn't have enough to do with the people involved in it. "The best melodrama," he maintained, "is when the case you're working on becomes an expression of your character, like Paul Newman in *The Verdict*. I didn't see that there."[19] It was directed by Harold Becker instead. Lumet, meanwhile, turned his attention to *Family Business*. Like *Daniel* and *Running on Empty*, it carried the theme of children paying for the sins of their fathers. This didn't strike Lumet until after he'd finished making it.[20] In this humorous crime caper, Sean Connery, Dustin Hoffman and Matthew Broderick play father, son and grandson—three generations of a family whose "business" is crime.

Jessie (Connery) thinks of it as a great career. Vito (Hoffman) has made a brief foray into it that embarrasses him; he now has a respectable job at a meat factory. He's trying to get his son Adam (Broderick) to stay in college. But Adam is tiring of his studies. His head is turned by Jessie and the exciting world of crime that he represents. Vito allows himself to be sucked back into criminal activity through the persuasion of Jessie.

It was Connery's fifth collab-

Lumet sets up a shot from *Family Business*. Despite its array of talent, it couldn't seem to make up its mind if it was a comedy or a drama (Larry Edmunds Bookshop).

oration with Lumet and the actor was happy to play Hoffman's father even though he was only seven years older than him. This didn't bother Lumet either. (Connery had recently played Harrison Ford's father in *Indiana Jones and the Last Crusade* despite being only 12 years older.) Lumet liked Connery, one of many actors who came back to him time and again. His fellow New York directors Woody Allen and Paul Mazursky also liked working with the same people in different films. They built up a relationship with them that made directing empathetic, even clairvoyant.

Hoffman had wanted to work with Lumet for some time now. He admired his predilection for lengthy rehearsal schedules. "At the start of any film," Hoffman maintained, "there's a kind of barrier separating the actors. The way Sidney works, when you start shooting, you're at a place you wouldn't be in most pictures until you were halfway through them."[21]

Vito was an unusual character for Hoffman to take on but he welcomed that too: "I want people to go into a cinema and not know what I'm going to do."[22] Lumet liked his tendency to question everything. The director didn't see this as being "difficult," a term often used for fastidious actors. "Difficult," for Lumet, was when someone didn't know their job, or had ego, or fluffed their lines, or walked off set. An actor interested in the finer points of a script gladdened Lumet: "My feelings are always that an actor is the one that's up there. If he needs two hours of discussion to get a scene right, have the two hours of discussion. You might learn something."[23]

Connery initially refused his role, feeling it would have been better suited to

Sean Connery telling his screen son Dustin Hoffman how to be a *real* criminal in *Family Business* (Jerry Ohlinger).

someone like Burt Lancaster.[24] He changed after Ann Roth, who did the costume design, had kitted him out. "She's given me the whole bloody character," he gushed.[25] He modeled the character on his grandfather.[26]

In the early scenes, there was a clash in acting styles between Hoffman, a Method actor, and Connery's more straightforward approach. As time went on, with Lumet refereeing, they compromised, matching one another "improvisation for improvisation."[27]

Apart from the age problem, Dustin didn't look anything like Connery. Neither did he have his height. "If he'd had Scottish genes," Connery laughed, "he would have been at least five feet taller."[28] This caused a problem for Lumet. Connery was six four and Hoffman only five six. To align them, and to save him from shooting into (or from) ceilings, he asked Connery to "do a Groucho," i.e., to lower his body so they seemed to be in line with one another.[29] He was happy to oblige, but the discrepancy was still there for all to see. David Edelstein asked, "Who was the mother—Dr. Ruth?"[30]

Connery and Broderick play things broadly, with Hoffman looking for the more sentimental angle. All three are shoehorned by the far-fetched plot and ill-conceived characterizations. The script is also smart-alecky in a way that precludes audience identification. It looks for attention; it's too pleased with itself. It presents us with a culture where crime is a solid career, a mixture of fun and profit. These are "ordinary decent criminals" but they still fail to inspire sympathy.

The film took too long to warm up. We're an hour into it before it justifies its thriller credentials. The "family tree" element also wears out its welcome pretty quickly. Lumet veers uneasily between comedy and farce and seems unhappy in both genres. A director who experimented with styles as much as he did was bound to come a-cropper at times and this is one such occasion. Sometimes he appeared to work better with lesser-known actors than famous ones. In the present venture, the reputations of Connery and Hoffman (if not Broderick) were too established. This made it more difficult for them to morph into their characters. Having two icons in the one cast meant Lumet was struggling with preconceived notions about them. He was also struggling with audience expectation. The film failed on both scores.

Jessie remains "proudly Nietzschean" in his view that the criminal is society's only true free man.[31] In one scene he humiliates Adam's real estate broker girlfriend when she reveals that she buys apartments at cut rates. This is because a friend of hers works in a hospital and gives her the addresses of terminal patients. Knowing they're going to be coming on the market before everyone else enables her to make early bids. Jessie is shocked at her opportunism. Her actions may be legal but to his way of thinking they're immoral. To him, this is a more cowardly form of underhandedness than robbing a bank, because there's no risk in it, or at least no risk of jail.

Elsewhere he says to Adam, in one of the film's funniest lines, "Your father robs the tax man. It's never been easy having a thief in the family." Lumet should have exploited the comedic elements of the film more. Mixing them up with the drama of the film weakened both. Lines like, "There's nothing like a good robbery to bring a family close" lose their bite because of this, as do ones like Jessie's "Anyone who's embarrassed about doing time is a goddamn snob."

Connery gets the best dialogue. Jessie is the most believable character for this reason. Neither Vito nor Adam really look like thieves. They're actors toying with the idea of robbery. Considering the fact that so much money was spent on the cast, it's ironic that it's this that weakens the film. Vito is the real problem. His decision to go back to crime, even if his motive is to preserve his relationship with Adam, doesn't ring true. The chemistry between Adam and Jessie works better. Broderick liked Connery as a person too. In fact, he was in awe of him. Connery seemed to almost expect this.[32]

Adam likes his grandfather because crime is more fun than college. The best time he had with Vito was when Vito made his brief foray into the underworld. For us to believe this, Lumet needed to cast a rougher diamond then the baby-faced Broderick. Though crime is "the family business," it doesn't look like it. This is probably because when we first see Vito, he's going straight. Watching Jessie draw Adam into his lifestyle is a nightmare for him. In one scene he tells Adam, "I broke my ass to give you everything my father never gave me." This makes it all the more unlikely that he would allow himself be enticed to dabble in crime again, thereby endangering everything he'd spent so many years building up.

Connery plays the film for laughs. When Hoffman is funny, it seems almost by accident, as if he's the straight man to him. Broderick looks frozen between the two of them, as perhaps befits his character. All three seem to be making a different film, which suggests that Lumet's rehearsal process didn't produce the dividends it usually did.

With "rat tail hair and sideburns like scimitars," Connery crowns the film, even while he's singing in the bath out of frame. Lumet made a misjudgment in killing him off at the end. He might be older than the other two but he exudes more life than them. "I have some differences with Sidney about how he resolved the end," Connery huffed.[33] He was entitled to them. It wasn't so much a resolution as a cop-out. Jessie has forgotten more about the world of heists than Vito and Adam will ever know. Audiences needed him to outwit the forces of law and order. His survival would have given the film an upbeat ending. But as Lumet often told us, he didn't particularly like happy endings. Maybe he should have made an exception in this instance.

There are two wakes in the film but Lumet doesn't exploit them for a lachrymose effect. This is especially apparent in the second one, conducted for Jessie. He was such a cheery individual, it wouldn't have been right. "Given the opportunity to jerk your tears," wrote one critic, "he takes off his hat and backs out the door apologetically." Here he's at his best, giving us dignity without melodrama.[34]

The film is really about the breakdown of parental influence. Jessie tries to make Vito embrace a life of crime but fails, just as Vito tries to turn Adam away from it. Adam reverts the arc of influence back to his grandfather, thereby seeming to prove the inefficacy of parental control. Hoffman's brief descent into robbery results in him being caught. This makes him a failure for Jessie. His son "disappoints" him by not being able to be a successful career criminal. He tries to make up for that lapse with his grandson but fails. This is hardly surprising.

Broderick needed to be more rakish to convince us he would forego college privileges for escapades that could land him behind bars. He looks more like Hoffman's son than Connery's grandson. This is the film's main failure. He comes across as the preppy kid with the "geeky spectacles and the wimpy sweaters."[35] In *Ferris Bueller's Day Off*, he walked a similar tightrope.

Lumet was aware that *Family Business* had its share of flaws. He knew Hoffman didn't look like Connery's son and that the film went from frivolousness to tragedy too suddenly. After Adam is arrested and Jessie is sent to jail, it changes its tone, thereby confusing its audience. It was "neither fish nor fowl" in Lumet's estimation.[36] No wonder it flopped—though Connery thought people would have gone to it for its curiosity value if nothing else.[37] It would need to have been a massive hit to recoup its budget. The salaries of the three leads alone came to $12 million. It took many years to turn a profit. The critics lined up to tear it to pieces.

Lumet felt he might do better to return to material where he felt more sure of himself. He did that with *Q&A*, another gritty drama. The difference this time was that he came to it with his own screenplay. It brought him back to one of his favorite themes: police corruption. His back-up team included the ubiquitous Andrzej Bartkowiak; Philip Rosenberg, who'd designed ten Lumet films; and producer Burtt Harris, a veteran of nearly 20 Lumet offerings. They were all a part of this latest odyssey into the mean streets of New York.

It was based on a book by Ed Torres, the first Latino judge to work in New York State. Lumet knew he was a "tough mother," the type of man to say to a prisoner he was about to sentence, "Let me tell you, son, your parole officer hasn't been born yet."[38] His book was tough too. Lumet thought it was a devastating portrayal of racism.[39]

An Irish-American policeman (Nick Nolte with a walrus mustache) guns down a smalltime hood in cold blood and makes it look like self-defense. Timothy Hutton is the assistant D.A. looking into what appears to be a case of justifiable homicide. Nolte believes himself to be untouchable. He's a legend in the force because of his no-nonsense style of policing. Clint Eastwood's Dirty Harry is mild compared to this "shoot-first" cop with sociopathic tendencies.[40]

Lumet's familiar cast list of drug kings and drag queens are all present and correct in this grisly parable. It has strong echoes of *Serpico* and *Prince of the City* in its chronicle of a police system that seems to have evil woven into its fabric. Hutton does his best as the investigator zeroing in on Nolte but his performance doesn't have the conviction he showed in *Daniel*.

Lumet relaxing between takes on *Q&A*, another "bent cop" story. The difference this time was that he wrote the script as well, and even found a part in it for his daughter Jennifer (Eddie Brandt's Saturday Matinee).

His big scene comes near the end when he starts breaking windows in frustration that his attempt to bring Nolte down is doomed to failure. But even this falls flat. The film belongs to Nolte. Evil characters usually hold sway over idealistic reformers in films unless they're played by larger-than-life actors or have various shades of light and dark in them. Having said that, Nolte over-acts. He generally does. The film was there to be stolen from him if Hutton was able to give the kind of nuanced performance someone like Henry Fonda might have in a previous era. This is beyond his compass. He becomes too much of a goodie-two-shoes, and no match for Nolte as he shambles about the place like someone with a screw loose.

Lumet's daughter Jennifer appeared in the cast. (By now his other daughter, Amy, had married the acerbic author P.J. O'Rourke.) She'd had smaller roles in *Deathtrap* and *Running on Empty*. Here she plays Hutton's former fiancée. Hutton attempts to re-ignite his relationship with her but now she's with a Puerto Rican drug dealer (Armand Assante). Lumet credited her with enlightening him on many of the problems of racism that were prevalent at the time.[41] Her multi-ethnic background made her an ideal conduit for the treatment of this theme. It's one of the reasons she's parted from Hutton, as emerges in a very interesting scene where she tests him in a subtle manner.

Q&A received positive notices both for Lumet's writing and directing but its familiar plot and limited range meant he was hardly stretched by it. Its virtues were predictable ones. Was he in danger of repeating himself? He hoped not. What had always kept him going was the spark of originality.

He was at a crossroads. He was tired of trying new things that didn't work and equally tired of old things that did. He needed a challenge to prove to the up-and-coming talents that he was still capable of teaching them a thing or two.

He continued to be frustrated by most of the fluff that was being churned out by the major studios. He felt they were always reaching for the lowest common denominator of themes and genres. "It's a very tough time in Hollywood right now," he complained, "because the stakes are so high. The studios are going for safer and safer ground." Nobody could be sure they'd find a project worthy of their talent or, if they did, that it would be followed by another one half as good. Maybe it was always thus; maybe everyone needed a helping hand or a slice of luck. "Even Marlon couldn't do it alone," Lumet reflected. "He would continually pick parts that weren't worthy of him."[42]

He was slated to direct *What Makes Sammy Run*. It had been hibernating as a movie product for over a half century when Warner Bros. bought it from Budd Schulberg. It looked tailor-made for Lumet but it never happened, either due to the fact that his recent films hadn't performed well, or his age-old antipathy towards Hollywood kicked in. Producer Gene Kirkwood suspected the latter. "He's a New Yorker," Kirkwood said. "He never came out here and fought for the picture."[43] It was never made.

Lumet expressed interest in *Malcolm X*. He wanted to make it with Richard Pryor in the lead role but that didn't happen either. It ended up being directed by Spike Lee with Denzel Washington as the title character. Instead Lumet made *A Stranger Among Us*, scripted by Robert J. Avrech. Avrech was adamant that Lumet direct it. He admired the director for his herculean work ethic and the way he sidestepped the traps so many film people fell into when fame came their way. "I wanted a class director," he declared,

Lumet was accused of patronizing the Hasidic community in *A Stranger Among Us*, a film that was part love story, part thriller and part sociological tract. Melanie Griffith played against type as a policewoman going undercover to try and solve a murder before falling for Eric Thal, whose value system differed markedly from hers (Jerry Ohlinger).

"not someone who's made two films and now gets five million dollars because he knows how to work the room at Spago."[44]

Melanie Griffith plays a New York policewoman who goes undercover in a Hasidic community seeking the killer of a diamond dealer. She believes it to be an inside job so she infiltrates the Hasidim to find the perpetrator. In the process, she falls in love with one of its handsome young men, Ariel (Eric Thal). Her own name is Emily Eden. The original title of the film was *Far from Eden*, which transmitted its metaphorical intent.

Emily is a streetwise cop while Ariel is a pure spirit trying to come to grips with the strict codes of his people against her repeated urgings to break away from them. Though Lumet is respectful of the Hasidim and shows their culture in a dignified and celebratory manner, this is still one of his "cop undercover" movies, a kind of feminist *Serpico*. Considering that perspective, it might better have been entitled *A Stranger Among Them*.

Ariel's curiosity about Emily's world of easy sexual virtue conflicts with his own strict codes. He tries to see life from her point of view. At one point he even seems to be willing to abandon his lifestyle for hers, thereby deserting the woman who's been chosen for him by his own people, but deep down one feels this will probably be a bridge too far for him. Emily also has her own man, fellow cop Nick (Jamey Sheridan), but he doesn't play too much of a part in the proceedings after being wounded early on. Her heart lies with Ariel, if not her ideology.

In the middle of all this is the thorny question of who killed the diamond dealer. Lumet doesn't really seem that interested in this aspect of things and wraps it up rather perfunctorily in the last reel. His primary focus is the love story and the exploration of Hasidic customs. He leaves the whodunit part of the film to malinger on the sidelines as Emily and Ariel discuss sex and fulfillment—though not necessarily in that order.

The film was hated at Cannes, where Lumet first screened it, and it isn't hard to see why. The main problem was the uneasy fusion of romance and thriller. It could also have been accused of being part-documentary. The different strands failed to coalesce, which meant that in between enjoying Bartkowiak's lush cinematography, Rosenberg's extravagant sets and Avrech's economical script, we really don't know if we're meant to admire Ariel for his integrity or pity him for all the things they're missing out on in life—like marriage with Emily, for instance. Here's a woman who will entrance you with pillow talk one minute and rub out your worst enemy with her Magnum the next.

The film plays out like a poor man's *Witness*. It's a confusing treatment of primitiveness vs. modernity cloaked in a contrived murder mystery that becomes, like the treatment of the Hasidim, ultimately tokenistic. Neither does Griffith's baby voice help. She comes across as a kind of Marilyn Monroe for the '90s, a woman who tries too hard to satisfy her cold, alcoholic father. (She probably became a policewoman to please him.) She realizes too late that she'd probably prefer to be cuddled up with Ariel instead of keeping New York's streets safe. The fact that she chooses the latter role in the end gives the film a bittersweet edge. It saves it from Mills & Boon convenience, a territory it uneasily inhabits during some of the earlier romantic scenes between Emily and Ariel in which their conflicting mindsets are exemplified in too-broad strokes.

"Women are on a higher spiritual plane than men," we're informed at one point, but they're still the downtrodden "second sex" as far as the Hasidim are concerned. They place them on pedestals not so much to elevate them as to get them out of the way. Emily would threaten this hierarchy were she to marry Ariel so perhaps it's better that he aligns himself to his stage-managed bride in the finale. He can quote the Bible to her to his heart's content without Emily having to remind him of all the erotic pleasures he's missing out on in the pagan boulevards of Brooklyn.

In the end, Cupid's arrows fail to fly in this direction. Emily also rejects Nick's eleventh hour advances, which means that, like a female cowboy (she's referred to as one), she goes back to her lonely hacienda having rooted out the evil in the alien world she inhabited all too briefly. In actual fact, it's Ariel who fires the fatal bullet at the murderer, but only to rescue his sister Leah (Mia Sara), a woman who, like his bride-to-be, harbors no other ambitions in life than to be a wife and mother. "What could be more important?" she asks a bewildered Emily, who's no doubt already thinking of the next murder she'll have to solve with Nick when he gets back to full health. The tough cop is a vulnerable lover but ne'er the twain shall meet, as Lumet makes all too clear in the film's gently philosophical finale.

Another director might have given us a happy-ever-after between Emily and Ariel.

Not Lumet. He suggests she might be Ariel's bride by cleverly concealing the identity of the woman at the altar but then we see Emily standing alone, far away from it all. She is, it should be said, smiling, so it's all good really, her chaste little idyll consigned to her memory banks as duty calls.

As was the case with *The Morning After* and various other films before it, Lumet gave us a strong female character here. He concentrated on this in later films, having started his career with a preponderance of men in central roles. *Twelve Angry Men*, by definition, had this. *Long Day's Journey into Night* had a three-to-one ratio of men to women. Men also figured predominantly in *Fail-Safe, The Pawnbroker, The Hill, Bye Bye Braverman, The Anderson Tapes, Child's Play, The Offence, Serpico, Dog Day Afternoon, Equus, Prince of the City, Deathtrap, The Verdict* and *Power*. There were exceptions, of course, and when women had smaller parts, as in *Network* (Faye Dunaway and Beatrice Straight), they walked off with Oscars for their troubles. Nobody ever accused Lumet of being sexist but a director's early work is often what people look to when seeking to put someone in an easy box. Speaking of the decade in which he made *Twelve Angry Men*, he reflected wryly, "In those days, women could be excused from jury duty simply because they were women."[45]

After *A Stranger Among Us* was released, Griffith came in for a lot of criticism. Many people thought she was miscast but Lumet disagreed. He said he thought she was wonderful in the part and that he would work with her again "tomorrow" if the right script came along. As to whether she looked too sexy to be a policewoman, he said he and his friend Nick Paleggi were having a drink one night and Paleggi told him he knew a policewoman who reminded him so much of Griffith that he thought Lumet had based her on her.[46]

"There are 270,000 cops in this city," Emily says in a scene where, frustrated, she seeks some back-up from her colleagues. "I'm sure you can find the six that I need." She plows a lonely furrow for most of the time and herein lies the film's main weakness: It sacrifices the way normal policing would take place in favor of the dictates of her personal journey. Featuring a strong policewoman was a brave plot device for Lumet but making her the "only" cop in the force, as it sometimes seems, was an unwise move.

Emily needed some support in her investigative work if not her love life. Nick seems about as helpful in this department as Ariel would be if he found himself facing down the barrel of a gun.

Crime and Punishment

Guilty as Sin (1993), another fascinating Lumet thriller, gives the game away in the title but in this story of a man who's arrested on suspicion of killing his wife, we don't really mind.

Early on, we feel David Greenhill (Don Johnson) is probably guilty. He claims she committed suicide by throwing herself off a balcony, having written a letter beforehand claiming he was trying to kill her and sending it to the D.A. Could she be that sick? Or is he sicker? Right from the start, as he sits in court with a smug grin watching defense counselor Jennifer Haines (Rebecca De Mornay) go about her business, we think of him as the "slimy bastard" that Haines' boyfriend Phil (Stephen Lang) suggests he is.

He moves in on Haines pretty soon, not only for her legal services but personally as well, making himself familiar with her colleagues and even with Phil, of whom he's madly jealous. Or is he just mad, period? He later tells Haines he's always been attracted to her. In fact, he killed his wife so she could defend him. If this was indeed the motive behind the murder, it makes her a catalyst. What a fascinating premise for a movie: kill your wife because you fancy a lawyer and want an excuse to meet her. As an early newspaper headline puts it, "Ladykiller Kills Lady." The compulsive womanizer tells Haines in another scene, "God put too many damn attractive women on the Earth." His *modus operandi* seems to be to stalk them, mate with them and then murder them.

Haines eventually realizes Phil is right about Greenhill being slimy rather than slick. She asks to be relieved of the task of defending him but a tough judge prevents her withdrawal from the case, saying too much taxpayer money has been used to get it this far. She's caught in a bind. A man who's threatening her as well as trying to seduce her is her client and there's nothing she can do about it. "Is there anything better than winning?" she crows after an early victory in court, but as Greenhill becomes more of a thorn in her side, she realizes there is: losing. She wants him to be found guilty so she doesn't try as hard to defend him as she might. He notices this. After her closing speech to the jury, he moans, "You've done better." When they're deadlocked, she's distraught. It means another trial. But at least this time, she won't be his attorney. Will she be his corpse?

There are many Lumet staples here: the courtroom scenes, the knotty legal points, the "good friend" played by Jack Warden in a kind of rehash of the role he had in *The Verdict*. The performances are all top-notch. One expected this from De Mornay but Johnson, like many "ordinary" actors who worked for Lumet, steps up a notch for him.

This isn't the Johnson of *Miami Vice* but a man who conveys genuine menace, genuine derangement. In an early scene where he waves a knife around his kitchen in front of Haines, he could be Sharon Stone chopping up ice cubes in *Basic Instinct*. He looks mad here. It's the first time Haines senses this, the first time she tastes real fear.

There are some inconsistencies in the plot that Lumet should have addressed. Why, for instance, doesn't Haines report Greenhill for harassment to get out of having to defend him? That would have ended the tough judge's injunction to proceed. There are other implausible elements, like the manner in which some of the evidence is presented. Lumet admitted he used poetic license in his courtroom dramas going back as far as *Twelve Angry Men* so this doesn't come as a surprise. As Alfred Hitchcock might have said, "It's only a movie, Ingrid."

There are many Hitchcockian touches in *Guilty as Sin*. There are also a few Billy Wilder ones, at least if we think of the Wilder of *Witness for the Prosecution*. In that film, Tyrone Power confessed his guilt to his defense attorney Charles Laughton in an empty courtroom after his acquittal. Here, after a hung jury, Johnson does the same to De Mornay from the witness stand. "The worst thing about committing the perfect

A smiling Lumet on the set of *Guilty as Sin*, a stylish thriller which seemed to signal a change in his view of the legal system since *Twelve Angry Men*. In that film we witnessed a "hanging jury" becoming reformed, but here the world has changed so much guilty people can walk free if they're rich enough to be able to afford manipulative attorneys (Larry Edmunds Bookshop).

murder," he tells her early on, "is that you can't tell anyone about it." But here he does. Her blood freezes, as does ours. When he's finished, she gathers herself together enough to one of the film's great lines: "I have no further questions, the witness may step down."

There are pulp elements in *Guilty as Sin* but they're handled so slickly they're forgivable. As Lumet approached his seventieth year, he showed us he still had the mojo. Not too much had changed since *Twelve Angry Men*. The sets may have become more expansive and he'd moved into color but the same dynamics were at work. As well as presenting us with a Don Johnson we hadn't seen before, he helped De Mornay brilliantly convey the manner in which an accomplished attorney like Haines could allow her judgment to become impaired by the early sexual charge Greenhill held over her—so much so that the mention of other women in his life seemed to make her almost jealous.

His sexual charm works on Haines at this point but at the end of the film she reverts back to the woman she was at the beginning, someone who believes that, yes, there's nothing better than winning. This belief is strengthened when Haines tells her he's now going to see her off too. As he tries to push her to her death from a great height, her fighting spirit comes back. She grits her teeth at him like an animal, dragging him off with her.

The film now descends into drive-in-movie melodrama. The pair of them plunge downwards. Greenhill hits the floor first and breaks her fall so he actually saves her life. Blood gushes out of him as she groans beside him. She looks at the river of blood surrounding him with a mixture of shock and relief. As she's being carted off to an ambulance she tells Phil, "I beat him. Tough way to win a case." It's the first time Lumet has taken his foot off the gas to give us some light relief. Up until now, it's been tension all the way.

The film was mostly shot indoors. Unusually for Lumet, it doesn't really have a sense of place. This is probably because it was shot in Toronto but set in Chicago. Even so, it avoids a sense of claustrophobia. This is largely due to Andrzej Bartkowiak's cinematography. His camera is mostly trained on hi-tech glass structures. If *The Morning After* had its glossiness transmitted horizontally, here vertical structures reign.[1]

The film is most interesting for the complex relationship between the two main leads. As Michael Wilmington wrote in the *Los Angeles Times*, Greenhill is so arrogant, he believes outright confession can't even hurt him: "He's the stud without alibis." But neither is Haines without stain on her character. She does, after all, get evil men off. Their partnership is "a match made in courtroom hell."[2]

Rebecca De Mornay discussing a point with Lumet on the set of *Guilty as Sin*. She plays an attorney who has her confidence shattered by Don Johnson, "a ladykiller who kills ladies" (Eddie Brandt's Saturday Matinee).

Lumet combines elements of romantic comedy with erotic thriller in the film. Sometimes he dumbs himself down to the level of a Saturday night date movie at the local theater. The fact that this is intentional makes it a somewhat less than heinous crime. The one plot fault he can't seem to fix is why Haines, whose confidence is at such an all-time high in the early scenes, doesn't get herself out of defending a man she knows to be a killer. She doesn't want to be disbarred but what was to prevent her simply going sick? Or, as mentioned already, reporting him for harassment? Even if we hadn't seen her in *The Hand That Rocks the Cradle*, playing a character who would have made even David Greenhill wince, we would know she's formidable enough to somehow bring this about. Planting false evidence on Johnson to trap him is an amateurish (if not career-threatening) ruse.

After *Guilty as Sin*, Lumet took a break to write a book about his career. It wasn't very large but there was more meat in it than other books twice its length. As unpretentious and fast-moving as its author, *Making Movies* was a must-read for anyone interested in filmmaking. There were many anecdotes about sound, lighting, camerawork, the eccentric behavior of actors, the demands of studios, the grueling conditions under which he produced some of his greatest work. He took the reader into his confidence as he laid bare all his trade secrets. But it wasn't a kiss-and-tell book. Personal reminiscences were at a minimum. Neither was it a book in which he settled scores with people. Those he fell out with, or who fell out with him, weren't named. Only those he admired greatly—which is most of the people he worked with—were. Roger Ebert gave *Making Movies* due praise when he said, "If you are to read only one book about the steps in the making of a film, make it this one. There is not a boast in it, not a word of idle puffery. It is all about the work."[3]

He was right. The people who expected Lumet to rake up all the dirt about Hollywood Babylon, or his own many trips down the aisle, were sorely disappointed. The title said it all. It did what it said on the tin.

Lumet was never the type to betray confidences or divulge secrets. As far as the public was concerned, his art was his life. Having said that, his personality comes across in the book. It does so through his reflections on what he's spent his life doing, and his attitudes toward the people he worked with. But his main focus is on his craft, the manner in which he achieved so many brilliant effects over the years on limited budgets by his common sense and his flair for cutting corners without compromising his principles.

He appeared on Charlie Rose's TV show to promote it. Asked *why* he wrote it, he said it was out of a sense of frustration with people not understanding his work, especially the students he lectured.[4] So how did he choose his scripts? Often on instinct, he told Rose, making decisions after a first reading. Such instincts weren't always right, it had to be said. On two films he did, he realized on the second day of shooting that they were going to be disasters. By then it was too late to back out. Neither could he tell anyone in the cast that he'd lost faith in them. How could he? He'd picked them![5]

He talked about the way the film business was going, how it was increasingly motivated by money. "If a picture doesn't gross nine figures now, it's regarded as a flop," he contended—nine figures meaning at least $100 million. He said studios would prefer to make one film costing that amount than ten costing $10 million each. He saw the logic of this. It cut down on extraneous expenses. But it meant the industry was moving in a dangerous direction. Such figures were like telephone numbers. He usually worked with more modest budgets. If he had a hit, it enabled him to make three flops after it without being fired.[6]

In general he felt he'd had a charmed career. He'd worked with the best. And when they weren't at their best, he'd tried to get as close to that with them. In some ways, working with great actors placed a huge responsibility on a director, just as working on a great script did: "There's nothing worse than a bad *Hamlet*."[7]

He'd been lucky to have had Pacino when he did. It was at a time before people knew what he was capable of. He had the volcanic energy of Brando. Lumet hadn't got Brando himself in his prime, but he still *got* him. Second-rate Brando was better than no Brando at all. He wasn't easy to work with but Lumet had such awe for him he put that to the back of his mind. When you employed Brando, you employed the whole package.[8]

Henry Tischler, who interviewed Lumet around the same time, thought he looked more like 60 than 71. The director was as bubbly as ever: "His friendly manner and unassuming smile make him seem like the favorite family uncle rather than a high-powered Hollywood film director."[9] Asked why he titled his book *Making Movies*, he said it was because there was a lot of nonsense talked about "film." At the end of the day, it was a mass market medium. That didn't mean it couldn't be art but the motor that drove it was money.[10]

He didn't have any preconceptions when reading a script: "I let it wash over me. I become a blank page." He talked about David Picker, the man who ran United Artists for a time. Picker once said to Lumet, "If over the years I'd said 'Yes' to all the pictures I said 'No' to and 'No' to all the pictures I said 'Yes' to, the results would have been identical." Lumet thought it was a revelatory anecdote. In other words, nobody knew anything, as William Goldman famously asserted. It was all a lottery.[11]

Tischler asked him if there was anyone he would like to have worked with that he hadn't. He cited Michelle Pfeiffer, Robert De Niro, Sissy Spacek, Tom Hanks and Winona Ryder. Where did he see movies going from here? He didn't know. Technology was taking over the industry. The money was frightening ("I believe *The Lion King* will do a billion dollars"). People were also losing their way, becoming swamped under the size of things. There were also too many producers working on films today: "I've seen as many as eight." Things were becoming faceless. We were living with devolved responsibility. Nobody wanted to carry the can any more, or accept the blame for anything that went wrong. They all had different titles: "associate producer, executive producer, line producer, chief producer." When you had that many of them, it meant there was no real job there.[12]

Lumet didn't rush into a new production after he finished promoting his book. He was winding down now so he took a break, to build up enthusiasm for his next project. He liked to give everything to a film. If his energy levels faltered, as they could be expected to at his age, it meant he wouldn't have been able to give of his best.

There was a four-year gap between *Guilty as Sin* and his next film, *Night Falls on Manhattan*, another courtroom drama. Again it explored the vagaries of the law against the backdrop of a love story. It was based on the novel *Tainted Evidence* by Robert Daley (Daley had also written *Prince of the City*).

Andy Garcia played Sean Casey, assistant to the tough District Attorney Morganstern. At the beginning of the film, ruthless Jordan Washington (Shiek Mahmud-Bey) kills two policemen to avoid arrest. Casey's father Liam (Ian Holm) is subsequently shot by Washington during a stakeout. He presents himself to a defense lawyer, Sam Vigoda (Richard Dreyfuss). Peggy (Lena Olin) falls in love with Casey. Lumet cast James Gandolfini in a smaller role. The director saw potential in the future star of *The Sopranos*.

Lumet calls out instructions to his crew during the shooting of *Night Falls on Manhattan*, another police drama that blurred the lines between virtue and vice on "the force" (Eddie Brandt's Saturday Matinee).

Lumet always liked to cast against type. Garcia usually played Latino roles. Here Lumet had him as a black Irishman. He was aware of Garcia's sense of purity before he cast him; it was one of the reasons he did so, apart from the fact that he believed he was one of the best actors of his generation.

Lumet had met the actor at a party. After conversing with him for two hours, he was stunned by the fact that Garcia hadn't used even one four-letter word in all that time. "Are you a religious man?" he asked. Garcia said he was. Lumet was heartened by the fact that his instincts were right. He said he wanted to bring that element of his character into the film.[13]

Holm, who was British, was also surprised at being cast. Lumet had seen him give an "instinctive" performance in *The Madness of King George*.[14] This was probably what swung it for him. Another reason was the fact that he thought that Holm would work well with Garcia. The two of them met in his office one day and Lumet was impressed by the bond they seemed to have.[15] Father-son relationships were always important in his films, going back as far as *Long Day's Journey into Night* and extending into his two "generational guilt" films, *Daniel* and *Running on Empty*.

Ron Leibman, who played Morganstern, was married to actress Jessica Walter, whom Lumet had worked with in *The Group* and *Bye Bye Braverman*. He ran into them two years before shooting began in a restaurant in East Hampton. "I have a part for you," he told Leibman on that occasion. Leibman knew he was a man of his word but after the two years had elapsed he was beginning to wonder. Then the phone rang. It was Lumet, calling to tell him about *Night Falls on Manhattan*. That was how far he looked ahead.[16]

When Leibman was asked how he prepared for the role, he replied, "By living in New York all my life!" He was impressed by Lumet's concern for him on the set. There was one scene where he had to jump up on a table and give a speech. He was trying hard to prepare himself for it but not having much success. Lumet was at the other end of the room, some distance away, but he sensed Leibman's discomfiture. The cameras were ready to roll but Lumet didn't shout "Action!" Instead he yelled up to Leibman, "Just tell me when you're ready." Leibman was amazed at the fact that he knew he was having a problem. "That's not just respect," he said. "That's intelligence."[17]

Lumet cast Dreyfuss for his sense of confidence, a quality necessary for defending a man like Washington with so much damning evidence against him. Dreyfuss liked the way Lumet worked, staying in the background without asserting himself too much, just putting in a word here and there as he saw fit.[18] He also liked his unique style of filming. Lumet panned his camera around the courtroom instead of cutting from shot to shot, preferring the continuity that afforded. "It's like a visual metronome," he said. He knew he might have to use cuts at some stage—as when a prosecutor was questioning a witness—and he preferred to keep the "luxury" until then. "It's like fuel that you might need later on," he claimed, "so you don't use it up."[19]

It was Mahmud-Bey's first film. It took him a while to get into the part but when he did, Lumet found him ideal for the role. The way he grew into it demonstrated once again the importance of rehearsals. As the film went on, Mahmud-Bey developed an expression of arrogance. This was what Lumet was looking for. He wanted "no hint of vulnerability." He loved the casual way Mahmud-Bey moved, like a lion prancing around a jungle.[20]

Lumet didn't balk at the fact that he was black. Everyone knew villains came in all colors. To insist on him being white would have been a kind of inverse racism, a pandering to the clichéd image prevalent at the time both in British and American films of "the marvelous colored man."[21] In some ways his color helped Vigoda in his defense. Like the lawyers defending O.J. Simpson, he could now play "the black card."

As well as assembling the best cast he could, Lumet chose the extras for the courtroom scenes with great care. He liked his final choice, feeling they gave the film "specificity." All types were represented here: "slobs, shyster lawyers, people whose clothes didn't fit." New York extras belonged to the Screen Actors Guild and Lumet gave them all the respect that engendered.[22]

There was one plot flaw. Why did Washington turn himself in after committing such a horrendous crime? Lumet said it was because he was afraid of being killed by some "street punk." That didn't seem in-character. Even if we accept it, the scene of him turning himself in should have been shown. It was a highly dramatic point of the film and it was glossed over, something Lumet didn't seem willing to accept.[23]

Lumet could never have been accused of prudery but he didn't have any sex scenes in the film, even after Sean and Peggy move in together. He never liked what he called "humping" scenes because he didn't believe they looked authentic.[24] He got around it with Garcia and Olin by showing them having breakfast. This was like a throwback to a pre–liberal era where censorship ruled—except here it was Lumet's choice, not that of the Production Code. He'd done something similar in *Guilty as Sin* when Rebecca De Mornay and Stephen Lang went to bed. We only see them the morning after. Is Lumet's reticence here because he thought sex scenes looked false in films or was it a result of shyness on his part? Sex scenes are very infrequent in his work. When they occur, like in *The Pawnbroker* or *Network*, it's only when they're absolutely endemic to the plot. Perhaps he had more of Andy Garcia's austerity than he thought.

Garcia found it a productive learning experience working with him. "He deals in very simple lines," he said. Dreyfuss added, "He knows how to seduce an actor rather than to beat him up."[25] Both of these stars had worked with impolite directors in their time. They appreciated the relaxed atmosphere of a Lumet set. Every problem was listened to and every suggestion addressed.

Neither was Lumet afraid to praise his actors. What he liked most about Garcia was the way he built up intensity from the inside and then let it out. He could be fiery when he wanted. Then there was his gentle side. He showed this mainly in his scenes with Olin. It was also evident when he visited Morganstern in hospital, and his father after he'd been shot. He did something Lumet liked in this scene, burying his head at Holm's bed to show his devastation. This gesture wasn't in the script. "Some people might have felt he left it there too long," Lumet remarked, but he didn't. For him it worked beautifully.[26]

Sean Casey was another one of Lumet's "tarnished princes." He makes moral compromises but they're not major ones. Lumet seems to be saying that in some instances, the end justifies the means. He's not as compromised as *Prince of the City*'s Daniel Ciello but neither is he a Henry Fonda figure. He knows there are corrupt policemen protecting Harlem dope dealers, that corners are sometimes cut in catching criminals. But like Frank Serpico, he's still a "good cop."

Lumet praised the film's set designer Philip Rosenberg for a scene that takes place near the end. Holm, Garcia and Gandolfini are in Holm's house. Rosenberg modeled it on a house he visited with Lumet some time before. A retired policeman lived there. As soon as he went in the door, he knew this was the kind of place where Holm would have lived: the cheap throw on the sofa, the terrible material on the chairs, the inevitable commemorative plaque of John F. Kennedy that was in almost every Catholic home of the time. He nodded at Lumet when he went in. Lumet knew exactly what he meant: They'd found their final location. This cop had obviously never taken an illegal dime in his life.[27]

Lumet liked Holm's work in the film. Apart from his general performance, he was impressed with his accent. It wasn't just New York; it was New York Queens. Lumet feared he might lapse back into his British one in the final scene where there's a lot of shouting. That sometimes happened with actors during moments of high drama, but it didn't here. Lumet gave Holm the credit for this rather than himself: "People say I get great performances from actors. That's because I get great actors."[28] Of course it wasn't as simple as that. If it was, the people who performed well in his films would have done equally well in their other work. That wasn't the case with a lot of them.

He didn't know how to end the film. Would Sean Casey walk away from the force in disgust? That would have been too depressing. Would he set up a legal practice with Peggy? Lumet thought not. It would have been too "happy ever after." Lumet's solution was somewhere in the middle. He decided to end it as it began, in the building where Casey started his training. He's now training others. He tells them, "If you're not willing to take risks, get out." Lumet loved that line.[29]

Casey's decision to stay with an imperfect system puts him more in the tradition of *Prince of the City* than *Serpico*. He's become a realist. It would have been clichéd for him to leave like a cowboy leaving a corrupt town in another genre—the Gary Cooper of *High Noon*. Lumet wants him to stay, to tough it out like his father did. He'll be as good at being a district attorney as he was at being a cop. Nobody says to him, as they said to Danny Ciello at the end of *Prince of the City*, "I don't think I have anything to learn from you." Because they know they have. He's at the coalface of crime but he's not undercover. What you see is what you get, a man going about his job, immersing himself in the grime and trying not to become a part of it.

Lumet was proud of *Night Falls on Manhattan*. One of the reasons he wanted to make it was to frustrate people who thought he was finished with this type of film. When he made *Q&A*, a critic wrote, "This completes the Sidney Lumet trilogy of New York police stories that also contains *Serpico* and *Prince of the City*." Lumet wondered what gave anyone the right to presume such a trilogy existed. The three films had similarities on some levels but they weren't part of a trilogy. They were three separate films with separate emphases. Now he was making a fourth "Sidney Lumet police story." What would that critic have said now? What does one call a trilogy with four films in it? Definitions, for Lumet, were damaging to his vision. They put limitations on it. Critics who wrote like this tried to second-guess directors. They were unhelpful because they put limits on what someone might do in the future. Lumet was upset that everything had to be boxed in by some writers. For him, *Night Falls on Manhattan* was just another film. It wasn't part of anything but itself. If somebody wanted to call it the fourth part of a trilogy, well and good. As far as he was concerned, "I hope I have a fifth and a sixth [one]. It's an endlessly interesting subject."[30]

By now, as John Anderson noted in *Newsday*, the "Zola of cinematic New York" had all but accepted corruption as the norm and the triumph of goodness as near miraculous.[31] In such circumstances, the judicial system was in a post–O.J. Simpson media landscape.[32] Dreyfuss had been cast as a kind of celebrity lawyer in the Alan Dershowitz–William Kunstler mold. He was someone who could make money talk and bullshit walk. Villains ruled the roost. The "good guys," meanwhile, hovered between life and death after being wounded in stakeouts, like Liam Casey, or maybe they suffered heart attacks and sat in wheelchairs, like Morganstern. Which isn't to say Casey or Morganstern were angels. They made compromises, even if their intentions were basically honorable.

The film was a pleasant working experience for all concerned. Garcia praised Lumet's preciseness, his instincts, his professionalism. He thought it was a pity he wasn't making three films a year like he used to. So did Lumet. Asked what would happen if he became too old to work, he said he found this prospect too horrible to even contemplate.[33]

The sad fact of aging was central to his next film, *Critical Care*. It was another radical departure for Lumet, being a satire of the health system.

James Spader played Werner Ernst, a doctor who's keeping an old man in a vegetative condition on a life support machine. His two daughters, meanwhile, contemplate their forthcoming inheritance from his sizable fortune. Felicia (Kyra Sedgwick) stands to inherit it if he dies immediately. Connie (Margo Martindale) will get the money if he survives a little longer. Each denies they're after his estate. They insist they're motivated by concern for his wellbeing rather than their bank balance. Ernst's focus is on the welfare of the patient himself. His attempts to help him are frustrated by the greed of the two women and also that of the alcoholic head consultant of the hospital, Dr. Butz (Albert Brooks). Helen Mirren plays Stella, a kindly intensive care nurse.

This is a world of *Future Shock*, a world where state-of-the art technology keeps terminally ill patients alive. They're treated as dollar signs. Computers replace bedside manners. The key item of interest is where inheritances go after "the loved ones" shuffle off their mortal coils.

The tagline said, "At Memorial Hospital no one ever dies ... until their insurance runs out." Lumet explores a world where people's purses are more important to the medical establishment than their pulses. It returns him to the compromised culture of *The Verdict*. Here, though, the tone is more satirical than impassioned.

With a little more imagination—or insanity—this could have been up there with *Coma* and *The Loved One*. Unfortunately, Spader plays it too straight. We needed a scene where he lets loose, a scene where he tells us, like Howard Beale, that he's as mad as hell and isn't going to take it any more. That scene never comes, even in the finale where, like Solomon in the Bible, he devises a plan to see both women share the inheritance. This is too prosaic by far.

The closest to hysteria we get is when Felicia goes through her meltdown, but even this is fabricated. When she tells us she can't stand the pain of watching her father in his vegetative state, what she means is she isn't able to take that he might live a little too long and deny her the money Connie is also claiming. In the end, it turns out they're only half-sisters, reminding us of the half-brother situation affecting the inheritance in *The Last of the Mobile Hot Shots*.

In the middle of the movie, Ernst becomes involved in a sexual relationship with Felicia. She films the pair of them cavorting on a bed, Lumet panning to the blinking red light of the camera much as he panned to the face of Charlotte Rampling in James Mason's office in *The Verdict*. Here's another traitor. She bribes Ernst, threatening to destroy his career by exposing the film unless he does what she wants with her father.

Under Butz's instructions, he keeps the old man alive. A gastrostomy is discussed. This prolongs his life by having him fed through a tube. Connie wants it. Felicia doesn't. They both employ high-priced lawyers who threaten to sue the hospital if their wishes aren't adhered to. The hospital will be sued by Connie's lawyers if it "yanks his tubes" and by Felicia's ones if it performs the gastrostomy.

Ernst is caught in the middle of all this. He represents the voice of reason in a mad world. But it would have been better for the film if he was a little mad himself. Butz tries to be, with his Coca-Cola glasses and his Groucho Marx mustache. He chomps on a cigar and says things like, "Next time his heart stops, let's kiss his ass goodbye."

In this faceless world, only Ernst and Stella—or the divine nun played briefly by Anne Bancroft—are humane. We wait for the moment when everything blows up but the film ends tamely, failing to deliver on its dystopian premise. In the last scene, a young boy on roller skates has an accident and Ernst runs to his aid. As he does so, Butz yells out of a car, "Make sure he's got insurance!" The boy says to Ernst, "Are you a doctor?" He has to think for a moment before he replies, "Yeah."

It isn't a bad film but it would have been much better if Lumet added more drama to it. He fought against it being a TV movie but it has the look of one. There are very few outdoor shots. It looks like it was made on a shoestring.

It isn't just a satire of the medical profession because Felicia and Connie are as mercenary as Butz. It's a broadside against greed in general. Its polemical overtones are too obvious in lines like Stella's, "I have seen the enemy and he is us." Do people speak like this in real life? Especially people involved in life-and-death situations on a daily basis? There's too much of an acceptance of the evil surrounding them by Ernst and Stella. They're the conscience of the film but evil plays better, especially when it's being essayed by someone like Brooks in his Mad Scientist persona.

The subsidiary characters (the cancer victim who wants to die, the woman who answers "Eisenhower" to every question) could have been fleshed out more. Lumet prefers to concentrate on the tug-of-cash situation between Felicia and Connie, and on the slick lawyers who officiate over such matters, protecting their backs. He tries to give us a more corrosive spin on Arthur Hiller's *The Hospital*—which was scripted by Paddy Chayefsky—with mixed results. His barbs are pungent, to be sure, and lines like Ernst's "I have lettuce in my refrigerator with a better chance of becoming conscious than this guy" hit the mark for a society that has replaced Obamacare with Trump Non Care, but sometimes it's too obvious in its intentions. Satire is always better when it's subtle.

Lumet's concern about corruption in the health services, which was a theme almost as dear to his heart as corruption in the police force, reached its nadir here. He was asked in an interview if he was cynical about doctors. In his youth, he replied, they were kind figures making house calls but now it was all different:

> They're not saviors any more. Recently my son-in-law's sister had a terrible accident. She busted four ribs and suffered head contusions. She was in intensive care for six days but was discharged without a neurological examination. She had to go back to the hospital because she suffered headaches. Every once in a while she started talking gibberish. Episodes like that show our system is in the toilet. I think people get a lot of their reality about television from *E.R.* They get an abrupt awakening when something goes wrong with them.[34]

His sentiments were heartfelt but *Critical Care* didn't fare well either with the critics or the public. It had its adherents but at the end of the day it simply wasn't powerful enough. The fact that it fizzled out at the end was largely due to Spader's flat performance. If he was any more laid back, he would have been horizontal.

Lumet wondered what he might do next. One thing was for sure, he wasn't going to retire: "They're going to have to carry me out," he growled.[35] In 2005, he received a Lifetime Achievement Award. "When you get to my age," he joked, "you're revered, like a building." He didn't let it go to his head. It was being given to him, he said, simply because he'd survived.[36]

Elia Kazan also received an Honorary Oscar that year. He was 89. It was 47 years since he'd named names to HUAC but most people remembered that. Abraham Polonsky, one of the directors whose career plummeted as a result of his testimony, said he hoped somebody shot him.[37] Some people applauded him as he took the award but others didn't. It was presented to him by Martin Scorsese and Robert De Niro. Lumet remarked on how awkward everyone looked. Scorsese and De Niro, he thought, were trying to hide behind him. He thought Kazan himself looked senile.[38]

Kazan became famous before Lumet but many people saw Lumet as his heir. Lumet thought Kazan was better at getting the neurosis out of people than he was.[39] He didn't know how he felt about his HUAC actions. How could anyone say how they would behave if put in his position? Kazan was one of the busiest directors in Hollywood in the '50s. It was a lot to give up if he stayed silent. Lumet knew the feeling. He'd been hauled before the committee once. Luckily, they'd mistaken him for someone else. What if it was him they were looking for? Would he have ratted on his friends? He hoped not. On the day of his questioning, he remembered, he behaved well. "On another day, who knows? I might have crawled."[40] His honesty in admitting the possibility was commendable.

Lumet embarked on *Gloria*, a remake of a 1980 John Cassavetes film which starred Cassavetes' wife Gena Rowlands. She played a mobster's ex-mistress trying to avoid the clutches of a gang of Mafia hoods. She's accompanied by a young boy whose parents were murdered by the hoods. They need to catch him because he has a disc containing information about their operations that would incriminate them if it came to the attention of the law. In Lumet's remake, Sharon Stone took on the Rowlands role. She played it well but the film was stolen by Jean-Luke Figueroa as Nicky, the young boy.

"This is one tough-talking broad," Stone said of her character. Her co-star was no slouch in that department either. Even though he was only six years old, he was "a total wiseguy."[41]

Stone wasn't regarded as being in the same class as Rowlands. Figueroa earned the most praise from the critics. Lumet thought she deserved a large part of the credit for

Lumet getting a shot ready for *Gloria*, the film in which he gave Sharon Stone a chance to do a gangster's moll turned surrogate mother (Larry Edmunds Bookshop).

this: "She got the performance out of the kid because of her bond with him." She never patronized him, treating him like an equal. She also had a lot of fun with him. When he wanted to do a particular scene again, she said, "We can't without more pay and more chocolate—more pay for him and more chocolate for me!"[42]

When we first meet Stone's character, she's just done time for her mobster boyfriend for an offense he committed. She expects him to pay her for this. When he doesn't cough up, she runs off with the boy—and the disc. This is Stone as we've never seen her before, "owning" a film without using seduction or leg-crossing maneuvers at police interrogations. The closest we get to the sex-soaked overtones of her screen past is when Nicky says to her, "I like sleeping with you." She gives him an ambiguous look and replies, "You're not the first person to tell me that." Lumet allows her this in-joke as an indulgence. Elsewhere he focuses more on her maternal instincts as she effectively adopts Nicky during their flight from the hoods.

As was the case with *Family Business* and many of Lumet's other crime films—even *Dog Day Afternoon*—he treads a delicate line between thriller and comedy here. Sometimes he over-steps the mark. This is the case in an early scene where Gloria pulls a gun on the villains. She orders them to take off their clothes before making her getaway with Nicky. It's difficult to imagine ruthless killers being forced into this humiliation by Hollywood's iconic sex symbol.

Thereafter she goes on the run with the little tyke. One doesn't have to be a genius to predict this will turn into one of those bonding parables where an unlikely relationship develops between the moll who's seen it all and the child who's about to. Lumet's winning card is the fact that he doesn't play it cute. Nicky helps him achieve this in a number of ways. For starters, he's Puerto Rican rather than American. When he says things to Gloria like, "You talk too much," it works. In some ways he's as streetwise as she is. When she snaps back at him, "You're the only kid I ever met who makes a big deal out of breathing"—he suffers from asthma—we could be forgiven for imagining we're listening to a bickering married couple.

This Sharon doesn't have a heart of Stone. Is she any more credible on that score? Maybe if she made *Gloria* before *Basic Instinct*, it would have been easier to accept her in this mode. Her interpretation of the part owed a lot to Rowlands in the original. That film wasn't liked much. For Jack Mathews, the remake was a case of "ham imitating ham."[43] This was unfair. Stone built on the confidence she'd gained from films like *Casino*—not everyone could act opposite Robert De Niro, at least at that time, without looking like a hole on the screen—to make the film her own.

Which isn't to say it didn't have faults. It was saccharine. It was derivative. It was *faux*-tough. And Stone's "dese," "dem" and "doze" delivery rankled at times.[44]

But the performances were good enough to make you forget such things. The dialogue was also above par as it chronicled her journey from crime to redemption. "Every time I should have made a right," she tells us, "I made a left." Her time with Nicky is definitely a right.

In the end, we know that when it comes to a toss-up between handing her young ward over to a posh school or keeping her with him in her rundown pad in Florida, there's only going to be one outcome. Lumet negotiates it without too much schmaltz. All in all, it's a successful experiment, even if the villains are Runyonesque.

Stone appears in almost every scene. Many of them have her running through streets in a skirt so tight it's hardly designed for the purpose. But, being Stone, those legs—which appear at times to go up to her shoulders—have to be shown.

The film provided a small role for George C. Scott. (He had refused Lumet's earlier offer to appear in *Network*. Lumet had taken this personally at the time, feeling he hadn't wanted to work with him. He now knew that to be untrue.) He played an Irish-American gangster with romantic ties to Gloria. Lumet emphasized his sentimental side rather than his threatening one. He was in poor health when he made the film and spends more of his screen time sitting down. At one point, he stands but leans against Stone for support.[45] But he still exudes power in the role. The flesh may be weak but the spirit is willing. His face shows a lifetime of longing and under-expressed pain.

Final Surge

The new millennium dawned. Was there anything left for Lumet to do? Any other mountain to climb? He'd never sat idle but he was in his mid-seventies now. He couldn't expect too many more offers to come his way no matter how good he was. Film was a transient industry. There were too many new kids on the block. Apart from everything else, there were insurance issues to be considered. If he was on a multi-million dollar set, even though he was in good health for his age, production heads would be nervous.

He didn't wait for the phone to ring. Instead he went back to the medium where he made his name, directing the NBC-TV series *100 Center Street*. It aired in 2001. The material was familiar to him: a courtroom drama. It was little surprise, then, that he didn't only direct it but was also the writer, creator and executive producer.

He had a reliable leading actor in Alan Arkin. Arkin played Joe Rifkind, a kindly judge who sometimes erred on the side of leniency. This suggested a shift in Lumet's orientation since the days of *Twelve Angry Men*. "Let 'Em Go Joe" adopts his kid gloves approach to sentencing.

The title of the series was the address of the criminal division of New York's Supreme Court. La Tanya Richardson played Judge Sims, a lesbian African-American. Bobby Cannavale—he would marry Lumet's daughter Jennifer in 1994—was an assistant D.A. So were Joel de la Fuente and Joseph Lyle Taylor. Paula Devicq played attorney Cynthia Bennington. Manny Perez was Legal Aid attorney Roman Rodriguez. Michole White was another one, Fatima Kelly. Many episodes dealt with the personal lives of these people. Ramon is unfaithful to his wife; Fatima becomes a drug addict; Cynthia has a romance with Bobby Esposito, the assistant D.A. played by Taylor.

On the other side of the law, there were a motley crew of characters from New York's seamy side: the pimps, prostitutes and drug dealers that formed the supporting players of so many of Lumet's past crime dramas. Here they were featured in more downbeat mode.

He wrote and directed the pilot as well as two further episodes. They were replete with his trademark sensitivity. He worked hard at making them look authentic. "What I hope happens," he said, "is that the dilemmas will be so real, people will realize that what gets lost in the separation of law and justice is our humanity. Each one of us loses."[1]

Executive producer David Black spoke more bluntly about the series' kitchen sink overtones. "You don't need a life-and-death situation," he asserted. "The issue about keeping your job is more important than a dead body. Somebody working a double shift to support his family is the real hero."[2] Black's comments reminded us of Lumet's work in *Danger* and all the other series he helmed as a rookie. He was back to micromanaging. The difference now was that he had a lifetime of experience to draw from for his scenarios.

The first episode ran for two hours. Subsequent ones were an hour each. As well as drama, there was romance and humor. The productions were slick. Technology had advanced hugely since Lumet's early days and he was happy to avail of its blandishments.

Despite his age, he was as alert as ever. "At one point," Arkin recalled, "he asked that they put me on a quareter-foot riser. By mistake they gave me a half-foot one. I decided not to say anything to see if he'd notice. Sure enough, as we're shooting, I hear him say, 'Hey, what have you got him on?' He has more energy at 75 than I had at 30."[3]

Arkin didn't need much persuasion to take the part after he learned who the director was: "When I heard his name, I just jumped."[4] Neither did Devicq. She wasn't a great fan of television "but with Sidney Lumet I'd have gone to Siberia."[5] Lumet didn't express any surprise at being back on the small screen. "I always felt I never left it," he claimed. "I felt it left me."[6]

In one episode, a drug addict rolls onto a courtroom floor as a bailiff tries to prevent her from swallowing her tongue. When she bites him, he curses her, fearing she might have AIDS. "I hate this job," he fumes. The episode was typical of the gritty nature of the series. Some viewers felt it was unworthy of Lumet, that he was doing it merely to have somewhere to go in the morning, but he vehemently disagreed. "I never did a job from hunger," he said.[7]

He believed the series had a lot to say about the lives of those who either didn't have chances in life or blew them. That might sound like routine fare but he put his indelible stamp on it to make it resonate. It was far superior to most of the dross that was being served up as entertainment for those coming home from work on a Monday evening who didn't want to watch the ballgames. Even when the plots didn't intrigue, one was always aware of a professional behind the camera. If Lumet wasn't seen as having the golden touch, Howard Rosenberg remarked, "Someone is color blind."[8]

Some of the episodes had *longueurs* but when they were imaginative—for example, the one where a Vietnamese man held the courtroom hostage in a ploy to "try" the soldiers who massacred his village—they gripped audiences. Overseeing them all was Arkin, garlanding them with his "innate *menschiness*."[9] Neither were the scripts all grim. Lumet insisted on a fair dollop of humor to be threaded through them. In one episode, a character expresses disapproval of a colleague's hairdo with the line, "I wouldn't mind issuing a warrant for your barber."[10]

The series ran for two seasons. The reviews weren't exactly ecstatic but they were usually favorable. It was shot in high definition video, resulting in a Golden Laurel award from the PGA for New Technology. Lumet was proud of it. In general, it reminded him of his fledgling days. A lot of water had passed under the bridge since then but in some ways nothing had changed. Whether one was working on the small screen or the big one, human stories were the same. The budget for television may have been smaller but that didn't mean the work had to be of a lesser quality. He'd never been snobbish about "the boob tube" and he certainly wasn't going to start now.

A subsidiary benefit of the series was the fact that it got him believing in himself again. A man couldn't live on his memories. No matter how many classics he'd made, he always felt a director was only as good as his next gig. You had to keep doing it to prove you still *could* do it.

After the series ran its course, he tackled the TV film *Strip Search* in 2004. It aired on HBO. Coming not too long after 9/11, it explored the controversial issue of intrusiveness into people's lives for security reasons in the aftermath of that tragedy. But didactic films rarely work. The plot, if such it could be called, seemed contrived.

In China, American student Linda Sikes (Maggie Gyllenhaal) is interrogated by a man called Liu Tsung-Yuan (Ken Leung). In New York, Arab student Sharif Bin Said (Bruno Lastra) is questioned by FBI agent Karen Moore (Glenn Close). The two episodes mirror one another almost to the word. It's easy to see what Lumet is getting at but the film was too obvious, too polemical. There were no nuances, just the repetition of twin scenarios that fell flat. After the horrors of 9/11, we deserved a more substantial treatment of an issue that angered Lumet intensely: the withdrawal of civil liberties in a time of political tension and the presumption of a person's guilt until they were proved innocent. Here the interrogator's intimidation of their quarries was old hat; we'd seen it done more effectively in dozens of films before this.

The bewildered pleading of the detainees also left something to be desired. Kafkaesque lines like, "You are not charged with anything" had potential but they weren't developed beyond the implication that the arrest was for a crime that could conceivably be committed in the future.

Lumet telegraphs his intentions in the pre-credit lists of legal misdemeanors which has seen people stripped of their civil rights for decades. This would have worked better if it appeared at the end of the film. Placed where it is, it more or less tells us what we're about to see, and indeed how to think about it. It's not like him to be this obvious. As a statement about democracy, it's fine. But as a work of art, it fails. As someone once said, if you want to send a message, go to Western Union.

Now that the clock was winding down on Lumet's career, people seemed to be in a rush to confer awards on him. It was as if they were trying to make up for the ones he should have received but didn't when he was at the height of his powers. He was given a Lifetime Achievement Award by the Savannah College of Art and Design at the 2005 Savannah Film Festival. For reasons unexplained, the award was later found hidden in a patch of shrubbery at a three-point intersection in Brooklyn. AMPAS presented him with an honorary award that year too, a step up on his 1987 citation. Al Pacino introduced him: "If you prayed to inhabit a character, Sidney was the priest who listened to your prayers and helped make them come true."[11]

He was predictably self-effacing on the night, joking that he'd been working on an Oscar speech for 48 years and now he could finally deliver it. When he did, it was modest in the extreme: "How do I thank Spielberg and Scorsese and Coppola? How do I thank Jean Vigo, Carl Dreyer, Willy Wyler, Kurosawa and Buster Keaton? And I'm not even mentioning the ones I really stole from!"[12] He went on to say he had "the best job in the best profession in the world."[13]

Buoyed by the recognition of AMPAS, he went back to the big screen for (surprise surprise) another courtroom drama. *Find Me Guilty* (2005) told the true story of Jack

Di Norscio, a mobster who was shot four times by his cousin and survived. He was later arrested for dealing drugs and sentenced to 30 years in prison. While serving his sentence, he was offered a deal by the authorities. If he informed on other mobsters, they would release him immediately. Di Norscio replied, "I'd rather stay in jail than rat on any of my friends."

Instead of informing on them, he challenged the U.S. State in a landmark initiative. It turned out to be the longest federal case in U.S. history. There were 20 defendants, 20 lawyers and 76 charges. With a fifth grade education, Di Norscio fired his attorney and undertook the case himself. His defense was, to say the least, unorthodox. He was frequently cited for contempt by the judge. His language sometimes seemed more suited to a bordello than a courtroom. But it amused the jurors. "A laughing jury isn't a hanging jury" is a kind of running joke in the film.

Di Norscio becomes the film's hero, or rather its anti-hero. The prosecutors are more like the villains. We root for him to get his friends off even though we're under no illusion that any of them are Boy Scouts. We enjoy their banter as we do Di Norschio's. They have vitality, the kind of vitality we saw in Lumet's ne'er-do-wells right back to the Sonny Wortzik of *Dog Day Afternoon*.

Al Pacino introduced Lumet when he was presented with an Honorary Oscar in 2005. He accepted it with the graciousness one had come to expect from a man ignored so unfairly for so long by the Academy (Larry Edmunds Bookshop).

Lumet originally wanted Joe Pesci to play Di Norscio but he wasn't available. He then fastened on Vin Diesel. This wasn't regarded as a wise move. Diesel's reputation had been built on mindless car movies where the emphasis was on how he looked instead of what was going on inside his head. Few people knew Diesel once expressed a wish to do a remake of *My Fair Lady*.[14] Lumet was happy to work an actor whose voice was described by one commentator as being so low, "it's a wonder it doesn't set off car alarms."[15]

He approached Diesel with an open mind, ignoring the Neanderthal kinds of performance he gave in the *Fast & Furious* films to get at the man beneath the grunting. He felt there was much more to him and his instincts proved right. He used Diesel's physique to enhance his presence on screen. Diesel wore a suit that was too large for him, to give himself extra heft. Skinny ties underlined that effect. A uniform can sometimes "create" a character. His bearing seemed more dignified as a result of these details than it did when he was dressed in jeans and sneakers in the *Fast & Furious* films.

Lumet said of Di Norscio, "He was a liar, a cheat and a whoremonger and yet he was likable." Di Norscio was dying of cancer when Lumet met him but he was still articulate and funny. Lumet believed it was his humor that won the case for him. He was a "gagster" as much as a "gangster." Di Norscio said of the people in the courtroom, "They love me and I love them."[16] Was he good or evil? Or something in between? Lumet ventured, "In his own moral universe, he was doing the right thing." A man who destroyed his life, he had nothing to lose by taking on the system. "When they fucked with me," Di Norscho blasts at one point, "they woke a sleeping giant." For Lumet, he had *omerta*. He thought Diesel was the right man to play him. "This film runs on pure diesel" ran the tagline. The actor took to Lumet from the very first day of rehearsals, trusting him implicitly. "He knows exactly what he wants," he said. "He's like Frank Sinatra in his pacing."[17]

Annabella Sciorra played his wife. She liked Lumet too. "There's nothing negative about him," she said. "I couldn't imagine him thinking badly of anyone. He doesn't ever criticize." Of his directing technique, she noted, "Maybe he didn't like what you did, but you're not going to know it."[18] He conveyed his dissatisfaction in subtle ways, by casual suggestion.

Find Me Guilty was well received. Diesel's performance was revelatory to most of his critics. It was a new beginning for him. As for Lumet, many people were surprised that he was still making films. Some even thought he'd died. It was reassuring to know that he was still fighting for the outsider against the system, even if this was a significantly more imperfect outsider than any of his forbears.

Vin Diesel was a surprise casting choice for Lumet. He saw something in him beyond the Neanderthal grunting of the *Fast and Furious* movies. Diesel gave a convincing portrayal of a hood with his own code of ethics in *Find Me Guilty* (Larry Edmunds Bookshop).

The fact that a known criminal like Di Norscio endeared himself to a jury was unprecedented. Lumet was asked how he felt about the jury system in general. Did he think it worked? He said yes, even with O.J. Simpson, a man most people believed to be guilty of murder despite the fact that he was acquitted: "Undoubtedly people have gotten away with something because of the system as it stood, but that was better than innocent people being convicted because of the absence of those laws."[19] In general, he thought it was better to have 12 people adjudicating on a case than one; if a judge didn't like you, he could throw your case out without having to answer to anyone. So why did Lumet make so many films about the justice system? Was it an obsession of his? He said he did it almost subconsciously: "I guess when you're a Depression baby, someone with a typical Lower East Side poor Jewish upbringing, you automatically get involved with social issues."[20] He'd certainly done that, year in and year out for five decades, on the small screen and the big one, with small budgets and large ones, with megastars and veritable nobodies.

Most people expected *Find Me Guilty* to be his last hurrah but Lumet had another surprise in him. The Depression baby wasn't finished yet.

The thriller *Before the Devil Knows You're Dead* (2007) had echoes of many of the father-son films he'd made in the past: *Running on Empty, Family Business, Long Day's Journey into Night, Daniel, Night Falls on Manhattan.* But it was different. It was more like a Greek tragedy. Lumet cited *Oedipus Rex* when talking about it. He chortled, "I would love to have been around for the shot of Oedipus, where he pulls his eyes out."[21]

Philip Seymour Hoffman heads the stellar cast as Andy Hanson, an accountant in dire financial straits. So is his brother Hank (Ethan Hawke). Hawke is sleeping with Andy's wife Gina (Marisa Tomei). Their parents, Charles and Nanette (Albert Finney and Rosemary Harris), run a jewelry store. Andy wants to rob it. The insurance will pay for this, he tells Hank. Nobody will suffer. It will be the perfect crime. Hank reluctantly agrees to do it but he doesn't tell Andy that he doesn't have the courage to do it himself and so he's bringing in a third party. This is the rock they will all perish on. When the third party shoots "Mom," who wasn't supposed to be working on the day of the robbery, everything comes unstuck.

Philip Seymour Hoffman (left) tries to persuade his screen brother Ethan Hawke to rob the family jewelry store to ease both of their financial burdens in Lumet's outstanding swan song, *Before the Devil Knows You're Dead* (Jerry Ohlinger).

Lumet handles the crumbling marriage of Andy and Gina with great professionalism, the laughter of the early scenes counterpointed with the sudden descent into chaos. Andy's face is blood-red as he screams, "It's not fair!" at her in a central scene. This would become the film's most famous line, almost up there with Peter Finch's "I'm mad as hell" from *Network*. When she tells him she's sleeping with Hank, he shows no reaction. A half hour later he's squeezing the trigger of a gun to kill him.

Lumet hadn't worked with Finney for 32 years but it might as well have been the previous day. His style of directing hadn't changed and neither had Finney's acting. The fact that Finney was made up to be 20 years older than his real age in *Murder on the Orient Express* made it seem as if less time had elapsed since their last collaboration. "He shoots just as fast now as he did then," Finney observed.[22]

Hoffman and Hawke were equally impressed with Lumet's vitality. "He grabs your shoulder," Hoffman recalled. "He touches your face, your hand. He wants his connection close. He doesn't play the withholding father type. Once you understand his rhythm, you're in it. You never feel rushed. You know when you're here that you're going to shoot."[23]

The film moves at a frenetic pace. Lumet proved he was up to the task of dealing with this. Not many people would have guessed he was 83 when he made it: "Thirty-three seemed more like it."[24]

He was asked why he chose Hoffman for the older brother. He said it was Hoffman's decision. Sent the script, Hoffman asked, "Which part do you want me to play?" Lumet said, "You pick." Hoffman laughed but Lumet was serious. "I told him he could play either brother. He can do anything." But when Hawke came on board, it obviously made more sense for Hoffman to play the older brother.[25]

The clumsy robbery mirrored that of another Hoffman (Dustin in *Family Business*). It was a trademark of Lumet's villains that they didn't ever seem too adept at their villainy. In *Family Business*, a comical element was present in the proceedings. Here it was more bleak. The film, as one writer put it, was "perilously alive with the wages of sin."[26]

When events spiral out of control after the tragedy of their mother's shooting, the film suddenly becomes melodramatic. Melodrama isn't something one normally associates with Lumet but this aspect of the story entranced him when he first read it. It also dictated the pace at which he directed it. "In melodrama," he explained, "the events of the story unfold quickly and without warning. Time is short and the pressure cooker is really cooking. There's no time to give the character a background or deal with his past. The storytelling is fast, lean and aggressive. Anything that doesn't advance it is unimportant." In most dramas, he pointed out, the story comes out of the characters but in melodrama that dynamic is reversed. We're more interested in the things people do than the people who do them.[27]

Before the Devil Knows You're Dead begins on an earthquake, to paraphrase Jack Warner, and works up to a climax. Everything about it is un–Lumetian: its plot-driven nature, its outrageous developments, the timeframe that jumps back and forward in pulp movie fashion, the fratricide-infanticide elements that seem more suitable for Greek tragedy than a modern-day thriller. Even the sex scene between Andy and Gina that begins the film is unusual for Lumet. It's uncharacteristically explicit.

If it weren't for the brilliance of the cast, it would all have been totally unacceptable. They all stretch themselves to their limits. They know what's demanded of them with this great director and deliver accordingly, pushing their emotional levels up many more notches than usual to match the Grand Guignol tableau.

This is a film in which anything can happen and usually does. Nothing is off the table. Once we accept the premise that two members of a respectable family would rob their parents, everything else—like Hoffman's double murder within minutes—becomes part of the same quasi-logical framework.

Lumet grabs us by the throat from the outset and doesn't let go until Charles, foaming at the mouth like a mad dog, murders the son who was responsible for the death of his wife and then walks away to whatever fate may await him. By now the lives of Hank and Gina are also destroyed. There are no winners in this tawdry bloodfest.

Within such parameters, amazingly, a real story gets itself told. We accept the fact that desperation—financial and otherwise—can drive quote unquote "ordinary" people to such depths of depravity. Andy's drug addiction—an ironic foretaste of how Hoffman's actual life would end—is one such stimulus. So is Hank's susceptibility to temptation. In theory, the "Mom and Pop" operation looks like a piece of cake but then film crimes usually do until they come unstuck.

"The easiest money you'll ever get," Andy promises Hank, and it seems like it will be, provided "Mom" doesn't turn up at the store unexpectedly and decide (fatefully) to take on the balaclava-clad robber. As she lies in a coma after being shot, it seems that none of her family can grieve properly for her. Her two sons are too consumed by fear and her husband by anger. Already we know this is not going to end well. From now on, the film becomes one more exercise after another in attempts at damage limitation. But they only increase the damage. The spiral of destruction goes out of control repeatedly. As the film's tagline so chillingly informs us, "Families can be murder."

The haphazardness we see on screen was contrasted with the discipline Lumet employed behind the camera. Hawke enthused, "What I took from Sidney was that he was the most prepared director I ever worked with." Tomei echoed Hawke's view. Everything was mapped out, she said—the bed, the furniture, where you stood, where you walked. It gave her a comfortable spatial sense.[28]

She was also impressed by Lumet's physical warmth: "He takes your hand. He touches your face. He gives you signals all along that he's in your corner." The film's producer, Michael Cerenzie, also felt that. Cerenzie had sent the script directly to Lumet without employing an agent. This in itself was unusual. The fact that Lumet agreed to meet him in his office on such a basis was unusual too. "You walk in and he embraces you," Cerenzie recalled. "There are no trophies, just him and a desk." Cerenzie was amazed that such an "iconic and powerful man" made him feel so much at ease.[29]

He pitched the project to him as a thriller but Lumet, as mentioned, preferred to think of it as melodrama. For Hawke, melodrama was another word for overacting. Lumet didn't see it like that. He wanted to push things to the point where belief was just about to collapse but didn't quite go over that border. This was the challenge. Hoffman said Lumet re-educated him about just how far you could go in a film and still be believable. This was because of its "heightened stakes."[30]

Lumet changed the script to make it more focused. In the original draft, Andy and Gina had a child. He removed that. Andy and Hank weren't brothers in the original script. Making it into a family drama—with one brother sleeping with the other's wife—ratcheted up the tension to the level he wanted to make the consequent overflow of emotion credible. When it does, in the scene where Andy prepares himself to shoot

Hank, the minimalism of the script beautifully underscores this. "You know I know," Andy says to Hank, pointing the gun at him. "What do you know?" Hank says. Andy replies, "I know." And then he shoots him.

Lumet ended the film with a poignant touch. In the opening scene, after the intense sex, Andy asks Gina to put her hand on his chest to feel his heart beating. In the closing one, Charles does the same thing to indicate it isn't. Sex and death collide in one motif as the family is sundered.

Lumet's first film had been a classic. His last one was as well. It was a fitting way to bookend a career. Some offerings in the middle failed to live up to the high standards he set himself but as he often said, he liked to keep working. In this case, his need to be active was validated in spades.

Before the film premiered at the New York Film Festival, he was celebrated at a "Director's Dialogue" interchange. The first thing the interviewer said to him was, "You must be getting used to these tributes." He replied, "It's strange, because I'm not dead yet." The interviewer said, "I noticed. And your Lifetime Achievement Award was three years ago." Lumet deadpanned, "Usually people get these three months before they die so I guess I'm doing okay."[31]

The interview touched on many of the issues that had consumed him over the years. One of these was his affection for New York. Many people felt the Big Apple was impersonal, but not this man. He felt the city was much more intimate than Los Angeles: "In L.A. there are no streets, no sense of a neighborhood." Our greatest problems today, he said, were caused by feelings of isolation. He accepted the fact that this had also crept into parts of New York. In fact, it was one of the reasons he moved from his original home on the East Side. Some years ago, he said, there used to be lots of people walking around at night but now there weren't. "After 8:40, nobody's walking any more. So I moved to the West Side. There are still people on the street there."[32]

He was asked about where he thought he belonged in the tradition of New York directors. He'd often been lumped together with people like Woody Allen and Martin Scorsese as part of a school. Did he feel part of a school? He said he didn't, either professionally or socially. Even if he was in the habit of meeting these people socially, he didn't like being categorized: "We were all doing our own thing. That stuff about a movement came later."[33]

He was asked where he saw the film industry going in the future. His reply was an anecdote: "We were shooting out in Astoria and one day I watched all these kids standing outside a school near the studio. It was just marvelous: Indian girls in saris, kids from Pakistan, Korea, kids from all over. So I think you'll see more directors from these communities telling their stories." Such multi-culturalism paralleled his own experience: "I started out making films about Jews and Italians and Irish because I didn't know anything else." By definition, people made films about their experiences. The contemporary experience was wider than it had ever been before because of so many cross-cultural reference points.[34]

Before the Devil Knows You're Dead was his final film. No matter how energetic he was, even he had to bow to the slowing-down of his body. After 2007, he spent most of his time at home. This would have been insufferable to him as a younger man but age brought acceptance. He saw its positives, as he'd always seen positives in everything during his life. It meant he had more of an opportunity to develop relationships with his grandchildren. He hadn't spent quite as much time with his daughters as he'd wanted. Now there was a chance to make up for that with the next generation. In other words, the family man in him was given full rein. Notwithstanding that, he had to accept the fact that his passion for life was diminishing. This meant he was under-reacting to both positive experiences and negative ones: "The joyful moments aren't as joyful or the painful ones as painful."[35]

He developed lymphoma in 2010. He experienced the first symptoms when he was invited to attend a special showing of *Twelve Angry Men* at the Fordham Law Film Festival. It had been organized to celebrate the induction of Sonia Sotomayor, the first Hispanic-American to serve on the Supreme Court. She'd seen the film as a child and said it inspired her to pursue a law career. Having said that, she found some aspects of it unrealistic. Lumet wasn't offended by this critique. Films, he stressed, weren't documentaries. It was their diversion from reality that gave them dramatic import.[36]

Despite the deterioration of his health, he retained his pleasant demeanor. He didn't expect to live long more but he had no regrets. He'd had a blessed life. He started to speak about his mortality but not in a dramatic way. Asked about how he wanted to "go out," he said, "I don't think about it. I'm not religious."[37] He'd always been frivolous about what might happen to him after he died. One thing he was sure of was that he didn't want to take up too much space, "Burn me up," he ordained, "and scatter my ashes over Katz's Delicatessen."[38]

Asked how he wanted to be remembered, he said he didn't like the question:

> People who worry about that get themselves into terrible trouble. You can't worry about history and posterity. Do your work and go home. What's going to happen is going to happen. The very question, "How would you like to be remembered?" implies you're dead already so what difference does it make?"[39]

Shortly before Lumet died, Gloria Vanderbilt visited him. They hadn't seen one another for many years. She wanted to tell him how much she'd always loved him, how much he'd meant to her. Lumet was glad to see her even though he'd been happy in his marriage to Mary Gimble. He wasn't as sentimental about his time with Vanderbilt as she was. She'd never really got over divorcing him. Their meeting, she said, freed her from the "tormenting guilt" she'd been agonizing about for years.[40]

Lumet's big heart finally gave out in 2011. He was 86. "May you be half an hour in Heaven before the devil knows you're dead," says an Irish toast. He'd used it for the title of his final film. He was so fast, one imagines his spirit would have had no trouble eluding the infernal serpent if it came to a race for the Pearly Gates.

In 1968 he said, "When I'm 84 I'd like to see 60 pictures behind me. If only two of these are great, I'll see myself as a great man."[41] He was entitled to. Many more than two were great. Elsewhere he said, "I don't know what my life is about; Maybe work is what my life is about."[42] And elsewhere again: "I get very nervous when people ask me what my work is about. The only time you know that is when you die."[43] Now he would have known.

He always eluded definition. Nobody could pin him down in life and neither would they be able to do so now that he was gone. He remained an inscrutable director, reinventing himself with each project. He'd made heroes of "bank robbers, suicidal TV anchormen, drug-addicted mothers and whistle-blowing cops."[44] He'd won Oscars for Katharine Hepburn, Peter Finch and Faye Dunaway but none for himself. It seemed appropriate. He never courted the limelight. If people wanted to see his epitaph, they could go to a cinema. He said it best himself: His life was his work.

Everybody who was anybody in the film industry paid tribute to him. Few people expected him to work after *Before the Devil Knows You're Dead* but a world without Lumet was very much a lesser one. Woody Allen nailed it when he said, "Knowing Sidney, he'll have more energy dead than most live people."[45]

His 40-odd films garnered more than 50 Oscar nominations. Who else could make that kind of boast? His legacy was secure. "I adored him," said Philip Seymour Hoffman. New York Mayor Michael Bloomberg labeled him "one of the great chroniclers of our city."[46]

Al Pacino was more upset than most actors at his passing. He'd witnessed the best of him (and vice versa). It would be difficult, he surmised, to imagine there wouldn't be any more films by Lumet. "All the more reason," he concluded, "to take good care of the ones he left behind."[47]

There were many of these. Were there too many? Some people felt he overworked, that quality sometimes varied inversely with quantity. But in every Lumet film, whether he was dealing with substandard material or not, there was always something you took with you from the cinema to chew on, be it the moral struggle of a character or the camerawork or a moment of epiphany that poured enlightenment on everything that went before. Pacino added that, as well as being a wonderful filmmaker, Lumet was "the most civilized of humans and the kindest man I have ever known."[48]

Steven Spielberg was also vociferous in his praise, describing him as "one of the greatest directors in the long history of film," his strong suit being "compelling stories and unforgettable performances."[49] Taylor Hackford said he had a "never-wavering enthusiasm for film technology and a true respect for the actor."[50]

Jane Fonda remembered his laughter from as far back as 1957 when she met him on the set of *Twelve Angry Men* (which starred her father). "He taught me to appreciate bagels," she said, "New York bagels." Three decades later, she received an Oscar nomination for *The Morning After*. "He was always very kind and generous with me," she recalled, "He was a master. Such control of his craft. He had strong progressive values and never betrayed them."[51]

Costume designer Tony Walton referred to him as "one of the most lovely people imaginable, and the closest and best collaborator and friend." Walton worked with him on several films and was amazed he that he (Walton) was encouraged to offer suggestions. No suggestion was ever dismissed.[52]

A *Los Angeles Times* writer said Lumet was less a stylist than a populist but he admitted that *Network*, which was seen by many as little more than a "bizarre Orwellian fantasy" when it was made, had a prescience that went on to define the era that followed. Not all of Lumet's films were great, the writer pointed out, but his "restlessness of spirit" drove him to make the best of what he was given.[53]

The *San Francisco Chronicle* was measured in its evaluation. He was no Antonioni, it noted, no Bergman. But if he was given a good script, he could make "the best possible movie" from it. And if he was given a good actor, he "just might" find a great one lurking within them.[54]

Why has Lumet not received the due recognition he deserves from the critics? People like Andrew Sarris and Pauline Kael had been most vehement in their denunciation of him. Others were lukewarm despite his plethora of Oscar nominations and Directors Guild awards. Was this because so many of his films had their sources in plays and novels? Or because his espousal of old-fashioned liberalism is regarded as passé?

Peter Blanner had another theory: "Great American artists are supposed to burst forth like supernovas and then quickly flame out like Orson Welles and F. Scott Fitzgerald. Or they're supposed to be magisterial and remote like Stanley Kubrick, spending ten years between projects, pondering." Lumet, to the contrary, made some 40 films in as many years. As a result, he inspired suspicion: "Instead of sitting around, he dived from one film to another, scrabbling for the emotional heart of each one, doing whatever it took to make an impact."[55] Whatever the reason, his star hadn't shone for the critics as brightly as it did for the likes of Scorsese or Coppola. Maybe the fact that he rejected Hollywood as a location—if not a cultural benchmark—was another factor.

Some of his critics accused him of being amorphous, which annoyed him. He huffed, "It's ridiculous to say I lack style because I don't have any identifiable look to my frames. Some dopes can only recognize cinematic technique if it's focused on a mountain or the sky. They keep confusing cinema with scenery."[56]

For Roger Ebert, the fact that Lumet's films lacked a noticeable visual style was a compliment: "He reduced every scene to its necessary elements and filmed them invisibly. You shouldn't be thinking about the camera. He wanted you to think about the characters and the story."[57] Alan Heim said he was like those baseball stars that played for 30 years. "He made three films every year when I worked for him. Nobody does that any more. Nobody *could* do that."[58] With such an output, nobody expected him to hit the target every time, least of all Lumet himself. "I don't fancy myself as the Second Coming," he said.[59]

His humility helped him disappear behind his work; it gave him the intellectual space to see the greatness in others: "The moments Marlon Brando gave me in *The Fugitive Kind*, or Sean Connery in *The Hill*, or Kate Hepburn in *Journey*, or Mason and Fonda or dozens of others I've worked with, those moments I couldn't have got from any other source."[60] He treated every job like his last one. If a film worked, somebody might employ him again. This was as far down the road as he looked.[61]

A lot of his films end sadly but he made no apology for this. As Ernest Hemingway once said, "Happiness writes white." Lumet wasn't a dour person by nature. "I enjoy life and pleasure and comfort," he said, "but obviously there's something in me that lets me know there are no such things as happy endings. When I read a script with one, I tend not to believe it."[62]

Even so, his films tend to leave one in an upbeat mood. Their circumstances may be sad but their tone isn't. This is probably down to the fact that he very much liked what he was doing. Asked why he became a film director, he replied, "Because it's a wonderful way to spend your life."[63]

His prolific output was the result of an absence of self-importance, a wish to get on with things without over-thinking them. "There's too much articulation about the meaning of movies today," he said.[64] He preferred a more straightforward approach, one that didn't show the wheels turning.[65]

He professed not to care about whether or not he would be remembered. He will be. Not only for his broad vision of the human condition but the way he located it in the hundreds of locations he portrayed so cerebrally. He captured New York, one critic wrote, like Picasso captured Barcelona in his paintings.[66] Owen Gleiberman maintained, "When he went into the New York streets, he made them electric."[67]

His legacy continued into the next generation, what with his daughter Jennifer scripting the critically acclaimed Anne Hathaway film *Rachel is Getting Married* (2008). In 2011, the Human Rights First organization inaugurated a Sidney Lumet award for Integrity in Entertainment. Four years later, Nancy Buirski made a documentary about his career, *By Sidney Lumet*, which contained many interviews by and about him. PBS devoted its American Masters series to him in 2017. Added to this was a plenitude of critical studies of his work.

The adulation he should have received when he was alive came to him when he wasn't around to enjoy it but he wouldn't have been bitter about that. If he was interviewed in that big studio in the sky about his enormous contribution to the world of art in film, he would probably wave the praise aside with a chuckle. One can see him shrugging his shoulders nonchalantly and saying, "You're too kind. I was just an ordinary guy doing his job in an extraordinary business. Better late than never."

Chapter Notes

Introduction

1. *Films in Review*, October 1984.
2. Sidney Lumet, *Making Movies* (London: Bloomsbury, 1996), 118.
3. Stephen E. Bowles, *Sidney Lumet: A Guide to References and Resources* (Boston: G.K. Hall & Co., 1979), 36.
4. *Films in Review*, October 1984.
5. Bowles, *A Guide to References and Resources*, 36.
6. *Night Falls on Manhattan* DVD, Spelling Entertainment.
7. Frank R. Cunningham, *Sidney Lumet: Film and Literary Vision* (Lexington: University Press of Kentucky, 1991), 14.
8. *New York Times*, April 9, 2011.
9. *BBC Omnibus*, February 26, 1991.
10. Lumet, *Making Movies*, 87.
11. Cunningham, *Film and Literary Vision*, 10.
12. *New York*, August 10, 1981.
13. *Ibid*.
14. *Village Voice*, October 23, 1984.
15. Andrew Sarris, *The American Cinema: Directors and Directions, 1929–1968* (New York: E.P. Dutton, 1968), 197.
16. Nancy Buirski, *By Sidney Lumet* (FilmRise, 2015).
17. Max Wilk, *Schmucks with Underwoods* (New York: Applause Theatre and Cinema Books, 2004), 295.
18. Peter Cowie, *50 Major Filmmakers* (South Brunswick, NJ: A.S. Barnes, 1975), 162.
19. *San Diego Union Tribune*, April 9, 2011.
20. Robyn Kearney, ed., *Who's Who in Hollywood* (London: Bloomsbury, 1993), 282.
21. Lumet, *Making Movies*, 8.
22. Ronald Bergan, Graham Fuller and David Malcolm, *Academy Award Winners from 1927 to the Present* (London: Prion, 1994), 252.

Beginnings

1. Robert J. Emery, *The Directors: Take One* (New York: TV Books, 1999), 364.
2. Buirski, *By Sidney Lumet*.
3. *New York Times*, January 20, 1974.
4. Buirski, *By Sidney Lumet*.
5. *Positif*, February 1982.
6. *New York Magazine*, September 24, 2007.
7. *American Film*, December 1982.
8. *New York Herald-Tribune*, August 22, 1965.
9. *New York Times*, January 20, 1974.
10. *Rolling Stone*, January 20, 1983.
11. Dave Itzkoff, *Mad as Hell: The Making of Network and the Fateful Vision of the Angriest Man in Movies* (New York: Henry Holt and Company, 2014), 73.
12. Kearney, ed., *Who's Who in Hollywood*, 202.
13. Cunningham, *Film and Literary Vision*, 15.
14. *Positif*, February 1982.
15. Buirski, *By Sidney Lumet*.
16. *New York*, November 22, 1976.
17. David Garfield, *A Player's Place: The Story of the Actors' Studio* (New York: Macmillan, 1980), 146.
18. *Ibid*., 52–3.
19. *Positif*, February 1982.
20. Cunningham, *Film and Literary Vision*, 16.
21. *Ibid*.
22. Bowles, *A Guide to References and Resources*, 7.
23. *New York Times*, July 24, 1977.
24. *Hampton Star*, April 14, 2011.
25. *BBC News*, April 9, 2011.
26. *Films in Review*, October 1984.
27. Buirski, *By Sidney Lumet*.
28. Jhan Robbins, *Yul Brynner: The Inscrutable King* (London: W.H. Allen, 1988), 34–37.
29. *New York American Journal*, February 14, 1966.
30. *Films & Filming*, June 1965.
31. Tom Hutchinson, *Rod Steiger: Memoirs of a Friendship* (New York: Fromm International, 2000), 67.
32. Alexander Walker, *It's Only a Movie, Ingrid: Encounters On and Off Screen* (London: Headline, 1998), 112.
33. Hutchinson, *Rod Steiger*, 69–71.
34. Piper Laurie, *Learning to Live Out Loud* (New York: Crown Archetype, 2011), 163–4.

35. Buirski, *By Sidney Lumet*.
36. *BBC Omnibus*, February 26, 1991.
37. *American Masters*, July 26, 2006.
38. Shawn Levy, *Paul Newman: A Life* (London: Aurum, 2010), 86.
39. Emery, *The Directors: Take One*, 249
40. Shelley Winters, *The Middle of My Century* (New York: Pocket Books, 1989), 132–3.
41. *American Masters*, July 26, 2006.
42. *American Film 8*, December 1982.
43. *Ibid*.
44. Gloria Vanderbilt, *It Seemed Important at the Time: A Romance Memoir* (New York: Simon & Schuster, 2004), 82–3.
45. Anderson Cooper and Gloria Vanderbilt, *The Rainbow Comes and Goes: A Mother and Son on Life, Love and Loss* (New York: Harper, 2017), 166.
46. *L.A. Examiner*, February 28, 1956.
47. *Ibid.*, December 15, 1955.
48. Cooper and Vanderbilt, *The Rainbow Comes and Goes*, 166–7.
49. *L.A. Examiner*, August 28, 1956.
50. Vanderbilt, *It Seemed Important at the Time*, 86.
51. *Films in Review*, November 1973.
52. Peter Bogdanovich, *Who the Devil Made It* (New York: Alfred A. Knopf, 1997), 810.
53. Jerry Roberts, *Encyclopedia of Television Film Directors* (Lanham, MD: Scarecrow Press, 2009), 353.
54. Tab Hunter with Eddie Muller, *Tab Hunter Confidential: The Making of a Movie Star* (Chapel Hill, NC: Algonquin Books, 2005), 196.
55. Erik Barnouw, *Tube of Plenty: The Evolution of American Television* (New York: Oxford University Press, 1990), 16.

Moving to the Big Screen

1. David Shipman, *Movie Talk: Who Said What About Whom in the Movies* (London: Bloomsbury, 1988), 134.
2. Buirski, *By Sidney Lumet*.
3. *Journal of the Writers Guild of America*, October 1997.
4. Emery, *The Directors: Take One*, 365.
5. *Twelve Angry Men, Fresh Air*, 30.
6. www.herbertspencer12quotes.com.
7. Henry Fonda, *My Life: As Told to Howard Teichmann* (New York: New American Library, 1981), 267.
8. *Ibid*.
9. *San Francisco Chronicle*, April 14, 2011.
10. Lumet, *Making Movies*, 26.
11. Itzkoff, *Mad as Hell*, 74.
12. *New York Times*, July 15, 1956.
13. Lumet, *Making Movies*, 81.
14. John R. May, ed., *Image and Likeness: Religious Visions in American Film Classics* (New York: Paulist Press, 1992), 29.
15. Jay Boyer, *Sidney Lumet* (New York: Twayne, 1993), 3.
16. Barry Norman, *The Film Greats* (London: Futura, 1985), 93.
17. *Ibid.*, 93–4.
18. *Ibid.*, 103.
19. Fonda, *My Life: As Told to Howard Teichmann*, 267–8.
20. *Ibid.*, 268.
21. *Ibid*.
22. Joanna E. Rapf, ed., *Sidney Lumet Interviews* (Jackson: University Press of Mississippi, 2006), 146.
23. Buirski, *By Sidney Lumet*.
24. Rapf, ed., *Sidney Lumet Interviews*, 178.
25. *BBC Omnibus*, February 26, 1991.
26. Dick Cavett, *Talk Show: Confrontations, Pointed Commentary and Offscreen Secrets* (New York: St. Martin's Griffin, 2010), 65.
27. Shipman, ed., *Movie Talk*, 134.
28. Michael Kerbel, *Henry Fonda* (New York: Pyramid Publications, 1975), 98.
29. Lumet, *Making Movies*, 54.
30. Fonda, *My Life: As Told to Howard Teichmann*, 273.
31. Patricia Bosworth, *Jane Fonda: The Private Life of a Public Woman* (London: Robson, 2011), 103–4.
32. Bogdanovich, *Who the Devil Made It*, 802.
33. Bowles, *A Guide to References and Resources*, 13.
34. Bogdanovich, *Who the Devil Made It*, 805.
35. Bowles, *A Guide to References and Resources*, 13.
36. *New York Herald Tribune*, April 23, 1958.
37. *Films in Review*, March 1958.
38. *Variety*, February 26, 1958.
39. Bogdanovich, *Who the Devil Made It*, 806–7.
40. Lumet, *Making Movies*, ix.
41. Doug McClelland, ed., *Hollywood on Hollywood: Tinseltown Talks* (Boston: Faber & Faber, 1985), 59.
42. Hunter with Muller, *Tab Hunter Confidential*, 209.
43. *Ibid*.
44. *Ibid.*, 210.
45. *Ibid*.
46. *Ibid*.
47. *Ibid*.
48. *Saturday Review 5*, September 1959.
49. *New York Times*, September 12, 1959.
50. *Variety*, August 12, 1959.
51. *New York Herald Tribune*, September 12, 1959.
52. *Time*, September 21, 1959.
53. Hunter with Muller, *Tab Hunter Confidential*, 211.
54. *Ibid*.
55. *Films & Filming*, June 1965.
56. Sophia Loren, *My Life: Yesterday, Today and Tomorrow* (London: Simon & Schuster, 2014), 132.

57. Lumet, *Making Movies*, 186.
58. Bogdanovich, *Who the Devil Made It*, 799.
59. *New York Times*, May 8, 1960.
60. Bogdanovich, *Who the Devil Made It*, 799.
61. *Hollywood Reporter*, November 16, 1959.
62. *New York Times*, December 31, 1963
63. *Hollywood Reporter*, April 9, 2011.
64. Gregory D. Black, *The Catholic Crusade Against the Movies, 1940–75* (New York: Cambridge University Press, 1997), 224.
65. Buirski, *By Sidney Lumet*.

On the Wing

1. David Downing, *Marlon Brando* (New York: Stein & Day, 1984), 89.
2. Tony Thomas, *The Films of Marlon Brando* (New York: Citadel, 1992), 123.
3. Nellie Bly, *Marlon Brando: Larger Than Life* (New York: Windsor Publishing, 1994), 92.
4. Peter Manso, *Brando* (New York: Hyperion, 1994), 501.
5. Charles Higham, *Brando: The Unauthorized Biography* (London: Grafton Books, 1989), 260.
6. Susan L. Mizruchi, *Brando's Smile: The Life, Thought and Work* (New York: W.W. Norton & Co., 2014), 158.
7. Paul Ryan, *Marlon Brando: A Portrait* (London: Plexus, 1991), 97.
8. Manso, *Brando*, 498.
9. Maureen Stapleton and Jane Scovell, *A Hell of a Life* (New York: Simon & Schuster, 1995), 180.
10. Manso, *Brando*, 511.
11. Higham, *Brando*, 260.
12. Mizruchi, *Brando's Smile*, 159.
13. Manso, *Brando*, 503.
14. Ryan, *Marlon Brando*, 98.
15. Marlon Brando with Robert Lindsay, *Songs My Mother Taught Me* (London: Century, 1994), 260–2.
16. *Ibid.*, 262.
17. Manso, *Brando*, 502.
18. Bogdanovich, *Who the Devil Made It*, 797.
19. Stephen Randall, ed., *The Playboy Interviews* (Milwaukie, OR: M Press, 2006), 69.
20. Bogdanovich, *Who the Devil Made It*, 797.
21. Ron Offen, *Brando* (Chicago: Henry Regnery, 1973), 129–30.
22. Higham, *Brando*, 261.
23. Stefan Kanfer, *Somebody: The Reckless Life and Remarkable Career of Marlon Brando* (London: Faber & Faber, 2008), 166.
24. Ryan, *Marlon Brando*, 98.
25. Fred Baker, ed., *Movie People* (London: Abelard-Schuman, 1973), 46–7.
26. Manso, *Brando*, 506.
27. *Ibid.*, 507.
28. Darwin Porter, *Brando Unzipped* (New York: Blood Moon Productions, 2005), 567.
29. Lumet, *Making Movies*, 103.
30. Manso, *Brando*, 506.
31. Bly, *Marlon Brando*, 93.
32. *Ibid.*
33. Bogdanovich, *Who the Devil Made It*, 798.
34. *Ibid.*
35. *Ibid.*
36. *Ibid.*, 799.
37. Lumet, *Making Movies*, 82.
38. Manso, *Brando*, 506.
39. Porter, *Brando Unzipped*, 566.
40. Kanfer, *Somebody*, 166.
41. Manso, *Brando*, 505.
42. Stapleton with Scovell, *A Hell of a Life*, 181.
43. David Thomson, *Marlon Brando* (London: Dorling Kindersley, 2003), 102.
44. *Journal of the Writers Guild of America*, October 1997.
45. Thomson, *Marlon Brando*, 102.
46. Kanfer, *Somebody*, 167.
47. Manso, *Brando*, 512–3.
48. Thomson, *Marlon Brando*, 101.
49. Lumet, *Making Movies*, 82.
50. Manso, *Brando*, 513–4.
51. *Saturday Review*, April 23, 1960.
52. *Films in Review*, May 1960.
53. David Shipman, *Marlon Brando* (London: Sphere, 1989), 128.
54. Rene Jordan, *Marlon Brando* (London: W.H. Allen, 1975), 91.
55. Shipman, *Marlon Brando*, 127.
56. Alan Frank, *Marlon Brando* (London: Gallery Press, 1982), 43.
57. Bob Thomas, *Marlon: Portrait of the Rebel as an Artist* (New York: Random House, 1973), 156.
58. Offen, *Brando*, 131.
59. Donald Spoto, *The Kindness of Strangers: The Life of Tennessee Williams* (New York: Ballantine Books, 1985), 265.
60. Offen, *Brando*, 131.
61. *New York Times*, April 15, 1960.
62. *Film Comment*, August 1988.
63. Kanfer, *Somebody*, 167.

Peak and Valleys

1. Bowles, *A Guide to References and Resources*, 16.
2. Bogdanovich, *Who the Devil Made It*, 800.
3. Bowles, *A Guide to References and Resources*, 17.
4. Richard A. Blake, *Street Smart: The New York of Lumet, Allen, Scorsese and Lee* (Lexington: University Press of Kentucky, 2005), 47.
5. *Hollywood Reporter*, June 10, 1997.
6. *New York Herald Tribune*, January 23, 1962.
7. *New York Times,* January 23, 1962.
8. *Variety,* October 18, 1961.
9. *Saturday Review,* January 27, 1962.
10. *Time,* January 19, 1962.

11. *New Republic,* February 12, 1962.
12. Doug McClelland, *The Unkindest Cuts: The Scissors and the Cinema* (South Brunswick, NJ: A.S. Barnes, 1972), 102.
13. Mason Wiley and Damien Bona, *Inside Oscar: The Unofficial History of the Academy Awards* (New York: Ballantine Books, 1987), 343.
14. Manso, *Brando,* 434.
15. David Dresser and Lester D. Friedman, *American-Jewish Filmmakers: Traditions and Trends* (Urbana: University of Illinois Press, 1993), 169.
16. Lumet, *Making Movies,* 24.
17. Hutchinson, *Rod Steiger,* 216–7.
18. Lumet, *Making Movies,* 68.
19. Cunningham, *Film and Literary Vision,* 124.
20. Lumet, *Making Movies,* 69.
21. *Film Quarterly,* Summer 1971.
22. *Ibid.*
23. Lumet, *Making Movies,* 70.
24. Charlotte Chandler, *The Real Kate: A Personal Biography of Katharine Hepburn* (London: Robson Books, 2012), 223.
25. Barbara Leaming, *Katharine Hepburn* (London: Phoenix, 1995), 482.
26. *Film Quarterly,* Summer 1971.
27. *Ibid.,* Autumn 1975.
28. *Ibid.,* Winter 1967–8.
29. Lumet, *Making Movies,* 65.
30. Rapf, ed., *Sidney Lumet Interviews,* 40–1.
31. Lumet, *Making Movies,* 162.
32. *Journal of the Writers Guild of America,* October 1997.
33. Rapf, ed., *Sidney Lumet Interviews,* 32.
34. William J. Mann, *Kate: The Woman Who Was Katharine Hepburn* (London: Faber & Faber, 2006), 411.
35. Cunningham, *Film and Literary Vision,* 123.
36. Mann, *Kate,* 412.
37. Pauline Kael, *Kiss Kiss Bang Bang: Film Writings 1965–1967* (London: Arena, 1987), 85.
38. *Newsweek,* October 15, 1962.
39. Anthony Holden, *The Oscars: The Secret History of Hollywood's Academy Awards* (London: Warner Books, 1994), 234.
40. *Time,* October 12, 1962.
41. Lumet, *Making Movies,* 89.
42. *Films and Filming,* June 1965.
43. *Saturday Review,* October 6, 1962.
44. *Time,* October 12, 1962.
45. Vanderbilt, *It Seemed Important at the Time,* 90.
46. Anderson and Vanderbilt, *The Rainbow Comes and Goes,* 181.
47. *Ibid.,* 175–6.
48. Gail Lumet Buckley, *The Hornes: An American Family* (New York: Applause Cinema and Theatre Books, 1986), 248–9.
49. James Gavin, *Stormy Weather: The Life of Lena Horne* (New York: Atria, 2009), 336–7.
50. *Daily News,* September 21, 1963.
51. Buckley, *The Hornes,* 249.
52. Gavin, *Stormy Weather,* 337.
53. Buckley, *The Hornes,* 249.
54. *Newsday,* May 7, 1963.
55. *Time,* October 9, 1964.
56. Desser and Friedman, *American-Jewish Filmmakers,* 170.
57. Kael, *Kiss Kiss Bang Bang,* 70.
58. *New Republic,* September 12, 1964.
59. David Mamet, *Bambi Vs. Godzilla: On the Nature, Purpose and Practice of the Movie Business* (London: Simon & Schuster, 2007), 172.
60. *Newsday,* May 7, 1963.
61. Philip Strick, *Science Fiction Movies* (London: Octopus, 1976), 92.
62. Allan Hunter, *Walter Matthau* (London: W.H. Allen, 1984), 55.
63. John Baxter, *Stanley Kubrick: A Biography* (London: HarperCollins, 1997), 175–6.
64. Strick, *Science Fiction Movies,* 91.
65. *Films & Filming,* May 1975.
66. Emery, *The Directors; Take One,* 367.
67. Kerbel, *Henry Fonda,* 110.
68. Shipman, *Movie Talk,* 134.
69. Peter Collier, *The Fondas: A Hollywood Dynasty* (London: HarperCollins, 1991), 178.
70. Bogdanovich, *Who the Devil Made It,* 805–6.
71. *New York Herald-Tribune,* October 9, 1964.
72. *Ibid.*

That Vision Thing

1. *Film Quarterly,* Fall 1971.
2. Desser and Friedman, *American-Jewish Filmmakers,* 165.
3. Lumet, *Making Movies,* 102.
4. *Ibid.,* 176.
5. Emery, *The Directors: Take One,* 268.
6. Lumet, *Making Movies,* 159.
7. *Films in Review,* November 1973.
8. *Films & Filming,* October 1964.
9. Hutchinson, *Rod Steiger,* 119–20.
10. *Ibid.,* 211.
11. *Ibid.,* 222.
12. Emery, *The Directors; Take One,* 368–9.
13. Hutchinson, *Rod Steiger,* 205–6.
14. John Eastman, *Retakes: Behind the Scenes of 500 Classic Movies* (New York: Ballantine Books, 1989), 254.
15. Morrissey, *Autobiography* (London: Penguin, 2013), 447.
16. Hutchinson, *Rod Steiger,* 209.
17. *Ibid.,* 49.
18. Lumet, *Making Movies,* 166.
19. *Saturday Review,* April 3, 1965.
20. Black, *The Catholic Crusade Against the Movies, 1940–1975,* 225.
21. Frank Miller, *Censored Hollywood: Sex, Sin*

and *Violence on Screen* (Atlanta: Turner Publishing, 1994), 197.
22. Julian Petley, *Censorship: A Beginner's Guide* (Oxford: Oneworld Publications, 2009), 20.
23. Miller, *Censored Hollywood*, 197.
24. David Shipman, *Caught in the Act: Sex and Eroticism in the Movies* (London: Elm Tree Books, 1985), 142.
25. Marshall Fine, *Bloody Sam: The Life and Times of Sam Peckinpah* (New York: Hyperion, 2005), 119.
26. *Ramparts*, September 1965.
27. *Variety,* April 4, 1965.
28. Barry Norman, *Talking Pictures* (London: BBC Books, 1987), 100.
29. Jeremy Pascall and Clyde Jeavons, *Sex in the Movies: A Pictorial History* (London: Hamlyn, 1975), 126–7.
30. *Newsweek*, December 28, 1964.
31. Frank Walsh, *Sin and Censorship: The Catholic Church and the Motion Picture Industry* (New Haven: Yale University Press, 1996), 318.
32. *Newsweek*, December 28, 1964
33. Eastman, *Retakes*, 256.
34. John Trevelyan, *What the Censor Saw* (London: Michael Joseph, 1973), 188–9.
35. *Exhibitor*, June 2, 1965.
36. Miller, *Censored Hollywood*, 199.
37. *Time*, December 3, 1965.
38. National Catholic Office of Motion Pictures, Press Release, December 8, 1965.
39. Jody W. Pennington, *The History of Sex in American Film* (Westport, CT: Praeger, 2007), 13–14.
40. Hutchinson, *Rod Steiger,* 117.
41. *Life*, April 2, 1965.
42. *Film Daily*, April 16, 1965.
43. *New York Herald Tribune*, April 21, 1965.
44. Hutchinson, *Rod Steiger,* 118.
45. *Nation*, May 10, 1965.
46. *Village Voice*, July 15, 1965.
47. *Variety*, September 15, 1965
48. Kael, *Kiss Kiss Bang Bang*, 161.
49. Leonard J Leff and Jerold L. Simmons, *The Dame in the Kimono: Hollywood, Sex and the Production Code* (Lexington: University Press of Kentucky, 2001), 259.
50. Hutchinson, *Rod Steiger*. 119.
51. Holden, *The Oscars*, 244.
52. Emery, *The Directors: Take One*, 369.
53. *Ibid.*, 370.
54. Joey Berlin, ed., *Toxic Fame: Celebrities Speak on Stardom* (Detroit: Invisible Ink, 1996), 8.
55. *Evening Standard*, October 30, 1964.
56. Bob McCabe, *Sean Connery: A Biography* (New York: Thunders Mouth Press, 2000), 69.
57. Lumet, *Making Movies*, 185.
58. *Ibid.*, 184
59. Cunningham, *Film and Literary Vision*, 210.
60. *Ibid.*, 200.
61. *Sunday Herald*, April 10, 2011.
62. Lumet, *Making Movies*, 153–4.
63. Baker, ed., *Movie People*, 39
64. *Ibid.*, 41.
65. Christopher Bray, *Sean Connery: The Measure of a Man* (London: Faber & Faber, 2010), 114.
66. John Parker, *Arise Sir Sean Connery: The Biography of Britain's Greatest Living Actor* (London: John Blake, 2009), 142–3.
67. Kael, *Kiss Kiss Bang Bang*, 82.
68. Lumet, *Making Movies*, 212.
69. *Ibid.*
70. McCabe, *Sean Connery*, 69–70.
71. Parker, *Arise Sir Sean Connery*, 143.
72. Baker, ed., *Movie People*, 40.
73. *Ibid.*, 38.
74. Bray, *Sean Connery*, 116.

Chameleon

1. Emery, *The Directors: Take One*, 370.
2. Kael, *Kiss Kiss Bang Bang*, 93.
3. *Ibid.*, 78.
4. *Ibid.*, 71.
5. *Ibid.*, 77.
6. *Ibid.*, 84.
7. *Ibid.*
8. *Ibid.*, 91.
9. *Ibid.*, 97–8.
10. Itzkoff, *Mad as Hell,* 75.
11. *American Film*, December 8, 1962
12. Kael, *Kiss Kiss Bang Bang*, 76.
13. *Ibid.*
14. *Ibid.*, 80–1.
15. *Ibid.*, 83.
16. Baker, ed., *Movie People*, 41.
17. *London Observer*, September 25, 1966.
18. Norman, *Talking Pictures*, 319.
19. *Newsweek*, May 29, 1967.
20. Sheridan Morley, *James Mason: Odd Man Out* (London: Weidenfeld & Nicolson, 1989), 142–3.
21. *Ibid.*, 143.
22. *Films & Filming*, May 1975.
23. *Positif*, February, 1982.
24. *Time*, March 13, 1968.
25. *Film Facts*, March 1, 1968.
26. Jared Brown, *Alan J. Pakula: His Films and His Life* (New York: Backstage Books, 2005), 81–2.
27. *New York Times*, June 8, 1968.
28. *Positif*, February 1982.
29. Lumet, *Making Movies*, 15.
30. Cunningham, *Film and Literary Vision*, 242.
31. *Films in Review*, November 1973.
32. Simone Signoret, *Nostalgia Isn't What It Used to Be* (London: Granada, 1978), 382–3.
33. Morley, *James Mason*, 151.
34. *Time*, January 3, 1969.
35. *New York Times*, June 8, 1968.
36. Signoret, *Nostalgia Isn't What It Used to Be*, 383.

37. Morley, *James Mason*, 151.
38. Lumet, *Making Movies*, 9.
39. *Ibid.*, 98.
40. Rapf, ed., *Sidney Lumet Interviews*, 190.
41. Buckley, *The Hornes*, 250.
42. Ernest Hemingway, *A Farewell to Arms* (London: Penguin, 1973), 193.

Misfires

1. Rex Reed, *People Are Crazy Here* (New York: Delacorte Press, 1975), 223.
2. *Ibid.*
3. Lumet, *Making Movies*, 14.
4. Parker, *Arise Sir Sean Connery*, 185.
5. *Film Facts*, Volume 14. No. 7.
6. *Newsweek*, July 17, 1971.
7. *Newsday*, June 18, 1971.
8. Manso, *Brando*, 734.
9. Kanfer, *Somebody*, 251.
10. *Los Angeles Times*, December 11, 1972.
11. *Washington Post*, February 3, 1973.
12. Morley, *James Mason*, 158.
13. Hutchinson, *Rod Steiger*, 143.
14. *New York Times*, June 13, 1987.
15. Porter, *Brando Unzipped*, 566.
16. Parker, *Arise Sir Sean Connery*, 196–7.
17. *Films & Filming*, March 1974.
18. Cunningham, *Film and Literary Vision*, 213.
19. Bray, *Sean Connery*, 176n.
20. Andrew Rissik, *The James Bond Man: The Films of Sean Connery* (London: Elm Tree Books, 1983), 113.
21. *Evening Standard*, March 24, 1972.
22. *Films in Review*, November 1973.
23. Baker, ed., *Movie People*, 35.
24. *Films in Review*, November 1973.
25. Shipman, *Movie Talk*, 134.
26. *BBC Omnibus*, February 26, 1991.
27. *New York Times*, May 15, 1966.
28. *Ibid.*, January 28, 1974.

Pacino on the Double

1. Andrew Yule, *Al Pacino: A Life on the Wire* (London: Warner, 1992), 89–90.
2. *Serpico* DVD, Paramount Home Entertainment, Special Features.
3. *Ibid.*
4. Yule, *Al Pacino*, 99.
5. *Ibid.*, 177.
6. *Ibid.*, 90.
7. *Time*, December 31, 1973.
8. Yule, *Al Pacino*, 90–1.
9. *Ibid.*, 91.
10. Bernard F. Dick, *Anatomy of Film* (New York: St. Martin's Press, 1978), 92–3.
11. *Positif*, February, 1982.
12. Lawrence Grobel, *Al Pacino: The Authorized Biography* (London: Simon & Schuster, 2006), 32.
13. *Filmmakers' Newsletter 7*, February 1964.
14. Yule, *Al Pacino*, 91.
15. *Newsweek*, September 29, 1975.
16. *New York Times*, January 20, 1974.
17. Yule, *Al Pacino*, 101–2.
18. Charles Winecoff, *Split Image: The Life of Anthony Perkins* (New York: Plume Books, 1997), 342.
19. *Ibid.*
20. *Ibid.*
21. *Ibid.*, 342–3.
22. *Murder on the Orient Express* DVD, Special Features.
23. *Ibid.*
24. *Ibid.*
25. Lumet, *Making Movies*, 71–2.
26. *Murder on the Orient Express* DVD, Special Features.
27. Alexander Walker, ed., *No Bells on Sunday: The Rachel Roberts Journals* (New York: Harper & Row, 1984), 113.
28. *Ibid.*
29. *Murder on the Orient Express* DVD, Special Features.
30. Lawrence Leamer, *As Times Goes By: The Life of Ingrid Bergman* (London: Sphere, 1987), 379–80.
31. Charlotte Chandler, *Ingrid Bergman: A Personal Biography* (London: Simon & Schuster, 2007), 247.
32. *Murder on the Orient Express* DVD, Special Features.
33. Chandler, *Ingrid Bergman*, 247.
34. *Ibid.*
35. *Films & Filming*, May 1975.
36. *Murder on the Orient Express* DVD, Special Features.
37. Lumet, *Making Movies*, 192.
38. *Ibid.*, 12.
39. Lynn Underwood, ed., *Agatha Christie* (Glasgow: Belgrave Publishing, 1990),
40. *Films & Filming*, May 1975.
41. Wiley and Bona, *Inside Oscar*, 498.
42. Bray, *Sean Connery*, 183.
43. *Ibid.*, 184.
44. Leamer, *As Time Goes By*, 384–5.
45. Chandler, *Ingrid Bergman*, 251.
46. Winecoff, *Split Image*, 344.
47. Yule, *Al Pacino*, 131.
48. Patrick E. Horrigan, Widescreen *Dreams: Growing Up Gay at the Movies* (Milwaukee: University of Wisconsin Press, 1999), 185.
49. Yule, *Al Pacino*, 133.
50. *Ibid.*
51. *Ibid.*, 134.
52. Grobel, *Al Pacino*, xii.
53. *Films in Review*, October 1984.
54. *Village Voice* 8, 1981.

55. *Women's Wear Daily*, October 2, 1975.
56. Lumet, *Making Movies*, 113.
57. *Ibid.*, 89.
58. *London Evening Standard*, December 18, 1975.
59. Yule, *Al Pacino*, 136.
60. *Ibid.*
61. Grobel, *Al Pacino*, 141.
62. Yule, *Al Pacino*, 139.
63. Lumet, *Making Movies*, 33.
64. Yule, *Al Pacino*. 137.
65. Grobel, *Al Pacino*, 31–2.
66. *Newsday*, December 8, 1982.
67. Vito Russo, *The Celluloid Closet: Homosexuality in the Movies* (New York: Harper & Row, 1987), 178–9.
68. *American Film*, 1982.
69. Wiley and Bona, *Inside Oscar*, 512.
70. Yule, *Al Pacino*, 138.
71. Emery, *The Directors: Take One*, 376.
72. *Positif*, February 1982.
73. Yule, *Al Pacino*, 141–2.
74. Steven Schneider, ed., *1001 Movies You Must See Before You Die* (London: Cassell, 2014), 591.
75. *Entertainment Weekly*, April 9, 2011.

The Mad Prophet

1. Shaun Considine, The *Life and Work of Paddy Chayefsky* (Lincoln, NE: iUniverse, 2000), 303.
2. Itzkoff, *Mad as Hell*, 65.
3. Elaine Dundy, Finch, *Bloody Finch: A Life of Peter Finch* (New York: Holt, Rinehart and Winston, 1980), 321.
4. *Ibid.*, 321–2.
5. Itzkoff, *Mad as Hell*, 71–2.
6. David Sheward, *Rage and Glory: The Volatile Life and Career of George C. Scott* (New York: Applause Theatre and Cinema Books, 2008), 266.
7. *Ibid.*
8. Considine, *Mad as Hell*, 317.
9. Dundy, *Finch, Bloody Finch*, 322.
10. Wiley and Bona, *Inside Oscar*, 529.
11. Lumet, *Making Movies*, 142.
12. Considine, *Mad as Hell*, 343.
13. Lumet, *Making Movies*, 41.
14. Faye Dunaway with Betsy Sharkey, *Looking for Gatsby: My Life* (London: HarperCollins, 1995), 297.
15. Boze Hadleigh, ed., *Diss and Tell* (Kansas City: Andrews McMeel, 2005), 173.
16. Itzkoff, *Mad as Hell*, 121.
17. Dunaway with Sharkey, *Looking for Gatsby*, 301.
18. *Sarasota Herald-Tribune*, July 16, 1974.
19. Itzkoff, *Mad as Hell*, 47.
20. Boyer, *Sidney Lumet*, 71.
21. Considine, *Mad as Hell*, 321–2.
22. *Ibid.*, 324.
23. Lumet, *Making Movies*, 122–3.
24. Considine, *Mad as Hell*, 322–3.
25. *L.A. Times*, March 18, 1982.
26. Cunningham, *Film and Literary Vision*, 223.
27. *American Cinematographer 58*, April 1977.
28. Lumet, *Making Movies*, 85.
29. Itzkoff, *Mad as Hell*, 113.
30. *Ibid.*, 133.
31. Lumet, *Making Movies*, 43.
32. *Ibid.*
33. Dundy, *Finch, Bloody Finch*, 325–6.
34. Itzkoff, *Mad as Hell*, 128.
35. Eastman, *Retakes*, 231.
36. Itzkoff, *Mad as Hell*, 105.
37. *Ibid.*
38. Dunaway with Sharkey, *Looking for Gatsby*, 295.
39. *Ibid.*, 295–6.
40. *Ibid.*, 300.
41. *Ibid.*, 293.
42. Considine, *Mad as Hell*, 319.
43. *Ibid.*, 321.
44. *Ibid.*, 324–5.
45. Wiley and Bona, *Inside Oscar*, 529.
46. Dunaway with Sharkey, *Looking for Gatsby*, 301–2.
47. Cunningham, *Film and Literary Vision*, 224.
48. Desser and Friedman, *American-Jewish Filmmakers*, 221.
49. Dunaway with Sharkey, *Looking for Gatsby*, 302.
50. Itzkoff, *Mad as Hell*, 127.
51. Roger Ebert, *The Great Movies* (New York: Broadway Books, 2002), 319.
52. Considine, *Mad as Hell*, 323.
53. *Ibid.*, 325–6.
54. Itzkoff, *Mad as Hell*, 120.
55. Dunaway with Sharkey, *Looking for Gatsby*, 296.
56. *Ibid.*, 302.
57. Itzkoff, *Mad as Hell*, 124.
58. Dundy, *Finch, Bloody Finch*, 322–3.
59. *New York Post*, March 22, 1976.
60. Considine, *Mad as Hell*, 326–7.
61. Dunaway with Sharkey, *Looking for Gatsby*, 312.
62. *Christian Science Monitor*, February 23, 1977.
63. *Film Journal*, January 1986.
64. Buirski, *By Sidney Lumet*.
65. Dunaway with Sharkey, *Looking for Gatsby*, 312.
66. Danny Peary, *Close-Ups: Intimate Profiles of Movie Stars by their Costars, Directors, Screenwriters and Friends* (New York: Galahad Books, 1978), 547.
67. *L.A. Times*, February 2, 1977.
68. Schneider, ed., *1001 Movies You Must See Before You Die*, 604.
69. Bowles, A *Guide to References and Resources*, 31.

70. Wiley and Bona, *Inside Oscar*, 529.
71. Jim Piazza and Gail Kinn, *The Academy Awards: The Complete Unofficial History* (New York: Black Dog and Leventhal, 2008), 207.
72. Considine, *Mad as Hell*, 330.
73. *Ibid.*, 330–1.
74. *Ibid.*, 331.
75. *Film Comment*, August 1988.
76. Itzkoff, *Mad as Hell*, 143.
77. *Ibid.*, 175.
78. Dunaway with Sharkey, *Looking for Gatsby*, 318–9.
79. Considine, *Mad as Hell*, 340.
80. *New York Daily Metro*, September 26, 1976.
81. *New York Daily News*, December 23, 1976.
82. Considine, *Mad as Hell*, 308.
83. Ebert, *The Great Movies*, 323.
84. Norman, *Talking Pictures*, 300.

Workaholic

1. *American Film*, December 1982.
2. *East Hampton Star*, April 14, 2011.
3. Lumet, *Making Movies*, 125.
4. Considine, *Mad as Hell*, 359.
5. Winecoff, *Split Image*, 359.
6. Graham Jenkins with Barry Turner, *Richard Burton My Brother* (London: Sphere, 1988), 288.
7. Winecoff, *Split Image*, 354.
8. Bowles, *A Guide to References and Resources*, 31.
9. *Films & Filming*, May 1978.
10. *New York Times*, July 24, 1977.
11. *Films & Filming*, May 1978.
12. Melvyn Bragg, *Rich: The Life of Richard Burton* (London: Hodder & Stoughton, 1988), 440.
13. Tom Rubython, *And God Created Burton* (London: Myrtle Press, 2011), 763.
14. Wiley and Bona, *Inside Oscar*, 541.
15. Michael Munn, *Richard Burton: Prince of Players* (London: JR Books, 2008), 221.
16. Wiley and Bona, *Inside Oscar*, 541.
17. Bragg, *Rich*, 440.
18. *Radio Times Guide to Films 2012* (London: BBC Worldwide, 2011), 374.
19. Hutchinson, *Rod Steiger*, 99.
20. *Films & Filming*, May 1978.
21. J. Randy Taraborelli, *Diana Ross: An Unathorized Biography* (London: Pan Books, 2007), 309.
22. *Ibid.*, 309–10.
23. Gavin, *Stormy Weather*, 406.
24. *New York Times*, July 24, 1977.
25. Gavin, *Stormy Weather*, 406.
26. McClelland, ed., *Hollywood on Hollywood*, 34.
27. J. Randy Taraborelli, *Michael Jackson: The Magic, the Madness, the Whole Story* (London: Pan Books, 2009), 168–9.
28. *Ibid.*, 178.
29. *Ibid.*
30. Diana Ross, *Secrets of a Sparrow* (London: Headline, 1993), 185–6.
31. *Ibid.*, 187.
32. *Ibid.* 190.
33. *Ibid.*, 195–6.
34. *New Yorker*, October 30, 1978.
35. Horrigan, *Widescreen Dreams*, 171–2.
36. *Ibid.*, 172.
37. Taraborelli, *Michael Jackson*, 179.
38. *Ibid.*
39. Rapf, ed. *Sidney Lumet Interviews*, 176.
40. Ross, *Secrets of a Sparrow*, 197.
41. Itzkoff, *Mad as Hell*, 212.
42. Taraborelli, *Diana Ross*, 523.
43. *Ibid.*, 313.
44. Emery, *The Directors: Take One*, 377.
45. Gavin, *Stormy Weather*, 413–4.
46. *Ibid.*
47. Vanderbilt, *It Seemed Important at the Time*, 96.
48. Cooper and Vanderbilt, *The Rainbow Comes and Goes*, 205.
49. Bob Collacello, *Holy Terror: Andy Warhol Close Up* (New York: Harper Perennial, 1991), 399.
50. Vanderbilt, *It Seemed Important at the Time*, 96.
51. *BBC Omnibus*, February 26, 1991.
52. Ali MacGraw, *Moving Pictures* (London: Bantam, 1991), 131–2.
53. *Wall Street Journal*, January 15, 2011.
54. MacGraw, *Moving Pictures*, 132.
55. *Ibid.*, 132–3.
56. *New York Times*, August 5, 1981.
57. Considine, *Mad as Hell*, 399.
58. He needn't have worried. Not only is his reputation secure, these are still two of the most quoted lines in films today.
59. *Newsweek*, August 24, 1981.
60. *Village Voice*, August 11, 1981.
61. Lumet, *Making Movies*, 55.
62. Williams said of his performance in *Hair* that he didn't so much want to get "into" the part as "under" it (*New York Times*, June 1979).
63. Cunningham, *Film and Literary Vision*, 227. It was nonetheless true. See *Positif*, February 1982 where Lumet says it himself.
64. Lumet, *Making Movies*, 55.
65. On the set of *Dog Day Afternoon* he went so far as to involve extras in a "participatory" relationship with the people who lived in the neighborhood (see *Making Movies*, 113).
66. *Vogue*, August, 1983.
67. *East Hampton Star*, April 14, 2011.
68. *Positif*, February 1982.
69. Lizzie Francke, *Script Girls: Women Screenwriters in Hollywood* (London: British Film Institute, 1994), 96.
70. Boyer, *Sidney Lumet*, 105.
71. *Ibid.*
72. BBC, *Omnibus*, February 26, 1991.
73. Boyer, *Sidney Lumet*, 105.

74. *New York*, August 1981.
75. *Ibid.*
76. Lumet, *Making Movies*, 96–97.
77. *Ibid.*, 134.
78. Rapf, ed., *Sidney Lumet Interviews*, 170.
79. *Entertainment Parade*, January 2, 2017.
80. Lumet prided himself on the fact that his actors worked in a "secure atmosphere." See *La Revue du Cinema*, February 1982.
81. BBC, *Omnibus*, February 26, 1991.
82. Cunningham, *Film and Literary Vision*, 240.
83. *Monthly Film Bulletin*, February 1983.
84. *New York*, December 20, 1982.
85. He added elsewhere that he was also dependent on "120 people knowing their work." This was another reason he debunked the auteur tag, and why he never liked the billing, "a Sidney Lumet film." See Cunningham, *Film and Literary Vision*, 236.
86. Baker, *Movie People*, 48.

Mixed Grills

1. *New York Times Magazine*, June 6, 1982.
2. Shipman, *Movie Talk,* 173.
3. Kael, *Kiss Kiss Bang Bang*, 86.
4. Emery, *The Directors: Take One*, 379.
5. *American Film*, December 8, 1982.
6. Shipman, *Movie Talk*, 134.
7. Emery, *The Directors: Take One*, 371.
8. *Monthly Film Bulletin*, September 1982.
9. Michael Caine, *The Elephant to Hollywood: The Autobiography* (London: Hodder & Stoughton, 2010), 210.
10. Russo, *The Celluloid Closet*, 295.
11. Christopher Reeve, *Still Me* (London: Arrow, 1999), 212.
12. Steve Stewart, *Gay Hollywood Film and Video Guide* (Laguna Hills, CA: Companion Publications, 1993), 60.
13. Yule, *Al Pacino*, 265–6.
14. *Ibid.*, 245–6.
15. Peter Hay, *Movie Anecdotes* (New York: Oxford University Press, 1990), 191–2.
16. Shawn Levy, *Paul Newman: A Life* (London: Aurum Press, 2010), 347.
17. Wiley and Bona, *Inside Oscar*, 617.
18. Levy, *Paul Newman*, 346.
19. Susan Netter, *Paul Newman and Joanne Woodward: An Unauthorized Biography* (London: Sphere, 1990), 157.
20. *Ibid.*
21. Morley, *James Mason*, 171.
22. Daniel O'Brien, *Paul Newman* (London: Faber & Faber, 2005), 248.
23. *New York*, December 20, 1982.
24. Les and Barbara Keyser, *Hollywood and the Catholic Church* (Chicago: Loyola University Press, 1984), 255.
25. Shipman, *Movie Talk*, 153.
26. O'Brien, *Paul Newman*, 245.
27. Lumet, *Making Movies*, 98.
28. *Ibid.*, 158.
29. Considine, *Mad as Hell*, 313.
30. Rapf, ed., *Sidney Lumet Interviews*, 145.
31. Wiley and Bona, *Inside Oscar*, 617.
32. *L.A. Times*, December 16, 1982.
33. *Women's Wear Daily*, December 7, 1982.
34. *Village Voice*, December 14, 1982.
35. *American Film*, December 1982.
36. *The Verdict* DVD, Twentieth Century Fox Home Entertainment, 1982.
37. O'Brien, *Paul Newman*, 255.
38. Wiley and Bona, *Inside Oscar*, 626.
39. *Ibid.*, 627.
40. *Ibid.*
41. Lumet, *Making Movies*, 6.
42. Levy, *Paul Newman*, 349.
43. *Sunday Star Ledger*, September 18, 1983.
44. *Films in Review,* October 1984.
45. *San Diego Union Tribune,* April 9, 2011.
46. *La Revue du Cinema*, February 1982.
47. Rapf, ed. *Sidney Lumet Interview,* 182.
48. *La Revue du Cinema*, February 1982.
49. Yule, *Al Pacino*, 248–9.
50. *New York Times*, August 31, 1983.
51. Cunningham, *Film and Literary Vision*, 59.
52. *New Yorker*, September 5, 1983.
53. *Village Voice*, September 6, 1983.
54. *San Francisco Chronicle*, October 4, 1983.
55. www.emanuellevy.com.
56. Desser and Friedman, *American-Jewish Filmmakers*, 214.
57. *Film Quarterly*, Spring 1984.
58. *Vogue*, August, 1983.
59. *Newsday*, August 26, 1983.
60. Lumet, *Making Movies*, 42.
61. *Films in Review*, October, 1984.
62. *Village Voice*, October 23, 1984.
63. John Parker, *Richard Gere: The Flesh and the Spirit* (London: Headline, 1995), 158.
64. *Ibid.*, 159.
65. *Ibid.*
66. *Newsday*, January 31, 1986.
67. *Monthly Film Bulletin*, August 1987.
68. *L.A. Times*, January 31, 1986.
69. *New York Post*, January 31, 1986.

To Hollywood—Finally

1. *Positif*, February 1982.
2. James Mason, *Before I Forget* (London: Sphere, 1982), 305.
3. Bogdanovich, *Who the Devil Made It*, 803.
4. *San Diego Union Tribune*, April 9, 2011.
5. McClelland, ed., *Hollywood on Hollywood*, 1986.
6. Lumet, *Making Movies*, 61.
7. Jane Fonda, *My Life So Far* (London: Ebury Press, 2006), 448.
8. *Ibid.*, 452.

9. *Ibid.*, 448.
10. Patricia Bosworth, *Jane Fonda: The Private Life of a Public Woman* (London: Biteback Publishing, 2011), 486–7.
11. *Stills*, February, 1987.
12. *New York Post*, December 26, 1986.
13. *New Yorker*, January 5, 1987.
14. Wiley and Bona, *Inside Oscar*, 691.
15. Robert Osborne, *80 Years of the Oscars: The Official Story of the Academy Awards* (New York: Abbeville Press, 2008), 336.
16. Lumet, *Making Movies*, 25.
17. Desser and Friedman, *American-Jewish Filmmakers*, 202.
18. Penelope Dening, *The River Phoenix Album* (London: Plexus, 1995), 44.
19. Yule, *Al Pacino*, 316.
20. Rapf, ed. *Sidney Lumet Interviews*, 181.
21. Ronald Bergan, *Dustin Hoffman* (London: Virgin, 1991), 248–9.
22. Michael Freedland, *A Biography of Dustin Hoffman* (London: Virgin, 1989), 205.
23. Emery, *The Directors: Take One*, 381.
24. Bergan, *Dustin Hoffman*, 250.
25. Lumet, *Making Movies*, 104.
26. Sean Connery and Murray Grigor, *Being a Scot* (London: Weidenfeld & Nicolson, 2009), 14.
27. Parker, *Arise Sir Sean Connery*, 284.
28. Bergan, *Dustin Hoffman*, 249.
29. Lumet, *Making Movies*, 114–5.
30. *New York Post*, December 15, 1989.
31. *Monthly Film Bulletin*, March 1990.
32. McCabe, *Sean Connery*, 132–3.
33. Bray, *Sean Connery*, 266.
34. *New York Post*, December 15, 1989.
35. Bray, *Sean Connery*, 265.
36. Emery, *The Directors: Take One*, 381.
37. McCabe, *Sean Connery*, 133.
38. Emery, *The Directors: Take One*, 382.
39. *Ibid.*
40. *New Yorker*, April 2, 1990.
41. *New York Times*, December 31, 1989.
42. Yule, *Al Pacino*, 352.
43. *L.A. Times*, January 27, 1991.
44. *Premiere*, August 1992.
45. Lumet, *Making Movies*, x.
46. Emery, *The Directors: Take One*, 383.

Crime and Punishment

1. *Sight and Sound*, January 1994.
2. *L.A. Times*, June 4, 1993.
3. www.rogerebert.com.
4. *Charlie Rose Show*, CBS, April 14, 1995.
5. *Ibid.*
6. *Ibid.*
7. *Ibid.*
8. *Ibid.*
9. www.authorspeak.com/lumet.
10. *Ibid.*
11. *Ibid.*
12. *Ibid.*
13. *Ibid.*
14. Ian Holm with Steven Jacobi, *Acting My Life* (London: Corgi, 2006), 363.
15. *Charlie Rose Show*, CBS, April 14, 1995.
16. *Night Falls on Manhattan* DVD, Spelling Films Entertainment.
17. *Ibid.*
18. *Ibid.*
19. *Ibid.*
20. *Ibid.*
21. *Films & Filming*, October 1964.
22. *Night Falls on Manhattan* DVD, Special Features.
23. *Charlie Rose Show*, CBS, April 14, 1995.
24. *Night Falls on Manhattan* DVD, Special Features.
25. *Ibid.*
26. *Ibid.*
27. *Ibid.*
28. *Ibid.*
29. *Ibid.*
30. Emery, *The Directors: Take One*, 383.
31. *Newsday*, May 16, 1997.
32. *New York Times Magazine*, November 23, 1997.
33. *Night Falls on Manhattan* DVD, Special Features.
34. *New York Times Magazine*, November 23, 1997.
35. *Hollywood Reporter*, June 10, 1997.
36. Rapf, ed., *Sidney Lumet Interviews*, 173.
37. Steve Pond, *The Big Show: High Times and Dirty Dealings Backstage at the Academy Awards* (New York: Faber & Faber, 2005), 197.
38. *Film Comment*, August 1988.
39. *BBC Omnibus*, February, 26, 1991.
40. Rapf, ed., *Sidney Lumet Interviews*, 185.
41. *Gloria* DVD, Mandalay Entertainment, Special Features.
42. *Ibid.*
43. *L.A. Times*, January 25, 1999.
44. *New York Post*, January 23, 1999.
45. Sheward, *Rage and Glory*, 343.

Final Surge

1. *TV Guide*, February 17, 2001.
2. *Ibid.*
3. *L.A. Times*, January 15, 2001.
4. *Ibid.*
5. *Ibid.*
6. *Christian Science Monitor*, February 23, 1977.
7. *L.A. Times*, January 15, 2001.
8. *Ibid.*
9. *L.A. Weekly*, March 1, 2001.
10. *Ibid.*
11. *San Diego Union Tribune*, April 9, 2011.

12. Piazza and Kinn, *The Academy Awards*, 328.
13. Osborne, *80 Years of the Oscars*, 369.
14. Michael Robin and Todd Rone Owens, *Vin Diesel Exposed* (New York: Roundtable Press, 2002), 13.
15. *Ibid.*
16. *Guilty As Sin*, Warner Home Video, Special Features.
17. *Ibid.*
18. *Ibid.*
19. Rapf, ed., *Sidney Lumet Interviews*, 147.
20. *New York Times*, December 31, 1989.
21. Buirski, *By Sidney Lumet.*
22. *Ibid.*
23. *Ibid.*
24. *San Francisco Chronicle*, April 14, 2011.
25. *New Yorker Magazine*, September 24, 2007.
26. *Entertainment Weekly*, April 9, 2011.
27. www.emanuellevy.com.
28. *Before the Devil Knows You're Dead* DVD, Capital Entertainment, Bonus Features.
29. *Ibid.*
30. *Ibid.*
31. *New Yorker Magazine*, September 24, 2007.
32. *Ibid.*
33. *Ibid.*
34. *Ibid.*
35. Buirski, *By Sidney Lumet.*
36. *New York Times*, October 17, 2010.
37. *Ibid.*
38. *Ibid.*
39. Emery, *The Directors: Take One*, 385.
40. Cooper and Vanderbilt, *The Rainbow Comes and Goes*, 181.
41. *New York Times*, June 8, 1968.
42. Lumet, *Making Movies*, 13.
43. Baker, *Movie People*, 49.
44. Piazza and Kinn, *The Academy Awards*, 328.
45. *BBC News*, April 10, 2011.
46. *Ibid.*
47. *San Diego Union Tribune*, April 9, 2011.
48. *Hollywood Reporter*, April 11, 2011.
49. *Ibid.*
50. *Ibid.*
51. *WENN*, April, 2011.
52. *East Hampton Star*, April 14, 2011.
53. *L.A. Times*, April 11, 2011.
54. *San Francisco Chronicle*, April 14, 2011.
55. Leonard Maltin and Susan Gray, *Writers on Directors* (New York: Watson-Guptill, 1999), 152.
56. Boyer, *Sidney Lumet*, 71.
57. www.rogerebert.com.
58. Itzkoff, *Mad as Hell*, 144.
59. *Variety*, January 1, 1970.
60. Publicity Release for *The Appointment.*
61. Lumet, *Making Movies*, 141.
62. Bowles, *A Guide to References and Resources*, 45.
63. *New York Times*, April 9, 2011.
64. *Films in Review*, November 24, 1973.
65. *Film Comment*, August 1988.
66. *Hollywood Reporter*, June 10, 1977.
67. *Entertainment Weekly*, April 9, 2011.

Bibliography

Baker, Fred, ed., *Movie People*. London: Abelard-Schuman, 1973.

Barnouw, Erik, *Tube of Plenty: The Evolution of American Television*. New York: Oxford University Press, 1990.

Barson, Michael, *The Illustrated Who's Who of Hollywood Directors*. New York: Farrar, Straus and Giroux, 1995.

Baxter, John, *Stanley Kubrick: A Biography*. London: HarperCollins, 1997.

Bergan, Ronald, *Dustin Hoffman*. London: Virgin, 1991.

Black, Gregory D., *The Catholic Crusade Against the Movies 1940–75*. New York: Cambridge University Press, 1997.

Blake, Richard A., *Street Smart: The New York of Lumet, Allen, Scorsese and Lee*. Lexington: University Press of Kentucky, 2005.

Bly, Nellie, *Marlon Brando: Larger Than Life*. New York: Windsor Publishing, 1994.

Bogdanovich, Peter, *Who the Devil Made It*. New York: Alfred A. Knopf, 1997.

Boorman, John, and Tod Lippy, *Fonda: Projections II: New York Filmmakers on New York Filmmaking*. London: Faber & Faber 2001.

Bosworth, Patricia, *Jane Fonda: The Private Life of a Public Woman*. London: Biteback Publishing, 2011.

Bowles, Stephen E., *Sidney Lumet: A Guide to References and Resources*. Boston: G.K. Hall & Co., 1979.

Boyer, Jay, *Sidney Lumet*. New York: Twayne, 1993.

Bragg, Melvyn, *Rich: The Life of Richard Burton*. London: Hodder & Stoughton, 1988.

Brando, Marlon, with Robert Lindsay, *Songs My Mother Taught Me*. London: Century, 1994.

Bray, Christopher, *Sean Connery: The Measure of a Man*. London: Faber & Faber, 2010.

Buckley, Gail Lumet, *The Hornes: An American Family*. New York: Applause Theatre and Cinema Books, 1986.

Burston, Paul, *What Are You Looking At? Queer Sex, Style and Cinema*. London: Cassell, 1995.

Caine, Michael, *The Elephant to Hollywood: The Autobiography*. London: Hodder & Stoughton, 2010.

Carrick, Peter, *Richard Gere*. London: Robert Hale, 1996.

Chandler, Charlotte, *The Real Kate: A Personal Biography of Katharine Hepburn*. London: Robson Books, 2012.

Clum, John, *Paddy Chayefsky*. Boston: Twayne, 1976.

Clurman, Harold, *The Fervent Years: The Group Theatre & the 30s*. New York: Da Capo, 1983.

Collier, Peter, *The Fondas: A Hollywood Dynasty*. London: HarperCollins, 1991.

Connery, Sean, and Murray Grigor, *Being a Scot*. London: Weidenfeld & Nicolson, 2009.

Considine, Shaun, *The Life and Work of Paddy Chayefsky*. Lincoln, NE: iUniverse, 2000.

Cook, David, *A History of the Narrative Film*. New York: Norton, 2004.

Cooper, Anderson, and Gloria Vanderbilt, *The Rainbow Comes and Goes: A Mother and Son on Life, Love and Loss*. New York: Harper, 2017.

Cowie, Peter, *50 Major Filmmakers*. South Brunswick, NJ: A.S. Barnes, 1975.

Cunningham, Frank R., *Sidney Lumet: Film and Literary Vision*. Lexington: University Press of Kentucky, 1991.

Daniel, Douglass K., *Anne Bancroft: A Life*. Lexington: University Press of Kentucky, 2017.

Desser, David, and Lester D. Friedman, *American-Jewish Filmmakers: Traditions and Trends*. Urbana: University of Illinois Press, 1993.

Dick, Bernard F., *Anatomy of Film*. New York: St. Martin's Press, 1978.

Downing, David, *Marlon Brando*. New York: Stein & Day, 1984.

Dunaway, Faye, with Betsy Sharkey, *Looking for Gatsby: My Life*. London: HarperCollins, 1995.

Dundy, Elaine, *Finch, Bloody Finch: A Life of Peter Finch*. New York: Holt, Winehart and Winston, 1980.

Eastman, John, *Retakes: Behind the Scenes of 500 Classic Movies*. New York: Ballantine Books, 1989.

Ebert, Roger, *The Great Movies.* New York: Broadway Books, 2002.

Emery, Robert J., *The Directors: Take One.* New York: TV Books, 1999.

Falk, Quentin, *Albert Finney: In Character.* London: Robson, 1998.

Faulkner, Trader, *Peter Finch.* New York: Taplinger Publishing, 1979.

Fonda, Henry, *My Life: As Told to Howard Teichmann.* New York: New American Library, 1981.

Freedland, Michael, *A Biography of Dustin Hoffman.* London: Virgin, 1989.

Friedman, Lester D., *Hollywood's Image of the Jew.* New York: Unger, 1982.

Gabler, Neil, *An Empire of Their Own: How the Jews Invented Hollywood.* New York: Anchor, 1989.

Garfield, David, *A Player's Place: The Story of the Actors Studio.* New York: Macmillan, 1980.

Gavin, James, *Stormy Weather: The Life of Lena Horne.* New York: Atria, 2009.

Grobel, Lawrence, *Al Pacino: The Authorized Biography.* London: Simon & Schuster, 2006.

Hay, Peter, *Movie Anecdotes.* New York: Oxford University Press, 1990.

Hershman, Gabriel, *Strolling Player: The Life and Career of Albert Finney.* London: History Press, 2017.

Higham, Charles, *Brando: The Unauthorized Biography.* London: Grafton Books, 1989.

Holden, Anthony, *The Oscars: The Secret History of Hollywood's Academy Awards.* London: Warner Books, 1993.

Horrigan, Patrick E., *Widescreen Dreams: Growing Up Gay at the Movies.* Milwaukee: University of Wisconsin Press, 1999.

Hunter, Allan, *Walter Matthau.* London: W.H. Allen, 1984.

Hunter, Tab, with Eddie Muller, *Tab Hunter Confidential: The Making of a Movie Star.* Chapel Hill, NC: Algonquin Books, 2005.

Hutchinson, Tom, *Rod Steiger: Memoirs of a Friendship.* New York: Fromm International, 2000.

Insdorf, Annette, *Indelible Shadows: Film and the Holocaust.* New York: Random House, 1983.

Itzkoff, Dave, *Mad as Hell: The Making of Network and the Fateful Vision of the Angriest Man in Movies.* New York: Henry Holt and Company, 2014.

Jenkins, Graham, with Barry Turner, *Richard Burton My Brother.* London: Sphere, 1988.

Kael, Pauline, *Kiss Kiss Bang Bang: Film Writings 1965–1967.* London: Arena, 1987.

Kanfer, Stefan, *Somebody: The Reckless Life and Remarkable Career of Marlon Brando.* London: Faber & Faber, 2008.

Kearney, Robyn ed., *Who's Who in Hollywood.* London: Bloomsbury, 1993.

Kerbel, Michael, *Henry Fonda.* New York: Pyramid Publications, 1975.

Laurie, Piper, *Learning to Live Out Loud.* New York: Crown Archetype, 2011.

Leamer, Lawrence, *As Time Goes By: The Life of Ingrid Bergman.* London: Sphere, 1987.

Leaming, Barbara, *Katharine Hepburn.* London: Phoenix, 1995.

Leff, Leonard J., and Jerold L. Simmons, *The Dame in the Kimono: Hollywood, Sex and the Production Code.* Lexington: University Press of Kentucky, 2001.

Levy, Shawn, *Paul Newman: A Life.* London: Aurum Press, 2010.

Lumet, Sidney, *Making Movies.* London: Bloomsbury, 1996.

MacGraw, Ali, *Moving Pictures.* London: Bantam, 1991.

Maltin, Leonard, and Susan Gray, *Writers on Directors.* New York: Watson-Guptill, 1999.

Mamet, David, *Bambi Vs. Godzilla: On the Nature, Purpose and Practice of the Movie Business.* London: Simon & Schuster, 2007.

Mann, William J., *Kate: The Woman Who Was Katharine Hepburn.* London: Faber & Faber, 2006.

Manso, Peter, *Brando.* New York: Hyperion, 1994.

Mason, James, *Before I Forget: An Autobiography.* London: Sphere, 1982.

May, John R., ed., *Image and Likeness: Religious Visions in American Film Classics.* New York: Paulist Press, 1992.

McCabe, Rob, *Sean Connery: A Biography.* New York: Thunders Mouth Press, 2000.

McClelland, Doug, ed., *Hollywood on Hollywood: Tinseltown Talks.* Boston: Faber & Faber, 1985.

Miller, Frank, *Censored Hollywood: Sex, Sin and Violence on Screen.* Atlanta: Turner Publishing, 1994.

Mizruchi, Susan L., *Brando's Smile: The Life, Thought and Work.* New York: W.W. Norton & Co., 2014.

Morley, Sheridan, *James Mason: Odd Man Out.* London: Weidenfeld & Nicolson, 1989.

Munn, Michael, *Richard Burton: Prince of Players.* London: JR Books, 2008.

Navatsky, Victor S., *Naming Names.* New York: Viking Press, 1980.

Norman, Barry, *The Film Greats.* London: Futura, 1985.

_____, *Talking Pictures.* London: BBC Books, 1987.

Parker, John, *Arise Sir Sean Connery: The Biography of Britain's Greatest Living Actor.* London: John Blake, 2009.

Pascall, Jeremy, and Clyde Jeavons, *Sex in the Movies: A Pictorial History.* London: Hamlyn, 1975.

Patrizia, Pistagnesi, *Anna Magnani.* Milan: Fabbri, 1988.

Porter, Darwin, *Brando Unzipped.* New York: Blood Moon Productions, 2005.

Quirk, Lawrence J., *The Complete Films of Ingrid Bergman.* New York: Citadel Press, 1989.

Randall, Stephen, ed., *The Playboy Interviews*. Milwaukie, OR: M Press, 2006.
Rapf, Joanna E,. ed., *Sidney Lumet Interviews*. Jackson: University Press of Mississippi, 2006.
Rissik, Andrew, *The James Bond Man: The Films of Sean Connery*. London: Elm Tree Books, 1983.
Robbins, Jhan, *Yul Brynner: The Inscrutable King*. London: W.H. Allen, 1988.
Roberts, Jerry, *Encyclopedia of Television Film Directors*. Lanham, MD: Scarecrow Press, 2009.
Roseblum, Ralph, and Robert Karen, *When the Shooting Stops, the Cutting Begins: A Film Editor's Story*. New York: Penguin, 1980.
Ross, Diana, *Secrets of a Sparrow*. London: Headline, 1993.
Rubython, Tom, *And God Created Burton*. London: Myrtle Press, 2011.
Russo, Vito, *The Celluloid Closet: Homosexuality in the Movies*. New York: Harper & Row, 1987.
Ryan, Paul, *Marlon Brando: A Portrait*. London: Plexus, 1991.
Sarris, Andrew, *The American Cinema: Directors and Directions, 1929–1968*. New York: E.P. Dutton, 1968.
Schneider, Steven, ed., *1001 Movies You Must See Before You Die*. London: Cassell, 2014.
Sheward, David, *Rage and Glory: The Volatile Life and Career of George C. Scott*. New York: Applause Theatre and Cinema Books, 2008.
Shipman, David, *Movie Talk: Who Said What About Whom in the Movies*. London: Bloomsbury, 1988.
Signoret, Simone, *Nostalgia Isn't What It Used To Be*. London: Granada, 1978.
Spoto, Donald, *The Kindness of Strangers: The Life of Tennessee Williams*. New York: Ballantine Books, 1985.
Stapleton, Maureen, and Jane Scovell, *A Hell of a Life*. New York: Simon & Schuster, 1995.
Strick, Philip, *Science Fiction Movies*. London: Octopus, 1976.
Taraborelli, J. Randy, *Diana Ross: An Unauthorized Biography*. London: Pan Books, 2007.
____, *Michael Jackson: The Magic, the Madness, the Whole Story*. London: Pan Books, 2009.
Thomas, Bob, *Marlon: Portrait of the Rebel as an Artist*. New York: Random House, 1973.
Thomson, David, *Marlon Brando*. London: Dorling Kindersley, 2003.
Underwood, Lynn, ed., *Agatha Christie*. Glasgow: Belgrave Publishing, 1990.
Vanderbilt, Gloria, *It Seemed Important at the Time: A Romance Memoir*. New York: Simon & Schuster, 2004.
Walker, Alexander, *It's Only a Movie, Ingrid: Encounters On and Off Screen*. London: Headline, 1998.
Walsh, Frank, *Sin and Censorship: The Catholic Church and the Motion Picture Industry*. New Haven: Yale University Press, 1996.
Whale, Chase, ed., *Philip Seymour Hoffman: Brilliant. Troubled. Tragic*. London: Plexus, 2016.
Wiley, Mason, and Damien Bona, *Inside Oscar: The Unofficial History of the Academy Awards*. New York: Ballantine Books, 1987.
Wilk, Max, *Schmucks with Underwoods*. New York: Applause Theatre and Cinema Books, 2004.
Winecoff, Charles, *Split Image: The Life of Anthony Perkins*. New York: Plume Books, 1997.
Winters, Shelley, *The Middle of My Century*. New York: Pocket Books, 1989.
Young, Jeff, *Kazan: The Master Director Discusses His Films*. New York: Newmarket, 1999.
Yule, Andrew, *Al Pacino: A Life on the Wire*. London: Warner, 1993.

Index

Numbers in ***bold italics*** indicate pages with illustrations

Abry, Jonas 155
Abzug, Bella 111
Actors Studio 9–10
Adler, Richard 45
The Adventures of Helen and Mary 7
Ailes, Roger 147
Aimeé, Anouk 69–70
The Alamo 13
All the King's Men 24
All the President's Men 112
Allen, Jay Presson 80, ***125***, 128, 129, 132, ***134***, 135–6
Allen, Penelope ***91***
Allen, R.S. 57
Allen, Woody 3, 93, 125, 141, 145, 146, 159, 189, 191
Allied Artists 56
Allied International 56
Alpert, Hollis 26, 35
Altman, Robert 148
Altered States 115
American Buffalo 135–6
American Civil Liberties Union 149
American Masters 193
Anastasia 90
Anderson, John 175
The Anderson Tapes 3, 74, ***75***, 76, 166
Andersson, Harriet 65
Andrews, Harry 57, 58, 65, 66, 68
Antonioni, Michelangelo 70, 191
The Appointment 3, 69, ***70***
Archerd, Amy 44
Arkin, Alan 181, 182
Armstrong, Neil 47
Armstrong, R.G. 35
Arnold, Edward 98
Arnold, Gary 75
Assante, Armand 163
Autumn Fever 7
Avedon, Richard 14
Avildsen, John 81, 85, 112
Avrech, Robert J. 163–4, 165
Awake and Sing! 12

Baby Doll 56
Bacall, Lauren 88, 88–9
Bacon, Francis 54
Badman, John 118
Balsam, Martin 18, 75, ***87***, 88
Bancroft, Anne 44, 1445–6, 176
Bannen, Ian 78, ***79***
Barrymore, John 40
Bartkowiak, Andrzej 4, 128, 140, 143, 149, 1452–3, 154, 162, 165, 169
Basic Instinct 168, 179
Battleship Potempkin 54
Baum, Frank 117, 118
Beatty, Ned 101, 109, 112
Beatty, Warren 92
Beaver, Frank 102
Becker, Harold 158
Before the Devil Knows You're Dead 5, ***186***, 187–9, 191
Begley, Ed 18, 21
Belafonte, Harry 71
"Believe in Yourself" 121
Bennett, Richard Rodney 89
Benson, Sheila 149
Bergen, Candice 61, 100
Bergman, Ingrid 88, 89, 90–1
Bergman, Ingmar 112, 191
Berkeley, Busby 120
Berlin Film Festival 22
Bernstein, Walter 25, 26, 45
Best of Broadway 11
The Big Chill 67
Bill of Rights Award 149
Binns, Edward 18, 47
Bissett, Jacqueline 88
Black, David 181–2
Black, Karen 74
Blair, Linda 116
Blanner, Peter 192
Bloomberg, Michael 191
Bobby Deerfield 117
Bogdanovich, Peter 27, 37
Bond, James 3, 58, 59, 74, 79, 133
Bonnie and Clyde 101
The Book of Daniel 142
Booke, Sorrell 66
Booth, Margaret 59

Borgnine, Ernest 16
Bradbury, Ray 110–1
Bragg, Melvin 117
Brand, Neville 24
Brando, Marlon 9, 28–9, ***30***, 31, ***32***, 33–6, 39, 76, 78, 84–5, 88, 100, 105, 136, 163, 171, 192
Bray, Christopher 79
Bregman, Martin 81, 134–5, 141–2
The Bridge on the River Kwai 22
Bridges, Beau 76, ***77***, 85–6, 152
Bridges, Jeff 86, 152, 153
Bridges, Lloyd 13, 152
Brief Encounter 25
Broderick, James 95
Broderick, Matthew 158–61
Brooks, Albert 175–7
Brynner, Yul 11
Buchman, Sidney 62, 64
Bugs Bunny 107
Buirski, Nancy 193
Bunuel, Luis 70
Burdick, Eugene 2, 49
Burton, Richard 115, ***116***, 117
By Sidney Lumet 193
Bye Bye Braverman 3, ***66***, ***67***, 69–70, 166, 172

Caan, James 105
Caesar, Julius 13
Cagney, James 96
Caine, Michael 132, ***133***, 134
Caligula 37
Cambridge, Godfrey ***66***
Camus, Albert 37
Canby, Vincent 86, 110, 140
The Candidate 148
Cannavale, Bobby 181
Cannes Film Festival 43, 165
Cannon, Dyan 74, 75–6, 132, 133
Capote, Truman 124
Capra, Frank 138, 140
Capshaw, Kate 146, 149
Carnovsky, Morris ***38***
Carson, Kit 157
Casino 179
Cassavetes, John 5, 178
Castro, Fidel 135

209

INDEX

Cat Ballou 57
Cat on a Hot Tin Roof 74
Cavett, Dick 22
Cazale, John 92
CBS 1, 11, 13, 128
Cerenzie, Michael 188
Champlin, Charles 77
Chancellor, John 99
Chandler, Raymond 153
The Changing Ways of Love 12
Chapin, Kay 105
Chayevfsky, Paddy 5, 98–104, 106–113, 115, 126, 144, 149, 177
Chekhov, Anton 68, 69
Chicago Tribune 154
Child's Play 3, 76, **77**, 78, 152, 166
Chinatown 101
The Chinese Nightingale 7
Christie, Agatha 87, 89, 90
Christie, Julie 146–9
Chubbuck, Christine 101–2
Clift, Montgomery 10
Close, Glenn 183
Clurman, Harold 8
Cobb, Lee J. 8, 18–19, 20, 21, 22, 54, 57, 78
Coburn, James 72, **73**, 74
Cohen, Rob 117–8, 119, 121, 123
Columbia Studios 49, 50, 74, 75
Coma 176
Combs, Richard 148
The Confessions of Nat Turner 69
Connery, Sean 2–3, 57–60, 74, **75**, 78, **79**, 80, 87, 94, 133, 158, **159**, 160–2, 192
The Conversation 75
Cooper, Anderson 124
Cooper, Carter 124
Cooper, Gary 82, 85, 138, 174–5
Cooper, Wyatt 124
Coppola, Francis Ford 75, 145, 183, 192
Cortese, Valentina 90–1
The Cotton Club 147
Coulouris, Michael **87**, 88
Cox, Wally 76
Crawford, Joan 61, 153
Crist, Judith 50, 56, 67
Critical Care 175–7
Cronkite, Kathy 104, 111
Cronkite, Walter 13, 99, 111
Crouse, Lindsay 128, 139, **142**, 143
Crowley, Ed 94
Crowther, Bosley 36
Cukor, George 49, 61
Cunningham, Frank 127

Daddy Does It Best 56
Daily Express 36
Daily Mail 56
Daily Variety 140
Daley, Robert 126, 130, 171
Daniel 4, 5, 37, **142**, 143–5, 155, 157, 158, 162, 172, 186
Danner, Blythe **85**, 86
Darin, Bobby 25
Da Silva, Howard 145
Davis, Bette 44

Day for Night 90
Dead End 8, 15
Dead End Kids 8
The Deadly Affair 3, 65–6, 68, 141
The Deaf Heart 12
Dean, James 112, 119
Deathtrap 132, **133**, 134, 145, 163
The Deer Park 154
De La Fuente, Joel 181
De Laurentiis, Dino 81
De Mille, Cecil B. 14
De Mornay, Rebecca 167–8, **169**, 173
Denby, David 103–4
Dening, Penelope 158
De Niro, Robert 126, 130, 147, 171, 177, 179
De Palma, Brian 126, 141–2, 154
Dershowitz, Alan, 175
Devicq, Paula 181, 182
The Diary of Anne Frank 23
Diesel, Vin 5, 184, **185**
Di Palma, Carlo 70
Dr. Strangelove 2, 48–9, 101, 108, 142
Dr. Zhivago 57
Doctorow, E.L. 142, 143, 144
Dodge, Mary Mapes 16
Dog Day Afternoon 3, **91**, 92–3, **94**, **95**, 96–7, 102, 122, 127, 138, 166, 179, 184
"Don't Bring Me the Bad News" 121
Dreyer, Carl 183
Dreyfuss, Richard 117, 172, 173, 174, 175
Dunaway, Faye 100, 101, 104, 105, 106–7, **109**, 112, 113, 166, 191
Durk, David 81
Durning, Charles 93
Duvall, Robert 101, 104–5

Earth Dies Screaming 56
"Ease on Down the Road" 121
East of Eden 16
Eastman, John 56
Eastwood, Clint 140, 162
Ebert, Roger 108, 113, 153, 170, 192
Edelstein, David 160
Eden, Liz 96
Edward II 66
Eisenstein, Sergei 54
Elliott, Denholm 68
Equus 3–4, 115, **116**, 117
ER 177
Esquire 149
E.T. 50
The Exorcist 78
Exorcist II The Heretic 116

Face to Face 112
Fail-Safe 2, **46**, 47, **48**, 49–50, 75, 83, 101, 108, 142, 166
Falk, Peter 37
Family Business 5, 158, **159**, 160–2, 179, 186, 187
Far from Eden 164
Farquhar, George 10

Fast & Furious 184
Fellini, Federico 56, 70
Ferris Bueller's Day Off 161
Field, Sally 154
Fierstein, Harvey 145
Figueroa, Luke 178–9
Film Comment 36
Film Daily 56
Films in Review 24, 35, 79
Finch, Eletha 104, 112
Finch, Peter 3, 99, 100, 103, 104, 110, 111–3, 136, 186, 191
Find Me Guilty 5, 183–4, **185**, 186
Finney, Albert **87**, 88, 90, 186, 187
"Fire and Rain" 157
The First Salem Witch Trial 128
Firth, Peter 115, **116**
Fisher, Carrie 145
Fitzgerald, F. Scott 12, `192
A Flag Is Born 9
Fletcher, Louise 100
The Flying Monkeys 121
Fonda, Afdera 21
Fonda, Henry 17, **18**, 19–22, 23, 24, **46**, 47, **48**, 49, 65, 68, 99, 163, 174, 192
Fonda, Jane 23, 89, 100, 150–1, 152, 153, 154, 191
Foner, Naomi 155
Ford, Gerald 105
Ford, Harrison 159
Ford, John 2
Forman, Milos 127
Franciosa, Tony 13, 28, 29
Frankenheimer, John 2, 11, 13, 117
Freud, Sigmund 13
Friedkin, William 2, 112
Friedman, Stephen 86
Friendly Persuasion 85–6
The Fugitive Kind 2, 9, 28, **29**, 30–31, **32**, 33–36, 37, 76, 78, 192
Funny Girl 64
Future Shock 176

Gable, Clark 10
Gabor, Eva 44
Galilei, Galileo 13
Gam, Rita 10, 14
Gandhi 140
Gandolfini, James 172, 174
Garbo, Greta 145
Garbo Talks 4–5, 145–6, 148
Garcia, Andy 172, 173, 174, 175
Garland, Judy 117
Gaslight 90
Gazzara, Ben 71
Gelmis, Joseph 76
George, Peter 2, 49
Gere, Richard 146–9
Gielgud, John 88
Gingold, Hermione 145
Gleiberman, Owen 96, 193
Gloria 5, 178–80
Godard, Jean-Luc 70
The Godfather 76, 81, 84–5, 105
Going My Way 137
Goldman, William 171
Gone with the Wind 61, 118

Good Morning, America 111
The Goodbye Girl 117
Goodbye Mr. Chips 77
Goodyear Playhouse 90 11
Gordy, Berry 117–8
Gottfried, Howard 98, 106
Graham, Sheilah 44
Granger, Farley 13
Grant, Cary 26, 58
The Great Escape 59
Greco, Jena 143
Greenglass, David 143
Greenwood, Joan 23
Grey, Joel 85
Griffith, Melanie **164**, 165, 166
The Group 3, 9, 61–4, 68, 69–70, 100, 172
Group Theatre 8
Grusin, Larry 145
Guernica 54
Guilty as Sin 5, 167–8, **169**, 170, 171, 173
Guinness, Alec 87
Gyllenhaal, Jake 155
Gyllenhaal, Maggie 155, 183

Hackett, Joan 61
Hackford, Taylor 191
Hackman, Gene 146, 148
Hagman, Larry 47, 61
Hair 127
Hamlet 7, 171
The Hand That Rocks the Cradle 170
Hanks, Tom 171
Hans Brinker or the Silver Skates 16
Harper's Bazaar 14
Harris, Burtt 17, 162
Harris, Rosemary 186
Harrison, Rex 59
Hartman, Elizabeth 61
Hatch, Robert 56
Hathaway, Anne 193
Hawke, Ethan **186**, 187–9
Hays Code 56
Heaven's Gate 121
Hecht, Ben 9
Heim, Alan 108, 113, 192
Hello, Dolly! 69
Hemingway, Ernest 71, 192
Hendry, Ian 57, 59
Hepburn, Katharine 23, 39, 40, **41**, 42, 43, 44, 78, 129, 191, 192
Heston, Charlton 71
Hicks, Catherine 145
The Hiding Place 65
High Noon 82, 174–5
The Hill 2–3, 57–60, 61, 63, 74, 78, 133, 166, 192
Hill, George Roy 2
Hiller, Arthur 177
Hiller, Wendy 88
Himmelstein, David 149
Hirsch, Judd 155
Hirshfield, Gerald **48**
Hitchcock, Alfred 12, 19, 55, 66, 154, 168

Hoberman, Joe 4, 145
Hoffman, Dustin 136, 158, **159**, 160–2, 187
Hoffman, Philip Seymour **186**, 187-, 191
Holbrook, Hal 61
Holden, William 99, 100, 104, 105, 106–8, 109, 110, 111, 112, 113, 136
Holm, Ian 172, 174
Hooks, Robert 72, **73**
Hopkins, John 78, 79
Hopkins, Kenyon 35
Hopper, Dennis 25
Hopper, Edward 153
Horne, Gail 45–6, 70–1, 123–4
Horne, Lena 45–6, 70, 119, 124
Horrigan, Patrick e. 121
The Hospital 5, 98, 177
Houseboat 26
Howard, Trevor 78
Howe, James Wong 72
HUAC (House UnAmerican Activities Committee) 10, 14, 25, 177–8
Human Rights First 193
Hunter, Tab 16, 24–7, 86, 132
Hurt, William 115
The Hustler 137
Huston, John 78
Hutchinson, Tom 54
Hutton, Timothy 143, 144, 162–3

The Iceman Cometh 37, 39
Indiana Jones and the Last Crusade 159
International Federation of Catholic Alumnae 56

Jackson, Michael 4, 119, 120–1, 122
Jaffet, Albert **48**
Jagged Edge 154
Jaws 2 121
Jesus Christ 8
Joan of Arc 13
John Brown's Raid 65
Johnny Concho 15
Johnson, Don 167–9
Jones, Ed 140
Jones, James Earl 71
Jones, Quincy 4, 52, 72, 119, 122
Jory, Victor 35
Journey to Bethlehem 8
Julia, Raul 152
Jurow, Martin 28, 29, 31
Just Tell Me What You Want 124, **125**

Kael, Pauline 3, 5, 43–4, 47, 54, 57, 62–4, 77–8, 121, 132, 143, 192
Kahn, Madeleine 90
Kashfi, anna 28, 33, 34
Kaufman, Boris 17, 19, 25, 29, 31–2, 35, 40, 52, 58, 61, 69–70
Kazan, Elia 8, 16, 128, 177–8
Keaton, Buster 183
Kehr, Dave 154

Kelly, Grace 12, 14
Kennedy, John F. 45–6, 70, 174
Kennedy, Robert 70
Khruschev, Nikita 46, 71
King, Alan 67, 75, 124–6
King, David 147
King, Mabel 121
King, Martin Luther 70–1
King: A Filmed Record 71
The King and I 11
Kingsley, Ben 140
Kingsley, Sidney 8, 15
Kirk, Phyllis 15
Kirkwood, Gene 163
Kiss Me, Stupid 55
Klugman, Jack 18
Klute 153
Knight, Shirley 61
Krim, Arthur 21–2
Krol, Archbishop John 56
Kroll, Jack 84
Krost, Barry 99
Krupa, Gene 149
Kubrick, Stanley 2, 48–9, 192
Kuntsler, William 175
Kurosawa, Akira 24, 183
Kurtz, Marcia Jean 94

Ladd, Diane 90
Lahti, Christine **155**
Lancaster, Burt 71, 136, 159–60
Landau, Ely 17, 37, 39, 40, 52, 55, 56
Lang, Fritz 91
Lang, Stephen 167, 173
La Noire Rosetta **142**
Lansing, Sherry 122
Last of the Mobile Hot Shots 3, 72, **73**, 74, 176
The Last Picture Show 86
Lastra, Bruno 183
Laughton, Charles (actor) 168
Laughton, Charles (non-actor) 96
Laurie, Piper 12
Lawrence, Carol 38
Lawrence of Arabia 57
Lean, David 16, 22
Le Carré, John 65
Lee, Spike 163
Legion of Decency 55–7
Leibman, Ron 172–3
Lemmon, Jack 85, 140
Lennon, John 22
Leone, Sergio 68
Leto, Phil 86
Let's Pretend 7
Leuci, Robert 126, 129, 130, 149
Leung, Ken 183
Levin, Ira 132
Lewis, Bobby 9
Lewis, Jerry 14
Lewis, Roger 52
Life 56, 91
Lincoln, Abraham 71
The Lion King 171
Little, Monsignor Thomas 56
Living It Up 14
The Living Theatre 92

INDEX

Lollobrigida, Gina 24, 31–2
London Observer 64
Long Day's Journey into Night 2, 39–40, **41**, 42–4, 63, 68, 69, 78, 117, 129, 166, 172, 186, 192
Lord of the Flies 77
Loren, Sophia 24–7, 31–2
Lorre, Peter 91
Los Angeles Times 35, 76, 77, 169, 191
Loudon, Dorothy 145
The Louisiana Purchase 13
Love Is a Many-Splendored Thing 16
Love Story 145
The Loved One 176
Lovin' Molly **85**, 86–7, 88, 91, 152
Loy, Myrna 176
Luke, Eric 16
Lumet, Amy 71, 141, 150, 163
Lumet, Baruch 7
Lumet, Jennifer 141, 150, 163, 181, 193
Lumet, Sidney: acting career 7–10; Actors Studio 9–10; anti-Semitism 8, 23, 52, 100, 144; army years 9–10; attention to detail 58, 63, 120; communist sympathies 8, 14, 20, 128; concern for actors 12, 33–4, 88, 172–3; crusades against the system 4, 93, 98, 126–31, 140, 185; depression era 7; discipline 114–5; divorces 14, 45, 123–4; economy 2, 11, 12, 24, 58, 170–1; energy 3, 5, 33, 79, 80, 114, 191; "happy accidents" 16, 31, 114–5, 149; HUAC 10, 128, 177–8; HUAC investigations 10, 128, 177–8; improvisation 11, 30, 31, 34, 114; legal system 4–6, 17–22, 167–70, 171–5, 181–6; leisure pursuits 114; marriages 10, 15, 45–6, 124; New York affiliation 3, 8, 25, 27, 38, 47, 64–5, 92, 96, 118–21, 150, 189, 193; Oscar experiences 5, 6, 21, 22, 30, 44, 57, 84–5, 90, 96, 111–3, 117, 140–1, 154, 166, 183, 191; perfectionism 59, 67, 105; popularity with actors 2–3, 58, 95–6, 125, 129, 133, 174, 182, 185, 187; poverty-stricken youth 7–8; pressure as stimulant 12, 64; radio experiences 7; rehearsal routines 29–30, 40, 68, 101, 120, 125, 138, 159; same actors used repeatedly 18, 68, 92, 128, 159; social conscience 8, 14; social mobility 8; speed 2, 11, 15–16, 93, 105, 114–5, 124, 139, 187, 190; suspected suicide attempt 45; symbolic use of camera 4, 20, 24, 34, 42, 53, 104, 107, 128, 129, 138–9; television 10–13; theatre as influence 1, 3–4, 7, 28, 37–44, 68–9, 117; versatility 85, 89,

96–7, 131, 141; work ethic 1, 7, 114, 189
Lynn, Vera 49

M 91
Maas, Peter 81
MacGraw, Ali 124, **125**, 126, 145
The Madness of King George 172
Madsen, Harry 94
The Magic Christian 49
Magnani, Anna 24, 28–9, **30**, 31, **32**, 33–6
Mahmud-Bey, Shiek 172, 173
Mailer, Norman 106, 154
Making Movies 170–1
Malcolm X 103
Malden, Karl 10, 57
Malina, Judith 92
Mamet, David 47, 135–6, 139
The Man with the Golden Arm 15
Mangano, Silvana 24
Mankiewicz, Joseph L. 56
Mann, Delbert 2, 16, 17
Mann, William J. 43
Marasco, Robert 76, 77
Marjorie Morningstar 23
Markfield, Wallace 66
Marquand, Richard 154
Marshall, E.G. 10, 18, 37, 146
Marshall, Herbert 23, 24
Martin, Dean 14
Martindale, Margo 175
Marty 16, 21, 126
Marvin, Lee 57
Marx, Karl 7, 118
Mason, James 65–6, 68, 69, 76, **77**, 78, 136, 140, 150, 176, 192
Mason, Marsha 124
Mathews, Jack 179
Matthau, Walter 46, 47, 49
Matusow, Harvey 128
Maurice Schwartz Acting Group 7
Mazursky, Paul 3, 159
McCarthy, Sen. Joseph 14, 20, 128
McCarthy, Kevin 10
McCarthy, Mary 3, 9, 61, 62, 63
McLuhan, Marshall 92
McMurtry, Larry 85, 86
McQueen, Steve 125
Medavoy, Mike 98
Melnick, Dan 106
Mengers, Sue 106
Menjou, Adolphe 23
Merchant, Vivien 78
Merrick, David 76
Merrill, Dina 125
Miami Vice 168
Miles, Vera 154
Miller, Arthur 9, 37–8
Mills, Stephanie 117
Minnelli, Liza 68
The Miracle Worker 44
Mirren, Helen 176
Missing 140
Mr. Roberts 16
Mitchell-Smith, Ilan **142**, 143
Mitchum, Robert 100

Mix, Tom 89
Monotheatre Varieties 7
Monroe, Marilyn 165
Monterey, Carlotta 37
Monthly Film Bulletin 148
Mooring, William 56–7
The Morning After 5, 150–1, **152**, 153–4, 166, 169, 191
Morning Glory 23
Morris, Oswald 58
Morrissey 54
Motion Picture Association of America 55, 56
Motown Productions 117
Mulligan, Robert 61, 67–8
Muni, Paul 134
Murder on the Orient Express **87**, 88–91, 96, 104, 134, 187
Murphy, Dudley 8
My Fair Lady 49, 184
My Favorite Year 140
My Heart's in the Highlands 8
My Son, My Lover 56

The Nation 56
National Catholic Office of Motion Pictures 56
NBC 10, 181
Neal, Patricia 10
Network 3, 10, 98, **99**, 101–2, **103**, 104–8, **109**, 110–3, 115, 126, 132, 136, 148, 154, 166, 173, 180, 186, 191
The New Republic 39, 47
New York Herald Tribune 23–4, 26, 39
New York Times 36, 39, 81, 86, 110
Newman, Paul 4, 13, 29, 71, 89, 92, 99, **135**, 136, **137**, 138–41, 153, 158
Newman, Scott 136
Newsday 76, 175
Newsweek 56, 65, 90, 141
Nichols, Barbara 25
Night Falls on Manhattan 5, 171–5, 186
"Night of the Auk" 50
Night People 14
Nixon, Richard 22, 149
Nolte, Nick 162, 163
Norman, Barry 113

Obama, Barack 177
Odets, Clifford 12
Oedipus Rex 56, 186
The Offence 3, 78, **79**, 80, 166
O'Herlihy, Dan 47
Olin, Lena 172, 173, 174
Oliver, Thelma 53, 55
On the Waterfront 17, 18,, 57, 154
Once Upon a Time in the West 68
One-Eyed Jacks 28, 30–1, 34
One Flew Over the Cuckoo's Nest 100
100 Center Street 181–3
One Third of a Nation 8
O'Neill, Eugene 37, 39, 43–4
O'Neill, Terry 113

Index

O'Rourke, P.J. 163
Orpheus Descending 28, 30, 32
Oswald, Lee Harvey 45
O'Toole, Peter 117, 140
Oulahan, Richard 56
The Ox-Bow Incident 19, 20

Pacino, Al 3, 4, 81–2, **83**, 84, **91**, 92–4, **95**, 96, 102, 117, 126, 128, 130, 138, 142, 158, 171, 183, **184**, 191
Pakula, Alan J. 67, 112
Palance, Jack 14
Paleggi, Nick 166
Parker, Dorothy 45
Parkinson, David 117
Parks, Hildy **63**
Patinkin, Mandy 142–3
The Pawnbroker 2, 5, 51, **52**, 53–7, 63, 98, 144, 157, 166, 173
Peary, Danny, 110
Peck, Gregory 14, 67–8, 86
Peeping Tom 102
Pellegrin, Raymond 38–9
Penn, Arthur 2, 12
Pennebaker Productions 28
Perez, Manny 181
Perkins, Anthony **85**, 86, 88, 91, 115, 154
Pesci, Joe 184
Pettit, Joanna 61
Pfeiffer, Michelle 171
Philco Television Playhouse 12
Phillips, Julia 115
Phoenix, River **155**, 156, **157**, 158
Photoplay 26
Picasso, Pablo 54
Pickens, Slim 49
Picker, David 171
Picnic 16
Pierson, Frank 96
Pike, Bishop James A. 56
Pinter, Harold 79
Pisoni, Ed 138
Pitts, ZaSu 89
Plato 13
Play of the Week 11, 37
Plimpton, Martha 155
Plummer, Amanda 143
Plummer, Christopher 23
Polonsky, Abraham 177
Ponti, Carlo 24–7
Power 4–5, 146–9, 166
Power, Tyrone 168
Preston, Robert 76, **77**
Prince of the City 4, 126, **127**, 128–31, 132, 140, 142, 143, 145, 162, 166, 171, 174, 175
Production Code 54, 56–7, 173
Production Code Association 55
Production Code Review Board 55
Pryor, Richard 119, 163
Psycho 85, 86, 88, 89, 91, 154

Q&A 5, 162–3, 175
Quinn, Anthony 71

The Rabbi from Brownsville 7
Rachel Is Getting Married 193
Rainier, Prince 14
A Raisin in the Sun 37
Rampling, Charlotte **135**, 137, 139–40, 176
Ran 24
Red Alert 2, 49
Red Desert 70
Redd, Mary-Robin 61
Redford, Robert 37, 135, 148
Redgrave, Lynn 72, **73**, 74
Reeve, Christopher 132, **133**, 134
Revlon Theatre 12
Rice, Elmer 8
Rich, Frank 117
Richardson, La Tanya 181
Richardson, Les 94
Richardson, Ralph 40, **41**, 42
Riesel, Victor 128
Rigby, Ray 57
Ritchie, Michael 148
Ritt, Martin 11, 117
Robards, Jason 37, 40, 42
Robert Montgomery Presents 12
Roberts, Meade 30, 33, 35
Roberts, Rachel 88
Robertson, Cliff 28
Robeson, Paul 143
Rocky 112
Roisman, Owen 105
Rose, Charlie, 170
Rose, Reginald 12, 17, 21, 37
The Rose Tattoo 16, 30
Rosemary's Baby 77
Rosenberg, Ethel 142, 143
Rosenberg, Howard 182
Rosenberg, Julius 142, 143
Rosenberg, Philip 17, 162, 165, 174
Rosenfelt, Deborah 110
Ross, Diana 4, 117–23
Ross, Ted 119
Roth, Ann 160
Rowlands, Gena 178, 179
Running on Empty 5, 154, **155**, 156, **157**, 158, 163, 172, 186
Russell, Gail 151
Russell, Ken 115
Russell, Nipsy 119
Russell, Rosalind 61
Russo, Vito 96
Ryder, Winona 171

The Sacco and Vanzetti Story 37
The Salem Witchhunts 13
Salt, Waldo 81
San Francisco Chronicle 191–2
Sanders, George 24, 26
Sara, Mia 165
Sarandon, Chris, 94
Saroyan, William 8
Sarris, Andrew 4, 56, 96, 131, 192
Saturday Night Fever 118
Saturday Review 26, 39, 44
Save the Tiger 85
Scarface 134–5, 141, 142, 158
Schell, Maximillian 65–6
Schulberg, Budd 163

Schuler, Fred 105
Schumacher, Joel 118, 123
Sciorra Annabella 185
Scorsese, Martin 3, 96, 145, 177, 183, 189, 192
Scott, George C. 98–9, 180
Screaming Popes 54
Screen Actors Guild 173
Sea of Love 158
The Sea Gull 68–70
Sedgwick, Kyra 175
Segal, George **66**, 67
Serpico 3, 4, 81–2, **83**, 84–5, 93, 96, 126, 128, 130, 144, 162, 164, 166, 174, 175
The Seven Descents of Myrtle 72
Shaffer, Peter 3–4, 115
Shakespeare, William 10, 37, 117, 129
Sharif, Omar 69, **70**
Shaw, George Bernard 10
Sheridan, Jamie 165
Sheridan, Richard Brinsley 10
Sherman, Lowell 24
Sheward, David 99
Shewey, Don 14
Shipman, David 35
Shire, Talia 90
Shurlock, Geoffrey 55
Sidney, Sylvia 8
Sign of the Pagan 14
Signoret, Simone 65–6, 68, 69
Silberstein, Robert 119
Silent Nights 65
Silver, Ron 145, 146
Simon, Neil 124
Simpson, O.J. 173, 175, 186
Sinatra, Frank 14–15, 136
Socrates 13
Sontag, Susan 44–5
The Sopranos 172
Sorel, Jean 38
Sotomayor, Sonia 190
The Sound of Music 57
Southern, Terry 49
The Spa 15
Spacek, Sissy 171
Spader, James 175, 176, 177
Spielberg, Steven 183, 191
Spillane, Mickey 153
"Splish Splash" 25
Springer, Jerry 105
The Spy Who Came In from the Cold 65
Stage Struck 2, 23–4, 25, 28
The Stalking Moon 67–8
Stallone, Sylvester 112, 113
Stapleton, Maureen, 9, 28, 29, 31, 33, 38, 39
Star Wars 117
Stark, Ray 64
Steiger, Rod 11–12, 40, **52**, 53–4, 57, 58, 98, 117, 144
The Sterile Cuckoo 68
Stewart, James 138, 140
The Sting 85
Stockwell, Dean 40, **41**, 42
Stokowski, Leopold 14, 124

Stone, Judith 56
Stone, Oliver 135, 141
Stone, Sharon 5, 168, 178–80
Straight, Beatrice 10, 100–1, 109, 112, 113, 146, 148, 166
A Stranger Among Us 5, 163, **164**, 165–6
Strasberg, Lee 9, 23
Strasberg, Susan 23–4
A Streetcar Named Desire 36, 74
Strip Search 183
Studio One 11, 15
Summertime 16
The Swan 14
Sylbert, Dick 52

Tainted Evidence 171
Take the Money and Run 93
Taxi Driver 112
Taylor, James 157
Taylor, Joseph Lyle 181
The Ten Commandments 14
The Tenth Man 109
Thal, Eric **164**
That Kind of Woman 2, 24–7, 28, 86
Theodorakis, Mikis 81, 82
They Shoot Horses, Don't They? 153
"This Little Light of Mine" 143
Three Days of the Condor 101
Three Empty Rooms 12
The Three Faces of Eve 30
Time 26, 39, 44, 56, 67, 69, 134, 140
The Times 69
Tischler, Henry 171
To an Early Grave 66
Tomei, Marisa 186, 188
Torres, Ed 162
The Towering Inferno 100
Tracy, Spencer 41, 112
Tragedy in a Temporary Town 13
Travolta, John 126

Trevelyan, John 56
Truffaut, François 90, 128
Trump, Donald 111, 177
Twelve Angry Men 2, 5, 17, **18**, 19–22, 24, 25, 28, 37, 46, 47, 54, 63, 78, 90, 132, 144, 152, 166, 168, 181, 190, 191
Two Doors to Doom 49

United Artists 21–2, 52, 79, 98, 117, 171
Universal Studios 117–8, 121
Unman, Wittering and Zigo 77
USA 8

Valenti, Jack 56
Vallone, Raf **38**, 39
Vanderbilt, Gloria 14, **15**, 44–5, 100–1, 124, 190
Van Devere, Trish 98
Variety 26, 39, 44, 86, 96
The Verdict 4, **135**, 136, **137**, 138–41, 143, 145, 153, 154, 158, 166, 167, 176
Vidal, Gore 72
A View from the Bridge 37, **38**, 39
Vigo, Jean 183
Village Voice 124
Visconti, Luchino 70
Vogue 96

Waiting for Lefty 10
Walken, Christopher 74, 75
Walker, Jimmie 119
Wallach, Eli 10
Wallant, Edward Lewis 51
Walter, Jessica 61, 172
Walton, Tony 88, 128, 191
War of the Worlds 50
Warden, Jack 18, 25, 66, 94, 136, 167
Warner, David 68
Warner, Jack 23, 187
Washington, Denzel 146, 163

Washington Post 147
Watergate 105
Waterworld 121
Weaver, Fritz 12, 47
Wedding Breakfast 13
Weller, Peter 125
Welles, Orson 89, 192
West Side Story 120
Wexler, Norman 81
What Ever Happened to Baby Jane? 44
What Makes Sammy Run 163
Wheeler, Harvey 2, 49
White, Michole 181
Who's Afraid of Virginia Woolf? 117
Widdowes, Kathleen 61, 68
Widmark, Richard 88
Wilder, Billy 55, 168
Williams, Tennessee 9, 28, 30, 32–3, 35, 36, 72, 74
Williams, Treat 4, 126, **127**, 128–31
Wilmington, Michael 169
Wilson, Cecil 56
"Winter Dreams" 12
Winters, Shelley 13
Wiseman, Joseph 66
Witness 165
Witness for the Prosecution 168
The Wiz 4, 117–22, **123**, 124
The Wizard of Oz 117, 118
WNTA-TV 37
The Women 61
Woodward, Joanne 29, 30, **32**, 33, 35
Worth, Irene 134
Wyler, William 183

York, Michael 88, 89
You Are There 12–13, 99
The Young Lions 88

Zinnemann, Fred 27
Zorba the Greek 81

www.ingramcontent.com/pod-product-compliance
Lightning Source LLC
Chambersburg PA
CBHW060342010526
44117CB00017B/2937